Aerial view of Fairmont, c. 1930.

An Ornament to the City:
Historic Architecture in Downtown Fairmont, West Virginia

Debra Ball McMillan

An Ornament to the City:
Historic Architecture in Downtown Fairmont, West Virginia

By Debra Ball McMillan

All Rights Reserved

Copyright © 1996 by Debra Ball McMillan

All Rights Reserved, including the right to reproduce this book, its photographs, graphics or artwork in any form whatsoever without permission of the author, except customary privileges extended to the press or other reviewing agencies.

ISBN
0929915186

Library of Congress Catalog Card Number: 96-78848

For Information Address:
Debra Ball McMillan
217 Braddock St.
Fairmont, WV 26554

Headline Books, Inc.
P.O. Box 52
Terra Alta, WV 26764

PRINTED IN THE UNITED STATES OF AMERICA

> This book is dedicated to:
>
> my parents, Harry and Cecilia Ball,
> for their love and guidance all these years;
>
> and especially to:
> my husband, Todd Stewart McMillan, the love of my life.

I wish to thank the following people for their assistance in my book:

Bob Heffner and John Piscitelli, Fairmont State College, for their assistance with photography.

The late Rodney Collins, West Virginia State Historic Preservation Office, for his assistance and mutual interest in architectural history.

Elizabeth and Thomas Earl Windsor for their friendship and the use of photographs by their father, J. Earl Windsor.

and the following libraries and their staff:

Fairmont State College Library, Fairmont, West Virginia.

West Virginia and Regional History Collection, West Virginia University Libraries, Morgantown, West Virginia.

State Archives and Historical Library, Charleston, West Virginia.

Library of Congress, Washington, D. C.

Times newspaper advertisement, May 9, 1923

Table of Contents

Introduction	7
A Brief History Of Fairmont	10
Maps	12

Part I—Adams Street—(also called Main Street) 18
Chapter 1—100 Block Adams Street, even numbered buildings 19
Chapter 2—100 Block Adams Street, odd numbered buildings 42
Chapter 3—200 Block Adams Street, even numbered buildings 57
Chapter 4—200 Block Adams Street, odd numbered buildings 79
Chapter 5—300 Block Adams Street, even numbered buildings 96
Chapter 6—300 Block Adams Street, odd numbered buildings 110
Chapter 7—400 Block Adams Street, even numbered buildings 126
Chapter 8—400 Block Adams Street, odd numbered buildings 141

Part II—Cleveland Avenue —(previously Barney Street and Parks Avenue) 149
Chapter 9—100 Block Cleveland Avenue, even numbered buildings 150
Chapter 10—100 Block Cleveland Avenue, odd numbered buildings 155
Chapter 11—200 Block Cleveland Avenue, even numbered buildings 158
Chapter 12—200 Block Cleveland Avenue, odd numbered buildings 159
Chapter 13—300 Block Cleveland Avenue, odd numbered buildings 165
Chapter 14—400 Block Cleveland Avenue, odd numbered buildings 170

Part III—Monroe Street 174
Chapter 15—200 Block Monroe Street, even numbered buildings 174
Chapter 16—200 Block Monroe Street, odd numbered buildings 180
Chapter 17—300 Block Monroe Street, even numbered buildings 194
Chapter 18—300 Block Monroe Street, odd numbered buildings 198

Part IV—Jefferson Street 207
Chapter 19—200 Block Jefferson Street, even numbered buildings 208
Chapter 20—200 Block Jefferson Street, odd numbered buildings 218
Chapter 21—300 Block Jefferson Street, even numbered buildings 222
Chapter 22—300 Block Jefferson Street, odd numbered buildings 237

Part V—Madison Street—(also called Bridge Street) 239
Chapter 23—200 Block Madison Street, even numbered buildings 240
Chapter 24—200 Block Madison Street, odd numbered buildings 241
Chapter 25— 300 Block Madison Street, even numbered buildings 244
Chapter 26—300 Block Madison Street, odd numbered buildings 248

Part VI—Quincy Street 253
Chapter 27—400 Block Quincy Street, even numbered buildings 254
Chapter 28—400 Block Quincy Street, odd numbered buildings 257

Part VII—Locust Avenue and Jackson Street 261
Chapter 29—Locust Avenue 262
Chapter 30—100 Block Jackson Street, even numbered buildings 267
Chapter 31—100 Block Jackson Street, odd numbered buildings 269
Chapter 32—300 Block Jackson Street, odd numbered buildings 272
Chapter 33—400 Block Jackson Street, even numbered buildings 279
Chapter 34—400 Block Jackson Street, odd numbered buildings 281

Part VIII—Washington Street 285
Chapter 35—200 Block Washington Street, even numbered buildings 287

APPENDIX A—BUILDING INDEX 289

APPENDIX B—BIBLIOGRAPHY 294

APPENDIX C—PHOTOGRAPH CREDITS 295

INDEX 297

Times newspaper advertisement, May 13, 1923

Introduction

"It would require a book of a thousand pages of the most intensely interesting reading to record the advancement Fairmont has made from 1890 when the city first began to grow, a period of 40 years," stated Mr. Henry C. Sample, a prominent Fairmont businessman, in a newspaper interview in 1929. He had operated the Fairmont Press weekly newspaper years before. "To undertake to write about the business people and business concerns that have come and gone within these 40 and 30 years, would employ the time and intelligence of an able historian ... what a fund of interesting history for the generations now on the stage of action and for the generations to follow! Why not someone undertake the work?" [1] I read these words as I was finishing my research to write this book, and I had to laugh about the undertaking to which I had committed myself.

The kernel of thought to write this book began in 1992, when I was researching information to place the Masonic Temple Building on the Register of Historic Places. I am not a native Fairmonter, so I went to the library to find a book about the wonderful historic architecture that proliferates in this town. To my surprise, there was none. So, it became my task, my quest for the holy grail, to write the book that did not exist, and to document the buildings of which I have become so fond. I do not know if I can live up to the qualifications in the vision of Mr. Sample some 66 years ago and I do not know if the book will be a thousand pages long. I only know that I want to tell the story of these historic structures that has been unknown and forgotten for so many years.

The focus of my research is on the very period to which Mr. Sample refers: 1890 to 1930. From the census records, this was the period of astronomical growth for Fairmont, when the population rose from 1,023 to 23,159,[2] and the period in which the majority of monumental buildings were constructed. The quality of these buildings reflects the wealth of the city at that time, as very expensive buildings were constructed. These buildings survive today because of the substantial manner in which they were constructed. There was also a concern with aesthetics. Many new buildings were designed by noteworthy architects of the time; and, upon completion, a new building was referred to as an ornament to the city, or as the newest jewel in Fairmont's crown.

I have limited the geographical area of my research to the historic downtown as it was determined in 1819, which I refer to as the "Presidents' Grid;" this is the area bounded by Jackson Street on the north, Quincy Street on the east, and Cleveland Avenue on the south and the west. I have strayed slightly from these boundaries to include some of the separate-but-not-very-equal structures dictated by segregation at the time. The "colored" churches and schools were pushed to the fringe of the historic downtown area, and I have included them. I also included the first block of Locust Avenue, which was at times referred to as Jackson Street. It was connected both physically and functionally to the commercial activity in the downtown area.

Originally, I wanted to discuss the commercial structures in the downtown area. As my research began, I realized that the city, any city really, is not just its commercial structures. So I have included the churches, schools, banks, and institutional buildings that were all integrated into the fabric of peoples' lives and into the fabric of the city at the time. The commercial structures were the glue that held them all together.

My initial idea was to address the buildings in chronological order because, of course, this is history. However, some of the historical information, though scant, predates 1890; and, when known, I have also included information after 1930. Instead of chronologically, I have presented the buildings street by street in blocks, which will be less confusing; this is especially important for the buildings no longer in existence.

To alleviate confusion regarding street names, I want to clarify the changes that have occurred during the years. Adams Street was historically referred to as "Main Street," and was so in spirit as well. Madison Street was referred to as "Bridge Street" because the first bridge (constructed in 1852), the old suspension bridge, linked the southern end of it to the East Side of Fairmont (referred to as the First Ward and originally the town of Palatine). Cleveland Avenue was originally named Barney Street from Adams Street north, and Parks Avenue from Adams Street south and east (did I somehow miss a "President Barney?"). Ogden Avenue was Hull Alley, and Meredith Street was Porter Alley.

I have used the street address numbers from the 1927 Sanborn map, since it shows Fairmont in its most complete state: after all the major buildings have been constructed and before the demolitions began. This may be slightly different than the street numbers of the buildings today. The numbering system has changed throughout the years on the Sanborn maps, and I have tried to be consistent with the buildings themselves, rather than simply the street number.

When referring to compass directions, I have assumed Adams Street running east to west; in my research, I found references to it running both east-west and north-south, since Adams Street actually runs east-north-east to west- south-west. I have also attempted to include the street address of buildings mentioned in the text to help clarify matters.

I have made references to Sandborn maps in my text. These are maps of cities made for fire insurance companies to help them determine the dollar amount of loss from a fire in a building. Not only do they show the physical location and size of the structure on the site, but provide additional information about the building, such as the height, number of stories, materials, and use. For some of the more important structures in the city, the name of the business in the building was also given. These have been invaluable for me to trace the evolution of the city. Sandborn maps for Fairmont exist for the years 1884, 1892, 1896, 1902, 1906, 1912, 1918, 1927, and 1950 (correction of 1927).

I hope this information will heighten the awareness of the citizenry of Fairmont of the wealth of historic architecture in our city. Sadly, half of the structures that once completely lined the city's streets are gone. If the current trend of taking the wrecking ball to historic structures in Fairmont to create parking lots does not end, there will be little left in Fairmont to give it a sense of place and of history. These buildings were constructed as ornaments to the city; let us cherish them as such.

---

[1] *Fairmont Times,* 8/4/1929, supplement p. 11.
[2] Hoffman, p. 113.

A Brief History Of Fairmont

Fairmont was founded in 1819 as Middletown, Virginia on Boaz Fleming's farm, and was regularly laid out in a grid. In those days, it served as a stopping place when traveling between Morgantown and Clarksburg. It was named Middletown because it was in the middle of those two existing cities, or to commemorate the home town of Boaz Fleming's first wife, Elizabeth Hutchinson, who was from Middletown, Delaware.

Marion County was formed in 1842 from parts of Harrison and Monongalia Counties, Virginia, and named after General Francis Marion, from the Revolutionary War. Fairmont became the county seat in 1843, and the name of the city was changed at that time because a Middletown, Virginia already existed. The name Fairmont was chosen as an abbreviated form of "Fair Mountain." As the county seat, the Courthouse became the center of attention on court days, when there was an influx of people in town. Court days developed into market days, when buyers and sellers came to the city. This added to the growth of the city.

Two events occurred which spurred Fairmont to great future growth. First, the Baltimore and Ohio Railroad was completed in 1852. This provided transportation to and from the city, and made it possible to export the area's natural resources, especially coal. Fairmont became a railroad hub.

The second event also occurred in 1852. This was the construction of the suspension bridge between Fairmont and Palatine (now the east side of Fairmont). It was located at the base of Madison Street (also called "Bridge Street"), and was replaced by the existing metal span in 1908 (which is currently in a state of disrepair and closed). This further enhanced transportation to and around the city.

The state of West Virginia was born in the throes of the Civil War. Although most of the fighting did not affect Fairmont, one skirmish occurred in 1863 when Confederate General Jones raided the area to destroy bridges to cut the Union supply lines, and to steal horses and food for his men. The raiding party succeeded in destroying a railroad bridge south of the city, but the men could not demolish the suspension bridge over the river. Because Governor Pierpont's residence was in Fairmont on Quincy Street, the raiders took his books from his library and burned them on the street. Several casualties occurred, but the exact number is not definitely known. Jones' men left town before Union soldiers arrived to help.

Around the time of the Civil War, Fairmont was a city of wooden buildings. These were used as residences and as businesses. On April 2, 1876, a great fire took place. It started in a stairway between two buildings at the northwest corner of Adams and Madison Streets, and was thought to be incendiary in nature. The fire spread to the south side of the street because of the wind, and it burned both sides of Adams Street between Madison and Jefferson Streets before it was extinguished. In one sense, the fire was a great tragedy because of the loss of property; in another sense, it was an opportunity to rebuild the wooden buildings with more substantial structures.

Fairmont outgrew the original grid of the city around the turn of the century. A metal bridge was constructed over Coal Run Hollow in 1892, and the city expanded along Fairmont Avenue, thanks to the Fairmont Development Company. Electric lights came to the city in 1890, and natural gas in 1892. Streetcars were introduced in 1900.

The population of the city grew. In 1850, there were 683 people. By 1890, it had almost doubled to 1,023, in only 40 years. Another forty years, 1930, would see it escalate to 23,159. These families needed homes, businesses needed stores, residents needed entertainment and banking facilities, and travelers needed hotels and restaurants. Monumental architecture flourished in Fairmont between 1890 and 1930.

The first decline in architecture in the city occurred with the first World War. Material and labor were siphoned off to construct factories which produced war materiel; all other construction came to a virtual standstill. After the war, it took several years for construction to grow; but the Great Depression, followed by troubles with the coal market, put an end to the construction of monumental buildings in Fairmont. It is now a struggle just to retain the remaining structures, which are falling prey to lack of maintenance, fires, and the pressure to create parking lots. Preservation efforts in the city, spearheaded by the Main Street Fairmont program, are making headway in stemming this tide and preserving these structures, the ornaments to the city, which grace our sidewalks to provide a link to our past.

This drawing by "Scotty" Nelson, was made for *The Times* last year in connection with the Decoration Day Celebration in this city. It is typical of and appropriate for the ceremonies that will be observed in the city on Tuesday.

Times newspaper illustration, May 28, 1922

Map of Middletown, Virginia, 1819—1843. From Now and Long Ago, *p. 426.*

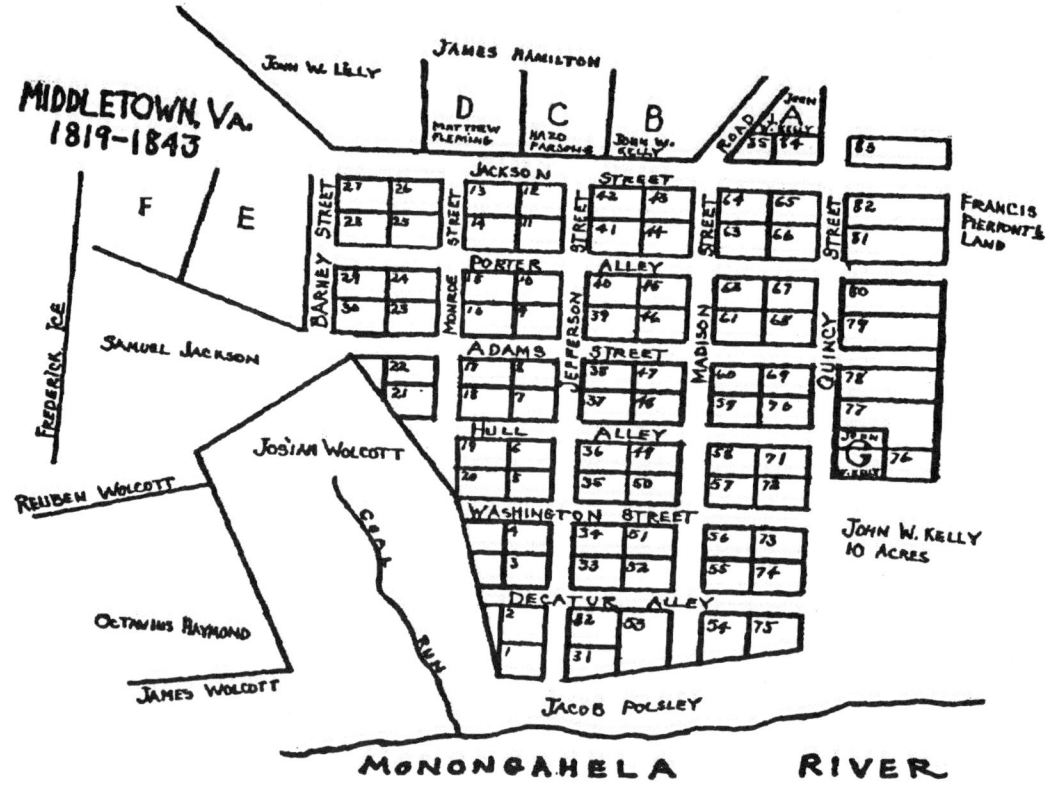

Map of Middletown in Monongalia County, Virginia, March 15, 1832 by William Haymond. From Memories of Fairmont.

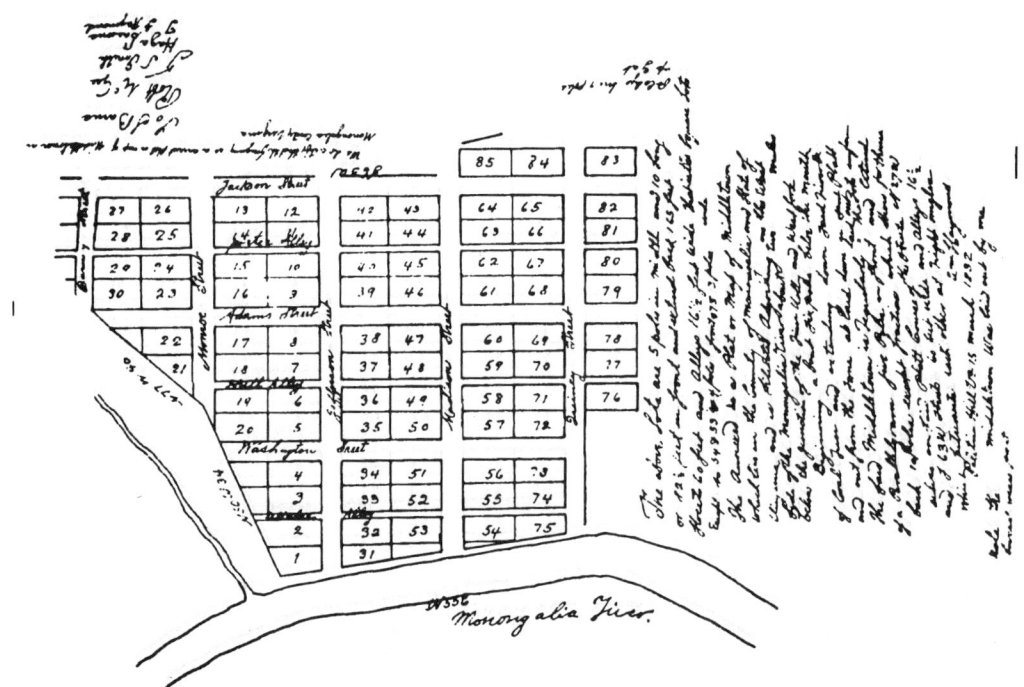

Portion of map, Fairmont, Marion County, 1886. From Atlas of Marion and Monongalia Counties, West Virginia *by D. J. Lake and Company.*

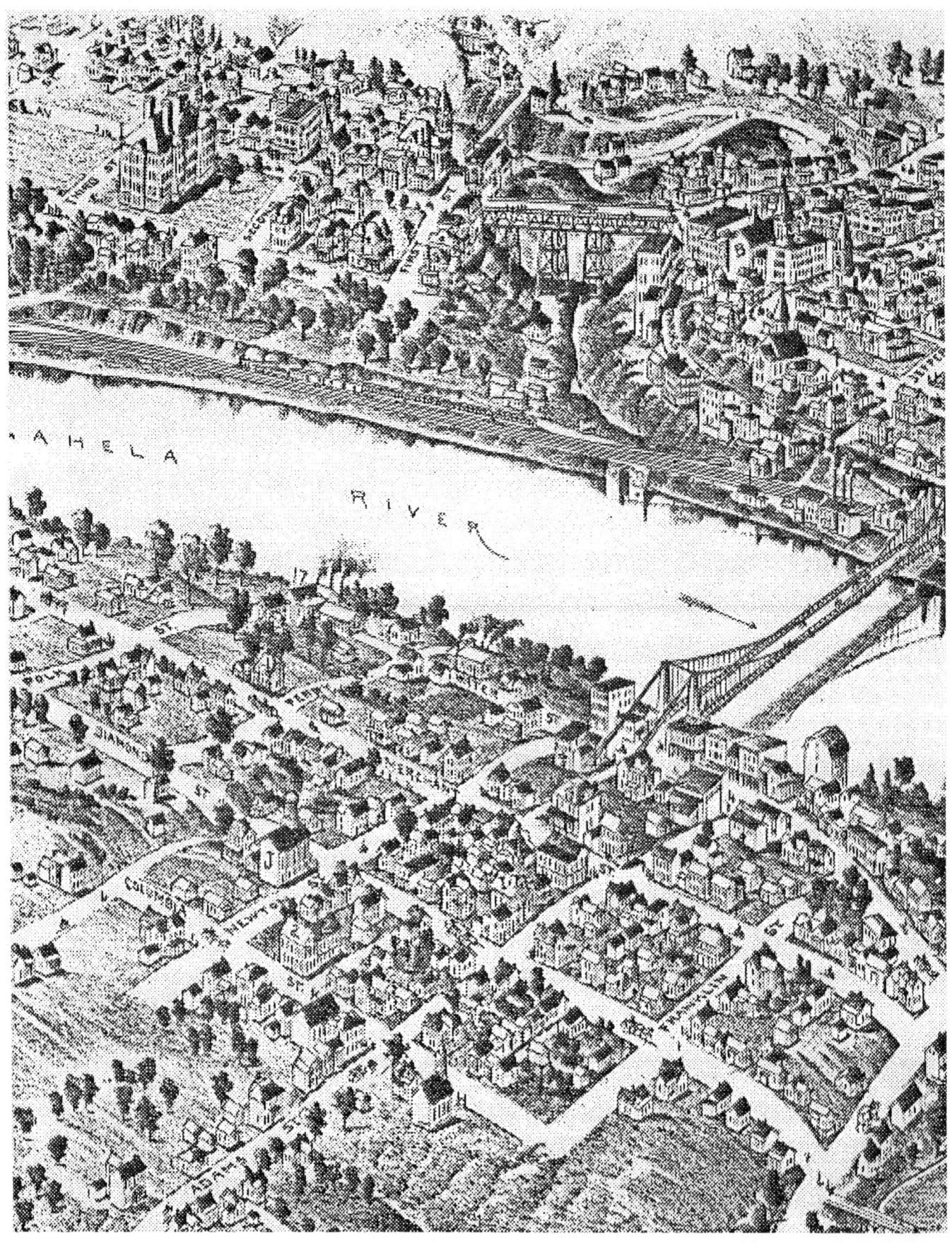

Portion of map, Fairmont, West Virginia, 1897. by T. M. Fowler and James Moyer.

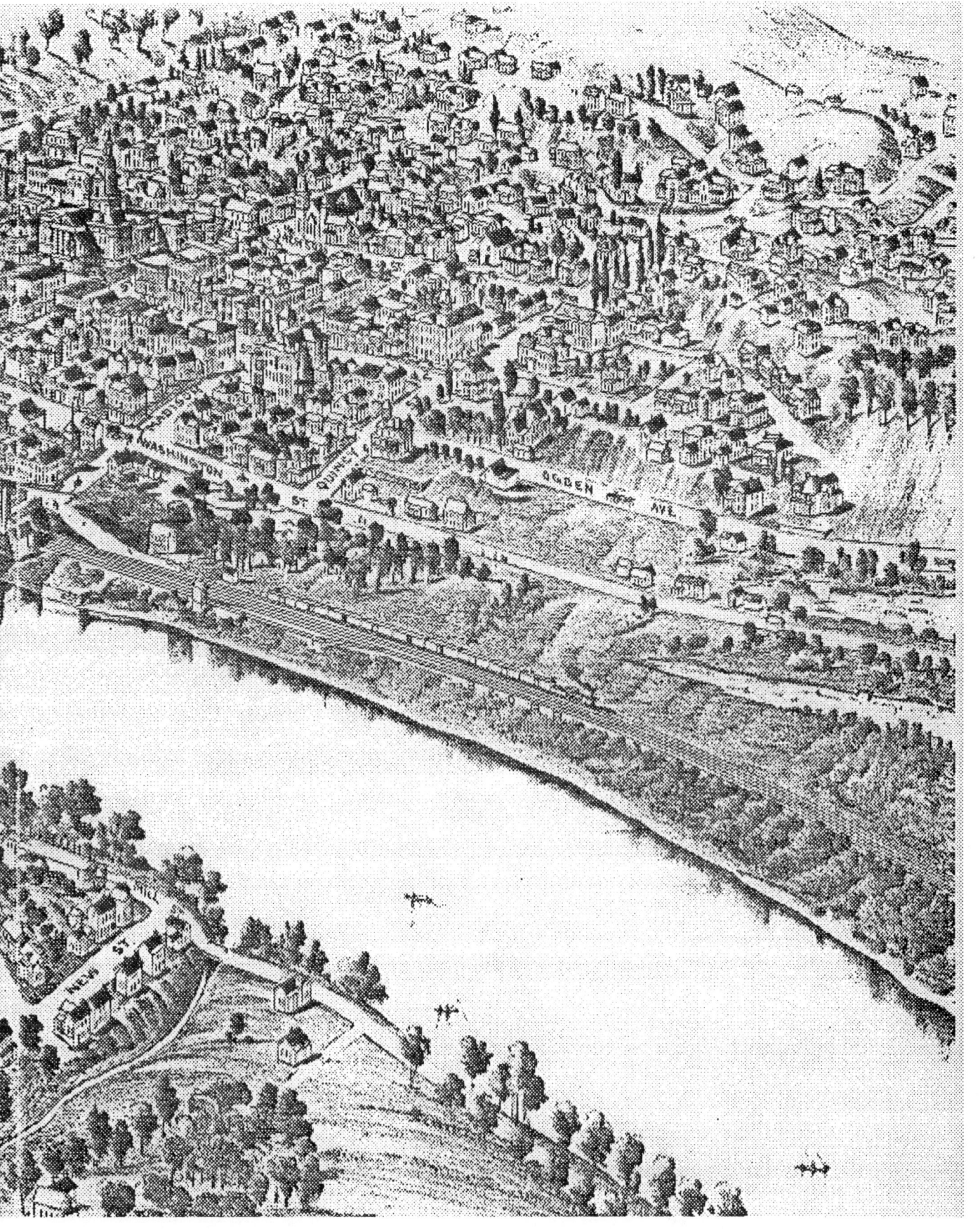

Map of Fairmont, West Virginia, April 1919, by E. B. Tucker and M. A. Williamson.

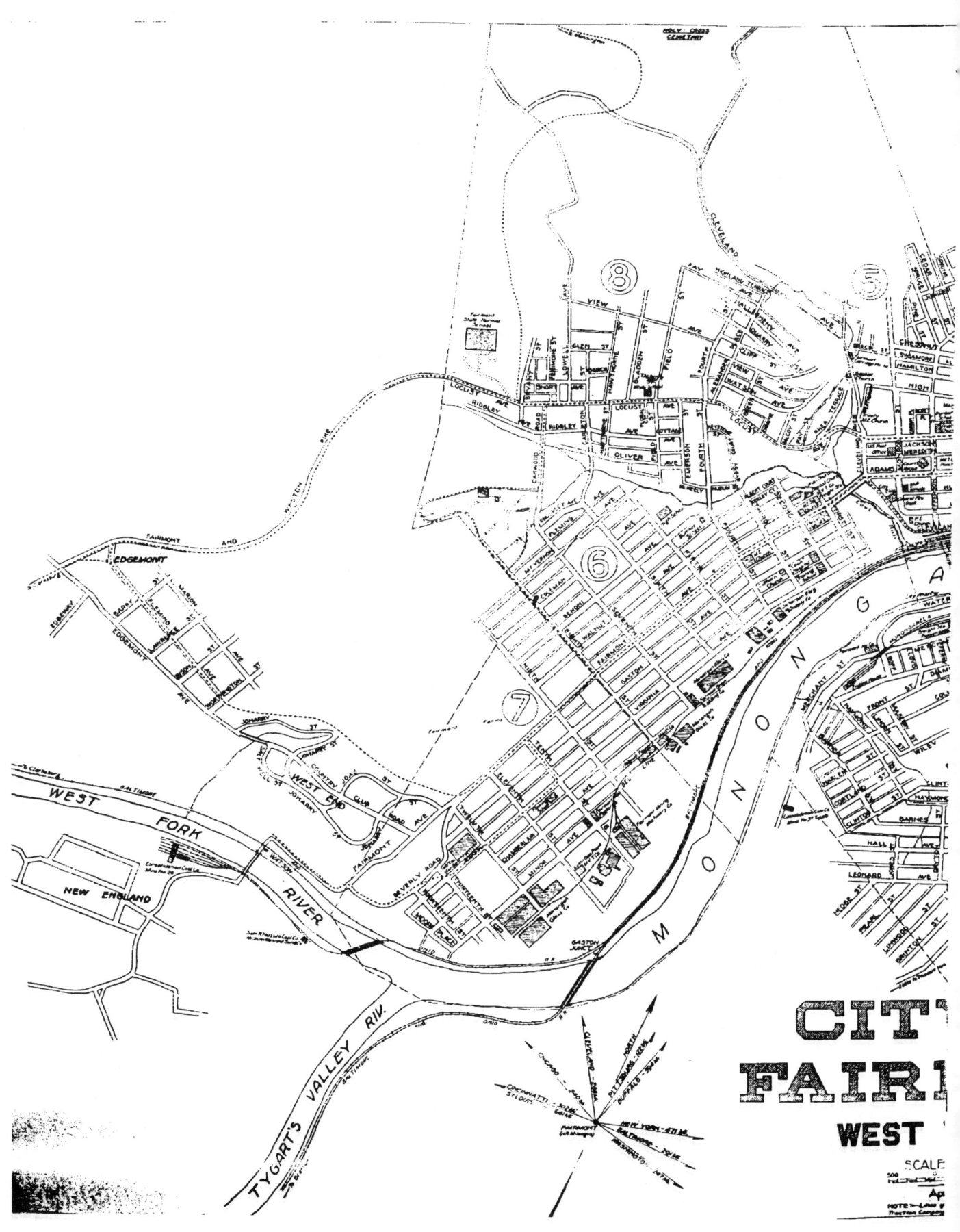

From Report of the Several Departments Under Commission Form of Government, Fairmont, West Virginia.

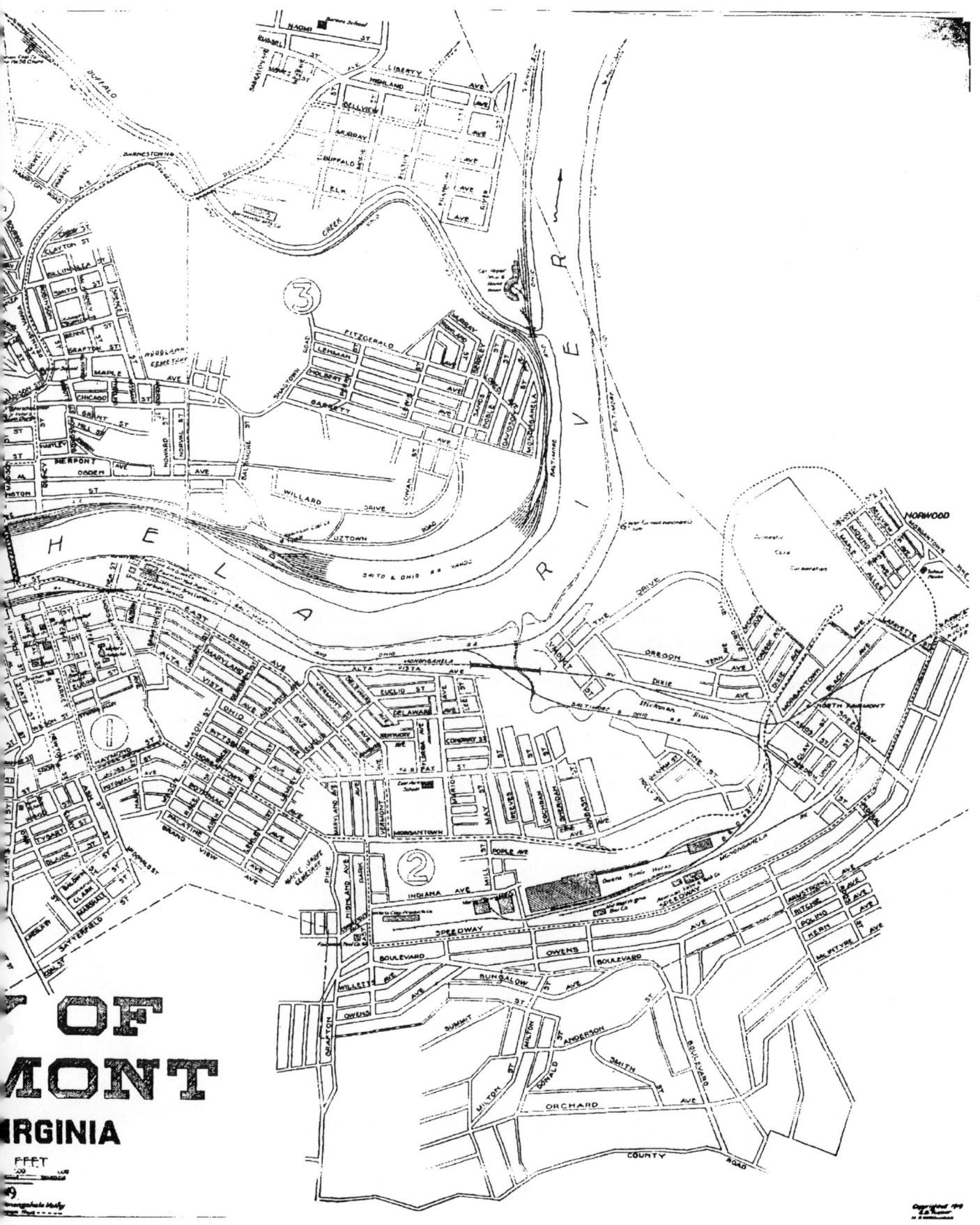

Part I—
Adams Street
(also called Main Street)

From the beginning of the city to today, Adams Street is the primary street in the downtown area. It was "the business address" for any enterprise. It is the most level street at the highest elevation in the downtown. Another reason for its prominence was that the Marion County Courthouse was located on it. Because court days brought many people to the city, merchants took advantage of the influx of people, and established their businesses in the vicinity of the Courthouse. Almost half of the buildings in this work are on Adams Street.

To further highlight the importance of Adams Street, illuminating arches were added to the intersections in 1907. Bulbs were placed in these metal arches to light the intersections of Adams and the following streets: Barney (Cleveland), Monroe, Jefferson, Madison, and Quincy. The street was then referred to as "The Great White Way."[1]

The city began its existence as small wood-frame structures, most houses; these lined the street. Because they were used as businesses, they were referred to as "business houses." Even large-scale structures that were constructed as commercial endeavors were called "business houses," perhaps because of the origin of the first commercial structures in the area. The small, wood-frame structures gave way to brick commercial structures in the period of growth, 1890 to 1930; brick structures were required in the city after the Great Fire of 1876.

Adams Street, 100 block in 1916.

Chapter 1

100 Block Adams Street, even numbered buildings

1. Carr Building, 1900. Andrew C. Lyons, architect. 100-102 Adams Street

The Carr Building was located on the corner of Adams Street and present-day Cleveland Avenue (at that time called Parks Avenue). The architect of the structure was Andrew C. Lyons of Fairmont.[2] From a photograph of the times, it was a three-story brick structure, with the unique feature of a truncated corner entrance; this was to face the traffic from the bridge over Coal Run Hollow, which was constructed in 1891-2.[3] There were store front windows on the first floor, rectangular windows on the second floor, and Roman arched windows on the third floor; there was a classical cornice at the roof. Above the third floor on the truncated face, the word "Carr" and the year 1900 were inscribed. The building was almost triangular in shape to fit the irregular site created by the intersection of the two streets. The Union One Price Clothing Store was the first business to occupy the new building[4]; historically, the two store fronts housed clothing stores, while the upper rooms were medical offices, according to city directories. Businesses were also located in the basement.

The building was demolished in 1973 for the present one-story structure on the site.

Carr Building (right), 100-102 Adams Street, c. 1902

2. George M. Jacobs Building, Citizens' Dollar Bank, Fairmont State Bank; 1900. Andrew C. Lyons, architect. 104 Adams Street

The site originally contained a dwelling prior to this structure. This building was one of several constructed by George M. Jacobs of Fairmont, and designed by the architect Andrew C. Lyons.[5] It was built of brick and Vermont granite, and was finished throughout in hardwood, "a fine specimen of modern architecture and ... a credit not only to its builder, but to the city of Fairmont."[6]

The structure was three stories high and had three bays. On the first floor, the center bay contained the doorway, and the two flanking bays were store front windows, flanked by engaged Corinthian columns. The upper floor windows were surrounded by two-story engaged Corinthian columns and topped by Roman arches. At the top of the structure was an Italianate balustrade with the year 1900 inscribed in the center segment. "Geo. M. Jacobs" was originally carved in high-relief letters below this, but must have been removed, as later photographs (c. 1919) show the letters "19 BANK 03" inscribed in its place. On the Sandborn Insurance maps of 1902, 1906, 1912, and 1918, it was labeled as one of the "Skinner Buildings" (along with 106-108 Adams Street).

When it opened, the first floor originally housed The Twin Rouss Store,[7] a clothier. It was occupied in 1902 by the Citizens Dollar Savings Bank, until it went defunct in 1915. This is probably when the inscription on the building was changed.

A new bank named the Fairmont State Bank was organized in July of 1917, and it bought the former Citizens building for its banking house.[8] The bank opened on November 17, 1917 in the redecorated rooms, with the directors and officers in attendance to welcome the patrons and visitors at the opening.

The Fairmont State Bank was remodeled by W. H. Spedden in March of 1924, necessitated by the increase in business. The entrance was moved from the center of the building to the east side of the front, which had been a large window; the steps were eliminated. The front door was bronze and plate glass. In the lobby, there were two rooms for the cashier, one the private and the other the public office. Alabama marble was used for the interior work. The existing vault was moved back, and an additional vault and safety deposit boxes were added in the basement; this room fronted on Cleveland Avenue.[9] The bank remained at this location until 1926.[10]

The building was demolished in 1973 for the present one-story structure on the site.

NOTE: The two buildings located at 106-108 and 110-112 Adams street were both referred to as the "Skinner Buildings" in book and newspaper references, and on the Sandborn maps of 1902, 1906, 1912, and 1918. Care has been taken to try to attribute the enterprises to the correct location through addresses and through the labeling of building uses on the Sandborn maps. However, it is a confusing situation, to say the least. Andrew C. Lyons is attributed with designing the "Skinner Block,"[11] which may be one or both of these buildings.

Fairmont State Bank, 104 Adams Street, c. 1919

3. "Skinner Buildings" (see note previous), c. 1895. Andrew C. Lyons, architect?
106-108 Adams Street

This was a three story, five bay structure. It had a large cornice at the roof line, Roman arched windows on the third floor, rectangular windows on the second floor, and two store fronts on the first floor. The store fronts were separated by a Roman arched opening for the stairs to the upper floors. Engaged columns ran from the second floor to the bottom of the arches for the third floor windows. Although the building does not appear adjacent to the Skinner Building in a newspaper photograph of 1894,[12] it appears on the Sandborn map of Fairmont in 1896. The two distinct store fronts on the first floor had various occupants throughout the years.

The first occupant at the 106 Adams store front (the west side), was the Post Office, having moved from its previous location at 204 Adams Street. Postmaster Carr received permission from the Postal Department to move into the "new Skinner building," which took place before the first of March 1896.[13] An addition was made to the rear of the building in December of 1902,[14] and more space was acquired early in the next year by moving the front of the office up to the door. The work was done without disturbing the regular work in the office. New racks were installed in the back room to hold forty-eight bags of mail, taking the place of the previous ones that only held a dozen. A new electric canceling machine was also noted as a great labor saver. In all, the working space of the facility was doubled by the changes.[15]

The clamor to build a new Post Office began in 1905, when it was noted that it was badly needed, and that other towns, the nearest being Washington, Pennsylvania (1900 census population 7,670), was scheduled to receive one. Several sites in Fairmont were considered; the "First Warders" (east side residents) were especially anxious to have it located on their side of the river, even offering free sites.[16] However, it was announced in 1906 that the new location for the Post Office would be on the ground floor of the new Masonic Temple Building (316-320 Jefferson Street).[17] The Post Office vacated the "Skinner Building" and moved on December 17, 1906.[18]

The 108 Adams store front was first occupied by the D. F. Everett drug store;[19] it continued to be used as a drug store by several different proprietors for approximately the next twenty years. One of the druggist, Martin Brothers, bought out the A. L. Parrish drug store in October of 1907.[20] In the spring, they renovated the store, adding a soda fountain and ice cream factory.[21]

It appears that the second floor of the structure housed offices of varying types. One of these was the Italian consulate, which was housed in the "Skinner Building" for a period of time around 1903. Because of the large number of Italian immigrants who came primarily to work in the mines, a consulate was opened to aid them with their problems. John W. Marianna served as the consul for approximately three years (c. 1903-06). He intervened on their behalf, served as the translator at the Post Office for the "foreign mail," and even opened up a foreign bank. Although the consulate was first located in the old Peoples Bank building (123 Adams Street), and later on Madison Street,[22] the Italian flag flew in front of the Skinner Building, even on the fourth of July as the law allowed, to the chagrin of some citizens.

The third floor of the entire building was occupied by the Elks Club, from the building's opening until it moved into its new location at 421 Adams Street in 1904.[23]

After the Post Office relocated, the 106 Adams store front was occupied by the city's first moving picture house, the Electric Theatre. Admission was a nickel,[24] which must have been an introductory price, because it was soon raised to a dime.[25] The moving picture business was a dangerous proposition in those days; at one time, the film exploded at the Electric Theatre and the hall of the building was slightly damaged.[26] Six months later, fire again ruined films and set the playhouse on fire, though the building was said to be in no danger.[27]

In October of 1908, the Electric Theatre was sold to McCray and Fletcher, who completely renovated and redecorated it.[28] It was given a new name, the Lyric Theatre, and provided vaudeville and picture shows on its newly enlarged stage.[29] Entertainment acts included Little Nemo, the barrel jumper; the equilibrist;[30] Miss Agnes Truesdale in a child's character singing act; the Westons, of national fame, in Japanese balancing and globe rolling; as well as motion pictures and illustrated songs, all which changed daily.[31]

Ownership of the Lyric Theatre was transferred again, this time to Turk Linn and M. Earle Morgan, representing the company which owned and operated the Dixie Theatre (230 Adams Street).[32] A new exit was subsequently added to the theatre through the adjacent Martin Brothers Drug store (108 Adams),[33] probably due to the concerns of theatre fires, which had been plaguing major cities in the country and costing many lives.

January 1913 brought big changes to the building; it underwent improvements to accommodate new businesses. The vacant Lyric Theatre space (106 Adams Street) was newly occupied by the United Woolen Mills of Parkersburg,[34] where it remained until it moved to the Carr Building (100 Adams Street) at the end of 1917.[35] Other tailoring and clothing enterprises follow in that location.

The room vacated by the Martin Brothers, Druggists (108 Adams Street) was newly occupied by L. T. Feaster, Jeweler, of Elkins.[36] The opening of the store was on March 3, 1913. Workers had been remodeling for several weeks prior to this; they had newly papered and painted the interior, installed new electrical fixtures, and installed new cases and other equipment for the display of jewelry and other lines of goods. Mr. Feaster was an optician as well as a jeweler, and furnished a room in the rear of the store to fit glasses and do other work.[37] This business was located here until it closed around 1915.[38]

The confusion concerning the two "Skinner Buildings" deepens in 1916, when Courtney's, a women's wear store located in the adjacent store front in the Skinner Building at 110 Adams Street, leased the store front vacated by L. T. Feaster and connected the two big store rooms in the different buildings with archway openings. Two openings, one toward the middle and one toward the back wall, are visible on the 1918 Sandborn map. This enabled Courtney's to enlarge its quarters, which had been crowded because of the increase in their trade; the store was enlarged by eighteen hundred feet, doubling the original size of the store. T. L. Burchinal, a well-known contractor in Fairmont, was in charge of the remodeling work. The new furnishings were in the Mission Style, and a new electric lighting system was installed, with the very latest improved lights.[39]

The entrance facade of the new "room" was finished to correspond with the front on the original store. In a photograph of Courtney's store front from a 1921 newspaper, one sees a unified front. The only evidence that these store fronts are from two adjacent though separate buildings is seen in the transom area, which shows different proportions of the transom windows.[40]

Courtney's store was purchased by E. Deitz, his brother J. H. Deitz, and Mr. Markowitz of Clarksburg in June of 1922.[41] The J. H. Deitz store opened on September 6, 1922, at the still combined store fronts at 108-110 Adams Street. The opening was held from 7 to 10 in the evening, and it was reported that "great throngs" of people passed through the building. Skinner's orchestra occupied a corner in the rear and played popular music throughout the receiving hours. Souvenirs in the form of stately gladioluses were given to the ladies; and asters and other smaller flowers were given to the men. Although the whole interior had been redone, the connection between the two store fronts remained. In listing in which areas of the store one could find the different departments, it was noted that the step which had connected the two buildings had been disposed of, and a slope built to make an easy access between the rooms.[42]

Kinney Shoe Store opened in April of 1925 in the store room formerly occupied by J. H. Deitz Company. Although it was stated that the store room was large for this kind of store, it gave ample room for carrying a large stock with proper display.[43] This indicates that the shoe company probably occupied the two rooms in the connected store fronts.

At some point in time, the connection between the two buildings was removed or covered, because it was noted that later in 1925, four different businesses occupied the first floor store fronts of the Skinner Buildings: Dan Block, tailor (106 Adams Street), the Dollar store (108 Adams Street), Kinney Shoes (110 Adams Street), and Martin and Leaf Grocers (114 Adams Street).[44]

The Dollar Store space was vacated and the C. A. House music store moved in it from across the street at 115 Adams street. The music store had been at it former location for ten years, but was forced to move in 1928 because the O. J. Morrison's store had purchased the property to erect a large department store building on the location. A number of sound-proof booths were built for the accommodation of the record business of the company, and the entire room was redecorated throughout. The front was set off by the addition of a handsome electric sign.[45]

The building was demolished in 1973 for the present one-story structure on the site.

4. Skinner Building (see note previous), 1892-3. Andrew C. Lyons, architect ?
110-114 Adams Street

On the rear of this site is believed to have been the location of the first meeting room of Fairmont Lodge No. 9 A. F. & A. Masons. According to Mr. E. C. Kerr, the lodge met on the second floor of a small building located here, when he joined the lodge in 1850. Mr. Kerr stated this at the cornerstone ceremonies held in 1906 for the Masonic Temple Building (316-320 Jefferson Street), at which he was the oldest living member of the local lodge. He said that the small building was in the rear of what in 1906 was Nuzum Grocery, which was located in the Skinner Building.[46] The lodge next moved to the old Presbyterian church on the corner of Jefferson and Adams Streets in 1854.

Charles L. Skinner had this "business house" constructed, with John F. Phillips of Fairmont as the contractor.[47] It was planned as a three-story business block. The third story was under construction during the second week of October 1892,[48] and the brick on the new structure was done at the beginning of December.[49]

The "new business house" was constructed near the new iron bridge, and was called one of the most handsome and most substantial buildings ever erected in Fairmont. It was constructed with a pressed brick front and rock-faced sills and lintels.[50] The ornamental pediment at the center of the roof cornice which read "1893 SKINNER" has been lost. The third floor has Roman and segmented arched windows, and the second floor has rectangular windows.

When the Skinner Building opened around the first of April, 1893, there were two fine store rooms on the first floor, one occupied by The Fair, a "queensware" store at 110 Adams Street; and the other by J. D. Davis, who carried dress goods, shoes, and clothing at 114 Adams Street. Both rooms were very large and commodious, with embossed steel ceilings and elegant counters and fittings.[51]

The second floor was divided into a merchant tailor's shop and cutting room on one side, and offices on the other. Fred T. Martin had the front office on the second floor and Clark Coal & Coke Company and the Natural Gas Company had the offices in the rear. The third floor was wholly occupied by W. C. Shafer's Photograph and Art Studio;[52] at their grand opening on June 10, 1893, everybody was invited to call.[53]

Stoy the Tailor also relocated his business to the "new Skinner building" in June of 1893. "Go there! Get measured there. Ah, there!," the advertisement read.[54] Stoy's business had grown steadily in the three years he had been conducting business in Fairmont. The number of his employees rose to a dozen first-class workmen, and he sold the finest goods to be bought in the eastern markets. He guaranteed fit in every case.[55]

Martin Brothers Cash Grocers moved into the 114 Adams Street store front sometime around 1896,[56] then proceeded to acquire the other store room as well when they opened their new dry goods and notions store in the room formerly occupied by The Fair at 110 Adams Street.[57] For the next twenty years, groceries and dry goods were the respective uses for the two store fronts, though the ownership of the stores changed. G. L. Jolliffe purchased the 110 Adams Street store front in July of 1904, which had previously been run by the Martin Brothers. His establishment sold a full line of ladies' and children's furnishings.[58] He had remodeled the store in both 1906 and 1908.[59]

The telephone exchange was located in the Skinner Building around 1896, having its office in the rear of the building, according to the Sandborn map of 1896. During an electrical storm in May of 1903, the Bell Telephone Company was almost burned out of business and home, when an electric light wire crossed a telephone wire on the pole in front of the telephone exchange. Flames shot twenty to thirty feet in the air, and it looked like the whole street was in danger. One of the "hello girls" (telephone operators) went to the nearby Marietta Hotel (128-130 Adams Street) and turned in the fire alarm; the fire department arrived in short notice to extinguish it. There was no damage to the building, but it took time to put the wires back in order.[60]

A few days after the fire, it was noted that Manager Mansfield of the Bell Telephone had rented the entire second floor of the Skinner Building over Jolliffe's store (110 Adams Street). The exchange boards were put in the rear of the building and the private booths in the front. The company also underwent substantial improvements of the telephone lines, spending about thirty thousand dollars to rebuild them. The switchboard was put on a new pattern, to save the "hello girls" lots of work and the public lots of waiting.[61]

There were further improvements in the operating department of the Bell Telephone Company in 1913, when they remodeled the rest rooms.[62] However, the quarters eventually became cramped and the rapid enlargement of their subscribers list indicated a need for new quarters. It was announced on January 7, 1916 that a new office building was to be constructed for the Bell Telephone Company around the corner at 214 Monroe Street;[63] they moved out of the Skinner Building on May 25, 1917 to their new structure.[64]

This building has recently been rehabilitated for office use, and houses the Marion County Chamber of Commerce.

Skinner Building, 110-114 Adams Street, c. 1894

5. Methodist Episcopal Church; 1854, 1896.
Hennen Building; 1911, 1916. 118-122 Adams Street

The earliest record of the site of the Hennen Building exists in an inventory of 85 lots, a portion of Boaz Fleming's 254 acres of property which he owned along the Monongahela River, laid out as the city of Middletown, Virginia in the year 1819. Lot 22 was bought by Hazo Parsons (with an extra parcel) for $30 on December 18, 1822. Parsons built a good house on it and sold it in 1835 to Harriet Henderson for $150. Harriet fixed up the place and sold out in 1837 to C. B. Bristol, for $350.[65]

The earliest accounts of a non-residential structure on this site was the Methodist Episcopal (M. E.) Church. The church was established in the year 1837 and first met in a schoolhouse on the corner of Jackson and Monroe Streets. A brick church at 220 Washington Street was constructed in 1842 (later sold to the Protestant Episcopal Church, currently the Union Mission Chapel), and the congregation met there until 1854, when they moved to their new building, on the site of the present-day Hennen Building.[66]

The M. E. Church on Adams Street was constructed in 1853-1854. According to the 1884 Sandborn map, the two-story structure was set back from the street line of buildings by approximately seven feet, had forty feet of frontage on Adams Street, and had a depth of approximately sixty feet. It was 30 feet to the eaves, had a shingle roof, a wood cornice, and was constructed of brick. From photos of that time, it was a Neoclassical structure with a gable-end facade with three bays, topped with a central hexagonal tower with a dome. The vertical second floor windows were rectangular in shape and had shutters on the front. It had a seating capacity of approximately six hundred.[67] The cost of the construction was $5,000.[68] The church appeared unchanged in the 1892 Sandborn map.

By 1896, the church must have been inadequate for the congregation's needs or must have seemed "old fashioned," because an extensive remodeling occurred in this year. "The work of tearing out the old front of the M. E. Church was begun Monday morning. This work had been delayed by the recent bad weather. The handsome new front will be put in as rapidly as possible and when completed will be an ornament to the town."[69] "The brick work is being laid on the M. E. Church, which is undergoing improvements."[70]

The remodeled church was such a radical change from the first that it is hard to believe it was the same structure, though nowhere was it noted that the old church was demolished. Photos from this time show a Gothic style church, similar to the Methodist Protestant Temple constructed nearby at 216-218 Monroe Street in 1896-7. According to the 1896 Sandborn map, the central tower was replaced by 50 foot tall bell tower on the north-east corner; it had a tall, pointed spire topped with a finial. A smaller tower balanced the front on the opposite side of the entrance door below the gable end of the roof. The rectangular windows had been replaced with Gothic arched windows with stained glass. More importantly, the structure has been extended toward the street by seven feet and lined up with other structures on Adams Street. Although it still had wood cornices and was still two stories tall, it was 36 feet to the eaves, and had a slate roof.

The M. E. Church appeared the same on the Sandborn maps dated 1902 and 1906. However, in 1905, the structure had become inadequate for the accommodation of the large church membership, and it had been placed in the hands of Real Estate Agent H. H. Lanham to be sold. One proposition was to sell it to the City of Fairmont for $30,000 for use as the new City building; this would have consolidated the various city departments which were scattered throughout the city.[71]

Mr. Lanham had employed Andrew C. Lyons, a locally outstanding architect, to sketch the church building as remodeled for the city's use. "According to the plans, the fire department and jail cells are on the ground floor, which has a large front opening. On the second floor are the various city offices, council room, etc. This sketch was drawn simply to show what could be done and should the council decide to purchase the building many changes could be made in the plans."[72]

This proposition was looked upon favorably by some of the councilmen, which caused the church trustees to look for a new lot to build a new church. At that time, they owned a lot on the corner of Fairmont Avenue and Fourth Street. "Many members of the congregation have objected to having their church at the present location, where the noises of the street interfere with their worship and will rejoice to get to a more quiet spot. While at first the new location will seem a little out of the way, the people will soon be accustomed to it."[73]

Although the sale to the city fell through, T. W. Hennen bought the M. E. Church property on August 4, 1910, paying approximately $32,000 for the property. Although he took possession of the property at once, the building was still used for the church services for several months until the new church was completed. Mr. Hennen was expected to "convert the church building into a modern structure to be used for business purposes."[74]

By May 1911, Mr. Hennen's purposes were more solidified. He had leased the property to a group of men, Charles E. McCray, Jr.; Dr. R. E. McCray, and M. B. Criss, for a period of ten years, and they were to convert it into a theatre. "The entire interior and exterior of the building will be gone over, alterations and improvements will be made and the structure placed in condition for its new use. A new stone front is to be put in and the house when altered will have a large stage and a seating capacity of 925 persons." It was to be known as the Church Theatre.[75]

The alterations made at that time must have been radical, for the two story church structure had become a three-story building, according to the Sandborn map of 1912. However, there is no statement that the church was demolished, and the exterior dimensions of the building on the map are unchanged. This must have been the time at which the beam at the second story ceiling was added to support the third floor. Remnants of masonry walls in the northeast corner of the basement may have supported the now-demolished tower.

The theory that the 1896 church was still an integral part of the theatre building is further supported by a newspaper article from the *Fairmont Times* in June 1911. "An injunction was yesterday secured by T. Wilbur Hennen and others against Thomas A. Deveny, to restrain Mr. Deveny from building on a strip of land, ten feet wide, on either side of the old M. E. church building on Main street. The case will come up for trial at the July court, when a suit is also set for trial. It is claimed, that although Mr. Deveny owns the land in question there is a provision in the deeds that no buildings were to be erected nearer the church building than ten feet. It is the contention of the defendant that this meant while the building was in use as a church, and that now the church having sold the (b)uilding for use as a theatre, the terms do not have force. The plaintiff claims that terms hold force forever ... It is understood that Mr. Deveny wished to enlarge his hotel building" (the Marietta Hotel, currently the site of the Deveny Building) "the width of the alley next the church building, which is now being reconstructed to make a theatre building."[76] Though no subsequent article regarding the outcome of the case was found, the 1918 Sandborn map shows the alley in contention to the east of the Hennen Building as being filled in with a structure.

Another article in support of the theory that the church building was still part of the building appeared in the *Fairmont Times* on June 21, 1911. It was noted that the contents of the cornerstone of the 1853-4 church that was discovered when the front of the building was torn down. No photos of the building as a theatre have yet been located.

The 1912 Sandborn map now shows a three-story, forty-two foot tall brick building with a composition roof and metal cornice. The first and second floors "in one" were used for moving pictures, the third floor for "photo," for which a skylight had been installed. On the first floor, partitions were added at the front; a florist had a small area in the northeast corner, a tailor had a small area in the northwest corner, and the entrance to the theatre was in the middle. A stage and scenery area were designated in the back. Subsequent advertisements in the Fairmont Times noted a first and second balcony; prices for balcony seats were five cents and main floor seats were ten cents, though in later years they were raised to balcony seats ten cents, main floor seats twenty cents.[77]

The name "Church Theatre" never materialized. Perhaps it seemed sacrilegious to use a former church as secular structure such as a theatre, perhaps they didn't want the people to remember the building's previous use. In any case, the Colonial Theatre opened on December 12, 1911.[78]

The opening was not without problems. The original opening date was advertised for Friday, December 9, 1911; but it was postponed because of "their moving picture machine not being there." At the opening, the police chief, fire chief, and mayor closed the theatre during the second show due to inadequate fire exiting. "When the building was put up the proper exits were planned and were put in the building, but because they did not own the property on either side of the building, the owner of the property" (Mr. Deveny) "goes to work and builds obstructions on the outsides of the doors so that they could not be opened outward as the law requires. The owners of the Theatre had carpenters remove the hinges from the doors so that they would be opened inward in a moments time, but the officials did not think this lawful, and ordered the Theatre closed on this account."[79] From these comments and the previous injunction, it appears that the new theatre was not a welcome addition to its next door neighbor.

Those among the large crowd who had been at the opening were pleased with the building. "The interior of the new building is very attractive and the decorations are beautiful. The architecture of the place is excellent, and the balcony is so placed that all can see perfectly, either from the balcony, the second balcony or the ground floor. Their new curtains are very pretty and the outer curtain contains little advertising."[80]

The structure became known as the Colonial Theatre Building. The Fleming Flower Store, Egan's Shoe Store, Johnston's Studio, and the Main Street News Stand were some of the businesses located there between 1912 and 1916; at the same time, McCray's Colonial Theatre operated.

Times became tough in 1916, however. Part of this was due to the fierce competition of theatres in the city; the Grand Theatre (325 Monroe Street, formerly the Grand Opera), the Dixie Theatre (230 Adams Street), the Nelson Theatre (316 Adams Street), the Ideal Theatre (308 Jefferson Street), the Princess Theatre (220 Jefferson Street), and the Hippodrome (413-415 Adams Street) were all competing for business. The Colonial promoted itself in new and different ways, offering free gifts, having boxing matches and amateur nights, and booking vaudeville acts. But the advertisements in the newspapers slowly became smaller in size, and then stopped. The last one appeared in September 30, 1916.

In October 1916, T. W. Hennen applied for a building permit in the amount of $6,000 to rebuild the interior of the Colonial Theatre Building.[81] Beginning in February 1917, it was referred to as the New Hennen Building. The Sandborn map of 1918 shows some of the remodeling; the first floor was divided by a wall to create two storefronts, though the exterior dimensions, number of stories, and the height of the building were unchanged from the last map of 1912. It is assumed that the two balconies were removed at this time to provide a continuous second floor for business uses; the second floor joists probably bear on the new first floor wall, which is supported in the basement by metal columns. The unusually tall second floor ceiling height (approximately 13 feet) was probably due to the previous ceiling height of the church, subsequently the theatre with two balconies.

Again, no photos have been found of the building at this time, but it is assumed that this remodeling provided the current appearance of the Hennen Building. It is a three- story beige brick structure with six bays of large rectangular windows. There were two store fronts on the first floor. A stone door sill can be seen near the ceiling of the basement at the front of the building, which may have been at the entry to one of the two first floor storefronts. Weber's Flowers moved into the "new Hennen Building" in February 1917.[82]

The Western Union offices also moved into their new offices in the Hennen Building that spring. "As one enters the lobby from Main (Adams) street, he sees a standing writing desk and a writing desk where the writer may sit to compose his message. Inside the counter will be two large flat top desks and deeper in the office the telegraph table with six stations ... Back of the telegraph table is the telephone table where clerks take messages over the phone and send out messages in the same manner. In the rear of the room is the messenger quarters ... In the basement are storage rooms, storage batteries, and other things that are connected with the operation of the office."[83]

Wilbur Hennen died suddenly on November 27, 1920; he was forty-two. "Mr. Hennen had

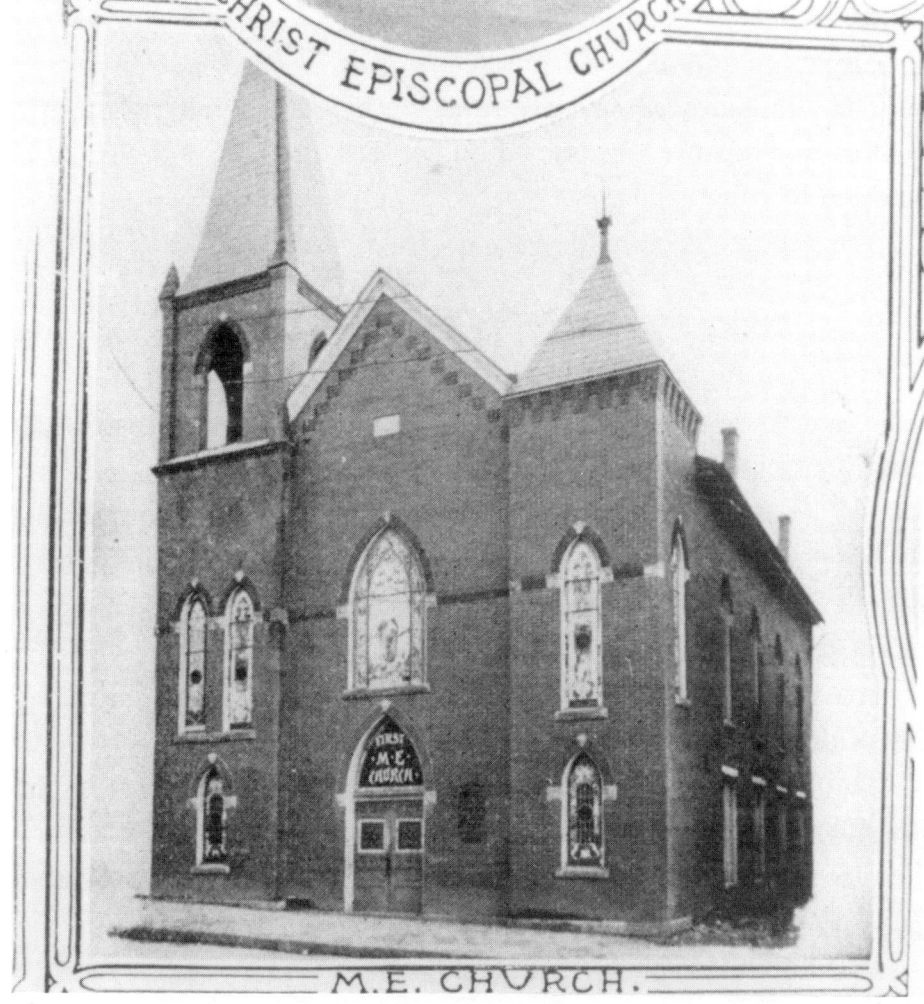

Methodist Episcopal Church, 118-122 Adams Street, c. 1908

been among his friends that day previous exchanging the greeting of the festive season and was apparently in his usual health, strong and robust as he always appeared to be. He, however, had not been well for a few weeks but it was not thought to be anything serious. The immediate cause of his death as pronounced by the physicians was dilation of the heart." He had been stricken at the breakfast table and fell over in an unconscious state; his death was "instantaneous."[84] He was a prominent citizen, and a leader in business, church and lodge affairs. T. Wilbur Hennen was remembered in the Maundy Feast of the Masons in April 1922.[85] According to the City of Fairmont's tax assessor's record, the property was deeded to Thomas W. and Dora F. Hennen, his only son and daughter-in-law.

From the time the original M. E. Church was constructed in 1853, there has been no mention of any structure on the site being demolished as the building evolved from a church to a theatre to a commercial building. It has been "extended," "improved," "altered," "reconstructed," and new "fronts" have been added; but from all evidence, the historical fabric of the previous buildings is part of the current Hennen Building.

The building is currently undergoing renovation for offices.

6. alley infill building, c. 1917. 124 Adams Street

The site had been an alley from the city's beginning. The infill building, one story in height, was probably constructed by Mr. Deveny after the dispute over his right to do so as contested by Mr. Hennen in 1911.

The building is currently vacant.

7. Marietta Hotel Annex, c. 1898. 126 Adams Street

When the accommodations at the adjacent Marietta Hotel became too small for the increased patronage, a three-story, two-bay brick annex was erected by Mr. Thomas A. Deveny around the year 1898. It "was fitted up and furnished in modern style and provided with lavatories, toilet rooms, and other accessories to comfort." It brought the total number of bedrooms for the hotel to forty.[86] It had a simple cornice at the roof and a sign reading "Hotel Marietta" was located above the third floor windows. Originally, there was an alley between it and the Marietta Hotel; this alley was eliminated when the Deveny Building was constructed to the edge of the Hotel Annex.

Sam B. Iseman moved his burgeoning clothing business from the Watson Hotel Building (402-408 Adams Street) to the Marietta Hotel Annex in 1899, where he remained until 1904 when he moved to 204 Adams Street.[87] The Union Clothing Store occupied the building in 1923.

This building is currently vacant.

Marietta Hotel Annex (right), 126 Adams Street and Marietta Hotel (left), 128-130 Adams Street, c. 1902

8. Continental Hotel, Marietta Hotel, c. 1840. Deveny Building, 1916-17.
John Burchinal, architect. 128-130 Adams Street

The first structure on the site of the present Deveny Building was the Continental Hotel. It was said to have been built by Jas. Burns;[88] a newspaper article, recalling some of the building's history prior to its demolition for the Deveny Building in 1916, stated that it was constructed in 1840.[89] From photographic evidence, the structure was a three-story, hipped roof brick building with five bays on the front. From the side elevation on Monroe Street, it appears to have been constructed in two distinct sections: the front part was three bays deep and the rear section was seven bays deep. It had an ornamental balcony on the Adams Street front at the second and third floors. Both sections of the building appear on the Sandborn map of 1884.

Additional information about the original building came to light in a newspaper article in 1921, five years after the Continental Hotel, later called the Marietta Hotel, was razed to make room for the Deveny Building. One of the first schools to be established in Fairmont was founded when the W. R. White School opened in the Marietta Hotel building, in the room of the hotel which was used as a restaurant. The school flourished from May 4, 1856 until sometime in the 1860's.[90]

The Continental Hotel came under new management after April 1, 1886, when George W. Manley became the proprietor; "No pains nor expense will be spared to render the entertainment first-class in every particular," read the newspaper advertisement.[91] It was successfully managed by him until his death, sometime prior to 1894; afterwards, it was managed by his family under the direction of his administrator. However, it was offered for sale by W. E. Arnett, Real Estate Agent. The notice stated that it was lighted with electric light, heated with natural gas, and had a bath room on the second floor. It offered a free bus to and from all trains, all for the rate of $2.00 per day.[92]

In 1894, a fire occurred in the wash house of the Continental Hotel, which was an addition to the hotel. The alarm was sounded and the Fire Company and a large number of citizens responded at once. The "hose boys" had it under control in less than an hour, and their work was commended; had it not been for the Hose Company, the hotel would have been doomed. The loss was about $500, and the building was fully insured.[93]

Some time between 1894 and 1895, the name was changed to the Marietta Hotel, according to the Sandborn map of 1896. A man named Marcus Marietta owned the building for a time, and conveyed the property to Colonel Thomas A. Deveny on August 10, 1895. Mr. Deveny conducted the hotel in good style: "The table is substantial; the meals well cooked and well served; cleanliness rules in every nook and corner of the building and every department of the hotel. ... These are the things that render a stay—short or long—at the Marietta pleasurable to the traveler."[94] When the hotel became too small for its business, Mr. Deveny had an annex erected around 1898 adjoining it at 126 Adams Street.

In 1906, W. D. Wood and Charles Berns became the new proprietors of the famous Marietta Hotel.[95] Colonel Deveny had leased his property to the two gentlemen when he was elected to the presidency of the Tygarts Valley Brewing Company of Grafton. The lease was based upon the hotel when it had a bar in connection with it, and the rent was a "handsome figure," though not publicly known.[96]

Though Berns and Wood were popular hotel men who conducted the hotel to the fine standards set by Colonel Deveny, the Marietta Hotel, under the terms of the contract, reverted to its owner in 1908. The proprietors were said to have become in arrears in rent; the hotel became a "losing proposition" when the saloons were voted out of Fairmont.[97] When the Moose Lodge was being organized in 1909, it had met in the Marietta Hotel.[98]

Milan Glumicich became the proprietor in 1914, and he planned many improvements for the Marietta Hotel. The plans called for interior alterations including removing the partition in back of the hotel office to provide a smaller office leading directly from Adams Street to the old hotel dining room. The old dining room was being remodeled into a first class restaurant, complete with new equipment and furnishings. The rooms on each side of the Adams Street office were remodeled and show windows were installed to convert the two rooms into stores. The former bar was converted into a lunch counter in connection with the existing soft drink counter.[99]

The Marietta Restaurant opened on August 18, 1914. It was fitted with marble tables, and had entrances from both Adams and Monroe Streets. Dinner was served from 11 to 2 in "the new ladies and gentlemen's dining room."[100] It had become a popular place, with new innovations such as having late musical hits play on the Victrola during dinner.[101]

More remodeling was done in 1915 by Proprietor Glumicich. A barber shop with three chairs was added as well as "shower baths;" after a shave, haircut and shampoo, one could enjoy a shower bath at a nominal price. The newest fad in conjunction with having the Victrola playing during one's meal was to have the daily menu announced on the Victrola as well. This was to save the waiters a little time and to make the patrons hungry.[102] Telephones were also added to the hotel and restaurant.[103]

The foreign bank exchange and ticket agency were located at the Marietta. "Here, men of all nations and every walk of life gather. Here they can buy tickets for their homes in the foreign lands and send their messages to loved ones across the sea; here the men of all nations gather and talk about the great European war; here is the place where they may send money to the poor and needy in the war-stricken country. In fact, history is made every day in the little banking room at the Marietta."[104]

Many functions were held at the Marietta to draw in the public. The hotel held a reception in May of 1915, and had 3,000 visitors. Of course, there was free ice cream and cake, and Bossie's Orchestra played.[105] In the following month of June, they held a cabaret at the Marietta, which was a big success; there was talk of fitting the hotel with a regular stage for repeat performances.[106] Nola Ingram of Columbus, Ohio was "sweetly singing" at the Marietta Restaurant that July.[107]

In spite of all of these efforts, a change in management occurred in November of 1915, perhaps as a sign that all was not well at the hotel. Mike Glumicich became the manager of the hotel, and Boyd Anderson, an experienced restaurant man from Shinnston, leased the restaurant from Mr. Glumicich and became the restaurant manager. It was stated in the newspaper that Mr. Anderson's new position "is assurance that the Marietta is due to become known over the state as one of the truly good places to eat." Further upheaval included managerial changes; Mr. Anderson brought his own experienced force of waiters with him, and made many changes to the menu.[108]

All these efforts to rejuvenate the aging hotel in the era of the "dry" city were for naught; Colonel Thomas A. Deveny announced in April of 1916 that the antiquated Marietta hotel building would be razed to make way for a skyscraper office building on the site. He planned a three story structure worth $56,000, but the foundations would be massive enough to hold ten stories as they were needed. The first floor was to be occupied by stores, the second by offices, and the third by apartments. It was to be constructed of the latest improved pressed brick and an elevator would be installed between the lobby and the apartments. Eventually, he thought a building from eight to ten stories high and extending to the Colonial Theatre Building (118-122 Adams Street) would be built on this corner.[109]

The demolition began on May 1, 1916, and was expected to last more than a week. "With its passing, Fairmont loses one of her landmarks for the old brick pile has been standing since 1840."[110]

Shortly after this, the Fairmont Elks began discussions regarding whether or not they should sign contracts with Colonel Deveny to build them a home in his new block to be erected. A large turnout of members met for the discussion; some claimed that the new location would be more convenient that their current one (419-420 Adams Street), which was just outside the business section of the city.[111]

On May 5, 1916, it was announced that the Elks were "going to have new and very modern quarters in the new Deveny building." Papers were to be signed to authorize Colonel Deveny "to so arrange his plans as to give the lodge possibly the finest home in West Virginia."[112] These papers were signed a few days later, and Colonel Deveny planned to outfit the fifth and sixth floors of his new building "in a very lavish manner for the boys." The Elks' existing club building (421 Adams Street) was to be offered for rent.[113]

An agreement between Colonel Deveny and the J. C. McCrorey & Company was announced for the company's occupation of the first floor and basement of the proposed Deveny skyscraper, with a twenty-one year lease. The 6,500 square feet of floor space would be used for a "1 to 25 cent store." The ten-cent store in the McCrorey Building (218-220 Adams Street) was to be continued. No other floors had been leased at this time, other than the two top floors for the Elks' Club. It was still undecided whether the building would be topped with six or seven stories. John Burchinal, architect of Fairmont, was "laboring daily at his office ... drawing out a finished and practical piece of construction."[114]

The contract was let on February 28, 1917 for the construction of the buff brick, steel frame building, which was to cost $110,000; C. D. Keiser of Bellaire, Ohio was the lucky bidder. The price for the six story, 60' by 100' building did not include the plumbing, electrical work, or heating; they were contracted separately. Both the brick and the steel had already been ordered, to arrive in a timely manner, for the building to be completed in the contracted time, by October 1, 1917.[115]

At this time, the Woolworth store had leased the first floor, and the Elks Club the two upper floors. On the other floors, sixty-five fine offices were to be located and equipped. The construction of the superstructure began as soon as the materials arrived; the weather was thought to be favorable for construction, and the building was to be finished before the next winter set in. Mr. Deveny's project was to provide offices for many of the business concerns seeking a place for their headquarters; he had taken a keen interest in the development of the city.[116]

The Elks were already planning how they were going to outfit and use their new rooms. The present lodge building was to be disposed of, and the lodge would be in position to expend large sums in furnishing and fitting the new quarters. The fifth floor was planned to house the lodge room which would also be used for an assembly room and dance hall; the kitchen, billiards rooms, cards rooms, lounging rooms and the parlors would also be on this floor. The sixth floor would house eleven bedrooms, each equipped with shower baths, which would be rented to members or visiting Elks.[117]

The steel for the skyscraper arrived and was brought to the site in March 1917. One hundred tons of steel were used in the structure. The brick to be used came in steadily to the site. The excavation work was almost complete in that month, as was the remainder of the foundation.[118]

As with any construction project, the actual work is noisy and messy. In April, the West Virginia Publishing Company had secured a mandamus (writ) to clear the obstruction of the streets and sidewalks in Monroe and Adams Streets about the site of the proposed building. It seems that the contractors had erected a frame building within the fire limits of the city (not allowed after The Great Fire of 1876) and also on the streets of the city. In addition, they had violated the laws by fencing up the sidewalks and by putting steel on the streets. It was understood that Mayor Bowen had given official permission for these acts, but the complainant was taking the matter into the courts to force the city to enforce its own laws.[119]

The completed six-story brick structure has five bays on Adams Street, and eight bays as well as the main entrance to the upper floors on Monroe street. Brick pilasters extend from the second through fourth floors. A decorative cornice separates the fourth and fifth floors. The first floor had large store front windows (which have since been filled in). Originally, there were two-story Roman arched windows which stretched from the fifth to sixth floors; these were located on the five bays on Adams Street, and the first three bays from the corner down Monroe Street, as seen in an early photo. The remaining windows were rectangular in shape with sandstone lintels.

In spite of the October 1 deadline, the Woolworth Store did not open until November of 1917. It had opened earlier in the month for business, even though there was no sign over the door and no window lights; the customary one-day sale extended for an entire week. The official opening occurred on November 14, 1917.[120]

The Elks' move was delayed even more; they did not occupy their new home until the end of March 1918. The public reception occurred around April 1, 1918. The following description of their lavishly decorated fifth floor quarters appeared in the newspaper as follows: "All of the floors are of hardwood and the Elks have one of the nicest and coziest little lounging rooms and libraries that can be seen anywhere. Along one of the walls a fireplace is provided above which is the emblem of the order, 'the hour of remembrance,' which is symbolized by the hands of the clock pointing to 11.[121]

"The ladies parlor is furnished in walnut and the upholstering is of blue satin. The chandelier is of the candle arrangement and the globes are blue with silk shades to blend with the general color scheme.[122]

"The lodge room is one of the finest in the entire state. The furnishings are very elaborate and costly. The indirect lighting system is installed. The walls are finished to represent stone and contain all the familiar markings to produce that effect. The exposed pillars also show up very handsomely. In the center of the hall the 'star of fidelity' has been placed at intervals.. The lodge room is of sufficient size as to take care of the present needs as well as the future. The floor is of hardwood and several runners of carpets will be spread there. Among these are several Persian rugs. The draperies that will be strung across the room will be exquisite and very costly. They will be of velvet and satin and will be in harmony with the precepts of the order.[123]

"A private telephone booth is also located in the Elks' rooms. The pool and billiard room is especially fine. The three pool tables and one billiard table in use are constructed of steel entirely except a wooden railing, which extends around them ... There (sic) are the first all-steel tables in this section of the state, having only recently being (sic) manufactured by the International Company. The indirect lighting system is also in use in this room. The indirect lighting system is regarded as being very advantageous because no shadows are cast by the lights. This is an entirely new idea for a pool and billiard room. The tables are of a walnut finish to match the other furniture. The draperies about the windows are very handsome. Five sixteen-inch oscillating electric fans have also been installed in this room."[124]

The Elks occupied their two floors of the building until 1925, when they moved into temporary quarters in the Sample Building (221 Monroe Street) while awaiting the completion of their "new" quarters at 419-421 Adams Street; in fact, the Adams Street building was the location of their lodge quarters prior to moving into the Deveny Building.

After the Elks vacated the fifth and sixth floors, the lodge quarters were made into offices. It was at this point in time that the windows on the fifth and sixth floors were probably revised from the two-story Roman-arched shape to the single-story, rectangular windows currently on the building, and the two-story lodge room space was divided into two floors. The cornice at the roof also appears to have been added at this time.

Thomas A. Deveny, aged 65 years, died in his home on April 5, 1926 at 10:30 pm. He had been in failing health, suffering from "an incurable malady which had been slowly ebbing his life away." At the time of his death, he was known as prominent local citizen and a leading hotel man of Fairmont. It was noted that he had owned and managed the Marietta Hotel, closing it out to build the present Deveny business building; he was shrewd in his manners and of a congenial disposition.[125]

The Deveny Building is still partially used for offices.

Continental Hotel, 128-130 Adams Street, Index newspaper advertisement January 3, 1894

---

[1] *Fairmont Times*, 5/8/1907, p. 1.
[2] *Industrial Fairmont in 1908*, p. 66.
[3] Fleming, p. 15.
[4] *Fairmont Free Press*, 10/25/1900.
[5] *Industrial Fairmont in 1908*, p. 66.
[6] *Twentieth Century Edition*, p. 20.
[7] ibid.
[8] *Fairmont Times*, 7/27/1917, p. 2.
[9] ibid., 3/25/1924, p. 4.
[10] Fleming, p. 38.

Deveny Building (in background), 128-130 Adams Street, c. 1918. Note original Roman arched windows on fifth/sixth floors.

Deveny Building, 128-130 Adams Street, c. 1930. Windows on fifth and sixth floors have been replaced.

[11] *Industrial Fairmont in 1908*, p. 66.
[12] *Fairmont Index*, 1/3/1894.
[13] ibid., 2/7/1896.
[14] *Fairmont Times*, 12/1/1902, p. 1.
[15] ibid., 1/8/1903, p. 1.
[16] ibid., 8/1/1906, p. 8.
[17] ibid., 12/4/1906, p. 1.
[18] ibid., 12/17/1906, p. 1.
[19] *Fairmont Index*, 5/26/1896.
[20] *Fairmont Times*, 10/8/1907, p. 1.
[21] ibid., 3/21/1908, p. 1.
[22] ibid., 3/2/1906, p. 1.
[23] ibid., 4/26/1904, p. 8.
[24] ibid., 4/20/1907, p. 8.
[25] ibid., 1/1/1908, p. 1.
[26] ibid., 4/27/1908, p. 1.
[27] ibid., 10/2/1908, p. 3.
[28] ibid., 10/19/1908, p. 5.
[29] ibid., 9/27/1909, p. 3.
[30] ibid., 1/7/1910, p. 6.
[31] ibid., 1/5/1910, p. 1.
[32] ibid., 8/1/1911, p. 6.
[33] ibid., 4/8/1912, p. 8.
[34] ibid., 1/23/1913, p. 2.
[35] ibid., 12/10/1917, p. 1.
[36] ibid., 1/23/1913, p. 2.
[37] ibid., 3/1/1913, p. 2.
[38] ibid., 7/3/1915, p. 1.
[39] ibid., 1/10/1916, p. 1.
[40] ibid., 5/29/1921, sect. 2, p. 2.
[41] ibid., 6/25/1922, p. 1.
[42] ibid., 9/7/1922, p. 1.
[43] ibid., 4/10/1925, sect. 2, p. 1.
[44] ibid., 7/5/1925, p. 6.
[45] ibid., 2/5/1928, p. 10.
[46] ibid., 4/10/1906, p. 1.
[47] *Fairmont Index*, 8/26/1892.
[48] *Fairmont Free Press*, 10/11/1892.
[49] ibid., 12/2/1892.
[50] *Fairmont Index*, 1/3/1894.
[51] ibid.
[52] ibid.
[53] *Fairmont Free Press*, 6/9/1893.
[54] ibid., 6/2/1893.
[55] *Fairmont Index*, 1/3/1894.
[56] ibid., 12/1/1896.
[57] ibid., 4/19/1898.
[58] *Fairmont West Virginian*, 7/28/1904, p. 2.
[59] *Fairmont Times*, 3/23/1906, p. 2; 12/31/1908, p. 6.
[60] ibid., 5/23/1903, p. 1.
[61] ibid., 5/25/1903, p. 7.
[62] ibid., 3/7/1913, p. 2.
[63] ibid., 1/7/1916, p. 1.
[64] ibid., 5/25/1917, p. 1.
[65] Lough, pp. 420-422.
[66] *Welcome Westinghouse,* front sect., p. 9.
[67] *Fairmont Index*, 1/3/1894.

[68] *Hardesty's Historical and Geographical Encyclopedia*, p. 309.
[69] *Fairmont Republican*, 8/6/1896.
[70] *Fairmont Index*, 8/25/1896.
[71] *Fairmont Times*, 11/1/1905, p. 1.
[72] ibid.
[73] ibid., 11/8/1905, p. 2.
[74] ibid., 8/4/1910, p. 1.
[75] ibid., 5/1/1911, p. 1.
[76] ibid., 6/17/1911, p. 11.
[77] *Fairmont West Virginian*, 12/7/1911, p. 8.
[78] ibid., 12/11/1911, p. 4.
[79] *Fairmont Times*, 12/12/1911, p. 2.
[80] ibid.
[81] ibid., 10/10/1916, p. 1.
[82] ibid., 2/3/1917, p. 3.
[83] ibid., 4/24/1917, p. 1.
[84] ibid., 11/27/1920, p. 1.
[85] ibid., 4/14/1922, p. 11.
[86] *Twentieth Century Edition*, p. 40.
[87] *Fairmont Times*, 3/18/1923, p. 9.
[88] Fleming, p. 13.
[89] *Fairmont Times*, 5/2/1916, p. 1.
[90] ibid., 5/8/1921, sect. 2, p. 1.
[91] *Fairmont Index*, 7/16/1886.
[92] ibid., 1/3/1894.
[93] ibid., 3/7/1894.
[94] *Twentieth Century Edition*, p. 40.
[95] *Fairmont Times*, 4/26/1906, p. 1.
[96] ibid., 7/14/1908, p. 1.
[97] ibid.
[98] ibid., 5/28/1909, p. 1.
[99] ibid., 8/6/1914, p. 6.
[100] ibid., 8/18/1914, p. 8.
[101] ibid., 8/26/1914, p. 8.
[102] ibid., 2/1/1915, p. 2.
[103] ibid., 6/23/1915, p. 6.
[104] ibid., 2/1/1915, p. 2.
[105] ibid., 5/27/1915, p. 8; 5/28/1915, p. 4.
[106] ibid., 6/7/1915, p. 4.
[107] ibid., 7/23/1915, p. 3.
[108] ibid., 11/24/1915, p. 4.
[109] ibid., 4/19/1916, p. 1.
[110] ibid., 5/2/1916, p. 1.
[111] ibid., 5/3/1916, p. 1.
[112] ibid., 5/4/1916, p. 5.
[113] ibid., 5/10/1916, p. 1.
[114] ibid., 5/12/1916, p. 1.
[115] ibid., 2/28/1917, p. 1.
[116] ibid.
[117] ibid., 3/14/1917, p. 2.
[118] ibid., 3/26/1917, p. 1.
[119] ibid., 4/15/1917, p. 2.
[120] ibid., 11/2/1917, p. 6.
[121] ibid., 3/30/1918, p. 4.
[122] ibid.
[123] ibid.
[124] ibid.
[125] ibid., 4/6/1926, p. 1.

Chapter 2

100 Block Adams Street, odd numbered buildings

1. Mansbach's Store, c. 1897. 101 Adams Street

This corner structure was a two story, three bay brick building. The second floor had Roman arched windows. The building was not shown on the Sandborn map of 1896, and a reference in an 1898 newspaper announced the location of L. Mansbach's store in the "new building" at the corner of Main and Barney (Cleveland Avenue) Streets.[1]

H. H. Mansbach established the Mansbach Store in Fairmont in 1897 at this location, and it handled men's and boy's clothing and furnishings.[2] Although it was a principal place of business in Fairmont, it was not a large enough city for the business to thrive as the owner desired; therefore, in 1908, the business closed.

Leopold & Company clothing store located in the rooms vacated by Mansbach, "on the korner."[3] The rooms had been renovated for this purpose. Reitman's Market was subsequently located there, as well as Adams Office Supply from 1950—1972.[4]

The building was demolished around 1975 to make way for the Community Bank & Trust Company Building, presently Huntington Banks.

2. Home Savings Bank, 1897-1898. Andrew C. Lyons, architect. 103 Adams Street

The architect of this three story, three bay brick and stone structure was Andrew C. Lyons,[5] which is evident in the classical detail shown in the cornice and in the store front level. The windows on the third floor had Roman arches; the windows on the second floor were rectangular; and the windows on the first floor consisted of two openings, the door opening narrower than the display window opening. Both first floor openings had stone segmented arches. The building was constructed for the Mutual Home & Savings Association in 1897—1898, which they first occupied on April 1, 1899; the institution became the Home Savings Bank on January 1, 1900. The

Left to right: Mansbach's Store, 101 Adams Street; Home Savings Bank, 103 Adams Street; Fitch Block, 105 Adams Street; Old Fred Fleming Building, 107 Adams Street; Hartley's, 109-113 Adams Street.

ground floor was occupied by the offices of the bank, the second floor was used as professional offices, and the third floor contained a large hall which was leased to the Ancient Order of United Workman.[6] The Home Savings bank occupied the building until 1918 when it purchased the former First National Building (210 Adams Street) and moved.[7]

The building was demolished around 1975 to make way for the Community Bank & Trust Company Building, presently Huntington Banks.

3. Fitch Block, c. 1898. 105 Adams Street

W. E. Hawkins was awarded the contract to construct the two story, three bay structure for the "new Dr. Fitch building" in November of 1897.[8] Dr. D. P. Fitch had purchased the parcel of land for his office and home from the Fleming family.[9] The building had Roman arched windows on the second floor, and one store front on the first floor. There was a decorative, classical cornice at the roof. The property was subsequently sold to Ben Nathan of Parkersburg in 1911 for $14,000.[10] It was remodeled and then leased to different shoe stores, including Stout's Shoes[11] and Alford-Graham Shoes.[12] This was also the first location of Adams Office Supply, from 1932 until they moved in 1950 to 101 Adams Street.[13]

The building was demolished around 1975 to make way for the Community Bank & Trust Company Building, presently Huntington Banks.

4. Old Fred Fleming Building, c. 1900. 107 Adams Street

The first appearance of this three story, two bay structure was on the Sandborn map of 1902, so it is assumed that it was constructed between 1896 and that year. It had rectangular windows and a simple cornice at the roof. The 1901 City Directory lists its occupant as Fleming Jewelry. Shurtleff & Welton, a shoe store, was located in the building from the beginning of their establishment on April 1, 1905 until they moved out in 1907.[14]

On April 12, 1922, a fire broke out in the building. It was believed to have originated from a gas leak in a third floor apartment. No one was home at the time, and damage was slight.[15]

In 1929, a new front to the building was constructed at a cost of $1,500; for the Shertleff and Welton Shoe store, which relocated here. It had to vacate its store in the adjacent American Building when Hartley's moved its entire operation into the building.[16]

The building was demolished around 1975 to make way for the Community Bank & Trust Company Building, presently Huntington Banks.

5. Fleming Building, American Building, 1911-12; Hartley's, 1929; Emil R. Johnson, architect. 109-113 Adams Street

This site originally had a residence on it, which was the small cottage home of Allison Fleming, dating from the 1880's. In 1911, T. W. Fleming decided to demolish the house to build a large commercial building approximately thirty-five feet by eighty feet, and three stories high.[17] The eight bay structure was divided into two store fronts on the first floor. All upper story windows were rectangular, and there was a decorative classical cornice at the roof.

J. L. Hall Hardware Company moved into the 109 Adams Street store front on September 19, 1912; they had outgrown their quarters in the Jacobs-Hutchinson Block (211 Adams Street).[18] The store room was 30 feet wide and 165 feet deep; the basement was used for storage and for surplus supplies and heavy hardware, such as farm implements and builders' supplies. This gave them three times the space in the Jacobs-Hutchinson Block.[19]

The other merchant who occupied the new Fleming building at its opening was E. C. Jones, who moved his business from his previous location at 331 Adams Street. His store room was 51 feet wide and 165 feet deep, and covered the first two floors as well as the basement. The vestibule was set back 20 feet from the street to give the building the largest show windows in the city. The store included a system of seven telephones that connected all parts of the building; a writing desk with stationery for public use; a Lamson cash carrier system with twenty-two stations, the largest installed in the state; retiring rooms; and free automobile delivery to all of the city and the suburbs. Each of the store's nine separate departments was under the management of a department head.[20]

The opening of the Jones' Store on September 19, 1912 "brought out several hundred of the fair sex," as well as a fair number of men. Omen's Orchestra entertained the crowds during the afternoon and evening. It was "an auspicious event."[21]

E. C. Jones moved his store out of the Fleming Building in July of 1917 because he had outgrown the space. His new location was in the former Banker's Residence at 208 Adams Street, which had been renovated for the purpose. Sales at the store had cleared out most of the merchandise.[22] Shurtleff & Welton Shoes occupied the store subsequently.[23]

On the third floor of the Fleming Building was a hall, which was occupied by the Knights of Pythias; they had moved from their previous hall in the Smith and McKinney Building (313-317 Adams Street). The main hall was thirty by fifty- eight feet, the banquet hall was twenty-two by forty feet and the kitchen was fourteen by sixteen feet. In addition, there was an ante room, lobby, and property rooms. They also planned to sublet the quarters to other societies in the city.[24] One of these organization was B'nai B'rith, who used the lodge rooms for their activities.[25]

The Fleming Building was purchased by J. Lee Hall on March 2, 1919. One of the things that was contemplated at this time was a three-story addition to the top of the building, since the foundations and the walls of the building had been designed and constructed to carry many additional stories. This would be designed for apartments, which were greatly needed in the city at the time due to the expanding population and housing shortage. However, this addition was not undertaken at this point in time.[26]

The Hall Hardware store expanded into the basement under the shoe store (formerly the Jones' Store) and into the rear of the first floor; an archway opening was cut into the wall to connect the two spaces. An entrance on Meredith Street was also constructed for the hardware store. This made the store the largest retail store in the city. The second floor that had been used by the Jones' store was converted into offices space.[27] At this point in time, the building became known as the American Building.

In March of 1926, Hall Hardware remodeled its store to place the larger items in the basement, and all smaller goods on the first floor. A new system of display was developed by constructing sixty seven-foot tables, the tops of which were divided into plate glass bins where practically every article that could be displayed was shown. For the opening of the remodeled store, an orchestra was engaged to provide music, souvenirs were distributed, and J. L and Homer Hall were present in person to meet and greet the visitors to the store. Many manufacturers of nationally known goods were there to give demonstrations and expert advise to the visitors.[28]

The building was sold by the Halls to J. M. Hartley & Son on November 23, 1927. Mr. Hall decided to retire from the hardware business, and the stock of the store was closed out.[29]

In May of 1928, it was announced by Hartley's that the property would be used for their new furniture store. A sale at the Jacobs-Hutchinson Block ensued to eliminate the need to move the existing furniture stock to the location.[30] The opening of the store occurred on June 28, 1928. Though there was no orchestra or prizes, the crowds were impressed when the false front that had stood before the store for many weeks was removed. It was a signal for the crowds, who had braved a steady shower to enter, and they paraded through the store. "It was reminiscent of a 'first night' at some famed New York theatre." Everyone was deeply impressed by the store's atmosphere and the displays that they saw. Nationally advertised furniture companies had sent representatives to attend the opening as well.[31]

Hartley's subsequently decided to rebuild the furniture store building, adding additional stories that had been anticipated when the building was designed and constructed, to make it the home of the entire Hartley's store. Of course, there was a great sale at the furniture store to clear the merchandise so the work could begin.[32]

The actual work on the building began on May 16, 1929. The architect for the project was Emil R. Johnson, a former Fairmont man who was the official architect for the American Department Stores Corporation. It was noted that Mr. Johnson had attended Fairmont State Normal School from 1905 to 1906, that his family were well known brick manufacturers, and that he had receive his technical training under Charles G. Badgley, a noted architect from Baltimore (who had designed St. Peter's Catholic Church at 401-407 Jackson Street).[33]

The contract was awarded to the John M. Kisner Lumber Company of Fairmont for $135,000 for the labor and materials for the reconstruction of the building; this cost did not include the sprinkler system, three modern elevators, and the heating, plumbing and wiring. The total cost was thought to be close to $200,000. The Fairmont Mining Machine Company furnished the steel, the S. M. Kisner and Sons Company furnished the roofing, and the Hammond Fire Brick Company furnished the brick.[34]

Two additional floors were added to the building, making it a five-story structure. The facade was divided into nine bays and had rectangular windows. The stairway and walls separating the first floor, as well as the partitions on the second and third floor, were removed. The floors were leveled, and an entire new front of light color brick, limestone and granite was constructed.[35]

"The Facts" of the new building, for those people interested in the technical details of the building, were published in early November 1929, prior to the buildings opening; this seemed to whet the interest of the usually inquisitive townspeople. The new store would be the largest in Fairmont, having 72,000 square feet of floor space. There were three Otis elevators, two for passengers and one for freight. There were 766 electric light outlets, and 60,000 feet of wire (almost 12 miles) in the store. A special low pressure vapor steam heating system would keep the store at an even temperature in the winter, a special cooling system for the first floor and basement would keep them cool in the summer, "for shopping comfort!" A total of 1,167 automatic sprinklers would insure complete protection against fire. There was a drinking fountain with pure cold running ice water on every floor.[36]

Two hundred and fifty tons of steel, 250 tons of structural steel, and 47,000 pounds of steel joints were used in making the foundation and the skeleton work for the store. Sixty-six tons of limestone, 52,600 face bricks, 40,000 hollow tiles, and 245,000 common bricks were used in the building. The ventilating system for the store required motors that aggregated 72-1/2 horsepower. The lights in the new building would develop 263,000 candle power. "If all these lights were put into one great searchlight, it would throw a beam clear across the state of West Virginia."[37]

An elaborate program was planned for the opening of the new store. The weekly radio program, featuring "high class musical entertainment," was given on Monday, November 18th and Tuesday, November 19th. This was broadcast on the local station, WMMN, from its studio in the YMCA Building on Fairmont Avenue. The doors of the old Hartley's store closed at 4:00 on Tuesday, November 19, 1929. It had been home to Hartley's for 27 years, one of the first tenants when the new Jacobs-Hutchinson Block opened in 1902. Wednesday, November 20th, was set aside to put the finishing touches on the new store. Hartley's customers had to "mark time," with the old store closed and the new one not yet opened.[38]

There was a special reason for opening the store on Thursday, November 21, 1929. Thursday was considered Hartley's lucky day, because Thursday had always been an eventful day in the history of the store. All of the special sales of the store had been held on Thursday. But the greater reason was that Thursday was the 27th anniversary of the opening of the Hartley's old store and the 52nd anniversary of the founding of Hartley's store in Fairmont in 1877 by J. M. Hartley.[39]

Hartley's opening was an event in the life of Fairmont; the entire program was broadcast over station WMMN. Large crowds of people attended the opening, and at 10 am the doors of the store opened. A long list of speakers contributed to the program, including H. J. Hartley, former Senator M. M. Neely, Sheriff W. W. Conoway, Fairmont State Normal School President Joseph Rosier, Judge Emmet Showalter, and many more. Throughout all the speeches ran the common thread of a tribute to J. M. Hartley, who had founded the business and conducted it

Fleming Building, 109-113 Adams Street in 1916. This building was remodeled into Hartley's Store.

with integrity; he had died on June 25, 1926. The concluding feature of the program was dedicating the building to J. M. Hartley and the unveiling of the bronze tablet which bore the inscription of dedication, unveiled by Mrs. H. Glen Greer, his daughter. A basket of roses stood beneath the bronze tablet as a tribute to Hartley by his former employees. An excellent likeness of Mr. Hartley hung above the tablet. Many baskets of flowers were sent by friends and business firms to grace the event, and they added to the beauty of the store; and many telegrams of congratulations came from businesses and individuals.[40]

According to the county assessor records, Hartley's bought and expanded into the store at 117-119 Adams Street, formerly Morrison's Department store, in 1959.

Hartley's Department store operated successfully at this location until it closed in May 1985, after 108 years of business in Fairmont. The owners cited declining sales as the reason for closing.[41] The building was subsequently remodeled, along with the adjacent buildings at 115 and 117-119 Adams Street to create the West Virginia Office Complex in 1986, as designed by Omni Associates of Fairmont.

6. Nuzum Building Annex, c. 1880, 1901. 115 Adams Street

This modest two story, one bay structure with a second story bay window, first appears on the Sandborn maps in 1884 as a tin shop. In 1901, it was acquired by the adjacent Nuzum furniture store, which needed room to expand its successful mercantile business. At this time, an addition was made to the rear, extending it back to Porter Alley (Meredith Street). It became part of the "Nuzum Block" (117-119 Adams Street).[42]

On May 12, 1922, E. "Mannie" Deitz opened The Clothes Shop at this location. Mack's Orchestra supplied the music for the occasion, and flowers and cigars were distributed to the hundreds of visitors.[43]

When Shurtleff and Welton were forced to vacate their premises next door in the American Building (109-113 Adams Street), they moved their business to this location in May of 1929. The newly installed windows for the store were seen as being an unusual type, the metal part was gold finished bronze. These were the first windows of this type installed in Fairmont. The base was Carrara glass with onyx finish, and the woodwork was birch, but finished to imitate walnut. The main door was a French door with windows on either side.[44]

This building was demolished in the renovation of the two adjoining buildings for the West Virginia Office Complex.

7. Nuzum Block, 1865; Morrison's Store, Hartley's Store, 1928. 117-119 Adams Street

The original building on this site was thought to have been constructed in 1865, and housed a number of small business ventures, including a grocery and meat shop[45] The original building was a two-story, three bay wood frame structure, the gable end of which faced the street.

Sam R. Nuzum, "the Furniture King," began business in Fairmont at this location in 1887, which was formerly occupied by James F. Hough. Though many people had embarked on the furniture business in Fairmont and lost money, Mr. Nuzum was successful.[46] In 1892, his store was too small for his growing business, so he bought more ground to the east of his existing store to rebuild and enlarge the establishment, referred to as "The Mammoth."[47] It became a two-story, five bay flat-roofed brick structure; a pediment raised above the roof line cornice was inscribed "Sam R. Nuzum," and an insert in the brick below was inscribed "1892." The glass store front expanded to 33 feet wide and the store was 85 feet deep. The first floor housed the display and store room for parlor furniture and heavy furniture. The second floor housed chairs of all kinds, as well as oil paintings and picture frames. The two delivery teams shortly increased to three.[48] H. C. Sample began publication of the Fairmont Free Press in September 1892, using a rear room on the second floor of this building until 1903.[49]

Mr. Nuzum retired from the business in 1900, and was succeeded by Charles E. Nuzum (his cousin), William W. Karnes, and William C. Lyons; the company became known as the Fairmont Furniture Company.[50] In 1901, the business was growing so rapidly that they added the adjacent two-story building (115 Adams Street) to their business, and constructed an addition to it which extended back to Porter Alley (Meredith Street); this gave the business a total of 10,000 feet of floor space.[51]

H. J. Ross purchased half interest in the company in 1904, and the firm became Nuzum & Ross, proprietors of the Fairmont Furniture Company[52] In 1911, the firm became Ross Furniture; the store moved to the Masonic Temple Building in 1915 to occupy the space of the former Post Office[53] From the early part of 1916 until August 1917, the building was leased by

Nuzum's Store, 117 Adams Street, c. 1888.

the Anderson Restaurant and then the C. A. House music store. The Farley Clothing Store assumed occupancy of one of the ground floor rooms in 1920.[54]

The property was purchased by O. J. Morrison in December of 1927 for $100,000. His intent was to demolish the building to construct his ninth clothing store in the state.[55] Work on the demolition began on March 1, 1928, to make room for the modern three story building to house the Morrison Department Store.[56]

The matter of razing the old structure was seen as a relatively simple matter, but the excavation for the new building was a more considerable job. The building was to have a frontage of 40 feet and extend back 180 feet. There had been no excavation done near the area in a long time, so no one quite knew the character of the soil that would have to be removed.[57]

A large hole was excavated for the foundation of the new building, and this was the source of great interest to the citizens of Fairmont, especially those of the male gender. "What is there about a steam shovel tearing out great mouthfuls of yellow clay that draws old men, young men, little boys and even women to it as a magnet entices a nail?"

The crowds on the sidewalk in front of the site made it difficult to pass, sometimes being three or four people deep.[58] The excavation was finished in the early part of April 1928. The area adjacent to the street was difficult to dig because it was hard shale; and a great deal of time was taken in buttressing the earth and walls of the adjoining buildings which were on the line of excavation. The earth was removed without a break or crack in the adjoining walls, nor a slip in any of the adjoining foundations.[59]

Morrison's grand opening of the four-story, seven bay brick structure occurred on October 5, 1928. Thousands of men and women attended the opening, as well as O. J. Morrison and his 90 year old father, G. P. Morrison, head of the corporation. Just before the opening, the sidewalks and the street were crowded for half a block with people. Al Hartman's Orchestra provided the music for the opening, and brushes were given as souvenirs. The basement, first floor and second floor, as well as mezzanines on the first floor, were filled with merchandise; the third floor was devoted to stock. The building was equipped with an elevator and two stairways. Although this was a new enterprise in Fairmont, they were given a warm welcome by the people of the community.[60]

The building was taken over by Hartley's in 1959 as they needed more room to expand their business. This building, as well as the adjoining buildings, were renovated into the West Virginia Office Complex in 1986.

Nuzum Building Annex (left), 115 Adams Street; Nuzum Store (right), 117-119 Adams Street, c. 1902.

8. store, c. 1894. 121 Adams Street

First appearing on the Sandborn map in 1896, this two story, three bay modest structure was used as an office and as a barber shop, according to subsequent Sandborn maps of 1896 to 1918, inclusive. It had simple rectangular windows and one first floor store front.

The Dixie Shoe Store opened at this location in 1925. Its business was distinct in that it only sold men's shoes and at one price: $3.00. The new store front that was added was an "outstanding feature;" all of the company's stores had the same front, which was an imitation of the front of a southern cottage, with red brick front and fancy roof. Two small windows projected from the roof, between which a red illuminated sign was placed, which had on it a large figure three with the dollar mark. T. C. Loue, an architect from Baltimore (from where the store chain originated), put in the store front.[61]

The Smart Shoppe opened here in the summer of 1926, which was operated by Rose Osgood, whose husband was the proprietor of the Osgood's Store (222-224 Adams Street). It carried a line of women's and girls' dresses "at popular prices, in other words at moderate prices, to meet the demands of the average buyer."[62]

This building was demolished in the 1980's for the open space beside the West Virginia State Office building.

9. People's Bank, Palace Restaurant, c. 1854. 123 Adams Street

The two story, three bay brick structure with a gable roof that existed on this site was constructed prior to 1854, when it was occupied by the Fairmont Bank, which then reorganized and became the First National Bank in 1865. Although it was an unpretentious brick structure, it had a decorative store front with pilasters of classical columns and ornamental second story window hoods. In 1875, the First National Bank moved to its new quarters at 210 Adams Street; this building was then acquired by Farmer's Bank, which functioned here until it was liquidated in 1891. The location was then sold to the People's Bank of Fairmont on June 30, 1891.[63] When they took over the facility, the People's Bank remodeled the building into a "modern" banking facility. The floor throughout was made of tile, the ceiling of embossed steel, and the counter and desks were of quartered oak. In the rear of the main room was the vault and director's office.[64] People's Bank's business expanded and the quarters became too small. At first, discussions were to demolish the building and replace it with a six-story structure.[65] But in August of 1903, the bank acquired the corner "house" of the Jacobs-Hutchinson Block (201 Adams Street), and the bank moved there in March of 1904.[66]

The question arose of what was to be done with the building that previously housed the People's Bank. One idea was that the Masons, who were looking for a new home, would demolish the building and construct an eight-story building on the site; the first floor would be used for a business place, and the rest for the lodge. There were 250 to 300 Masons in the city at this time,[67] and their lodge at 330 Adams Street was becoming too small. This idea, however, did not come to pass, as the Masons built their home at 320 Jefferson in 1906-7.

The property was leased in 1904 by the Italian consul J. W. Mariana, who opened an Italian bank at the location.[68] In 1909, the Busy Bee Restaurant subsequently opened its doors at this location.[69] The Hub Clothing Store took over the building from the Busy Bee Restaurant in 1912, and remodeled the store to become a clothing business. The business operated successfully here until 1916, when it went out of business.[70]

The Anderson Restaurant moved to this location on March 16, 1917, and the building was extensively remodeled to make a "first class" restaurant. A kitchen was installed to the side of the rear, and outfitted for the business. The tables from the old location were brought here. It was thought that the restaurant would seat 125 people. A large electric sign on front of the building not only advertised the business, but greatly improved the appearance of the "Great White Way," as Adams Street was known.[71]

Mr. Spiro Gotses obtained control of the restaurant on June 17, 1919, and it then became the famed Palace Restaurant. The building underwent a major renovation at the end of 1926, and the opening of the newly-refurbished restaurant occurred on January 3, 1927. Mack's Orchestra furnished the music for the 2,500 Fairmonters who attended, and favors were given to them. They hardly recognized the new Palace; there were new tables and chairs, and the new style collegiate booths installed. The counter and table tops were all of a black onyx finish in a marble substitute. The renovations included many new pieces of kitchen equipment as well.[72]

More space was needed for the restaurant because of its success. An addition was constructed to the rear of the building that was 14 feet by 65 feet; this was to accommodate refrigeration units, which would leave more room for the kitchen in the existing building.[73] The restaurant was known state-wide for the highest quality of food and the well-trained, courteous employees. It was open every day of the year, 24 hours per day.[74]

The demolition crew put an end to the building on February 1, 1986. The *Times-West Virginian* newspaper photographer captured the images of the building as it came down, so that the site could be utilized in conjunction with the West Virginia State Office Building.[75] It is now part of a parking lot.

Nuzum Building (left), 117-119 Adams Street; store (middle), 121 Adams Street; People's Bank (right), 123 Adams Street, c. 1894.

10. store, c. 1905. 125 Adams Street

This one story structure was constructed around 1905, and appears to have been used as a restaurant, perhaps in conjunction with the adjacent Palace Restaurant. It has been demolished, and is now part of a parking lot.

11. Hall Block, 1893-5. 127-135 Adams Street

In January of 1893, Mr. S. W. Hall had not yet decided on what he would do about building on his Adams Street lot. He expected to build, but he was not sure how large a building it would be. He was considering a three story structure that would have four business rooms on the first floor, fronting on Adams Street.[76] By February, construction of a temporary building, to house Mr. Hall's drug store during construction of the large business block, had begun.[77] In July of 1895, the stone work had begun[78] and the sewer connection was made between the new building, stretching down Monroe Street to connect with the sewer in Jackson Street.[79]

The eighty foot by seventy foot building was three stories high. The brick structure was divided into four store fronts on Adams Street. Arched corbeling in the brickwork occurred above the third floor windows. A large pediment with the words, "Hall Block" rose above the roof line and cornice, and an oriel was placed at the roof line on the corner of the building.

Two of the business that moved into the new brick business block in 1896 were Tetrick and Randall, who dealt in dry goods, and John H. Hough's hardware store.[80] Mr. J. H. Beckman had established his dry goods store in the Hall Block in 1898 and occupied the store for eighteen years until 1916.[81] Sherman Wise opened his grocery establishment in the Hall Block around 1905[82] Martin Brothers Drug Store, who moved out of the Skinner Building (106 Adams Street) in 1913, took the store location of Mr. Wise on the corner of Monroe and Adams street, and then eventually that of Mr. Beckman. A soda fountain was installed at Martin Brothers Drugs, and they planned to install a ice cream factory and manufacture their own ice cream for the summer season.[83]

A. G. Martin relocated his stationery and cigar store to the Hall Block in 1904;[84] his store was 20 feet wide and 70 feet deep.[85] In 1915, a new store front was installed; the new display windows were "beautiful plate glass affairs."[86]

Extensive remodeling occurred at Martins Drugs in 1928. The walls were redecorated and more room added by removing some of the showcases. Because of the increasing demands of the luncheon business, new fixtures were installed which increased the seating capacity, and reduced the delay and crowding.[87]

As if it were an eerie prediction, a small blaze was discovered in the Hall Block in May of 1928, which threatened the structure with destruction. The fire originated in a rubbish room at the top of the rear stairs on the second floor, and spread upward to the third floor. The cause was unknown. The building filled with smoke, and many of the tenants, who resided on the third floor of the building, leaned out of the windows and even threatened to jump to the street. The firemen soon had the flames out, and the damage was not very extensive.[88]

It was fire that eventually contributed to the demise of the building. On November 27, 1973, fire gutted the Hall Block, causing an estimated $200,000 damage to the building. It was believed to have been electrical in origin, and apparently began in the rear of the building. There were 35 fire fighters who worked to bring the blaze under control; two of them were injured battling it. The top floors of the building had been vacant for some time, and the roof and walls of the structure collapsed in the blaze.[89] A few days later, it was determined that the building would have to be razed; the damage was estimated to be worth $215,000, and it was insured for only $65,000.[90] The site is now a parking lot.

Hall Block, 127-135 Adams Street, c. 1930.

---

[1] *Fairmont Free Press*, 3/31/1898.
[2] *Fairmont West Virginian*, 7/25/1904, p. 2.
[3] *Fairmont Times*, 2/8/1909, p. 1.
[4] *A History of Marion County, West Virginia*, p. 386.
[5] *Industrial Fairmont in 1908*, p. 66.
[6] *Twentieth Century Edition*, p. 23.
[7] *Fairmont Times*, 1/9/1918, p. 7.
[8] *Fairmont Index*, 11/5/1897.
[9] Fleming, p. 22.
[10] *Fairmont Times*, 5/4/1911, p. 1.
[11] ibid., 7/29/1911, p. 3.
[12] ibid., 3/18/1913, p. 6.

[13] *A History of Marion County, West Virginia*, p. 386.
[14] *Fairmont Times*, 7/8/1922, p. 6.
[15] ibid., 4/13/1922, p. 1.
[16] ibid., 3/19/1929, p. 2.
[17] ibid., 5/3/1911, p. 1.
[18] *Farmers Free Press*, 6/27/1912, p. 1.
[19] *Fairmont Times*, 12/13/1912, p. 16.
[20] ibid., p. 14.
[21] ibid., 9/20/1912, p. 1.
[22] ibid., 7/28/1917, p. 2.
[23] ibid., 3/21/1919, p. 1.
[24] ibid., 10/31/1912, p. 8.
[25] ibid., 1/20/1913, p. 1.
[26] ibid., 3/21/1919, p. 1.
[27] ibid.
[28] ibid., 3/25/1926, p. 1; 3/26/1926, p. 1.
[29] ibid., 12/7/1927, p. 11.
[30] ibid., 6/6/1928, p. 4.
[31] ibid., 6/29/1928, p. 8.
[32] ibid., 4/17/1929, p. 3.
[33] ibid., 5/17/29, p. 1.
[34] ibid.
[35] ibid.
[36] ibid., 11/8/1929, p. 3.
[37] ibid.
[38] ibid., 11/17/1929, p. 1.
[39] ibid., 11/18/1929, p. 1.
[40] ibid., 11/22/1929, p. 1.
[41] *Fairmont Times-West Virginian*, 4/30/1985, p. 1.
[42] *Fairmont West Virginian*, 8/9/1902, p. 2.
[43] *Fairmont Times*, 5/13/1922, p. 1.
[44] ibid., 5/5/1929, sect. 2, p. 1.
[45] ibid., 12/25/1927, p. 12.
[46] *Fairmont Index*, 1/3/1894.
[47] ibid.
[48] ibid., 4/15/1892.
[49] *Fairmont Times*, 12/25/1927, p. 12.
[50] *Twentieth Century Edition*, p. 8.
[51] *Fairmont West Virginian*, 8/9/1902, p. 2.
[52] *Industrial Fairmont in 1908*, p. 55.
[53] *Fairmont Times*, 5/5/1915, p. 3.
[54] ibid., 12/25/1927, p. 12.
[55] ibid.
[56] ibid., 3/1/1928, p. 2.
[57] ibid., 3/5/1928, p. 8.
[58] ibid., 3/30/1928, p. 1.
[59] ibid., 4/9/1928, p. 8.
[60] ibid., 10/6/1928, p. 1.
[61] ibid., 4/11/1925, p. 8.
[62] ibid., 7/21/1926, p. 6.
[63] Fleming, pp. 34-36.
[64] *Fairmont Index*, 1/3/1894.
[65] *Fairmont Times*, 12/26/1902, p. 1.
[66] ibid., 8/1/1903, p. 1.
[67] ibid.
[68] ibid., 5/26/1904, p. 1.
[69] ibid., 4/19/1909, p. 1.

[70] ibid., 12/6/1916, p. 9.
[71] ibid., 3/17/1917, p. 2.
[72] ibid., 1/4/1927, p. 2.
[73] ibid., 9/17/1928, p. 8.
[74] *Welcome Westinghouse*, sect. 3, p. 2.
[75] *Fairmont Times-West Virginian*, 2/2/1986, p. 1.
[76] *Fairmont Free Press*, 1/20/1893.
[77] ibid., 2/10/1893.
[78] *Fairmont Republican*, 7/11/1895.
[79] ibid., 7/18/1895.
[80] *Fairmont Index*, 5/26/1896.
[81] *Fairmont Times*, 11/5/1925, p. 5.
[82] *Industrial Fairmont in 1908*, p. 44.
[83] *Fairmont Times*, 1/17/1913, p. 3.
[84] *Fairmont West Virginian*, 5/26/1904, p. 8.
[85] *Industrial Fairmont in 1908*, p. 37.
[86] *Fairmont Times*, 10/11/1915, p. 2.
[87] ibid., 4/2/1928, sect. 2, p. 2.
[88] ibid., 5/17/1928, p. 1.
[89] ibid., 11/28/1973, p. 1.
[90] ibid., 11/30/1973, p. 1.

Chapter 3

200 Block Adams Street, even numbered buildings

1. Town Hall Theatre, T. W. Fleming Building, Odd Fellows Hall; c. 1870.
200-202 Adams Street

The first floor of this building was the mercantile store of the Flemings. The second story of the building, with a ceiling height of twenty-five feet, was added at a later date.[1] The building had three bays with very tall, vertical windows, an ornate cornice at the roof, and a smaller cornice above the first floor windows. The bottom floor had one store front. Access to the second floor was through a doorway on Monroe Street. The structure was referred to as the "Town Hall," and the second floor functioned as Fairmont's first theatre. A stage was placed at the Adams Street end of the hall, a curtain was provided, and chairs were placed in the "auditorium." For many years, the local entertainments were given here, including the Noss Family, a famous troupe of musicians; the "new story of the south," Uncle Tom's Cabin; and Robert Downing, a great American Shakespearian actor.[2]

Because Fairmont was small and there was little transportation at the time to convey professional acts, many local talents were also provided here. One such event was the "Merchants' Carnival," presented in the early 1870's. Included in the program was music by Dowden's Orchestra, recitations by Dr. Cowdan, march and sword drills by Company C of the Davis Light Guards, a tableau titled "Ten Virgins," and a song by Miss Frankie Pitcher titled "Thou Brilliant Bird." At the bottom of the program, there was an invitation: "Ice cream, cakes, sandwiches and coffee will be served. Don't miss the gun drill of Company C which will occur while refreshments are being served."[3]

The theatrical performances moved to "The Rink" (312 Madison Street), and the second story of the building was sold in April 1881 to the I.O.O.F. (International Order of Odd Fellows),[4] which they occupied until 1922 when they purchased the old Grand Opera House (325 Monroe Street).[5]

The upper part of the building was subsequently sold to John F. Phillips and Clarence L. Robinson, who utilized the extremely high ceiling by making two floors out of the one story.[6] A drawing of the building in 1923 shows the tall upper story divided into two stories; this is further supported by the Sandborn maps; the 1918 map lists it as a two-story structure, the 1927 map as a three story structure, although the overall height of the building remains the same.

The building was renovated in 1924 by Phillips and Robinson for use as offices for the C. and M. Land Company. Members of the Odd Fellows were invited to visit the new offices. The party of 450 people were amazed at the transformation of the building. First, the previous straight-run stairs had been replaced by stairs that rose part way to the second floor, and then turned left at a landing. The big room that had for years served as the lodge room had been divided by many partitions, to create what was then thought to be the best offices in the city. They were noted as being well lighted, airy, spacious, and convenient.[7]

Communtzi's Confectionery opened on the first floor of the T. W. Fleming Building in January 1911; the lower walls of the building were done in white carrara enamel.[8] At the grand opening, a small glass with the firm's name engraved on it was given out as a souvenir.[9] The company grew to be one of the largest confectionery stores in northern West Virginia, featuring soda fountain drinks, fancy baked goods, and a complete line of delicious choice candies which were manufactured on site. All of the ice cream served there was also manufactured in the establishment, made fresh daily and from pure ingredients. Light lunches, regular dinners, and breakfast were served as well.[10]

After Nicholas J. Comuntzis died in 1919, his widow, Cornelia, became the owner and manager, continuing the business. In 1926, Mrs. Comuntzis sold half of her interest in the store to William A. Frangos, George Frangos, and George Samas, who planned to remodel the store. The purpose of the change was to make the store and restaurant better than before; it encompassed enlarging the baking and candy departments, expanding the business into catering, and making it a more sanitary place. It was also renovated and redecorated for the grand reopening.[11]

Alas, Comuntzis went bankrupt and the establishment was sold to Nicholas Costianes, who "brought a corner of Grecian beauty to Fairmont ... at his restaurant at 200 Adams Street," which opened in February of 1928. He had spent $40,000 to remodel the restaurant property throughout its entirety, installing the most modern restaurant equipment. This included modern booths, tables, and panel work with inlaid pilasters. Each booth had a French plate mirror and two lights. The soda fountain, the lunch counter, and the back bar had porcelain backs and trimmings in monel metal. The twenty-five booths and panel work was of American walnut, and the tables had black decorated vitriolite tops. One hundred and fifty persons could be served at one time.[12]

The soda fountain was supplied with electrical refrigeration. Mr. Costianes made his own ice cream in the ice cream plant in the basement, capacity 300 gallons per day. He employed an expert chef from Cleveland, and also hired a French pastry chef.[13]

After Costianes vacated the room in 1929, the Great Atlantic and Pacific Tea Company announced that it would open West Virginia's finest A. and P. Store there, obtaining a three-year lease from T. W. Fleming for the first floor and basement.[14] The grand opening occurred on March 23, 1929; it was estimated that 6,000 people attended the official

ODD FELLOWS HALL.

Odd Fellows Hall (right), 200-202 Adams Street and T. W. Fleming Building (left) 204 Adams Street, c. 1894.

opening, and that more that 10,000 customers shopped in the store. Thirty-five clerks and food handlers were provided, but they were hardly sufficient to accommodate the trade. In remodeling the store, the wood work was finished in light oak, the floor remained a fine matched tile, and the walls were green and white. There were roomy display windows in the front of the store.[15]

This building is still in use today as offices.

2. T. W. Fleming Building, Iseman's Store; c. 1870. 204 Adams Street

This structure was also owned by T. W. Fleming. Originally, there was a projecting bay on the east side of second story and two additional windows to the west of it, all with segmental arched windows; the bay has since been replaced by the wide window in existence today. The first floor consisted of one store front. There was an ornate classical cornice at the roof. The Sandborn map of 1884 lists the building as being used for both a variety store and as the Post Office; the Sandborn map of 1892 lists it as being used for the Post Office only. It is assumed that the Post Office was at this location until it moved to 104 Adams Street around the year 1895.

An addition to the rear was added in 1904 to extend the building by forty feet; when completed, Sam B. Iseman, clothier and men's outfitter, moved into the quarters from his location in the Marietta Hotel Annex (124 Adams Street).[16] The grand opening occurred on September 20, 1904, and a large crowd attended the opening.[17]

Sam B. Iseman was known as Fairmont's leading clothier. His clothing establishment was the largest and most completely stocked in the city. Everything from shoes to hats for men and boys could be found in the establishment. While there was nothing "cheap" on sale, the prices were such as to attract trade from all classes. Every square foot of the 4,420 square feet of floor space was covered with merchandise. "The man who cannot be suited here, can be suited nowhere."[18]

Evidence of Sam B. Iseman's business recently resurfaced when renovations were being done in an adjacent small store at 206 Adams Street in 1994. This was originally an alley, and Iseman used the exterior wall of his store as advertising space, painting the figure of a dapper man in a suit and the words "SAM B. ISEMAN Clothier, Hatter and Furnisher" on the brick wall.[19] Although the painting cannot be dated exactly from viewing it, the man and his attire are similar to drawings of men in newspaper advertisements in 1913.[20]

Business was going well for Sam B. Iseman into the 1920's. In 1923, however, Mr. Iseman suffered a stroke and was thought to be at death's door. "Taking Mr. Iseman out of the daily life in Fairmont leaves a void that is being felt in business and social lines. He is one of the city's oldest merchants and a citizen who has been an honor to his chosen community."[21]

Because the stroke left him paralyzed, Sam B. Iseman was forced to discontinue business. Although he had improved considerably from the serious condition he had been in, he was no longer able to conduct his business. In March of 1924, Iseman sold his store to the Sharp-

Hamilton-Arnett company, who were well known young businessmen in the city. Several improvements were made in the store, including the erection of an electric sign, and there were substitutions in the line of goods sold, including custom-made suits in addition to the ready-to wear already stocked.[22]

Still in use today, the structure has housed many commercial enterprises over the years.

3. alley infill, c. 1940. 206 Adams Street

The construction of this one-story building eliminated the alley, and it is inside of this store that one can see the Sam B. Iseman advertisement that was painted on the wall around 1913 when it was still in the alley. The building was recently renovated.

4. First National Bank Cashier's Residence, 1875; Jones' Store, 1917. 208 Adams Street

The First National Bank of Fairmont was organized in 1853 as the Bank of Fairmont. On July 4, 1875, its handsome bank building (210 Adams Street) with the attached cashier's residence (208 Adams Street) was completed, at the total cost of $35,000.[23] The two buildings were 2-1/2 story Victorian buildings with dormer windows on a mansard roof. Ornate window hoods surrounded the windows, which were segmental arched windows on the second floor, and Roman arched on the first floor. The Cashier's Residence was set back from the front of the adjacent bank building by approximately fifteen feet, according to the Sandborn maps. It had a bay that extended from the first floor to the top of the mansard roof; a rondele window was set in the middle of the bay in this roof. The roof can still be seen atop the present building.

In 1898, a lot adjoining the bank to the east, on the opposite side of the cashier's residence, was acquired. The present building was erected to extend the frontage of the bank building to both the new and existing lots (210-212 Adams Street); the Victorian cashier's residence remained intact.[24]

In 1917, the Fairmont Trust Company purchased the bank building and the Cashier's Residence. The front of the Cashier's Residence was extended out to line up with the adjacent buildings and a new front was constructed to accommodate its use as a store. E. C. Jones, proprietor of Jones' Department Store, signed a lease for the space, and moved his business from its previous location at 113 Adams Street.[25] Mr. Jones used all three floors of the building, and installed a large plate glass show window on the second floor for the display of goods.[26] There is decorative brickwork below the large overhanging cornice. The roof of the Victorian house is mostly hidden by the new front. This is the building's appearance today. T. L. Burchinal of Fairmont was awarded the contract to perform the work, which cost $10,000. The date set in the contract for completion was September 1917.[27]

The opening of Jones' Store was in the middle of September, as scheduled. There was no special demonstration other than opening the doors to the public; E. C. Jones needed no introduction to the public, since it had been a well-established firm in the city since 1906. The interior of the store was remodeled to include cream ivory walls with mission finishings and furniture. There were many plate glass mirrors and windows; especially beautiful was the second floor window. It was so unusually large that it filled the center front and could be seen from a great distance.[28]

Within six months, the Jones's Store was enjoying a splendid trade. One of the attractive features was the policy of "No two garments alike," which appealed to the woman who wanted to be exclusive, as well as the policy of "Something new every day," which reflected the day to day incoming of new stock for every department.[29] The store was even mentioned in the *Garment Weekly*, a retail merchants publication in New York, as having Fifth Avenue standards on Main Street; the publication was surprised to find such a beautiful and original shop in such a small city.[30] Jones' business was so successful that it expanded into the second floor of the adjoining bank building (210-212 Adams Street) in 1924. Later, it took over all three floors above the first floor banking quarters.

To celebrate the twenty year anniversary in 1926 of the establishment of his store in Fairmont on March 15, 1906, the Jones' Department Store displayed the contrasting fashions from 1906 and 1926. Some local women contributed their "treasured frocks" to the display, mostly hand-sewn, as "bought" dresses were not in vogue as they were in the 1920's. The long trailing skirts, numerous petticoats and high waist lines of 1906 were no longer acceptable to the women of 1926; "The modern women of today will not permit of so much flubdubbery."[31]

Jones' Department Store occupied the building until it relocated to 203-209 Adams Street in the 1930's. The radio station WMMN located its broadcast studio and businesses office from the Holt-Rowe Building at 325 Adams Street, to the second floor of the building beginning on August 20, 1935.[32]

The first floor is currently used as a women's clothing store, and the second floor was recently renovated as offices.

First National Bank (left) and Cashier's Residence (right), 208-210 Adams Street, c. 1894.

FIRST NATIONAL BANK.

An Ornament to the City

First National Bank (left) and Cashier's Residence (right), 208-212 Adams Street, c. 1902.

Jones' Store, 208 Adams Street, 1923. This facade was constructed in front of the Victorian-style Cashier's Residence.

5. First National Bank, Fairmont Trust Company, Adam's Office Supply; 1875, 1898. 210-212 Adams Street

The First National Bank of Fairmont was organized in 1853 as the Bank of Fairmont. It was originally located at 123 Adams Street, where it remained until 1875. On July 4, 1875, its handsome bank building at 210 Adams Street with attached cashier's residence (208 Adams Street) was completed, at the total cost of $35,000.[33] The two buildings were 2½ story Victorian buildings with dormer windows on a mansard roof. The second floor windows of the bank were segmental arched windows with ornate window hoods; the first floor store front windows consisted of three Roman arches.

The bank outgrew its quarters and needed more space to keep up with the demands in the rapidly growing city. In 1898, the adjoining "Baker lot" to the east (212 Adams Street, which had a small two-story book store on it) was acquired, and the present bank building was erected on both lots (210-212 Adams Street), extending its frontage on Adams Street; the Victorian-style Cashier's Residence remained intact.[34] The new building is a three-story structure of stone and marble on the first floor, and brick above. The bottom floor is distinguished by three large Roman arches for the entrance and two store front windows, which are supported by four stocky, marble columns. Engaged Ionic columns of brick extend the height of the second and third floors, and support a large brick entablature. The windows on the upper floors are rectangular.

The banking room was handsomely fitted with modern counters and desks of highly finished mahogany, and the ceilings and walls were decorated with well proportioned massive mahogany beams. The floor was laid in marble mosaic. The counters and desks were protected by baseboards of Alpine green marble, and were surmounted by ornamental screen work of statuary bronze and chipped plate glass. The Director's room in the rear of the bank was also fitted with mahogany. The vault was lined throughout with heavy burglar-proof steel and beautified from without by copper-oxidized trimmings. It was also protected with the heaviest three-door vestibules manufactured at the time. The outer door alone was 5-1/2 inches thick, operated by the automatic bolt-operating device, and was protected by triple time lock.[35]

In January of 1916, the First National Bank property was for sale. This included the bank proper as well as the Cashier's Residence.[36] It had not sold by mid-May, and the stockholders decided to exert no further effort to sell the property, at least for sixty days. Their rationale was that the value of real estate in Fairmont was escalating so rapidly that they would get a more desirable sum for it later than if they rushed the sale.[37] Their patience paid off, and the bank and residence property was sold later that month to Clarence D. Robinson for $87,500.[38]

The Democratic State Headquarters announced in September of 1916 that it would be moving into the second floor of the building. There would be offices for the Democratic chairman and his campaign manager the stenographers and other attaches would have an office in the rear.[39]

In the following year, The Fairmont Trust Company bought the First National Bank property and remodeled it for their bank.[40] The actual moving day was February 22, 1917. The

Adams Street, 200 block, c. 1915.

banking room was repainted a brighter color, and other minor changes made.[41]

The adjacent Cashier's Residence (208 Adams Street) had been remodeled and purchased by E. C. Jones in 1917. He had expanded his store in 1923 by leasing the T. F. Hall building (214-216 Adams Street) on the other side of the bank building; this was known as the Jones' Dress Shop. By 1924, his trade was so successful that he took over the second floor of the Fairmont Trust Company building to create a "department of dresses;" this was "just a new growth to take care of the ever-increasing business." The new section adjoined the main second floor of the Jones' Store;[42] archway openings were cut between Jones' Store and the newly-leased space for easy and convenient access.[43] The rooms were entirely remodeled and repainted, using the Louis XVI style.[44]

Jones' Store expanded with 4,800 square feet more floor space when it leased all of the floors above the banking rooms on the first floor of the building. The second through fourth floors were converted from offices rooms into shop rooms for the increasing trade of the Jones' Store. The Jones' Dress Shop at 214-216 Adams Street was consolidated into the new space in the Fairmont Trust Company building. [45]

The Jones Fur Service,, which had been located in the McCrory Building (218-222 Adams Street), moved into the third floor space in 1927. They had the equipment and facilities for repairing, remodeling, and cleaning furs. Another part of the third floor was to be used by the display department, which produced the settings and display material used in all of the Jones shops.[46]

In January of 1928, the Fairmont Trust Company lobby and interior was remodeled. T. L. Burchinal, contractor, was in charge of the work. Parts of the granite columns at the entrance had to be chiseled away in order to make the improvement in the front. By rearranging the first floor, the bookkeeping department was removed from the front of the first floor to the basement, and the area was replaced with two teller windows. The stair to the left of the building was eliminated and the space was used in the lobby. Work on the project was slightly delayed because the mahogany woodwork to match that on the interior had to be obtained from Chicago.[47]

The Fairmont Trust Company and the Fairmont State Bank announced their merger in February of 1928. The business was conducted under the name of the Fairmont Trust Company, and located in this building.[48]

The first floor of the building is currently occupied by Adams Office Supply. The second floor was recently renovated (along with the adjoining second floor at 208 Adams Street) into offices. The third floor is vacant.

6. T. F. Hall Building, c. 1875. 214-216 Adams Street

Thomas F. Hall conducted a harness business at this location beginning in 1878. A short time later, he moved the business across the street under the old Mountain City Hotel, where he stayed for sixteen years.[49] This building appears on the Sandborn map of 1884 with the function noted as a dry goods and clothing store. On the 1892 Sandborn map, the 214-216 Adams Street location is noted as carrying groceries and "queensware."

Then, around the year 1894, Hall bought the building at his original location, and moved his business back to it. He also added an extension of twelve feet to make room for his increasing trade.[50] The Sandborn maps from 1896 to 1918 list the use as a harness shop.

Mr. Hall was the first man in Marion County to engage in the harness business on a large scale. He "carries a superb line of goods, comprising everything in the way of horse equipment, from the lowest to the highest priced, and an assortment of trunks, traveling bags, valises, suit cases, grip, etc., without a superior in the state. His emporium is a boon to the people of Fairmont."[51]

With all of the renovation activity occurring in Fairmont around 1910, T. F. Hall decided to update his building by constructing a new brick front for it. Workman had cut out the old front and built a temporary partition a few feet back to give the men a chance to work on the brick wall which was erected. The small two-story building located between its two towering neighbors, the First National Bank Building and the McCrory Five and Ten, would soon "stand up as proud as either of them."[52] This appears to be the store front that exists today. The building is a two-story brick structure with four bays on the second floor. A stone insert above the second floor windows reads, "T F Hall." The first floor store front has been extensively remodeled.

As progress, in the form of the automobile and the expansion of trade, came to Fairmont, the harness shop was "swallowed in the aeons of the past;"[53] E. C. Jones took a ten-year lease on the store to open a new department which would operate independently of but in conjunction with the Jones' Store (208 Adams Street). The new place was called the Jones Dress Shop. The old store room was thoroughly remodeled and had undergone a "complete metamorphosis." Jones and Nuzum, architects in Fairmont, made the plans for the remodeling. This included an entirely new front with higher, deeper, larger show windows for better display purposes. The remodeling took several months to complete.[54] "The inside of the shop will have an Adam period of architecture. The Robert and James Adam architecture is very dainty and was started in England following a trip by the historic Adam boys through Italy. It is a development of the classic style and is very charming."[55]

The Jones Dress Shop opened on March 10, 1923. There was no special ceremony for the opening, which was also the case when they opened its business at 208 Adams Street in 1917. The store room was called "the niftiest store room in the state." The sides of the display stages were constructed of imitation travertine marble; they were lighted by both foot lighting and overhead lighting, and could provide spot lighting, flood lighting, and combination color-effect lighting. The curtain and draperies for these "stages" was emblazoned with the trade sign used by the firm, and which was carried throughout its advertising. The floor was marbleoid.[56] The dress shop was "thronged" at the opening.[57]

Business was booming in the store, which led to another expansion. In 1927, the Jones' Store leased the rooms above the adjacent Fairmont Trust Company (210-212 Adams Street), and moved the Jones Dress Shop into that facility.[58] This location was then used for the Jones Economy Store.[59]

The building is still in use today, though the first floor has been divided into two narrow store fronts.

7. Fountain Saloon, c. 1866; McCrorey's, 1909. 218-220 Adams Street

The Sandborn map of 1884 shows a small, one-story marble cutter's business located on this site. This was said to have been the marble shop owned by the father of Bert Fleming and later operated by Bert Fleming. An unused tombstone from the shop, found under the window of the adjacent building at 222-224 Adams Street that was undergoing renovations in 1927, was engraved with a death date of 1866, dating the business to around that time.[60]

The first evidence of the Fountain Saloon is on the Sandborn map of 1892, the year W. J. Bryan acquired the property from Worth Fleming for the sum of $4,000.[61] The Sandborn map shows a small ice cream parlor set back from the building line by approximately sixty feet. The courtyard in front of the building was approximately sixty feet by forty feet, and a fountain (approximately ten feet in diameter), from which the building took its name, was located here. Mr. Bryan was the proprietor of the Fountain Restaurant and Bakery at the time, employing an "expert baker" from Ohio. He served meals and ice cream at all hours, and carried "a complete line of staple and fancy groceries."[62]

In 1894, the establishment was referred to as the Fountain Hotel, and was managed by Mr. J. H. Luther. Mr. Luther provided thirty-five cent meals, which were "popular with all classes." There were about sixteen guest chambers, and a billiard room was attached to the hotel. "The best of order prevails about it, and the hotel is run on correct and proper principals."[63]

The Sandborn map of 1896 shows an addition of a saloon to the east of the original building, which was used as a restaurant at this time. The property was acquired from Mr. Bryan by Mr. B. G. Williams in 1898 for the sum of $17,500, and was then sold to Mr. Henry P. Gilmore in 1901 for $29,600.[64] The establishment's reputation for propriety declined after that, as it was often the site of fires,[65] and gambling raids.[66]

H. T. Blair bought the Fountain Saloon building in 1903. There was talk of erecting a new building on the site,[67] but this did not materialize. Instead, it was the scene of a "shooting affair;"[68] subsequently, there was more talk of erecting a stone building on the site and tearing down the old one on the rear of the site.[69] Several years, and several more stabbings[70] and booze raids, ensued.[71]

A more serious fire occurred on April 30, 1909 at the Fountain Saloon, which endangered thousands of dollars worth of property on Adams Street. The old building, it was noted, had been on fire on several occasions. This one began in lodging rooms on the second floor, and was thought to have been caused by a crossed electrical wire. One of the occupants of the lodging rooms "made a high dive from the second story window of his room to the ground below, twenty feet and landed without injury." The fire department quickly extinguished the flames. The loss to the building was hard to compute, since it was so old and worn, had been gutted by the flames, and damaged by the water used to extinguish it.[72]

In August of 1909, the Old Fountain property was purchased from Mr. Gilmore for a sum of $36,500 by J. G. McCrory; he planned to construct a new five- and ten-cent store on the property. The new building was to be 40 by 165 feet, three stories on the front and one story on the rear. The upper floors would be used as offices. The property was seen as most desirable in Fairmont because of its location across from the Courthouse, and because it extended from Adams Street through to Hull Alley.[73]

Although the people would liked to have seen a skyscraper on the site, they were delighted to see the new building. "For a dozen years the old Fountain building has been an eye sore on Main street. Always regarded as a fire trap, it has caused the firemen no little work. It has also been associated with a great deal of the city's police history, and at least two men have been killed there."[74]

The excavations for the new building that September proved to be a dangerous, messy affair. The contractor found it necessary to tear down a large brick wall in the rear of the Hall Harness store (214-216 Adams Street), which adjoined the site on the west. This two-story high wall was about to topple into the excavations and was torn down for the safety of the workers. The wall of the Underselling Store (222-224 Adams Street), adjoining the site to the east, was torn completely down following an accident in which one worker was seriously injured; it was rebuilt when the foundation and wall of the new building was put up.[75] In November, the workers were rushing the work to completion to get the new store under roof, but were having problems getting lumber.[76]

The McCrory Building was opened in the summer of 1910. All of the offices in the upper part were leased when it opened, as its location in the city was seen as most desirable.[77] The

McCrorey's Store operated on the first floor.

The building is currently in use as a store on the first floor, and offices above, as originally planned.

Adams Street, 200 block, 1916. The McCrorey Building, 218-220 Adams Street, is behind the "c" in the banner.

8. Hatter Ben's Big Brick, Underselling Store, Goodman's Store; c. 1845. 222-224 Adams Street

This is thought to be the oldest building still in existence in Fairmont, and was perhaps the first brick building in the city. According to information obtained from "old timers" in the city in 1929, it was erected several years previous to 1848.[78] Another source stated that it was said to be the oldest brick building in Marion County.[79]

The building was known as "Hatter Ben's Big Brick," which had been built by Hatter Ben Fleming with two store fronts on the first floor; he occupied the right hand store room as a shop for the sale of hats, which he manufactured himself. The adjoining store room was used by the late James Burns, as a grocery store and later by C. J. Corbin as a cigar factory. "Hatter" Ben Fleming ceased to occupy the building around 1886.[80]

The erection of the building was a big sensation at the time, as big of an event as was the construction of the Watson Building in 1911, it was said. People came from far and wide to see this immense building under construction.[81] From a photograph said to be taken around 1876, it was a two- story, six bay structure; the eave end of the gable roof faced Adams Street.[82]

The second story was reached by an outdoor stairway on the east side of the building, which connected with a narrow portico which ran the length of the front of the building. This portico, which had an iron railing, often was used in early times for public speaking.[83] On days when the County Court was in session, persons who desired to address the residents of the county would stand on the porch of the second floor of Hatter Ben Fleming's building. The second floor was occupied around the 1870's by Hayden and McCoy, Attorneys, and later by Dr. Zedekian Kidwell; the first floor was used by Benjamin Fleming, who manufactured hats.[84]

Michael Blumberg's Underselling store opened in the east store front (224 Adams Street) in the beginning of April 1908.[85] The building owner, Thurston W. Fleming, planned to build a new, larger building to accommodate the burgeoning enterprise, to be ready for the fall,[86] but this did not materialize. Instead, the store received a new front with plate glass windows.[87]

In January of 1909, it was announced that the Underselling Store was to have a fine, modern home. They expanded into the adjacent west store front at 222 Adams Street, and an addition was added to the rear of the two store fronts that was 37 feet wide and 50 feet deep. T. L. Burchinal was the contractor for the addition. The new space gave the store 3,700 square feet of floor space. The entire front of the 222 Adams Street store front was altered and rebuilt to conform with the front of the original store front at 224 Adams Street.[88]

The Underselling Store experienced a devastating fire on Christmas Eve 1913. Much of its merchandise was damaged at the busy holiday season.[89] The store did not reopen until February 10, 1914 to allow for the repairs and renovations.[90]

Another improvement to the store front was planned though not implemented in the spring of 1921, which included moving the entrance to the middle of the building and placing show windows on either side of the new door. This would have allowed deep display windows with a single entrance, instead of the original two entrances and shallow display windows. It was also planned to level the floors between the two sides, which were different between the two separate stores. Some of the interior partitions were also planned to be removed at this time to unify the space.[91] Though contemplated, these renovations did not occur until 1927.

Fairmont's Underselling Store, which had been in business for fifteen years, went bankrupt in 1926. The Blumberg stores, including Fairmont's, were sold at auction.[92] The store reopened briefly in May for an inventory dissolution sale.[93]

Simon D. Goodman, formerly the manager of the old Underselling Store, became the owner of the new Goodman's Store which opened its doors at the site in April of 1927.[94] He was known as the king of publicity stunts, and he chartered every city street car in Fairmont to carry people free of charge to his store during the hour of his reorganization sale in July of 1926. In addition, he chartered three interurban specials which left Enterprise, Mannington, and Fairview, to carry guests free of charge to his store.[95]

The improvements to the store that had been contemplated in 1921 when it was the Underselling Store were finally realized under the management and ownership of Mr. Goodman, and they were said to be "metamorphic." Besides changing the store front to contain one door and large, deep display windows and bringing the floor levels in line, the upper part of the exterior wall was raised up eight feet to improve the appearance of the building by covering the "unsightly" eave end of the original gable roof. This upper part of the wall provided advertising space for signage. Lowering the floor on one side to make it even with the other side led to the nickname, "The Goodman Store on the Level."[96]

It was at the time of these changes that the building was said to be the oldest building in Fairmont, and that it had remained practically as originally constructed. One of the reasons that it had withstood the ravages of times was because it was built in such a substantial manner of brick. [97]

At the end of 1929, the Goodman Store held a Forced-to-Vacate Sale, stating that the building had been leased "right over our heads."[98]

Although the second story of the building has been covered over and is vacant, the building is still in use as a restaurant.

Hatter Ben's Big Brick (background), 222-224 Adams Street as Buffalo Bill came to town with the Fairmont Circus in 1916.

9. Fleming/Cochran Building, 1875-6. 226-230 Adams Street

The east store front (230 Adams Street) of this two story, seven bay brick structure was begun by B. A. Fleming in September 1875 and completed in March 1876, just one month previous to the Great Fire of April 2, 1876, which destroyed the nearby 300 blocks of Adams Street. A short while later, Nathaniel C. Cochran built the adjoining store front to the west (226 Adams Street), which was really a part of the Fleming Building, though it was separately owned and constructed. One interior stairway was used by both store fronts to gain entrance to the second floor (228 Adams Street). The building was the first flat roofed building to be erected in Fairmont, and the citizens were very proud of it.[99]

The building has seven bays of Roman arched windows on the second floor, topped with a decorative, classical cornice. Originally, it had two decorative triangular pediments which rose above the roof line; these are gone. The first floor had two store fronts.

Mr. Cochran operated a jewelry store in the 226 Adams store front, some time after the Fleming building was occupied. When Mr. Cochran died in 1904, his heirs sold his business to a Mr. Beard, who later went West for his health; he subsequently sold the business to A. B. Scott.[100]

Mr. Scott opened his jewelry store in the building in December 1906. "Not in the State of West Virginia, perhaps, is there an emporium of the same character that surpasses in the extent and value of its stock, that contained in the premises occupied by the firm named above" (A. B. Scott & Co.). The company also provided optician services.[101] Remodeling of the Scott store occurred in 1914, including new display windows in the front, new fixtures, new decorations, and new lights throughout the interior.[102]

The jewelry store was sold to the Fanus Jewelry Company in 1919,[103] who operated in this location until it went out of business in 1929.[104]

"Uncle Moose" Fleming's grocery store was located in the 230 Adams Street store front from 1876 to 1907;[105] he had moved his business from across the street in the Mountain City Hotel, where it had been for 21 years,[106] to this location. His store had a far-reaching reputation for the best groceries, and also for "throwing in a little" for "good measure" to its regular patrons.[107]

Will "Moose" Fleming had an interesting method of bookkeeping. No one was ever known to be refused credit at the Fleming store, and no one was ever asked to pay his account. Those who did settle their bills received no greater consideration from Mr. Fleming than did those who never had and never did make a payment on their accounts; and some accounts had run for a score of years or longer. When Mr. Fleming finally closed up his accounts and went out of business, his book accounts are said to have exceeded the amount of money he had taken in during the many years he operated his store by a very considerable figure. Despite his generosity, he made money by gradually accumulating real estate in the fledgling town; at his death his estate had grown to be worth a comfortable fortune.[108]

It was at Christmas that "Moose" Fleming was in his glory. He was the only man in Fairmont in those days who carried children's toys; when the Christmas season came around, his store was always crowded with the boys of the village who gathered to examine the new toys, try them out, learn how they worked, and speculate who would get the toys. [109]

There was an unwritten law among the boys of the village not to steal from the Fleming store. Occasionally, one boy would break the rule and one of his friends would report him to Mr. Fleming, who would say "Pshaw, dog-gone, that is wrong. Now, boy, don't you cry, but you musn't steal," and Mr. Fleming would give him some candy, then cakes, and finally the guilty boy would leave with far more than he had tried to steal. He would be so ashamed that he would never again steal from "Uncle Moose."[110] Unlike merchants of today, Mr. Fleming operated the store not so much for the material gain as it was a joyful task for him to serve and his reward was a long life of joy and happiness as well.[111] In April of 1907, the property of the Fleming store was sold to S. M. Casterline to become a "moving picture show;" [112] and so the Dixie Theatre began its operation at this location. There was stiff competition from the many other theaters in town, and the Dixie Theatre was constantly updating its facilities; it received new seats in 1912,[113] a new power plant in the basement in 1914,[114] and a new screen in 1915.[115]

In June of 1915, there was talk of building a new and modern theatre structure for the Dixie Theatre, which had simply outgrown its limitations. "Ordinary business fills the house's many performances each day, making it unwise for the management to book features for the reason that the patrons cannot be seated or made comfortable. The majority of the people who see the Charlie Chaplin pictures there each week, stand up during the performances." It was rumored

Adams Street, 200 block looking west, c. 1908.

the new building site would be on the lot of the theatre and adjoining property.[116]

The new building never materialized, but the owners continued to update the existing facility. New seats for 240 people were installed in the fall of 1915.[117] In 1919, a "typhoon fan" was installed on the roof to give the popular theatre "the best ventilation system of any play house in the city." The fan had two four-foot fan wheels and was operated by a three-horse power electric motor.[118]

A demonstration of colored pictures appeared at the Dixie Theatre on July 18, 1919. These were not the early colored pictures which were produced by tinting and shading the black and white photographs, but were the natural coloring of the subject taken with color film, which was achieved by the Prizma process. These pictures brought to the audience "in startling realism and without the use of artificial coloring the most beautiful delineations of nature that exist."[119] The Dixie Theatre existed at this location until the early 1930's.

The top part of the Fleming store was occupied as a dwelling by Lee Reinheimer and his family; it was later occupied by attorney Harry G. Linn and Judge W. S. Meredith.[120] The top part of the Cochran store front was first occupied by the *Fairmont West Virginian* newspaper, the Republican publication. The newspaper company had been located in an office over the old Carney drug store (300 Adams Street),[121] until it was burned out in the Great Fire of 1876. At that time, *The West Virginian* was moved into this building as soon as construction had been completed, [122] and remained here until in moved into the Jacobs Building at 316 Monroe Street in 1904.

The building is still in use today.

10. Commerford Building, c. 1878. 232-236 Adams Street

This building was constructed by Michael M. Commerford around the year 1878, and the store front at 236 Adams Street was occupied by Mr. Commerford as a drugstore in 1879. The building looked much as it does today: eight bays of segmented arched windows on the second floor, a decorative cornice at the roof, topped with a broken triangular pediment in the center. The first floor had two store fronts with tall panes of glass; these have been extensively remodeled.

The Great Fire of 1876 had destroyed the adjacent 300 blocks of Adams Street, which had originally housed the Commerford store; the stock was removed to the corner room in the Mountain City Hotel next to the old Marion County Courthouse until this building was completed. The drug store had been known as the Mountain City Drug Store, although it had changed hands several times. D. D. Albert had a jewelry store and watch repair shop in a corner of the room; a big watch hung in the entrance of the building to advertised Mr. Albert's trade.[123]

Mr. Booher and Mr. Watier came to Fairmont from Wheeling in the spring of 1893 and purchased the drug store from Mr. M. M. Comerford. They were experienced in the drug business, and made many additions to the stock and fixtures to create "the most complete drug store in all this section." Prescriptions were carefully compounded and they also carried a large line of toilet articles.[124] New awnings were added in April of 1897; they were said to be of the latest designs, and one of the nicest in town.[125]

Sometime prior to 1901, the Mountain City Drug Store was acquired by James A. Martin, and was known as "Jim Martin's." In addition to filling prescriptions and handling a full line of toiletries, he also conducted a large ice cream factory in conjunction with the store. The beautiful soda fountain was said to be one of the chief features of the store's fine fixtures. Mr. Martin also had a delivery wagon which was used in connection with both the drug store and the ice cream factory.[126]

The Mountain City Drug Store once again changed hands; in December of 1906, it was sold by W. S. Hamilton to Homer Hall.[127] Shortly after he took the reins of management, a complete transformation in the store interior was effected. The old fixtures were torn down, the soda fountain dismantled, and in their place handsome mahogany shelving, counters, new glass show cases, modern light fixtures, and other such accessories were added to the renovation, making a new store out of the old. In addition to prescriptions and toiletries, he had the Fairmont agency for the famous Rexall Remedies, for Huyler's celebrated chocolates, and had the best class of cigar trade.[128]

Mr. Hall made subsequent improvements, adding a Becker Iceless fountain in 1910.[129] An alcove was added to the rear of the store in 1913 to contain a half dozen model tables and chairs for the soda business, which was one of the important secondary functions of the drug store trade. The walls of the alcove were decorated with oil landscapes by a well-known artist and the woodwork was "novel and beautiful." The tables were round and equipped with a composition top in white. The chairs had V-shaped bottoms of such construction that when not in use they could be pushed close in under the tables, utilizing no more room than the table itself.[130]

Because this room was apart from the store room in the rear, it was very desirable for ladies. A bay window was installed in the room on the Jefferson Street side, and was very popular because it gave a splendid view of the busiest section of the city while enjoying the refreshment in this secluded apartment.[131]

A new store front for the Mountain City Drug store was installed in 1914. The windows were built upon a Carrara glass base with black border of the same material, making the effect most conspicuous by the tasty contrast of black and white. The plate glass was put together with beveled joints fastened with small clasps, eliminating the small frames used to hold the glass in place. The back of the window was mirrored about half way up and continued to the top with plate Prism glass above the large front plates and reflected much more light back into the room than could be obtained by using clear glass.[132]

On the interior of the store, new cases were placed on top of the original wall cases, making an unbroken line of cases from the floor to the ceiling; the cases ran the entire length of the room on both sides for added shelf and display area.[133]

The Mountain City Drug Store received a permit to erect an electrical sign in front of its place of business in 1923.[134] Later that year, Homer Hall retired from the drug store business, and it was purchased by Brooks S. Hutchinson and Earl Fortney.[135]

The store front at 232 Adams Street was occupied by J. L. Torrey as a boot and shoe mending shop.[136] In 1900, W. A. Fisher bought the jewelry store of T. H. Lloyd at this location, and conducted his jewelry business at this location.[137] He occupied the entire premises of the two story brick building. The main store was on the ground floor, and the second floor, which was reached by a staircase in the rear, had glassware and optical department.[138] Fishers Jewelry store conducted business here until 1913, when it was taken over by Berman and Polan.[139] In 1914, it became The Palace Jewelry Store.[140]

The store front stopped being used as a jewelry store when the Maunz and Crawford, tailor establishment and men's furnishing store, opened at this location on February 1, 1917.[141] Both the first and second floors were entirely refitted with new shelves, showcases and furnishings. New signs were painted on the building for the new endeavor.[142]

In the early days of the 1880's, a part of the basement under the corner building had an entrance on Jefferson Street, and it was occupied by the barber shop of John Jackson.[143] In January of 1896, Ed Shroyer opened the Busy Bee Restaurant (under what was then referred to as Booher's drug store). "This restaurant is up to date—has steam pans to keep all cooked meats and vegetables in—thus insuring what is served you to be in first-class condition. Give the Busy Bee a call."[144] Davy Levi's pool room was later located under the drug store in 1897.[145]

Part of the second story was occupied by *The Index* newspaper in the 1880's, which was a Democratic weekly.[146]

The building is still in use today.

Commerford Building (on the corner), 232-236 Adams Street and the Fleming/Cochran Building (right), 226-230 Adams Street, c. 1892.

[1] Fleming, p. 33.
[2] *Fairmont Times*, 5/27/1923, p. 1.
[3] ibid.
[4] Fleming, p. 33.
[5] *Fairmont Times*, 8/12/1923, p. 4.
[6] ibid., 5/27/1923, p. 1.
[7] ibid., 4/30/1924, p. 2.
[8] ibid., 1/14/1911, p. 3.
[9] ibid., 1/16/1911, p. 1.
[10] ibid., 3/18/1923, supplement.
[11] ibid., 2/26/1926, p. 10.
[12] ibid., 2/9/1928, p. 1.
[13] ibid.
[14] ibid., 2/17/1929, p. 9.
[15] ibid., 3/24/1929, p. 5.
[16] *Fairmont West Virginian*, 5/21/1904, p. 3.
[17] ibid., 9/21/1904, p. 1.
[18] *Industrial Fairmont in 1908*, p. 68.
[19] *Fairmont Times-West Virginian*, 5/4/1994.
[20] *Fairmont Times*, 3/28/1913, p. 5.
[21] ibid., 11/10/1923, p. 1.
[22] ibid., 3/1/1924, p. 1.
[23] *Hardesty's Historical and Geographical Encyclopedia*, p. 312.
[24] *Twentieth Century Edition*, p. 23.
[25] *Fairmont Times*, 2/1/1917, p. 1.
[26] ibid.
[27] ibid., 4/3/1917, p. 2.
[28] ibid., 9/17/1917, p. 8.
[29] ibid., 3/29/1918, p. 2.
[30] ibid., 5/6/1923, sect. 2, p. 1.
[31] ibid., 3/5/1926, p. 12.
[32] *Welcome Westinghouse*, sect. 1, p. 11.
[33] *Hardesty's Historical and Geographical Encyclopedia*, p. 312.
[34] *Twentieth Century Edition*, p. 23.
[35] ibid.
[36] *Fairmont Times*, 1/29/1916, p. 9.
[37] ibid., 5/13/1916, p. 1.
[38] ibid., 5/29/1916, p. 1.
[39] ibid., 9/12/1916, p. 1.
[40] ibid., 1/20/1917, p. 1.
[41] ibid., 2/23/1917, p. 2.
[42] ibid., 3/16/1924, sect. 2, p. 1.
[43] ibid., 11/22/1923, p. 6.
[44] ibid., 3/16/1924, sect. 2, p. 1.
[45] ibid., 11/5/1927, p. 9.
[46] ibid.
[47] ibid., 1/21/1928, p. 4.
[48] ibid., 2/22/1928, p. 1.
[49] *Twentieth Century Edition*, p. 34.
[50] ibid.
[51] ibid.
[52] *Fairmont Times*, 9/16/1910, p. 1.
[53] ibid., 1/2/1923, p. 12.
[54] ibid., 12/21/1922, sect. 2, p. 2.
[55] ibid., 12/31/1922, p. 3.
[56] ibid., 2/9/1923, sect. 2, p. 1.
[57] ibid., 3/11/1923, p. 7.

[58] ibid., 11/5/1927, p. 9.
[59] ibid., 1/12/29, p. 2.
[60] ibid., 3/20/1927, sect. 2, p. 1.
[61] ibid., 8/18/1909, p. 1.
[62] *Fairmont Index*, 6/2/1893.
[63] ibid., 1/3/1894.
[64] *Fairmont Times*, 8/18/1909, p. 1.
[65] ibid., 9/29/1902, p. 1.
[66] ibid., 11/10/1902, p. 1.
[67] ibid., 6/12/1903, p. 2.
[68] *Fairmont West Virginian*, 4/26/1904, p. 1.
[69] ibid., 11/16/1904, p. 1.
[70] *Fairmont Times*, 9/16/1907, p. 2.
[71] ibid., 5/18/1908, p. 1.
[72] ibid., 5/1/1909, p. 1.
[73] ibid., 8/18/1909, p. 1.
[74] ibid.
[75] ibid., 9/29/1909, p. 3.
[76] ibid., 11/20/1909, p. 2.
[77] ibid., 7/11/1910, p. 1.
[78] ibid., 8/11/1929, p. 12.
[79] ibid., 3/17/1927, p. 11.
[80] ibid., 8/11/1929, p. 12.
[81] ibid.
[82] ibid.
[83] ibid.
[84] ibid., 3/10/1929, sect. 2, p. 1.
[85] ibid., 4/13/1908, p. 1.
[86] ibid., 7/3/1908, p. 1.
[87] ibid., 8/29/1908, p. 1.
[88] ibid., 1/7/1909, p. 6.
[89] ibid., 12/24/1913, p. 1.
[90] ibid., 1/6/1914, p. 8.
[91] ibid., 2/20/1921, p. 12.
[92] ibid., 5/14/1926, p. 1.
[93] ibid., 5/27/1926, p. 1.
[94] ibid., 4/14/1927, p. 2.
[95] ibid., 7/29/1926, p. 1.
[96] ibid., 3/20/1927, sect. 2, p. 1.
[97] ibid.
[98] ibid., 11/13/1929, p. 8.
[99] ibid., 8/11/1929, p. 12.
[100] ibid.
[101] *Industrial Fairmont in 1908*, p. 26.
[102] *Fairmont Times*, 9/12/1914, p. 2.
[103] ibid., 5/11/1919, p. 3.
[104] ibid., 1/10/1929, p. 4.
[105] ibid., 4/15/1907, p. 8.
[106] ibid.
[107] ibid., 8/11/1929, p. 12.
[108] ibid., 1/12/1925, p. 8.
[109] ibid.
[110] ibid.
[111] ibid.
[112] ibid., 4/15/1907, p. 8.
[113] ibid., 4/8/1912, p. 2.
[114] ibid., 9/23/1914, p. 6.

[115] ibid., 2/1/1915, p. 5.
[116] ibid., 6/3/1915, p. 1.
[117] ibid., 10/1/1915, p. 2.
[118] ibid., 6/26/1919, p. 10.
[119] ibid., 7/18/1919, p. 12.
[120] ibid., 8/11/1929, p. 12.
[121] *Fairmont Index*, 1/3/1894.
[122] *Fairmont Times*, 8/11/1929, p. 12.
[123] ibid.
[124] *Fairmont Index*, 1/3/1894.
[125] ibid., 4/16/1897.
[126] *Twentieth Century Edition*, p. 26.
[127] *Fairmont Times*, 12/19/1906, p. 4.
[128] *Industrial Fairmont in 1908*, p. 53.
[129] *Fairmont Times*, 4/26/1910, p. 1.
[130] ibid., 4/28/1913, p. 2.
[131] ibid., 4/13/1914, p. 4.
[132] ibid.
[133] ibid.
[134] ibid., 1/16/1923, p. 10.
[135] ibid., 3/29/1923, p. 7.
[136] ibid., 8/11/1929, p. 12.
[137] *Fairmont West Virginian*, 8/17/1904, p. 7.
[138] *Industrial Fairmont in 1908*, p. 29.
[139] *Fairmont Times*, 10/17/1913, p. 6.
[140] ibid., 2/27/1914, p. 5.
[141] ibid., 1/22/1917, p. 1.
[142] ibid., 1/31/1917, p. 1.
[143] ibid., 8/11/1929, p. 12.
[144] *Fairmont Index*, 1/21/1896.
[145] ibid., 6/22/1897.
[146] *Fairmont Times*, 8/11/1929, p. 12.

Chapter 4

200 Block Adams Street, odd numbered buildings

1. Jacobs-Hutchinson Block: Peoples Bank Building, Hartley's Store, Jones' Store; 1901-1902. Andrew C. Lyons, architect. 201-207 Adams Street

The Jacobs-Hutchinson Block was designed by Andrew C. Lyons and constructed in 1901-1902 by Holbert & Spedden, Builders (S. Ray Holbert and W. H. Spedden).[1] The owners of the building were George M. Jacobs, J. M. Jacobs, M. L. Hutchinson, and Clyde E. Hutchinson[2] (Lyons had designed all of the men's private residences as well).[3] It is 92 feet by 80 feet and five stories high, and was built of Roman shaped pressed brick and trimmed with Euclid blue stone, with a terra cotta cornice. It had both a freight and passenger elevator.[4] At the cornice, two small segments of the entablature protrude beside the inscription "Jacobs- Hutchinson Block;" these areas read "19" and "02," which is the construction date. The building is Neo-classical in its detail.

Though it appears to be one unified block, the building was originally planned to be used as four separate business "houses," partitioned vertically; it was the largest commercial building in Fairmont when it was constructed. When it opened in November 1902, each of three firms occupied five stories plus basement: J. M. Hartley & Son occupied the two eastern quarters nearest the Courthouse; W. H. Billingslea, a furniture dealer, occupied the western corner quarter; and Casterline and Hoge, proprietors of the Racket Store, occupied the quarter in between the two other stores.[5]

J. M. Hartley & Son became the "anchor tenant" of the Jacobs-Hutchinson Block from the store's opening on November 20, 1902,[6] for which the Greater Fairmont band furnished music.[7] This business was founded in Fairmont in 1877 as J. M. Hartley's, then as Hartley & Company, Hartley & Morrow, and J. M. Hartley; it became J. M. Hartley & Son in 1901. It has been the hallmark of department stores in Fairmont from its beginning until its closure in 1985, one-hundred and eight years of commercial activity. Because of its very early success, the store moved from its original location at 302 Adams Street, which had become overcrowded, to the Jacobs-Hutchinson Block.

Casterline and Hoge's Racket Store had an opening to celebrate their new quarters as well, on November 29, 1902. One very popular feature of the opening was a baking contest; the girl under fourteen years of age who made the best biscuit was awarded a "pretty little stove." Nearly fifty children participated. Music for the opening was provided by C. E. MacArthur's Orchestra on the first floor; they played all afternoon and evening. Billingslea's opening was planned for early December.[8]

There was change of owners and tenants relatively soon after the building was occupied. In July 1903, T. W. Fleming bought the corner building of the Jacobs-Hutchinson Block for $50,000. It was reported the first floor was to be rebuilt for the permanent home of the Peoples

Bank, then located at 123 Adams Street. These rumors could not be verified, since Mr. Fleming had gone out of town and the bank officials refused to talk. Mr. Billingslea had only thirty days to move out of the place, and had a great sale to do so. He moved his furniture business to the Cunningham Block (308 Jefferson Street). The four floors above the street level were thought to be fitted up as offices, replacing the freight elevator with a passenger elevator.[9]

Upon his return to town, Mr. Fleming stated that he bought the building himself, but admitted the bank was likely to occupy it.[10] Four days later, it was announced the Peoples Bank had bought that quarter of the Jacobs-Hutchinson Block from Mr. Fleming. There were immediate plans to remodel the first floor to make it suitable for banking purposes, on the style of the noted Colonial Trust Company's building in Pittsburgh. A system of vaults were to be installed that would be "absolutely impervious to any explosive force." The directors would meet in a balcony room above and overlooking the general banking office. It was thought the work would cost $10,000, and the bank would be ready to be occupied by January 1, 1904.[11]

Although several businesses moved into the offices in the upper level of the People's Bank building earlier in the year, the bank itself did not open for business until March of 1904. Clark Safe & Vault Company of Pittsburgh installed double vaults with 150 safe deposit boxes. The fixtures were supplied by Ohmer Sons & Company, and were of solid mahogany with bronze trimming. The counters and wainscoting were of Italian marble with an English vein. Private booths were supplied for the cashier, teller, and collection clerk, as well as one for the patrons of the bank. The floor was laid with ceramic mosaic tile.[12] The Globe Rubber Stamps Works of Fairmont manufactured the bronze sign for the new building.[13]

The quarter of the Jacobs-Hutchinson Block that was originally occupied by The Racket Store was vacated when the store relocate to the adjacent Jacobs Building (312 Monroe Street); the store front was subsequently occupied by the Jacobs-Hutchinson Hardware Company beginning in March 1904. The company carried one of the largest lines of hardware in the state at the time. The enterprise occupied all six floors of their quarter of the block: the first floor housed a complete line of hardware; the second floor housed queensware, kitchen and household furniture; the third floor held stoves, ranges, brushes, and paints; the fourth floor had building supplies, such as doors and windows, as well as farming implements; and the fifth floor was used for stock.[14]

Early in 1907, Hartley's was on the move to acquire more space for its expanding business. The store secured a lease on the four upper floors of the store front occupied by the hardware store. The rooms were connected to the existing store by a series of arches. The two upper floors were used for stock, the upper floors of the original part of the store could be converted to salesrooms. This increased Hartley's floor space from 19,200 square feet to 25,800 square feet.[15]

A new front was installed at Hartley's to encompass the new area; this was completed in September of 1911.[16] According to the Sandborn map of 1912, the wall separating the two original "business houses" (nearest the Courthouse) was replaced with iron columns, opening up the space even further.

Hartley's business was wildly successful and needed more room to expand. The only area left in the Jacobs-Hutchinson Block were the rooms above the People's Bank Building, so Hartley's expanded into those rooms on the second, third fourth, and fifth floors by leasing them from the bank. An archway opening was constructed between these two "business houses" for circulation; these "annexes" were mostly used for stock rooms.[17]

As additional space was needed, Hartley's leased the first floor room and basement in the adjoining section of the Jacob's Building (312 Monroe Street).[18] The enlarged store was thrown open to the public on March 22, 1918, and it had increased its area 25%, from 30,000 square feet to 40,000 square feet. This event was referred to as an "at home," since it was seen as entertaining the many friends of the store.[19]

The newly-acquired space in the adjoining Jacobs Building gave the department store a Monroe Street entrance, and it was connected to the main building by an enclosed passage way. The entrance to the rooms upstairs in the Jacobs building were accessed from the second floor by an elevated passage way referred to as the "Bridge of Size" (a play on the words referring to the Bridge of Sighs in Venice, Italy), and it was planned to lower this bridge at a later date for convenience. There were no sales rooms added above the second floor at that time because it would have been impossible to transport customers until additional elevator service could be secured; it was seen as being out of the question at that time, as "it would be unpatriotic in the Hartley view to attempt to get huge elevators shipped into Fairmont with the present demands upon transportation facilities,"[20] due to the first World War.

A new elevator was installed in the Jacobs-Hutchinson Block in October of 1920, well after the war was over. An Otis electric elevator, entirely fireproof and made of iron, was erected in the rear of the main floor; after its installation, the old one was removed from the middle of the building, freeing up valuable sales space.[21]

Mr. Hartley was well-loved by his employees. He treated them well, giving 1% of Christmas sales to the clerks as a bonus,[22] having company picnics, and even entertaining the entire force of his store at the Country Club; this event occurred on April 25, 1922. The dinner for 95 included words of appreciation by Mr. Hartley to his employees, as well as remarks by other members of the Hartley firm and department heads, followed by dancing.[23]

All of Fairmont was in shock when word came of the sudden death of Joseph Milton Hartley, who was on route home from Denver where he had attended a Rotary convention. Heart failure had taken him on the train in Nebraska on June 25, 1926. He was 79 years old. The Hartley's store closed and remained closed until after the funeral, out of respect for the founder of Fairmont's largest retail enterprise.[24] His funeral was largely attended; at the head of the casket, there were 89 pink roses, one from each of his 89 employees. [25] The store was subsequently managed by his son, Harry J. Hartley, and his business partner, John H. Rownd.

Hartley's store was the first local firm to reach its 50th birthday, and had celebrations for the event. One of the activities was in conjunction with the Marion County Historic Society; they planned an exhibit that would contrast a kitchen, dining room and a parlor of 1877, the year Hartley's was founded, with a "modern" kitchen, dining room and parlor of 1927. Residents were asked to lend their possession from 1877 for the exhibit. The organizers were especially interested in articles that were purchased in the Hartley's of 50 years ago. They also had a fashion pageant contrasting the styles of 1877 with those of 1927.[26] In the midst of the celebration, J. M. Hartley was remembered and sorely missed. "It seems a pity that his life might not have been spanned the few short months that extended between the time of his demise and this very great anniversary in his business that his labors had made possible."[27]

In December of 1927, the American Building (109 Adams Street) was acquired by Hartley's.[28] The store opened its new furniture line at that location on June 28, 1928, in addition to its regular store in the Jacobs-Hutchinson Block. In September of that year, the American Department Stores Corporation in New York acquired five stores, one of them being Hartley & Son in Fairmont, West Virginia.[29]

Hartley's announced in the spring of 1929 that it would rebuild its furniture store at 109 Adams street, adding two stories and a new store front to the existing building, and move its entire operation to this new location.[30] On November 19, 1929 Hartley's closed its operations in the Jacobs-Hutchinson Block, which had never known its absence since it had moved there at the building's opening in 1902.[31]

During all the years of Hartley's business expansion, the People's Bank had been in its first floor corner location as the department store spread around it. In August of 1929, three banks in Fairmont merged: People's National Bank, the Fairmont Trust Company (210 Adams Street) and the Home Savings Bank (209 Adams Street), to be known as the Union National Bank.[32] It was decided the new consolidated bank would open temporarily in the old People's Bank location until the banking rooms of the former Fairmont Trust Company at 210 Adams Street were remodeled for the new bank.[33] The bank then moved out of this location.

Home of the People's Bank.

Jacobs-Hutchinson Block, 201-207 Adams Street, c. 1908.

Jones' Department Store moved from its location across the street at 208 Adams Street to the Jacobs-Hutchinson Block in the 1930's, where it remained until it closed in 1977. The structure was purchased in 1980 by the Spatafore family for use as the Friendly Furniture Store, its current use. The building was placed on the National Register of Historic Places in 1995.

2. Fairmont Trust Company, Home Savings Bank; 1904-1905. 209 Adams Street

In April of 1903, the Fairmont Trust Company announced that it had begun construction of its new entirely fire proof business block. Contractor Burchinal had prepared the plans, and the Brady Construction company had been awarded the contract for its construction. The structure was to have seven stories and a basement, and would have forty-eight office rooms above the banking room.[34] Nothing happened. In May of 1903, it was stated the structural steel building would soon be in the course of construction, and that they were waiting for the bids to come in for the project.[35] By December of that year, it was stated that work would probably begin in the spring and be "pushed to completion."[36] Again, no construction had begun.

After its tentative start, it does appear that construction finally began during the summer of 1904. The bank opened for business on May 1, 1905,[37] two years after it was said to be "pushing to completion." The front of the original building had two Roman arch openings, similar to the ones found on the side, but much larger in size. The exterior of the building is sheathed in iron mottled brick, the best product of the Ohio Brick Company, Zanesville, Ohio. The walls of the building are tied to the walls of the adjoining Jacobs-Hutchinson Block with 15 inch I-beams securely anchored into the brickwork at either end.[38]

This building is noteworthy as it appears to be the first structure built in the city with reinforced concrete floors, which provided the building its fire proof qualities. This was referred to as the Johnson system, and consisted of steel rods, wire meshing, cement, and fire-proof blocks.[39]

This new structural system was quite a novelty to the citizens of Fairmont, who were skeptical of its structural integrity. Specifically, the milling crowds did not think the floor would be strong enough. To prove themselves, the contractor made a test of the strength, loading a ten foot by twenty-two foot section of the floor with a load of thirteen tons, plus the weight of ten men standing on it. It was noted the deflection of the center of the floor did not exceed 1/8 inch, and the concrete did not show a crack or parting at the corners. Though only the floors of the building were being constructed with this system, it was noted that other buildings in the country were being completely constructed in this manner.[40] This occurred two years later in Fairmont, with the structure of the Masonic Temple Building (316-320 Jefferson Street) constructed entirely of reinforced concrete.

The seven story building is very narrow on the front facade, with only two bays. The first floor was made of rusticated stonework, and had two large Roman arches on the front, as well as four Roman arches on the side. The arches had crossettes forming the voussoirs of the arches. The rest of the building is constructed of red brick with terra cotta detail. The windows

Home Savings Bank, 209 Adams Street, c. 1919.

on the second through sixth floors are all rectangular, with ornamental "keystones" over each. The top floor has double windows in each bay, with more ornamental stonework surrounding them. The roof has a simple overhanging cornice.

The heating system was steam and the plumbing was known as "open work" and made of nickel throughout. The floors in the banking room, the lobby and the first flight of stairs were made of Tennessee marble, and the wainscoting in the banking room was of English vein Italian marble. The toilet room partitions and stair treads above the second floor were of slate. The stair work was made of iron, and was said to be one of the best jobs ever done in a Fairmont building.[41] In the banking room, the fixtures and furniture were of English oak, polished until one could see one's reflection. The marble work, which was white, contrasted with the black grill work, which rose from the marble. The ceiling was frescoes by Charles Yeager of Fairmont.[42]

The vault, twenty-one feet long and seven feet wide, protected the funds, books, and safe deposit boxes; it was constructed of Bessemer steel made of two layers of 3/4" steel with cement between them. The doors were built by the Molser Safe and Lock Company, and weighed 7,200 pounds apiece.[43]

"The Human Fly" performed in Fairmont by climbing to the top of the Fairmont Trust Company building in front of a crowd of thousands. "Starting at the pavement, equipped only with a pair of gym shoes and a pair of soft cotton gloves, he climbed from window to window until he had reached the top story of the building." The "Fly" was not a hit with the big crowd of young boys, who had expected something more spectacular. The "Fly" tried to explain that he climbed slowly because of the cold temperature in mid-February, but the dissatisfaction was reflected in the "collection," which did not reach more than $15.[44]

In 1917, the Fairmont Trust Company moved across the street to 210 Adams Street, and the Home Savings Bank moved into these banking quarters.[45] The Home Savings Bank conducted business here until 1929, when the bank merged with the People's State Bank and the Fairmont Trust Company to form the Union National Bank. This building was vacated by the former Home Savings Bank, first being temporarily located at 201 Adams Street until the renovations were completed at 210 Adams Street for the new bank.[46] It was later occupied by the Security Bank.

It is now used as offices.

3. Marion County Jailer's Residence and Jail, Marion County Historical Museum; 1909-1912. E. J. Woods, architect. 215 Adams Street

This was the first site upon which a public building was erected by the county in the young city of Fairmont, then Middletown; the county jail was built by Leonard Lamb in 1842 on land acquired from Matthew Fleming and James Kerns.[47] In 1877, a new jail was built on back of the site, along with the sheriff's residence at a cost of about $8,000.[48] These buildings were in the rear of the original courthouse and connected to it.

In 1909, the County bought the lot adjacent to the new Courthouse and next to the Jacobs Building (310 Monroe Street) for construction of a modern prison. The existing jail was to be demolished, and the new one constructed on the area of the new lot and the old lot. The jailer's residence would be a new and separate building in front of the jail and near the edge of the lot next to the Fairmont Trust Company Building (209 Adams Street). To accommodate the prisoners during construction when the old jail would be demolished, the "Farmers room" in the basement of the Courthouse was to be used as a temporary jail, with a guard there night and day.[49]

The Clarksburg architect E. J. Woods was chosen to be the designer of the two new structures, based on the sketches for the new buildings that he and a number of other architects had been invited to submit by the county commissioners. The two buildings were to cost approximately $100,000, and would both be of stone. The jail was to be a three story building with a basement, containing 32 cells. On the top floor, it was planned to have the hospital, juvenile cells and specials cells for both men and women. The jailer's residence was planned to be two stories with attic and basement, also of stone. The outer portions of the two buildings which faced Adams Street were planned to be constructed of stone to match the Courthouse, and the inner and back walls were planned to be made of "native stone."[50]

On August 6, 1909, work began on the excavations for the two buildings. The force of men was increased as soon as the rooms in the Courthouse were fitted up with cages to house the prisoners from the county jail. The old jail was then demolished and the excavations of the foundations "rushed through." When finished, few towns would have a better prison, it was stated.[51]

The Farmers Room in the basement of the Courthouse was prepared, the prisoners transferred, and work on tearing down the old jail began on August 30, 1909. It was said the buildings would be hurriedly completed, and well along before cold weather set in.[52] Ha.

On October 22, 1909, Contractor Howell had a large force of men working on the excavation and had the cement workers building the concrete foundation for the jail; they were "hurrying the work on the project." The ditch for the foundation was dug to a depth of nine feet and a four foot concrete foundation was built in this ditch. After the concrete floor was poured, it was ready for the masons. They also planned to begin the jailer's residence before the jail was completed.[53]

The project was not without mishaps. The lives of several workers and bystanders were endangered one day when the guy rope of a derrick broke; the derrick was being used to move the big stones for the jail. The derrick fell to the ground, but luckily no one was hurt. The derrick was replaced and made secure again for work. The contractor was "rushing along the work."[54]

Numerous delays ensued. On January 3, 1910, the Marion County Court decided not to let the contract for the construction of the new jail and sheriff's residence until January 20. It was decided that certain sections of the specifications needed to be revised before the contract was let, and the five bids were returned to the bidders. This was met with considerable surprise, though there had been rumors the contract would be held up. It was said that parts of the specifications for the material did not enable some contractors to bid, and there was not enough time allowed to furnish bond for the work.[55]

The bid was finally awarded to C. P. Howell of Clarksburg, with the low bid of $115,999.99. The highest bid was $131,963.00. Mr. Howell had already done the work of building the foundation for the jail and had his men and machinery on site, so the start up time for him would be minimal. The contract called for building the jail out of modern gray stone, fitted with all the latest jail accommodations. The sheriff's residence was to be made of gray stone, and both were to be built of first class materials, finished in hard wood, to be "first class," and to the satisfaction of the court.[56]

Let the snipping begin. S. Ray Holbert, one of the unsuccessful bidders on the project, became upset over the awarding of the contract, and set forth alleged facts concerning its award. He alleged the jail would not be constructed according to the specifications, and the architect was a friend of C. P. Howell who was awarded the contract. Further, Commissioner Lilly had not attended the letting of the contract because he had gone south on a hunting trip.[57]

In reply to his allegations, County Clerk J. F. Phillips stated that the County Court was entirely honest in the letting of the contract. Commissioner Lilly had stayed at the session long enough to determine which of the bids was the lowest and when he left he knew just what the decision of the court would be.[58]

In spite of the sour grapes, that contract was executed with Howell for the construction, to be completed in eight months on September 28, 1910.[59] The new jail was sorely needed, since the temporary one was filled to capacity. There were many escapes from the makeshift quarters.

By January of 1911, the buildings were not yet completed. The work was proceeding very slowly, which was beyond the control of the contractor and the County Court; it was the financial condition of the county that was to blame. "It is hoped that money matters will shape themselves so the building will be completed without any further delay than is absolutely necessary."[60] All the while, prisoners were continuing to escape from their temporary quarters in the basement of the Courthouse.

At long last, the Marion County Jail and Sheriff's Residence were opened on March 12, 1912, "rushed to completion," eighteen months behind schedule. The Jailer's residence is a two and one-half story structure of ashlar masonry, which matched the material of the adjacent Courthouse. It is Italianate in character, with its bracketed overhang and baskethandle windows. The Jail, not visible from Adams Street, is constructed of rough-hewn stone, with medieval battlements completing its Gothic fortress-like image.

Hundreds of people visited the structures during the public inspection of them. The woodwork in the floor of the jailer's residence, some of the beautiful windows, and the wood work in the building were the best that could be made or obtained. The Jailer's Residence was so constructed that it was completely shut off from the jail, so that none of the sounds of the jail were transmitted into the residence. A complete system of call bells, telephones and alarms made it impossible for any prisoner to make a move without the sheriff's office knowing, with indicators showing from what part of the jail the alarm or call had come.[61]

The jail was completely fire proof and sanitary. The walls were built of stone with a tile finish on the interior, making it "cheery yet sanitary." The stairways were made of iron and the floors were made of concrete. The cells were adequate to accommodate 100 prisoners, each about six feet square, with bars of five ply steel. There were fold-down racks for the beds so they could be folded up against the wall during the day. There was one cell that was not lighted at all, called the dungeon, for unruly prisoners; and two padded cells for the insane.[62]

It was remarked at its opening the new jail would end up costing about $130,000,[63] which ironically was the approximate amount of the highest bid given for the project back in 1910.

The Jail is still used for its original purpose; the Jailer's Residence currently houses the Marion County Historical Museum. The Jailer's Residence, though not the Jail, was placed on the National Register of Historic Places in 1979.

4. Marion County Courthouse, 1844; Mountain City House, 1849; Marion County Courthouse, 1897-1900. Yost and Packard, architects. 217-221 Adams Street

This site originally contained two significant structures before the construction of the present courthouse: the original courthouse and the Mountain City House, a hotel.

The original courthouse was constructed by Daniel M. Thompson for the sum of $3,150.75,[64] and was completed in 1844. The two story structure was constructed of red brick and had a cupola which contained a bell. The gable roof was supported by wood columns, and the front of the building facing Adams Street had a Greek temple front. The land for the courthouse, like the adjoining jail, was acquired from Matthew Fleming and James Kerns.[65]

The first story of the Courthouse contained the county offices of the clerk of the county court and the circuit court clerk's office. On either side of the hallway leading to the back of the building were various other offices. The second floor contained the large court room and two jury rooms. In the front of the building was a large yard with shade trees, and in the rear was the jail and sheriff's residence.[66]

The Courthouse had become dilapidated and the quarters were cramped for the expanding uses that came with the growing population. It was also thought of as a thing of the past that had outlived its usefulness, and unfit for the then present-day uses of the citizens. Even in 1894, there was a call for the construction of a new courthouse to better accommodate the litigants and the jurymen, and to better preserve the county papers and property records. The old Courthouse was cited as being dangerous and an injury to the pride of the county citizens. There was a call for a vote to issue bonds for the construction of a new courthouse, even in the unpopular light of increased taxes for the citizens to finance the new building.[67] The unpopularity of additional taxes must have outweighed the matter of civic pride concerning the condition of the courthouse, for nothing was done about it. Therefore, a group of citizens decided to take the matter into their own hands.

"Old Courthouse Torn Down," read the newspaper headlines. On the night of January 12, 1897,[68] a group of about eighty men gathered and lit into the old place with crowbars, axes, and mattocks, doing much damage to the walls, roof and floors. "Certain Fairmont 'big-wigs' bought the whiskey, and a certain well known party made a speech saying, 'This old building's a disgrace. What we're doing is good for the county. So, come one, let's get it done'," stated Sanford "Bucky" Fleming, one time county commissioner of Marion County. "Lots of people were mad about it, but things soon settled down, and when the new courthouse was finished most people were glad about what was done to the old one."[69]

Further explanation in the newspaper said the building was dangerous and had once caught on fire. The county court, therefore, believing that a risk of loss of life should not be run, ordered the courtroom proper to be torn down. A short time after the court adjourned in the evening, a large force of men was put to work; by midnight they had torn away the rear portion of the first story. There was considerable opposition throughout the county due to the action of the court, but everybody in the county knew that a new building was needed. It was thought the objections would soon be withdrawn. However, many persons believed the courthouse could have and should have been repaired, and questioned whether the late-night wrecking party had actually been authorized by the court.[70]

The other significant building that was demolished to make room for the new courthouse was the Mountain City House. This three story wood structure stood on the corner of Adams and Jefferson Streets, and was built in 1849. Made of two wings, the L-shaped building had the eave ends of the gable roofs facing the two streets. It had seven bays on Adams Street and nine bays on Jefferson Street. The hotel was the center of both social and business life in Fairmont for many years.[71] The first floor of the structure was used for small commercial enterprises such as a harness shop, a barber, and a stationery store; the sleeping room were on the two upper floors.

John W. Irwin was one of the well-known proprietors of the establishment. A newspaper advertisement said it all: "Elegantly repaired, refurnished, and equipped! Conveniently located and having splendid sample rooms, this house is specially adapted for use of commercial travelers, and offers superior accommodations to the general public. Ladies' entrance on Jefferson Street. Free bus attends all trains for passengers and baggage. Good feed stables attached."[72]

After the old courthouse had been severely damaged on January 12, 1897, arrangements were made for the construction of the new courthouse. The court made arrangements for the architecture firm of Yost and Packard (Joseph Warren Yost and Frank L. Packard) of Columbus, Ohio to design the new structure. On March 22, 1897 work began on removing the old courthouse.[73] A notice from Abram Page, the contractor in charge of tearing down the remains of the old courthouse and other property for the sum of $450,[74] appeared in the newspaper warning "persons loafing near where the Court House is being torn down that they do so at their own risk."[75] The court had been removed to another location for the duration of the new construction. The firm of Sturm and Watkins was the lowest bidder for the foundations of the new courthouse at the cost of $7,485, and they were awarded the contract on May 7, 1897.[76]

The contract for the construction of the courthouse was awarded to James Westwater & Company of Columbus, Ohio. Their bid was:

For furnishing material and doing work as specified:

	$130,743.10
If cast iron is used for main cornice, add:	$6,500.00
If stone is used in tympanums, add:	$1,500.00
If original plans for steps is used add:	$2,900.00

This order was entered on June 10, 1897. On June 11, 1897, Mr. George W. Mayers moved the Court to set aside and annul the order awarding the contract and on the next day he filed a new bid for the work, which was lower than the bid that had won the contract. The Court refused to vacate the order. For the fiscal year 1897-1898, $25,000 was budgeted for the construction of the Courthouse out of a total budget of approximately $47,000. The levy to meet this budget was 55 cents on the $100 valuation in Fairmont and West Fairmont, and 65 cents in all other districts in the county.[77]

Sour grapes by a contractor who was not awarded the contract occurred, just as with the construction of the adjacent Jail and Jailer's Residence. Mr. Mayers, who had resubmitted his bid in hopes of acquiring the contract, wrote an open letter to the newspaper in which he questioned the quality of the work in progress, whether the work conformed to the specifications, and whether the taxpayers of Marion County were getting their money's worth in the construction of the Courthouse.[78]

The cornerstone of the building, located on the southeast corner, was laid by the Lodge Number 9, A. F. & A. M. on November 17, 1897; the building was completed in 1900. According to the Sanborn map of 1912, it was constructed of stone, brick, steel and concrete. All interior wall were made of brick, and the floors were steel girders encased in hollow tile and concrete. The dome was made of steel frame, not fire protected, and had wooden stairways, floor and beams. The roof covering of the dome was copper laid on wood sheathing.

The original construction of the building provided a light well from the first floor (referred to as the "basement") through the center of the building to the dome. In the dome was a decorative chandelier. On the Adams and Jefferson Streets sides of the building are two large porches with pediments containing sculptural relief, the roofs of which are supported by huge stone Corinthian columns. On top of the building is a huge dome, which houses a clock which can be seen from all sections of the city. On top of the dome is the blindfolded figure of Justice, with a sword in one hand and scales in the other. An overpass on the second floor (referred to as the "main floor") connected the Courthouse with the adjoining jail;[79] this is no longer there. The original county courtroom is located on the third floor.

A handsome public drinking fountain was installed on the Courthouse Square, just off Jefferson Street on the edge of the Courthouse paving, in the spring of 1905. The bronze statue, which formed a beautiful column, was built by J. L. Mott Iron Works of New York.[80]

"Wonderful changes" had come to the Courthouse in the summer of 1911 after Democratic officials had taken charge. During the years of Republican administration, the interior and exterior of the building were allowed to go to "wrack and ruin." The corridors had been accessible at all hours of the night and "midnight loafers" made it their rendezvous, leaving it in a filthy condition. Complaints to the Republicans were of no avail. The sanitary conditions were so bad that some of the women clerks were made ill. The floors were filthy and the air filled with foul odors. The cornice and roof were neglected and leaking. After the Democrats took office, they began the task of cleaning the "Augean stable." The building was secured against the loafers, competent janitors were hired to clean the building, the roof damage was repaired, and the walls were painted. This was completed in only six months during the Democratic administration. "It stands as an indictment of the inefficiency of the preceding Republican administration," stated the Democratic newspaper, "and as a commendation of the wisdom of the people in putting an active and efficient body of men in office."[81]

An additional courtroom was added to the building sometime between 1906 and 1912, according to the Sandborn maps of those years. It was added on the second floor (referred to as the "main floor"), directly below the original courtroom on the third floor (referred to as the "second floor").

In the spring of 1912, the Circuit Courtroom was refurbished by the County Commissioners. The walls upon which there were handsome paintings were retouched by Mr. Frank Lloyd, a local artist; and the ceiling had been cleaned. New carpet was placed inside the rail; and the chairs, which were falling to pieces, were retouched so they looked like new. An electric chandelier was installed over the part of the room occupied by the attorneys and court officers; previously, on gloomy days, it was hard to read in this area.[82]

Renovation work also occurred in 1917. That spring, there was an effort to restore the building to its "old-time splendor" that age and use had deteriorated. There was a thorough cleaning of the walls, floors and ceilings. The bulk of the work, however, was being done in the "basement" (first floor), from which unpleasant smells emanated. The Farmers Room, which once had given the "country people of the county a place to gather and meet while they are in the city," was used as the county jail during the construction of the adjacent Jail and Jailer's Residence (215 Adams Street) in 1909-1912; this area had fallen into "disrepute and neglect" through this function. In addition, public toilets had been installed there, and these were to be renovated, refitted, and maintained by a janitor to keep them in a sanitary condition.[83]

Another feature that was the pride of the people when the building was new was the two oil paintings on the stair landing between the first and the second floors; these were restored. One depicted the old Marion county courthouse which "gave up the ghost" to make room for the present one, the other was a painting of the map of the county. Constant elbowing and leaning on these works of art, it was stated, had erased their lines and shadows, and it couldn't be discerned exactly what they represented before this restoration.[84] The paintings no longer appear there.

Later in the fall of 1917, it was decided to use the old Farmers Room in the "basement" (first floor) of the courthouse as a museum. "A corps of pretty young ladies" installed the display in the newly cleaned and painted room. The display consisted of family heirlooms and memoirs of other days, including an old fashioned bed, a spinning wheel, firearms of a century ago, and other objects. The collection was to be enlarged from time to time, and open to the public.[85]

An iron fence was erected around the rear of the porch of the Courthouse, which was connected to the adjacent jail via the "Bridge of Sighs," a bridge on the second floor. The porch had been originally unprotected, even though it was ten or twelve feet off the ground. This was seen as dangerous to a stranger who might walk off the edge, but also was a security concern: prisoners could escape while being taken to and from the courtroom.[86]

A new records room was installed in the Courthouse in the latter part of 1925. The county clerk at the time, Lee N. Satterfield, had been short on storage space for two years; he drew up his plans for increased storage, submitted them to local builders, and received the approval of the county court for the changes. The contractor was Mr. Burchinal of Fairmont. The old vault was converted into a storage room and a meeting room for the county commissioners. Adjacent to this room was the office work room. The new vault room was entered from the main office by stairs which lead to it on the floor below. A hand elevator was used to connect the clerk's office and the vault room and to remove the record books from room to room as needed. The room was constructed to be fire proof, with a steel entrance door, and windows which were screened and fire-proof. "The building might be destroyed by fire but the record room would remain intact with the records safe." New steel book shelves were installed, as well as new lighting and ventilation, which were deemed "perfect." The floor was covered with battleship linoleum cemented to the floor. Tables and chairs were installed for the use of attorneys looking up records, with room for as many as twenty-five to work at the same time. The new arrangement was seen to be the "pride of every citizen of the county."[87]

New lighting in the central atrium was necessitated when the old light fixture, which was suspended from the center of the dome inside the building, dropped with a crash from three stories to the first floor. This occurred in the spring of 1926. The new fixture that was installed weighted 800 pounds, and was hung from steel hooks and attached to a steel cable with windlass equipment used to lower the huge fixture. The new fixture included downward lights, as well as upward lights to reflect upwards into the dome.[88] It does not appear that this fixture is still there.

There was much wasted space in the building, since it had been designed with an eye for beauty. However, as the population increased, there was an need for additional space in the Courthouse. One plan that was considered was to secure land across Meredith Alley to build an annex, but it was finally decided to cut up the interior of the building to create more room. In later years, a floor was constructed over the light well on the second floor, or "main floor," of the building. The light well now only extends from top of the dome to the second floor, instead of completely down to the first floor.[89]

The idea of the annex was finally realized in 1982, with the construction of the Harper-Meredith City County Building, designed by Silling & Associates of Charleston, West Virginia. The two buildings are connected at the second floor of the Courthouse, and the fourth floor of the Harper Meredith Building.

The building has undergone more recent modifications. The first floor of the Courthouse was renovated in 1960, with L. D. Schmidt of Fairmont as the architect. On the second floor, the Assessor's Office was renovated in 1973-74, and the County Commission Offices and Circuit Clerk Offices were renovated in 1977; again, L. D. Schmidt was the architect for both. The Division I Courtroom on the third floor was historically restored in 1987, under the direction of Ralph Pedersen, an architect in Clarksburg.

The building was placed on the National Register of Historic Places in 1979, and is still in use as the Marion County Courthouse.

Top photo next page: Original Marion County Courthouse (left), 215-217 Adams Street and Mountain City House (right), 219-221 Adams Street.

Bottom photo next page: Marion County Courthouse (right), 217-221 Adams Street and Jailer's Residence, 215 Adams Street, c. 1930.

Historic Architecture in Downtown Fairmont, West Virginia

Marion County First Courthouse.

[1] *R. L. Polk & Company Directory*, 1904, p. 2.
[2] *Twentieth Century Edition*, p. 20.
[3] *Industrial Fairmont in 1908*, p. 66.
[4] *Twentieth Century Edition*, p. 20.
[5] *Fairmont Times*, 11/19/1902, p. 1.
[6] ibid., 11/11/1902, p. 3.
[7] ibid., 11/19/1902, p. 1.
[8] ibid., 11/29/1902, p. 1.
[9] ibid., 7/15/1903, p. 1.
[10] ibid., 8/1/1903, p. 1.
[11] ibid., 8/5/1903, p. 1.
[12] ibid., 3/29/1904, p. 8.
[13] *Fairmont West Virginian*, 6/18/1904, p. 4.
[14] ibid., 8/22/1904, p. 1.
[15] *Fairmont Times*, 1/3/1907, p. 3.
[16] ibid., 9/16/1911, p. 2.
[17] ibid., 9/28/1912, p. 3.
[18] ibid., 10/19/1917, p. 2.
[19] ibid., 3/19/1918, sect. 2, p. 1.
[20] ibid.
[21] ibid., 10/10/1920, p. 8.
[22] ibid., 1/11/1915, p. 1.
[23] ibid., 4/26/1922, p. 11.
[24] ibid., 6/26/1926, p. 1.
[25] ibid., 6/30/1926, p. 1.
[26] ibid., 10/6/1927, p. 7.
[27] ibid., 10/16/1927, sect. 2, p. 1.
[28] ibid., 12/7/1927, p. 11.
[29] ibid., 9/21/1928, p. 1.
[30] ibid., 4/14/1929, p. 4.
[31] ibid., 11/17/1929, p. 1.
[32] ibid., 8/28/1929, p. 1.
[33] ibid., 11/29/1929, p. 1.
[34] ibid., 4/11/1903, p. 3.
[35] ibid., 5/12/1903, p. 1.
[36] ibid., 12/12/1903, p. 1.
[37] ibid., 5/1/1905, p. 4.
[38] ibid., 7/31/1905, p. 3.
[39] ibid., 11/2/1904, p. 2.
[40] ibid.
[41] ibid., 7/31/1905, p. 3.
[42] ibid., 5/1/1905, p. 4.
[43] ibid.
[44] ibid., 2/12/1917, p. 7.
[45] ibid., 4/3/1917, p. 6.
[46] ibid., 11/29/1929, p. 1.
[47] *A History of Marion County, West Virginia*, p. 44.
[48] Dunnington, p. 82.
[49] *Fairmont Times*, 7/12/1909, p. 1.
[50] ibid., 7/14/1909, p. 1.
[51] ibid., 8/7/1909, p. 6.
[52] ibid., 8/31/1909, p. 1.
[53] ibid., 10/22/1909, p. 1.
[54] ibid., 10/30/1909, p. 1.
[55] ibid., 1/4/1910, p. 1.
[56] ibid., 1/21/1910, p. 10.

[57] ibid., 1/26/1910, p. 1.
[58] ibid.
[59] ibid., 2/1/1910, p. 1.
[60] ibid., 1/24/1911, p. 1.
[61] ibid., 3/12/1912, p. 1.
[62] ibid.
[63] ibid.
[64] Dunnington, p. 81.
[65] *A History of Marion County, West Virginia*, p. 44.
[66] Dunnington, p. 81.
[67] *Fairmont Free Press*, 11/3/1894.
[68] *Fairmont Index*, 7/2/1897.
[69] Lough, pp. 449-450.
[70] ibid., p. 450.
[71] Balderson, p. 307.
[72] *Fairmont Index*, 7/16/1886.
[73] ibid., 7/2/1897.
[74] ibid., 6/18/1897.
[75] ibid., 3/26/1897.
[76] ibid., 5/7/1897.
[77] ibid., 6/18/1897.
[78] *Fairmont Free Press*, 3/31/1898.
[79] *Welcome Westinghouse*, sect. 5, p. 4.
[80] *Fairmont Times*, 9/8/1905, p. 5.
[81] ibid., 7/18/1911, p. 1.
[82] ibid., 2/26/1912, p. 8.
[83] ibid., 3/29/1917, p. 3.
[84] ibid.
[85] ibid., 9/1/1917, p. 2.
[86] ibid., 2/9/1925, p. 2.
[87] ibid., 12/6/1925, p. 1.
[88] ibid., 5/15/1926, p. 3.
[89] *Welcome Westinghouse*, sect. 5, p. 4.

Chapter 5

300 Block Adams Street, even numbered buildings

The Great Fire of 1876

On April 2, 1876, the dread of the citizens of Fairmont came true. For years, it was a concern that the buildings on Adams Street between Jefferson and Madison Streets were a fire hazard, since they were made of wood and made even more flammable by the years of weather that had seasoned them. At approximately 3:30 a.m., the alarm was sounded.

The fire was discovered in an open stairway between Swisher & Carpenter's Store and Thomas Prendergast's Saloon (located on the corner at 331 and 329 Adams Street, respectively). Those who witnessed the fire at its beginning stage believed that the stairway had been doused with carbon oil. In a very brief time, Prendergast's building and Brock's store next to it were enveloped in flame. The fire spread from the north side of Adams Street to the south side due to the wind. At one point in time, it was impossible to pass along Adams Street because the flames swayed back and forth in a solid sheet, and sparks and burning debris covered the ground. The fire burned up to Jefferson Street, and everything in the block burned like tinder. It was stated that the best fire department in the world would not have been able to stop it.[1]

The city had no "appliances" (fire engines) for fighting the fire, and the only means of dousing the flames was by buckets of water; even the women and children worked steadily at carrying water and salt, assisting to remove goods from burning houses or pulling down buildings.[2] Men came from all over town, bringing their buckets and axes. A water line was formed down Madison Street to the river, with men standing three feet apart and handing the pails of water upwards until they were dashed in the blaze.[3]

Some individuals and businesses had time to remove their stock and possessions; J. E. Fleming saved a small portion of his stock of groceries, F. M. Fleming saved the greater part of his stock of boots and shoes, and both M. M. Commerford and C. B. Carney saved a considerable portion of the stock of their drug stores. A portion of the material only of the Index Printing office was saved. The West Virginian, who published the news of the fire only five days afterwards, stated that a small portion of the material of their office was saved in such shape as to be available in the future. "We may here appropriately remark that with the utmost care and caution exercised there is more or less damage done in removing a printing office, but to move on the 'rapid transit' style is of incalculable injury to the best regulated printing office. We adopted the 'rapid transit' method last Sunday morning."[4]

Although a dispatch had been sent to Wheeling to solicit aid in fighting the fire, it had been brought under control at the corner of Adams and Jefferson Streets. At the time, it was a tremendous loss in the city. "It was no discreditable exhibition that strong men shed tears during the prevalence of that awful fire. The accumulation of years was melting rapidly away before their eyes, and they powerless to prevent it."[5]

A large part of the $75,000 loss was covered by insurance. Almost the entire burnt district had been rebuilt by 1880, and in the place of the old structures were elegant "modern" brick business blocks and residences. There was no town in West Virginia the size of Fairmont, it was stated, that could boast of as fine business houses. In retrospect, the citizens of the town scarcely considered the fire a calamity, since, from that time, they dated an era of improvements in Fairmont.[6] Another benefit of the fire was that the council prohibited the building of frame buildings within a certain radius of the city, and brick structures at once began to be constructed.[7] Handsome brick buildings became "de rigeur" in Fairmont. However, if the people of Fairmont thought they had solved the problem of fires, they were sorely mistaken. Although the exteriors of subsequent buildings were required to be brick, the interiors could be made entirely of wood. The insides of the buildings could and did go up in flames, and many of Fairmont's historic structures have been demolished after serious fires, in spite of their brick exteriors.

1. Christie's Drug, Hartley's Store; c. 1877. 300-302 Adams Street

It was stated that a drug store had been operating at this location since 1830 or before.[8] An early building on this site was the two-story brick store house of Mr. Compton, which was sold to G. L. Turney in 1866 for his drug and variety store.[9] Though this was one of the few brick structures on the block, it was ruined by the fire in 1876, and Dr. Christie's store (originally C. B. Carney's drug store) replaced the old building.[10]

Though the current building looks like one structure, it was built in two stages, and was both originally and currently owned by separate people. The 302 Adams Street store front, consisting of five bays, was built in 1877; the adjacent store front on the corner at 300 Adams Street was built shortly afterwards, which added a store front on the first floor and four matching Roman arch windows on the second floor. The brick structure is Italianate, with a large overhanging bracketed cornice at the roof, and heavy, decorative window hood moldings on the second floor windows.

J. M. Hartley had a half interest in this corner lot, which cost $1,500, according to the recorded deed.[11] This was probably the cost of the lot after the fire. Hartley constructed this building at 302 Adams Street for his mercantile store, in which he began his business in 1877; the business would grow until the name "Hartley's" would be synonymous with quality shopping in Fairmont. The dry goods house occupied the basement and two floors of the building.

The corner lot had historically been occupied by a drug store. C. B. Carney operated a drug store in the 300 Adams Street store front; then, it was purchased and managed by Neal Carney for a number of years. In 1900, he sold the business to Matt Christy.[12] Christy had been clerking there since 1879,[13] and was the nephew of Mr. Carney, from whom he had learned the drug trade from 1885 to 1890.[14]

As Hartley's business increased, he expanded his operation into the store rooms above Carney's drug store at 300 Adams Street, in the section of the building constructed on the corner lot.[15] Hartley's business was very successful, growing at the same astronomical rate as the city of Fairmont. Hartley's vacated this location, and on November 20, 1902, the store opened at its new location in the Jacobs-Hutchinson Block at 207-209 Adams Street. Highland's clothing and shoes store was the next occupant of the 302 Adams Street store front through the 1920's.

After Hartley's moved out of the adjacent store front in 1903, the rooms that the store had previously rented above the drug store were occupied by the YMCA. It was the first practical attempt made to establish a branch of the organization in Fairmont. The home consisted of five rooms: the parlor and reading room, the office, the game room, the gymnasium and a "bathing apartment." The parlor was in the very desirable location, situated in the front of the building over Christie's Drug store; it was furnished with a large center table and comfortable chairs. The office was behind the parlor. In the rear of the building was the game room and gymnasium.[16]

In 1913, Mr. Christy retired after 34 years of service, and sold the store to Clyde S. Holt,[17] who formed the Holt Drug Company. The store was completely remodeled; a new front was installed and fixtures of Circassian walnut placed in the store.[18] In 1918, Glen B. Hamilton and his brother took charge of the business, and since that time the firm name had been known as the H. & H. Drug Company.[19]

The Holt-Rowe Novelty Company opened a Gift and Art Shop on Jefferson Street under the H. & H. Drug Store in 1921; it carried greeting cards which were fashionable, as well as souvenirs for the ladies, gifts for the children, and other novelties.[20]

Although the two first floor store fronts have been extensively remodeled over the years, the building is still in use.

Carney and Hartley Building (right), 300-302 Adams Street and millinery store (left), 304-306 Adams Street, c. 1894.

CARNEY AND HARTLEY BUILDING.

2. millinery store, barber; c. 1880. 304-306 Adams Street

This two-story, four bay brick structure is assumed to have been built after the Great Fire. It is Italianate in style, with a bracketed classical cornice and prominent window hood moldings. Originally, there was a Roman arch doorway under the second floor window to the west, and a large store front beside that; the doorway also had a prominent hood molding, and the store front was topped by another projecting cornice. Although the Sandborn maps list its use as a millinery store from 1884 to 1902, inclusively, it was later occupied by Sherwood Barber Shop in 1903,[21] and through the 1920's.

The building is still in use today.

3. Chisler Building, c. 1880. 308 Adams Street

This two-story, four bay brick Neo-classical structure has Roman arched windows on the second floor, and a bracketed cornice at the roof. It was occupied by A. Howard Fleming's jewelry store, which began its operation in 1886. Assisted by Fred C. Fleming, he had a fine stock of jewelry, and well as watches, clocks, and fine silverware. In addition, he provided repairs and engraving.[22] It was then known as the Chisler Building.[23]

The firm was acquired by Alex Riheldaffer and Arch Brown in 1898. Mr. Riheldaffer had been employed by Mr. Fleming since 1894, and spent four years as a salesman and watch repair man until he and his partner bought the firm.[24] In addition to their reputation as a jewelry store, the firm was noteworthy because it was selected by the Baltimore and Ohio Railroad Company as the official inspector of employees' watches. This was seen as a sign of their trustworthiness, since the accuracy of railroad men's watches had much to do with the lives and safety of the train traveling public.[25]

In 1913, Riheldaffer & Brownfield improved the appearance of their store by installing a new and modern front, which was installed by Walter Eliason, contractor.[26]

The store was originally twenty-five feet wide and thirty-five feet deep. Because of expanding trade, an addition was made in 1924 which added a one-story section to the back, which was approximately twenty-eight feet deep. The watch-maker's table, which had always been next to the Adams Street window, was eliminated. The new room housed watch-repair men, as well as retiring rooms for both men and women, and storage. The entire store was remodeled with new floor coverings and new display cases.[27] The jewelry store functioned there through the 1920's.

The building is still in use today.

4. store, c. 1880, 1902. 310 Adams Street

In the 1880's and 1890's, the structure on this site was a two-story building, and functioned as a grocery or a dry goods store. Around the year 1902, it was remodeled or rebuilt to the existing three story, three bay brick structure. It has a bracketed cornice at the roof, and segmental brick arches above the windows on the second and third floors. There were finials on the two corners of the cornice, which are now gone. At this time, it was occupied by Lewis A. Herman's store, which carried ladies' dress goods, furnishings, and millinery.[28]

The Palace Pool Parlor occupied the basement of the structure around 1913.[29] It was still listed as an occupant here in the 1933 city directory.

The Economy Shoe Store opened in the first floor store front in 1928.[30] It was later occupied by Ronay Jewelry in 1933, according to the city directory of that year.

The building was recently rehabilitated and is fully occupied by offices.

Adams Street, 300 block in 1916.

5. Osgood's Store, c. 1880. 312 Adams Street

The building was originally a two-story brick structure. On the second floor, there was a projecting bay window to the east, with two narrower windows beside it. It had functioned from the 1880's through the 1930's as a clothing store. An addition to the rear was made around 1890, according to the Sandborn maps. There were also additions to the rear around 1918, and one that wrapped around 310 Adams Street around 1927.

Osgood's Store occupied this building in the 1910's. It remodeled the existing store by removing a partition to make it one large room.[31] Osgood's continued to enlarge its space in 1917 by expanding into the adjoining rooms at 314 Adams Street by cutting through the wall with an archway opening on the first floor.[32]

The building was later occupied by Ray's Jewelry. A fire occurred in this structure in 1963, which necessitated the removal of the second story. It has since been sheathed with blue panels, hiding its previous architectural character. The jewelry store still occupies the building.

6. G. C. Murphy Building; 1932, 1939. 314-320 Adams Street

There were four small buildings on this site prior to the construction of the G. C. Murphy Building. According to the Sandborn maps, the store front at 314 Adams Street was mostly used for a news stand or a stationery store. In 1917, Osgood's, which was in the adjacent store front at 312 Adams Street, expanded into this store front by cutting an archway opening on the first floor.[33] Osgood's vacated the space and it was then leased to Dan Block, tailor, for use in his business in 1928.[34] This store front was incorporated into the Murphy Building expansion in 1939.

The 316 Adams Street store front was used from the 1880's through the 1890's as a dwelling, according to the Sandborn maps. The 1902 and 1906 maps shows that it was used as a dwelling with a florist in the basement, but by the time of the 1912 map the florist shop had moved to the first floor. Weber's was one of the florists who was located there in 1913,[35] until they were forced to vacate the property in 1915. This was to make way for the new Nelson Theatre.[36] This store front was used for the lobby of the theatre, while the auditorium was added to the rear of both the 314 and 316 Adams Streets store fronts.

The Nelson Theatre was described as "Ultra modern in every respect," with extra wide aisles and 400 extra wide seats. The lobby had immense plate glass mirrors on the walls, with beautiful palms and statuary. The most important elements in the entire theatre were the projecting machines, which were the best obtainable and had been awarded the Grand Prize at the Panama Pacific Exposition; and the curtain was made of gold fibers to make the picture much clearer and more natural-like than the silver colored material, and was the first of its kind in Fairmont.[37] The lobby also had little colonial doors with white paint and glass, which opened into the lobby on each side of the colonial ticket booth. The railings at the rear of the theatre were colonial pillars and were finished in rich mahogany.[38] The Nelson Theatre opened on November 19, 1915, with George Klein's new drama, *The Spendthrift*, as the opening fare.[39]

The Nelson Theatre took its place in the vanguard of motion picture theatres across the country when it showed talking pictures in March 1929. It was the first theatre in Fairmont to do so. It had installed the new "Biophone" and "Cinephone" equipment, and a contract signed with Warner Brothers for sixteen talking picture shows. The "talkies" were at first mixed with the silent films, since many of the latter had been contracted for previously. Admission for the "talkies" was 10 to 25 cents for the afternoons, and 15 to 35 cents for the evenings.[40] This store front was incorporated into the Murphy Building expansion in 1939.

In the 1880's, the property at 318-320 Adams Street was occupied by a three-story brick house. In 1909, the house was encompassed by new construction to created two, two-story store fronts.[41] If you look on the roof of this building today, you can still see the original house that was on this site. Afterwards referred to as the Haymond Building, the 318 store front housed Daffin's Confectionery,[42] and Campbell's Shoes,[43] and later in the 1920's the Rowand's Store[44] and then Beckman's Store. Beckman's had been established in Fairmont for 28 years at several different locations in the city before the establishment was moved to this location.[45]

The 320 Adams Street store front housed Klaw's Department store around the years 1901 to 1919;[46] then it was occupied by Kline Shoes from around the years 1920 to 1930.[47]

The G. C. Murphy Building was first constructed in the area of the 318-320 store fronts in 1932, and later expanded to the area of the 314-316 store fronts in 1939.[48] The structure was a simple, brick commercial building, with two groups of four unadorned windows on each side of the second floor, and one rectangular window in the middle. The first floor consisted of a large expanse of store front windows. The detailing on the building is limited to simple brickwork patterns. The store operated on the site until it closed on June 25, 1982.[49]

The structure is currently vacant, though expected to be rehabilitated in the near future.

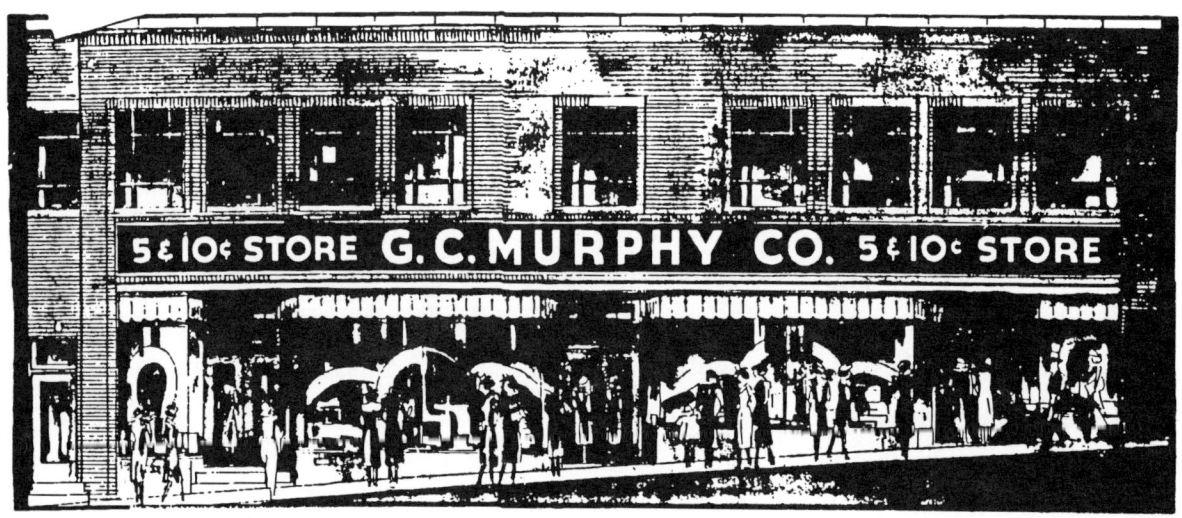

G. C. Murphy Building, 314-320 Adams Street in 1941.

7. Dowden Building, c. 1880. 322 Adams Street

This structure is a two-story, three bay brick building. It has a bracketed cornice at the roof, and Roman arched windows on the second floor. According to the Sandborn maps, it was used as a grocery and as a drug store in the 1880's and early 1900's. In 1918, it was occupied by The Exclusive Garment Shop, which specialized in exclusive clothes for women.[50] On November 13, 1926, Finger's Garment Store opened in the store front, and operated there through the 1930's.[51] The Virginia Theatre was constructed on the adjoining property at 324 Adams street and in the rear of this property in 1922.[52]

Although currently standing, the structure is slated for demolition.

8. Marion Hardware, Virginia Theatre, c. 1880, 1922. 324 Adams Street

This site had been the location of a hardware store from the 1880's, according to the Sandborn maps. Around the turn of the century, first Hood and Clelland Hardware, then Marion

Hardware were located in this building.[53] It is a two- story three bay brick building with a simple cornice over the windows and at the roof.

In April of 1921, it was announced that a new theatre for Fairmont was "practically a certainty." It would be constructed to the rear of the Dowden Building at 322 Adams Street and the rear of the Marion Hardware store, using the former hardware store as the entrance lobby for the theatre. The Marion Hardware Company moved to the first floor of the Manley Hotel Building (312-314 Jefferson Street).[54] The Linn Realty Company was formed by Russel Linn and Harry B. Clark, and the plan was to have a theatre to seat 900 persons. Jones and Nuzum of Fairmont were the architects for the building, which was going to be rushed to completion.[55]

Ground was broken for the construction on March 27, 1922 and was said to be opened for business on September 1, 1922. They planned to show high class motion pictures exclusively at the new theatre, though ample orchestra space was provided and the silver screen was to be placed upon a small stage which could be used for concerts.[56] The "structural iron" for the building arrived on the site on June 6th, and the work was to be rushed to completion for an opening in early October.[57]

The theatre was named "The Virginia," and its premier performance was planned for Christmas Day, 1922. The seating capacity was set at 860, with 331 of those in the dainty balcony. All seats were upholstered in fine leather.[58]

The lobby, which was the old Marion Hardware store, was a feat in itself. A soda fountain was installed, and candies, cigarettes, and cigars were sold. The foyer sloped down to the main floor. Between this floor and the balcony was an incline up to the mezzanine floor, which was seen as a perfect place to wait for someone, since it gave a full view of the lobby. Off of this was a rest room for the ladies. On the opposite side of the foyer was the manager's office and the projection room; the latter was equipped with the latest machinery, as well as 12 dimmers to control the lights. Colored lighting was used to create beautiful light.[59]

The interior of the theatre was decorated in green and gold with a touch of black. The walls were paneled. The proscenium arch over the stage was decorated with a niche in the wall on each side, in which large gold vases were set. Above the vases was to be the biggest decoration in the theatre: a great peacock with wide-spread tail. In each eye of the bird there was to be a crystal jewel backed with a mirror which would make it gleam like a thousand diamonds, as well as 60 jewels in the peacock's tail. The idea for this came from the "tower of jewels" at the San Francisco exposition.[60]

The peacock ornament never materialized. Upon hearing the intent of using the peacock in the theatre, numerous letters and calls came from superstitious women who would not sit in a house where a peacock was located. It was an old superstition that peacock feathers in a building meant that the women who were inside would be old maids. Therefore, the idea of the peacock decoration was abandoned and two very beautiful figures of alluring womanhood were painted in place of the peacock.[61] A variation of the women also appeared as a mural on the facade of the building, above the second floor windows.

The stage of the theatre was forty by ten feet; only prologues to the shows would be put on here. A twelve piece orchestra was prepared for the new theatre, which was housed in the orchestra pit that was two feet deep and seventeen feet long. A Hardman-Grand piano was also provided.[62]

On the exterior, an electric display with letters over two feet high spelled out "Virginia," and the sign was 17 feet above the top of the building. A canopy of copper provided a roof over the sidewalk for protection from the elements.[63]

A Typhoon Cooling System was placed on the roof for summer use, which could blow 100,000 cubic feet of air per minute into the theatre. Two seven-foot fans and two five-foot fans were used. An inter-communicating telephone system was installed which connected the manager's office, the projection room, the stage, and the orchestra. The basement of the theatre housed the bill room for the advertising manager, as well as the heating system, which was the "vacuum heating arrangement."[64]

In some of the pre-opening publicity, it was announced that "girl ushers" were to be employed in Fairmont's newest theatre. There would be six ushers and one head usher, with one colored girl to be chosen to take care of the colored section in the balcony.[65]

"New Playhouse is Wonderland for Fairmont. Vast Audience Dedicates Virginia Theatre." Hundreds of people came for the opening of the new theatre, with the opening feature of Charles Dickens' old masterpiece, "Oliver Twist" starring Jackie Coogan. Glenn Arnet and his orchestra were in the pit. In spite of the fact that all of the equipment was entirely new, the performances ran as smoothly as if the house had been in operation for months. This was credited to the training of the staff, which had worked at the old Dixie Theatre (230 Adams Street). Owners Linn and Clark, manager Robert E. Fisher, as well as the architects, Jones and Nuzum were in attendance; they were busy returning thanks for the compliments of the facilities, and keeping a watchful eye on the premier performances.[66]

The Virginia Tea Room opened over the entrance to the Virginia Theatre on April 7, 1923. This was an inviting eating place which could accommodate seventy-one persons. The music for its opening was supplied by Bud's Band, and roses were given for souvenirs.[67]

In November of 1925, controlling ownership of the Virginia Theatre was acquired by J. E. Watson, who also was president of the West Virginia Amusement Company, which operated the Fairmont Theatre (412 Adams Street). It was stated that the two theatres would be operated on a non-competitive basis, utilizing certain economies to maintain the high standards of both houses.[68]

A new Robert Morton organ, especially built for the Virginia Theatre, was installed in December 1925. The theatre was temporarily closed, as a foundation had to be constructed for its location under the stage; only the console was visible. The organ was to sound like an entire symphony orchestra, replacing Glenn and his orchestra. It was the first large concert organ installed in any theatre in the area. Although there had been other organs in the city, one in the Nelson Theatre (316 Adams Street), the other long dismantled in the Old Grand Opera House (325 Monroe Street), neither were the same type nor as costly as the $15,000 instrument purchased by the theatre corporation.[69]

Russel Linn, one of the original owners of the Virginia Theatre, died suddenly on April 6, 1926. It was rumored that his business dealings were in poor condition, and that he had taken poison.[70]

The rear portion of the building which was added in 1922 for the theatre auditorium has been demolished. The lobby of the theatre, formerly the hardware store, still exists, but it is scheduled for demolition.

The Virginia Theatre, 324 Adams Street in 1922.

9. market, Lipson Jewelry, c. 1880. 326 Adams Street

This two-story brick building originally boasted a bay window on the second story. According to the Sandborn maps, it had been used as a bakery from the 1880's until around 1910. It was later used for a meat market, then occupied by Lipson Jewelry around 1929.[71]

The facade had since been covered over with siding and wood, and the bay window replaced by one large window, losing its architectural integrity. It was demolished September 1996.

10. saloon, restaurant, c. 1880. 328 Adams Street

This two-story brick building functioned for many years as a saloon and a restaurant, according to the Sandborn maps.

Its facade had been completely covered over, and it was demolished September 1996.

Adams Street, 300 and 400 blocks, looking east, in 1919.

11. J. W. Lott Building, Masonic Temple; c. 1879. 330-332 Adams Street

The J. W. Lott building was a very distinctive three- story brick building; because it was located at the corner of Adams and Madison Streets, the corner of the building was truncated, and the decorative stone quoins placed on the corners of the truncation and on the corners of the rest of the building. It was six bays on Adams Street, one bay at the truncated corner, and six bays on Madison Street. The windows were segmented arched windows, separated by brick pilasters. At the roof was a bracketed cornice.

According to an old-timer in 1924, this lot sold for $1,000 after the Great Fire,[72] and the building was said to be the first rebuilt after the fire.[73]

The dedication of the new Masonic Hall, which was located on the third floor of the Lott Building, occurred in December of 1879.[74] Prior to this year, the Masons had their quarters in the second story of the Presbyterian Church when it was located at 301 Adams Street, facing Jefferson Street.

During the Masonic Convention held in Fairmont in November of 1902, it was noted that the hall was too small for the increasing numbers of members in the Lodge.[75] Discussions began in 1903 regarding the need for a new home. More than fifty Masons were interviewed regarding the idea, said originated by O. S. McKinney and T. W. Fleming, to build a great Masonic Temple; not one was against the idea. The new quarters were needed, the Masons of Fairmont had the money and the energy to build it, and it was thought to be the best time to proceed before all of the good locations in the city were gone. "That the Masons can erect it without the slightest monetary difficulty is evident to any one who will reflect that almost all the wealth of the hustling city is owned by Masons."[76] This comment by one of the members reflects the power and influence that the Masons had in the city. In December of 1903, a committee was appointed to investigate a suitable site for the proposed building, which was thought to house businesses as well as the Masonic functions.[77]

In the meantime, the lodge quarters were remodeled in the fall of 1904 in an attempt to make them more functional.[78] The 31st Annual Conclave was held in Fairmont in May of 1905 in these quarters, which were decorated in the Knights Templar colors (black and white), as well as the National colors; most of the buildings in downtown Fairmont also boasted these decorations in honor of the Masons. Decorative arches were set up at the principal corners of Adams Street with electric globes to light the intersections.[79] These lights may have been the inspiration for the lighted arches which were constructed at the intersections along Adams Street in 1907.

In July of 1905, a contract was closed for the Masons to purchase a lot on Jefferson Street for the construction of their new lodge building. It was to be "rushed to completion" for occupation by March 1, 1906;[80] the structure at 316-320 Jefferson Street was actually completed in June 1907. The Masons vacated their quarters in the Lott Building, and the Knights of Columbus occupied the third floor for their hall. They later moved into the Sample Building at 221 Monroe Street in March 1924; the Fairmont Post of the American Legion moved into the Lott Building at that time.[81]

The first floor store fronts of the Lott Building were used for commercial enterprises. The 330 Adams store front was used for a grocery and then a shoe store in the 1890's, according to the Sandborn maps. It became the site of a confectionery around 1904. This was when Commutzis Confectionery established an ice cream and candy factory in the basement,[82] then expanded operations for a candy store and soda fountain on the first floor later in the year.[83] Though the operations changed hands several times, it remained a confectionery through the 1930's.

One of the first tenants in the 332 Adams Street store front was Lee Reinheimer & Brothers Clothing, who moved into the quarters around 1880,[84] and remained there through the 1890's. In early 1903, it was occupied by the Fairmont Trust Company temporarily as they waited for their new building at 209 Adams Street to be completed,[85] which occurred in May 1905.

In early 1906, it was announced that a new drug store was to open in the corner room of the Masonic Temple. W. R. Crane renovated the rooms; he furnished them with mahogany fixtures, and plate glass display cases with bases of mottled blue marble. The ceiling was metal tinted in shades of coloring to harmonize with the furnishings. The prescription department was in the rear of the building, and the front of the building had a large illuminated jeweled mortar to advertise the new enterprise.[86] Crane's Drugs operated there through the 1930's.

The second floor of the Lott Building had varying uses. According to the Sandborn maps, it was used by the YMCA in 1896. Tailoring establishments were located there around 1902 to 1918. In the 1920's and 1930's, it was used for professional offices.

On October 15, 1972, fire destroyed this structure where Hando's Restaurant and Bobet News were located. At the time, locals remembered the Great fire of 1876, which also occurred on this block. "Well, it looks like the city will have another parking lot," an astute observer noted.[87]

The site is now a parking lot.

Masonic Temple, 330-332 Adams Street in 1905.

[1] *West Virginian,* 4/7/1876.
[2] Dunnington, pp. 119-120.
[3] *Fairmont Times,* 4/3/1916, p. 4.
[4] *West Virginian,* 4/7/1876.
[5] ibid.
[6] Dunnington, p. 121.
[7] *Fairmont Times,* 8/11/1929, p. 12.
[8] ibid., 4/1/13, p. 8.
[9] *Fairmont Commercial,* 1866-7.
[10] *Fairmont Free Press,* 11/26/1903.
[11] *Welcome Westinghouse,* sect. 3, p. 2.
[12] *Fairmont Times,* 3/18/1923, supplement.
[13] ibid., 4/1/1913, p. 8.
[14] *Industrial Fairmont in 1908,* p. 60.
[15] *Fairmont Index,* 1/3/1894.
[16] *Fairmont Times,* 6/17/1903, p. 1.
[17] ibid., 4/1/1913, p. 8.
[18] ibid., 3/18/1923, p. 2.
[19] ibid., supplement.
[20] ibid., 7/9/1921, p. 1.
[21] ibid., 5/16/1903, p. 1.
[22] *Fairmont Index,* 1892.
[23] *Fairmont Free Press,* 2/24/1898, p. 2.
[24] *Fairmont West Virginian,* 8/18/1904, p. 1.
[25] *Industrial Fairmont in 1908,* p. 44.
[26] *Fairmont Times,* 5/13/1913, p. 8.
[27] ibid., 6/19/1924, p. 5.
[28] *Fairmont West Virginian,* 8/13/1904, p. 5.
[29] *Fairmont Times,* 12/20/1913, sect. 2, p. 4.

[30] ibid., 10/12/1928, p. 1.
[31] ibid., 3/13/1913, p. 1.
[32] ibid., 6/26/1917, p. 8.
[33] ibid.
[34] ibid., 9/15/1928, p. 4.
[35] ibid., 10/24/1913, p. 3.
[36] ibid., 6/15/1915, p. 1.
[37] ibid., 10/23/1915, p. 8.
[38] ibid., 11/18/1915, p. 5.
[39] ibid., 11/19/1915, p. 1.
[40] ibid., 3/12/1929, p. 1.
[41] ibid., 11/12/1909, p. 1.
[42] ibid., 5/30/1910, p. 1.
[43] ibid., 5/9/1910, p. 1.
[44] ibid., 7/10/1921, p. 1.
[45] ibid., 11/5/1925, p. 5.
[46] ibid., 4/24/1913, p. 10.
[47] ibid., 1/17/1920, p. 7.
[48] *Welcome Westinghouse*, sect. 3, p. 2.
[49] Spevock, p. 71.
[50] *Fairmont Times*, 8/27/1918, p. 3.
[51] ibid., 11/14/1926, p. 12.
[52] ibid., 4/8/1921, p. 14.
[53] *Fairmont West Virginian*, 8/25/1904, p. 1.
[54] *Fairmont Times*, 4/8/1921, p. 14.
[55] ibid., 1/1/1922, p. 5.
[56] ibid., 3/26/1922, p. 1.
[57] ibid., 6/7/1922, p. 4.
[58] ibid., 11/12/1922, sect. 2, p. 1.
[59] ibid.
[60] ibid.
[61] ibid., 12/13/1922, p. 16.
[62] ibid., 11/12/1922, sect. 2, p. 1.
[63] ibid.
[64] ibid.
[65] ibid., 12/13/1922, p. 16.
[66] ibid., 12/26/1922, p. 1.
[67] ibid., 4/8/1923, p. 9.
[68] ibid., 11/3/1925, p. 1.
[69] ibid., 12/11/1925, sect. 2, p. 1.
[70] ibid., 4/7/1926, p. 1.
[71] ibid., 1/11/1929, p. 5.
[72] ibid., 8/3/1924, p. 1.
[73] *Fairmont Times-West Virginian*, 10/16/1972, p. 1.
[74] *Fairmont West Virginian*, 12/5/1879, p. 3.
[75] *Fairmont Times*, 11/12/1902, p. 1.
[76] ibid., 8/3/1903, p. 1.
[77] ibid., 12/8/1903, p. 1.
[78] *Fairmont West Virginian*, 10/4/1904, p. 5.
[79] *Fairmont Times*, 5/10/1905, p. 2.
[80] ibid., 7/5/1905, p. 1.
[81] ibid., 3/6/1924, p. 1.
[82] *Fairmont West Virginian*, 7/22/1904, p. 1.
[83] ibid., 12/2/1904, p. 1.
[84] ibid., 9/10/1880.
[85] *Fairmont Times*, 2/11/1903, p. 4.
[86] ibid., 10/10/1906, p. 7.
[87] *Fairmont Times-West Virginian*, 10/16/1972, p. 1.

Chapter 6

300 Block Adams Street, odd numbered buildings

1. Presbyterian Church: 1822, 1850; Bank of Fairmont, 1897; Watson Building, 1909-11. Horace Trumbauer, architect. 301-311 Adams Street

This site was the location for the first two Presbyterian church structures, before the church relocated to 301 Jackson Street. The lot was donated by Boaz Fleming and was located opposite the Courthouse.[1] The first frame structure was built in 1822 and was primitive in nature. There was no lath or plaster covering the walls or ceiling. The tallow candles in their candlesticks were fastened to the posts, or held in position against the wall by two nails driven into the studding.[2]

In 1850, this church was razed and replaced by a two-story brick structure with a simple gable roof; the gable end faced Jefferson Street.[3] Although the first floor was used for the church, the second floor of the building was used for the Masonic Lodge from 1854 to 1878, which rented it for $37.46.[4] "... the Historic and Festive Goat of the Masonic order roamed at pleasure when the brethren were called from labor to refreshment, confining himself to his own allotted chamber when a candidate was seeking an interview."[5] In 1879, the Lodge moved to the Lott Building (330-332 Adams Street).[6] There was also a graveyard in connection with the church. The edifice was torn down in 1878-1879, the dead in the cemetery moved, and the site sold for $1,000.[7] Some of the brick from this church were used in the construction of the new church at the corner of Jefferson and Jackson Streets in 1879.[8]

The next building on this site at 301-307 Adams Street was a two-story brick structure constructed in 1897 by Governor A. B. Fleming and B. A. "Moose" Fleming; they had decided that an office building here would be a good investment because of its prominent location. There was a "good sized" hill at this location on Jefferson Street, from Adams Street to the alley adjacent to the present-day Masonic Temple (320 Jefferson Street). The hill was taken away to make room for the structure (commonly known as the Coal Company Building), and it was seen at that time as one of the most important pieces of excavating done in Fairmont.[9]

The structure had eight bays on both Adams and Jefferson Streets, and a truncated wall with one bay at the corner. The windows had straight pediments over them on the first floor, and triangular pediments over them on the second floor; they were all rectangular except for a Roman arched window on the second floor on the truncated wall, which was above a Roman arched entrance door. On both sides of the building, extending along the second story, were long porches; these were the favorite vantage points for crowds to watch parades in town. The old building had been completely remodeled and had been given a new, modern front at one point in time.[10]

The Bank of Fairmont was chartered in 1895, and they opened their banking quarters on the second floor of this building; approximately two years later they moved the banking room to the first floor of the building.[11] In addition to the Fairmont Coal Company, many other important enterprises were located there, including the Traction Company (streetcars), the Western Union Office, and the Gas and Light Company.[12]

A small building was constructed adjacent to this structure at 309-311 Adams Street around 1900. It was a two- story, five bay brick building. It was used for various commercial enterprises, according to the Sandborn maps.

The quarters for the Fairmont Coal Company and the Bank of Fairmont were too small for the expanding businesses, and it was decided to construct a new building for them. The original idea in 1905 was to construct two new skyscrapers, the first an eight-story structure on Jefferson Street adjacent to this site, which would be the temporary home of the Bank and the Coal Company; the Masonic/ Lodge would be offered the top two floors of the building, with the rest devoted to apartments. After the first building was completed, the corner building, estimated to be a magnificent ten story structure, would be constructed as the permanent home of the Fairmont Coal Company and the Bank of Fairmont. [13] This plan never materialized, since the Masons decided to buy the adjacent property outright for a lodge building that they would own, rather than renting the top two floors from the Watson Company.[14]

In 1909, it was decided to construct an eight-story office building for the Fairmont Coal Company and Bank of Fairmont on the corner lot; the building would also house the Fairmont and Clarksburg Traction Company, and the Western Union Office.[15] The old bank building had to be vacated for its demolition to make room for the new skyscraper, and all of the enterprises in the old building found temporary "homes:" the executive offices and the legal department of the Fairmont Coal Company moved to the adjacent Smith and McKinney Building (313-317 Adams Street); the merchandise department, general superintendent's office, construction department, power and mechanical department, the Fairmont Mining Machine Company, and Mr. J. E. Watson's office were moved to the new Masonic Temple Building (316-320 Jefferson Street); and the auditing department was relocated to the People's Bank Building (201 Adams Street). The Bank of Fairmont moved to the Cunningham Building (308-312 Jefferson Street); the Traction Company and other offices of the Coal Company moved to the adjacent building at 306 Jefferson Street. The Western Union moved to the Hall Block (127-135 Adams Street), and the Gas and Light Company moved to the Fleming Building (107 Adams Street). With all of the businesses relocated, the work of razing both of the old buildings began around the first of August 1909.[16]

It was announced in September of 1909 that the Watson Company was to spend $300,000 on the new office building. They had closed on a contract with the Fuller Construction Company of New York for its construction. It was expected that the construction would be completed in eleven months.

Horace Trumbauer of Philadelphia was the architect, who was a famous designer of large business buildings and residences; he was the architect of J. E. Watson's residence, Highgate, on Fairmont Avenue.[17] There was an early change in contractors, as the Fuller Company had imposed some conditions which the Watsons did not accept; William Miller & Sons of Pittsburgh, who were building the residence of J. E. Watson, accepted the contract on the same basis that the Fuller Company had refused.[18]

Work began on the skyscraper on October 6, 1909. The contract for the excavation was let to George Adams of Fairmont. The building was planned to be 149 feet above the ground, with another 24 feet underground. It would front 90 feet on Adams Street and 70 feet on Jefferson Street. The exterior was Indiana limestone, with brick being used only on the side next to the Smith & McKinney Building (313-317 Adams Street) to the east. The building was to rest on a concrete foundation, and the base and curbing on the exterior was pink milford granite and light grey New England granite. All of the ornamentation including cornices, mouldings, and window sills were of Indiana limestone.[19]

The excavations proved to be a complicated job. First, the city was "threaten with clay plague;" the dozen or so teamsters working on the excavations did not equip their wagons with dust-proof bottoms, nor did they put side boards on them. The clay soil was dropped liberally on all the principal streets. A bit of rain made the streets a slippery hazard. The worst street was Jefferson Street, which had over an inch of clay on it when the rain began. The Commissioner put seven men to work cleaning the streets, and was indignant that the city would have to pay them each $1.65 to do the work; he threatened to take the offending teamsters to court.[20]

Another excavation controversy arose when it was thought that the area of excavation was within the boundary of the old Presbyterian Church cemetery. This was not true; the boundaries of the old cemetery were further down Jefferson Street than the construction area. The old cemetery, in which hundreds of the pioneer citizens were buried, had been excavated and the bodies relocated to Woodlawn Cemetery in 1878; the progress of the city made it necessary to demolish the old church building and relocate the cemetery to lay out the area in streets and lots. However, the citizens remembered when the excavations were being made for the Smith and McKinney Building around 1892, and a petrified body was found in the soils of the old cemetery. It laid exposed there for weeks, and people came from miles to see the sight. It, too, was then removed to Woodlawn Cemetery, though some of the petrified bones of the body were said to be souvenirs of some people in the city. Assurances were given to the citizens of Fairmont in 1909 that no other grisly discoveries like that would be made in the excavations for the Watson Building.[21]

Like the excavations in Fairmont before and after it, the Watson Building excavations were a source of wonderment to the citizens. The soil was being excavated by twenty men with picks and shovels and hauled away at the rate of 200 wagon loads per day. Bad weather initially had prevented the maximum amount of work from being accomplished, but this did not stop a steady crowd of gawkers at the site. From early morning until quitting time, there were from fifty to one hundred and fifty people watching the activity. "... the love of digging in the ground is strong in the breast of every man is being daily demonstrated. If a man cannot dig in the ground himself, he likes to see somebody else do it..." Some people predicted that quicksand would be discovered. Others said that the worked-out coal veins would be reached. Still others said that they might "strike it" before the excavations were done. None of it happened.[22]

A serious accident which did occur could have injured many workers, but all escaped harm when a huge beam of a derrick that was being erected crashed over them. A shout of warning from the foreman made the laborers crouch as low as possible in the hole, which saved their lives; although the mast crushed everything under it, it did not penetrate the hole.[23]

The work was progressing. By June of 1910, the steel work was done.[24] During September, the workmen were setting the stone for the arched windows and the iron panel work on the eighth story; the sculptor had been working on the ornamentation of the keystones over the windows and doors and the stone eagle over the Adams Street entrance. The keystones over the northeast windows had the carved adornments completed and the lettering "Watson Building" over the entrance was set.[25]

The completed Neo-classical structure is an eight story building, with four bays on Jefferson Street and five bays on Adams Street. On the first and eighth floors, the windows are Roman arched windows, while on the other floors, they are pairs of rectangular windows. There is ornamental stonework on the first floor, with crossettes carved into voussoirs around the windows. Stonework pilasters grace the corners of the building on the second through sixth floors. The seventh and eighth floors have carved pilasters not only on the corners, but also in between the bays. The building is capped with an overhanging classical cornice.

The arrival of the vault door for the bank was an event in Fairmont. It required sixteen horses and a traction car to transport the door frame from the B. & O. Freight Station on Parks (Cleveland) Avenue to Adams Street. To get the frame up the incline of Cleveland Avenue onto Adams Street required numerous blocks and tackles, as well as electric power. The route was crowded all day by sightseers, as many as five hundred at one point in time.[26]

By early April of 1911, both the Fairmont and Clarksburg Traction Company and the Fairmont Light and Gas Company were able to move into their new quarters on the first floor of the new Watson Building facing Jefferson Street.[27] By the end of the month, the offices of the Coal Company were being occupied by several of the departments, who were glad to be removed from their cramped temporary quarters.[28]

In a show of the "kindly feelings" that existed in the construction of the "big block," the construction engineer of the Consolidated Coal Company, who had supervised the construction, hosted a dinner at the Elks Club for the foremen of the various trades who had worked on the structure. Representatives of the City government and the Consolidated Coal Company were also in attendance. The dinner was greatly enjoyed by those present.[29]

The Fairmont Fire Department tested the city's water pressure in the event of having to fight a fire at the new skyscraper. The firemen were able to throw a stream of water to the top of the Watson Building, and the pressure was so strong that a window on the fourth floor was broken in the process. The test was watched by a large number of the citizenry. The fire chief was satisfied with the results, though the firemen and water authorities were slightly disappointed, as they had hoped to shoot the stream of water completely over the top of the building.[30]

"Magnificent Banking Room of National Bank of Fairmont Finished," the headlines declared. The facility was open to public inspection of the public on June 24, 1911. The banking room was wainscotted in Pavanazzo marble with bronze trimming, The inside furnishings were mahogany. The floor was of Italian marble, with cork flooring in the working space behind the counter. The vaults were of the most modern burglar-proof construction; they were lined with steel and reinforced by heavy masonry. The circular vault door was ten inches thick and weighed twenty-two tons, and it has four time locks for security. There was a large space in front of the counter running its length for general customers, as well as a separate ladies' department. Adjacent to the room was the President's office. The Bank opened for business on June 26, 1911.[31]

The new Chamber of Commerce moved into the Watson Building in August of 1911. It was seen as ideal quarters, and was located in the front of the second floor.[32]

The Watson Building symbolized the progress and success of the coal company and the coal industry in Fairmont. The image of the building was used extensively in advertisements for the Consolidated Coal Company and for the National Bank of Fairmont. Even their local baseball team was named "The Watson Skyscrapers."

Rumors began in 1927 regarding whether or not Consolidated Coal would abandon the Watson Building because it was too small for their operations. At first, it was thought that the Watson Building could have four additional stories added to it, but that was later found to be false. Another story was that the Bank desired more room, so the bank and the Traction Company would divide the Watson Building, with Consolidate providing quarters of its own. The most interesting story of the time was that the coal company would construct a "garden community," with general offices surrounded by ideal homes for the employees, to be located at some spot near Fairmont. The garden idea had come from England a few years previous.[33]

Consolidated Coal Company eventually moved its offices from the building, and subsequently the National Bank of Fairmont used the building, renting the upper floors as offices. It is still used as a bank and offices today.

Bank of Fairmont, 301-307 Adams Street, c. 1902.

2. Smith & McKinney Building, 1892.
313-317 Adams Street

This structure, built by Mr. C. L. Smith and O. S. McKinney, was completed early in 1892. It was an imposing three-story, seven bay brick structure 51 feet in length along Adams Street and 70 feet deep. The lots had been purchased from A. B. and B. A. Fleming. There were two projecting bay windows, each centered over the door of a store front below; there were decorative lintels over the windows. At the roof, there was a decorative classical cornice topped with finials and two rectangular pediments, again centered over the two store fronts.[34]

The first floor had two large storerooms: the 313 Adams Street store front to the west was occupied by the Bon Ton store, operated by J. E. Anderson; the 317 Adams Street store front to the east was originally occupied by George Morrow, for "The Ideal," his tailoring and men's furnishing store. There was a stair to the upper floors through a large hall in the center of the building. The second floor held the offices of the Fairmont Development Company on the east in the front. The rest of the second floor was used for the Fairmont Index Newspaper, though the printing presses were located in the basement, with materials sent up and down via an elevator in the rear hall. The third floor housed the lodge room of the Knights of Pythias to the west, and the rooms of Israel Forman, a photographer, to the east.[35]

After the Consolidated Coal Company vacated the rooms it had used on the second floor while the adjacent Watson Building (301-311 Adams Street) was under construction, the Bon Ton store expanded into that space in June of 1911. The store then occupied the basement, first, and second floors of this half of the building. The rooms were remodeled for the millinery department, and new display windows were added on the first floor.[36]

Watson Building, 301-311 Adams Street in 1913.

Rowand's Store, a men's clothing store, occupied the 317 Adams Street store front around 1910. They put in a new store front in 1913, doubling the size of the original windows.[37] Both the Newark Shoe Store and Schoolnics, a women's clothing store, opened in the store front in 1921[38]; it appears as though the original store was divided into two to accommodate them.

On September 25, 1926, Owen S. McKinney, leading newspaper man of Fairmont and former state legislator, died in his home after an illness of more than two weeks. He was seventy-seven years old.[39]

This building was demolished and the site is part of the bank parking lot.

"INDEX" OFFICE SMITH AND McKINNEY BUILDING

Smith and McKinney Building (left), 313-317 Adams Street and Fleming Home (right), 319 Adams Street, c. 1894.

3. Fleming Home and Building; c. 1890, 1929. 319 Adams Street

The building on this site was originally the home of Will "Moose" Fleming, who ran the Fleming Grocery store at 230 Adams Street. From the Sandborn maps, the house was constructed around 1890. It was a three-story brick structure with a projecting bay on the front that was topped with a turret.

Adams Street, 300 block looking east, c. 1906.

In 1929, it was decided to erect a modern store room and office building on the site. Walter Eliason of Fairmont was hired as the contractor to do the work. The building was to be used for The Palace Coffee Shop. It was managed by Spiro Gotses who, along with Sam Scarlats, operated The Palace Restaurant (123 Adams Street). The new establishment was said to be a great improvement over the Palace Restaurant.[40]

On November 18, 1929, the new Palace Coffee Shoppe was formally opened. More than 6,000 persons visited and inspected the new establishment of Spiro Gotses and Sam Scarlats; they had ordered 3,000 carnations for souvenirs for the visitors, which was exhausted before 8:00 pm. Many floral arrangements and telegraph messages were received carrying well wishes for the business.[41]

On the front window was the largest neon sign in Fairmont at the time, with "Palace Restaurant" in red and blue. The front window was finished in French bronze sash and white enamel paint, and the plate glass is artistically decorated.[42]

Four individual counters were provided for quick lunches, the establishment's specialty; and they were to be used by women as well as men. In addition, there were 78 seats at tables. The kitchen was large and sanitary, with an electric washing machine.[43]

The building was demolished and the site is used for the bank parking lot.

4. residence, Kaufman's Store, c. 1880. 321 Adams Street

The building was originally constructed as a one-story residence prior to 1884, according to the Sanborn maps. In the 1900's and 1910's, it was used for various stores: an electrician, plumbing and electrical supplies, a tailor.

In 1926, Harry Kaufman purchased the building and made extensive alterations to the building, having contractor W. H. Spedden remodel it throughout and install a modern front on it. Kaufman's Store opened in Fairmont in November of 1926. The store was thronged with shoppers, and the depleted supplies had to be augmented by the arrival of huge shipments of merchandise from New York. In the ladies' ready-to-wear-store, the first floor was devoted to dress, coats and accessories, while the new second floor was devoted to millinery.[44]

The building was demolished and the site is used for the bank parking lot.

5. Brownfield Building; c. 1880, 1923. 323 Adams Street

This building was originally the two-story residence of Dr. G. H. Brownfield, and was built prior to 1884; it was said to be one of the best residences in the city. In 1923, the building was remodeled to provide three separate store fronts on the first floor, Dr. Brownfield's offices and residence on the second floor, and 12 additional offices for rent on the newly-added third floor.[45] In addition to adding the third floor at this time, it also appears from the Sanborn maps that he infilled areas in the rear and along the west side of the irregularly shaped original house, making the building rectangular. This is evident on the interior on the second floor where there are windows in an interior hallway.

The Marvin Fink Store opened in the two western thirds of the three store fronts on September 28, 1923, and carried men's and boys clothing. Five thousand people attended the evening opening and the manager passed out cigars and cigarettes for the men, and flowers for the women. Skinner's Orchestra furnished the music or the evening.[46]

Horen's specialty shop opened in the remaining eastern third of the Brownfield Building on November 3, 1923. He carried a line of women's and children's clothing. Rosebuds were given out as favors.[47]

This building was recently rehabilitated, and the first floor is occupied by a restaurant.

6. Holt-Rowe Building; c. 1880, c. 1910, 1921. 325 Adams Street

The original part of this building consisted of the three east bays and the first two stories, which was constructed prior to 1884. The second story windows were Roman arched, and a curved pediment above the roof line contained the street number, 325. On July 15, 1895, Clyde S Holt opened a jewelry and novelty store in this building. Just three years after starting his business, the store was burglarized and the entire stock of jewelry was taken, except for one ring. In 1910, the store was remodeled, and a new store front was installed.[48]

The two-story, two bay building adjacent to the west was constructed sometime between 1906 and 1912, according to the Sanborn maps. In 1921, Clyde Holt and A. M. Rowe bought both buildings, added a third story to them, put in a basement, and installed a new front with a center door to access the upper levels.[49] This explains the difference in the brick on the facade of the present day building. The Holt Rowe Novelty Company operated here through the 1930's.

In 1931, the studio and businesses offices of radio station WMMN were moved to the second floor, although the transmitter and antenna remained at their original location in the Fairmont Hotel (200-214 Jefferson Street). The offices remained here until they moved to 208 Adams Street in 1935.[50]

The building is still occupied.

Holt-Rowe Building, 325 Adams Street, c. 1923

7. Brownfield Building, c. 1895, 1919, 1926. 327 Adams Street

The Brownfield Building was constructed around the year 1895, and it was a two-story brick structure with a projecting bay window on the second floor, and a bracketed cornice on the roof line. The first occupant of the building was D. L. Morrow's boot and shoe store;[51] it is thought to have been Fairmont's first boot and shoe store. Mr. Morrow later sold it to Joseph P. Fleming, who in turn sold it to E. Trickett, who conducted the shoe business in it for many years. Mr. F. J. Smith bought the establishment on March 1, 1907.[52] The store was enlarged by Mr. Smith in 1919 by a thirty-foot addition to the rear of the store, to enlarge the main sales room and the storage room for the shoe store. Three windows in the rear wall lit the building.[53]

Mr. Smith retired from the shoe business in 1926, after 19 years in the business. "You can't make money and keep up with the fads and styles of nowadays. Can't satisfy the flapper." He also blamed the advent of the automobile for the decline of the shoe trade, since "people ride too much and walk but little," thus not wearing out their shoes as quickly as before.[54] Thus, the site that had been continually used for a shoe store for forty years was remodeled for a new use.

L. L. Crawford relocated his meat market from across the street and opened it in the room formerly used by Smith's shoe store on July 28, 1926. The building was enlarged again with an addition to the rear, which was 80 feet deep and 35 feet wide; this was used for meat packing and refrigerated storage. The front of the store was used for the meat and grocery market.[55] Thousands of people attended the opening, and two policemen were utilized to keep the crowd from crushing the door. The people were given carnations as souvenirs, and many cooled off in the big meat refrigerating room on that hot July day.[56] Crawford's operated at this location through the 1930's.

The building has been recently remodeled and is currently used for a fur service.

8. Prendergast's saloon, c. 1890; Golden Brothers Annex, 1924. 329 Adams Street

In the 1870's, this was the site of Prendergast's saloon, and it was in an open stairway between this building and the adjacent building to the east (331 Adams Street) where the Great Fire of 1876 began.[57] After the fire, the lot was vacant until around 1890, when a two-story brick structure with a second story metal balcony was constructed.

T. W. Arnett opened his hardware business here in 1903,[58] and sold the business in 1910 to L. F. McCray for his home furnishings store.[59] In 1924, the adjacent Golden Brothers Department Store (331 Adams Street) bought F. Klaws Toggery Shoppe, which was located at this address, built a new three story building, and connected the two stores as one.[60]

This building no longer exists, and the area is part of a parking lot.

9. Swisher & Carpenter Store, c. 1870. Yeager's Store, Jones' Store, Harrison's Store, Golden Brothers' Store; 1896. Andrew C. Lyons, architect. 331 Adams Street

The Swisher & Carpenter Store was located here in the 1870's. The original building, as was much of Fairmont at that time, was a wood frame building. It was between this building and the one at 329 Adams Street, in an open stairway between the two buildings, that the Great Fire of 1876 began.[61] The building was destroyed. Afterwards, a new brick building was rebuilt on the site, which was two

Yeager's Store, 331 Adams Street, c. 1892.

stories in height, four bays wide, and had a decorative cornice at the roof. The second floor windows had segmented arches, and the first floor store front windows had Roman arches. Samuel S. Yeager established his mercantile store at this location in 1879. After his death in 1892, his son, George G. Yeager, took over the store.[62]

In October of 1894, Yeager & Company had a sale to close out the entire stock, first, to settle the estate of his father and second, to tear down the building that had been extensively damaged by the raising of the grade of Madison Street.[63] The new building was designed by Andrew C. Lyons,[64] and the plans and specifications for the new Yeager's store were available for bid in August of 1895.[65] The contractor for the new building was T. L. Burchinal.[66]

Yeager's new store was opened to the public on March 26, 1896. From 1:00 pm to

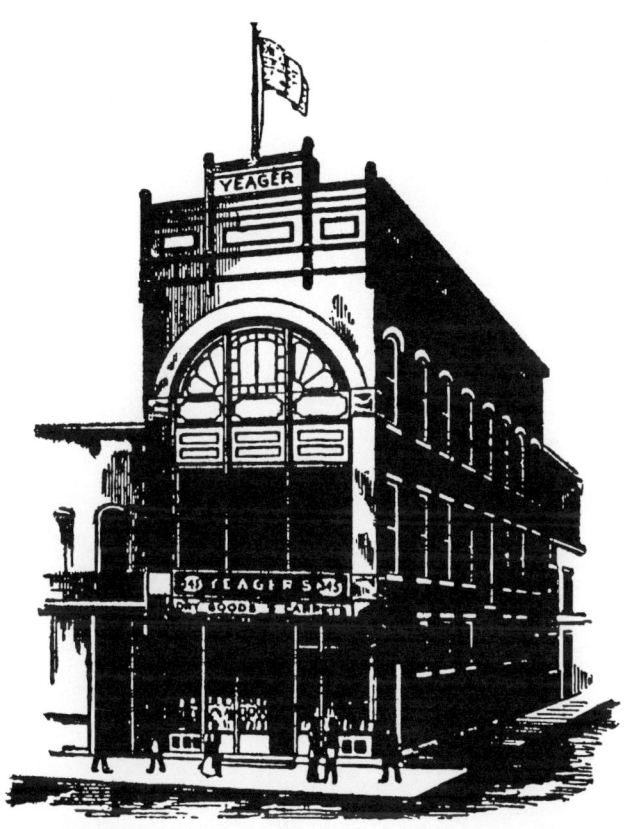

Yeager's New Store, 331 Adams Street, c. 1896.

10:00 pm, the building was thronged with visitors, who were delighted with the building which was deemed handsome both on the interior and exterior. It was thought to be the finest store in West Virginia.[67] There was also a new plan of doing business, marking the price of each article in plain figures. "Treating All Alike," their advertising read, "Exacting not a penny more from the smallest child than the shrewdish adult shopper visiting our store."[68]

The building was a three story brick structure. The front facade was distinctive with a Roman arch almost the entire width of the front that had rounded decorative glass at the third floor level, and which encased three windows on the second floor level. At the top of the roof, a rectangular pediment was raised in the center, with the name "Yeager" carved on it, topped with a flagpole.[69]

A stir was caused in the mercantile world in Fairmont when it was announced in November 1905 that George Yeager was retiring from business and leasing the building to Mr. E. C. Jones, who had a store in Mannington.[70]

E. C. Jones opened his first Fairmont store on March 14, 1906 in the former Yeager location. So many people came to the opening that there were crowds of people assembled on the street in front of the store, waiting to get in. As the ladies entered, they were given a souvenir carnation, while the men were given a souvenir hat brush. Omen's orchestra provided the music for the evening, which was seen as a great success.[71]

As Jones' Store grew with its success in the city, it outgrew the space in the building. In

Jones' Store, 331 Adams Street, c. 1908.

September of 1912, the store moved and opened in a portion of the new Fleming Building (109-113 Adams Street).[72] A. Harrison subsequently opened his department store at this site in March of 1913.[73] One improvement that Harrison's made was to create an entrance to the store off of Madison Street. [74]

To celebrate the seventh anniversary of their store, Harrison's Department Store had a monster cake baked for the occasion by Harry L. Gould. The total weight of the cake was 437 pounds and it was seven feet, one inch tall. Each of the seven layers represented one of its birthdays, and it was sliced into 5,000 pieces.[75]

Harrison's Department store was purchased by Golden Brothers Department store of Brownsville, Pennsylvania on January 15, 1921. Mr. Harrison's plans for the future were to "rest for two months."[76] The Golden Brother's Store was very successful at this site; the location became known as "Golden Corner," and images of the building were used extensively in their advertisements. The store remained at this location for many years.

Mr. George G. Yeager, son of the founder and himself subsequent owner of the Yeager Department store, died in Philadelphia on December 29, 1921 at the age of sixty-three. The body was returned to Fairmont for burial in Woodlawn Cemetery.[77]

On March 12, 1985, downtown Fairmont's famous Golden Brothers Store was demolished.[78] The site is now a parking lot.

Golden Brothers' advertisement in 1925.

1. *Welcome Westinghouse,* front sect., p. 5.
2. Dunnington, pp. 95-96.
3. ibid.
4. *Fairmont Lodge No. 9 A. F. and A. Masons, Fairmont, West Virginia: One Hundredth Anniversary 1849-1949,* p. 12.
5. *Fairmont Index,* 4/15/1892.
6. *Fairmont Lodge No. 9 A. F. and A. Masons, Fairmont, West Virginia: One Hundredth Anniversary 1849-1949,* p. 12.
7. *Welcome Westinghouse,* front sect., p. 5.
8. Dunnington, p. 96.
9. *Fairmont Times,* 7/27/1909, p. 1.
10. ibid.
11. Fleming, p. 37.
12. *Fairmont Times,* 8/6/1909, p. 1.
13. ibid., 4/16/1905, p. 1.
14. ibid., 7/5/1905, p. 1.
15. ibid., 5/15/1909, p. 1.
16. ibid., 8/6/1909, p. 1.
17. ibid., 9/13/1909, p. 1.
18. ibid., 9/22/1909, p. 1.
19. ibid., 10/6/1909, p. 1.
20. ibid., 10/15/1909, p. 1.
21. ibid., 10/16/1909, p. 2.
22. ibid., 10/21/1909, p. 1.
23. ibid., 1/8/1910, p. 6.
24. ibid., 6/16/1910, p. 1.
25. ibid., 9/15/1910, p. 1.
26. ibid., 3/10/1911, p. 1.
27. ibid., 4/7/1911, p. 1.
28. ibid., 4/19/1911, p. 5.
29. ibid., 4/27/1911, p. 5.
30. ibid., 4/29/1911, p. 5.
31. ibid., 6/23/1911, p. 1.
32. ibid., 8/2/1911, p. 6.
33. ibid., 2/8/1927, p. 1.
34. *Fairmont Index,* 1/3/1894.
35. ibid.
36. *Fairmont Times,* 6/27/1911, p. 3.
37. ibid., 11/20/1913, p. 8.
38. ibid., 7/13/1921, p. 1; 8/7/1921, sect. 2, p. 1.
39. ibid., 9/26/1926, p. 1.
40. ibid., 11/17/1929, supplement p. 1.
41. ibid., 11/19/1929, p. 1.
42. ibid.
43. ibid.
44. ibid., 11/17/1926, p. 12.
45. ibid., 9/13/1923, p. 2.
46. ibid., 9/29/1923, p. 2.
47. ibid., 11/4/1923, p. 5.
48. ibid., 3/18/1923, supplement.
49. ibid.
50. *Welcome Westinghouse,* sect. 1, p. 11.

[51] *Fairmont Index*, 7/16/1886.
[52] *Fairmont Times*, 4/25/1926, p. 1.
[53] ibid., 9/24/1919, p. 10.
[54] ibid., 4/25/1926, p. 1.
[55] ibid., 7/27/1926, p. 1.
[56] ibid., 7/29/1926, p. 1.
[57] *Fairmont West Virginian*, 4/7/1876.
[58] ibid., 8/23/1904, p. 3.
[59] *Fairmont Times*, 9/28/1910, p. 4.
[60] *Welcome Westinghouse*, sect. 2, p. 2.
[61] *Fairmont West Virginian*, 4/7/1876.
[62] *Fairmont Times*, 11/22/1905, p. 1.
[63] *Fairmont Index*, 10/13/1894.
[64] *Industrial Fairmont in 1908*, p. 66.
[65] *Fairmont Index*, 8/20/1895.
[66] *Twentieth Century Edition*, p. 37.
[67] *Fairmont Republican*, 4/2/1896.
[68] *Fairmont Index*, 2/18/1896.
[69] ibid.
[70] *Fairmont Times*, 11/22/1905, p. 1.
[71] ibid., 3/15/1906, p. 1.
[72] ibid., 12/13/1912, p. 14.
[73] ibid., 3/19/1913, p. 8.
[74] ibid., 8/6/1913, p. 2.
[75] ibid., 10/18/1917, sect. 2, p. 1.
[76] ibid., 1/15/1921, p. 2.
[77] ibid., 12/30/1921, p. 1.
[78] Spevock, p. 82.

Chapter 7

400 Block Adams Streeet, even numbered buildings

1. Shot Tower, c. 1834. Watson Hotel, 1894. Leiner & Faris, architects. 402-408 Adams Street

Tradition has it that "The Shot Tower" was built on this site in 1834, which was a smokestack-like structure used to make shot. By dropping molten lead through the tower, it formed perfect spheres for shot, because of the cohesive properties of the lead and the cooling effect of the air. By the time that the lead droplets had somewhat hardened on the surface, they hit a pool of water in a trough at the bottom of the tower, from where they were sorted and bagged. The tower was demolished by John Levell in May 1893.[1]

When talk began in January of 1893 concerning building a structure on the corner owned by Thomas F. Watson, it was first thought to be a new bank for Fairmont.[2] Watson later decided that he would build a hotel; plans and a picture of the proposed hotel showed it to be four stories and, without a doubt, a beauty.[3] Though the lot had been graded by September 1893, there was no sign of construction beginning, and observers were anxious to see the project begin.[4]

It was announced in January of 1894 that the Watson Hotel was a certainty, filling a great need in Fairmont at that time for a modern hotel. The architect was Mr. Faris of Leiner & Faris, Wheeling. The structure was planned to be either red pressed brick or re-pressed brick, trimmed with stone, and ornamented with carving and brick. The roof was to be slate and the style of the building distinctly Romanesque.[5]

The first floor of the hotel was to contain five store rooms, a banking room, and a drug store, as well as the hotel offices and elevators; the ceilings were to be twenty feet high here. The main entrance was planned for Madison Street, with ladies' entrances on both Adams and Madison Streets. The second floor was to contain dining rooms, parlors, and a kitchen, along with three or four suites of rooms with baths. The third and fourth floors would be similar to each other, and would contain the majority of the sleeping rooms. The top floor was allocated to rooms for the help and dry rooms. In all, the hotel was to have from 75 to 100 sleeping rooms; every room was to have an outside window and all the halls were to connect with the fire escapes. It was estimated to cost $60,000 to complete.[6]

Later that month, Architect Faris was in town to estimate the excavations and stone work. The excavations were to be made seven feet deep under the entire building, and it was suggested that the soil be placed at the head of Jackson Street to level it.[7] The architect also surveyed the site and drove in stakes to outline the building; it was to be 96 feet on Adams Street and 120 feet on Madison Street. The bids for the excavation and the masonry were to be considered soon after the architect's visit, and the excavation to commence shortly thereafter. This efficient schedule was to insure an early start of the construction in the spring, as it was thought that it would be one of the most extensive building years in Fairmont.[8]

The beginning of construction was delayed because the bids for the construction came in over the amount that the financing company wanted to pay. Therefore, Architect Faris changed the plans, decreasing the dimensions of the building to 75 feet along Adams Street and 115 feet along Madison Street, and lowering it to four stories in height. In subsequent bidding, the lowest bidder in the first round had given an estimate within the budget, and was chosen for the project.[9]

Work finally began on the project in April of 1894. John Dohney was in charge of the excavations, and Mr. McClaine was in charge of the construction.[10] By May, the stonework was progressing very rapidly.[11]

The Thomas F. Watson Hotel opened for business on January 24, 1895. It was an elaborate structure, with tall, square towers on the northwest and southwest corners, Roman arches in the brickwork on the first and fourth floors, as well as in the windows of the towers. Semi-circular balconies projected in the middle of the walls on Adams and Madison Streets. The thickness of the walls was emphasized with multiple layers of concentric Roman arches in the brickwork. It was indeed a Romanesque fantasy.

On the day previous to the opening, the hotel was opened to the general public for inspection, before any of the rooms were occupied; many of the citizens of Fairmont took advantage of it. The floors of the rotunda and hallways were made of laid-in mosaic marble, the finishings were in oak, and the ceiling was steel. The elevator traveled at the rate of one round trip per minute. The bedroom suites were all in oak, and every room in the building was private and had good light and ventilation. The rooms were heated with steam and lighted with electric lights. The furniture was purchased by the Mammoth Furniture House, and the dry goods were from J. M. Hartley's store. The special feature of the hotel was the dining room. It was large, pleasant, and well lighted; all of the china and silverware bore the mark "The Thos. F. Watson" on each piece.[12]

Sam B. Iseman of Baltimore had rented the corner room of the Watson Building even before the structure was completed, and opened his men's clothing and furnishing store there.[13] He conducted his business here until 1900, when he moved it to the Marietta Hotel Annex (126 Adams Street). This was only one of the many commercial enterprises that occupied space in the bottom floor business rooms.

The Watson Hotel was also the site of many social events in the life of Fairmont. One such event in the summer of 1897 was the Outing Club Dance, "one of the most enjoyable and brilliant dances ever held in Fairmont," which was given by "a considerable number of the Society Devotees of the city." The dance was held in the spacious dining room, which was well filled but not crowded. Guests came from Pennsylvania, Delaware, Maryland, Ohio, and West Virginia; "as they mingled together in costume of rare beauty and elegance, they presented a scene of dazzling splendor." It was intended to hold such dances twice a month through the summer and the next winter.[14]

The property changed hands after the death of Thomas F. Watson. It was sold to J. F.

Conoway for $100,000 in February of 1904 to settle the estate.[15] Mr. Conoway conducted the hotel successfully for many years.

In 1916, the Watson Hotel was sold for $165,000 to Joseph Moebs of Washington, D. C.; his intentions were to remodel the hotel, if the walls of the building were strong enough for the installation of modern furnishings and equipment. The cost of the remodeling was thought to be $40,000. If the building could not carry the weight of the remodeling, Mr. Moebs, a prominent contractor in Washington, D. C. and Boston, intended to tear down the entire structure and build a new hotel. In addition to the sales price, J. Frank Conoway was also given an apartment house in Washington when he sold the hotel to Mr. Moebs.[16]

It was later decided to improve the hotel rather than to demolish it, and a local man, John Biller, was hired to oversee the remodeling and operation of the hotel. Mr. Biller had experience with both the Marietta Hotel (128-130 Adams Street) and the Manley Hotel (312-314 Jefferson Street). The remodeling was to encompass removing all of the furnishings, redecorating the walls, recarpeting the floors, and installing new baths, with hot and cold water provided in each room. When completed, a large number of rooms were to have private baths and every sleeping compartment was to have hot and cold water.[17]

Before these plans could come to fruition, the Watson Hotel property changed hands. The Loch Lynn Construction Company, composed of several prominent local men, purchased the property in exchange for the Loch Lynn Hotel property at Mountain Lake Park, Maryland, which then became the property of Mr. Joseph Moebs.[18]

J. Vaughn Jolliffe leased the hotel and managed it. His plans to modernize it included installing a cafe, named the Cafe Watson, in a vacant store room to the east of the Adams Street entrance, which would have easy access from the lobby as well; and to convert the dining room into a ball room. The dance floor, under construction by August, was to be the center of "terpsichore," or dancing, during the winter society season. The remainder of the Watson would be operated as a hotel under the "European plan," which was a fixed rate for lodging only, and did not include meals, as did the "American plan."[19] Later, it was decided that the Woman's Club in the city was to use the ballroom for its club room. The old butler's pantry was converted into a store room for their paraphernalia, which could be moved from the floor in quick notice and be safely locked away during other uses of the ballroom.[20]

The Loch Lynn Construction Company, which owned the Watson Hotel, changed its company's name to the Mountain City Hotel Company in December of 1916. The name was chosen to perpetuate the memory of the Mountain City Hotel, which had been the best hotel in the country. It had been demolished to make way for the Courthouse on the corner of Adams and Jefferson Streets.[21]

Once again, the Watson Hotel came under new management, as it was leased by R. L. O'Neal and George Vonderhaas around 1918. Under their management, the hotel underwent the extensive repairs that had originally been planned in 1916: new furnishings, baths in many rooms, and hot and cold water for all rooms.[22] They also changed the name of the hotel to "Mountain City House," which was the wish of the owners, the Mountain City Hotel Company;

Watson Hotel, 402-408 Adams Street.

WATSON HOTEL, FAIRMONT, W. VA.
ilson's News Agency, Publishers, Watson Hotel Building, Fairmor

again, this was to honor the memory of the previous Mountain City Hotel. Another change in the Hotel was to remove the two main stairways leading to the second floor in the lobby and to construct a new flight of stairs. A new public wash room was installed as well. The old wall paper, sometimes seven layers thick, was removed and new paper put on. New window shades and new furniture was also provided.[23]

In November of 1919, the Fairmont Hotel Company formed, and it acquired both the Mountain City Hotel (formerly the Watson Hotel) and the Fairmont Hotel (200-208 Jefferson Street).[24]

The Watson Hotel was demolished in November 1956 by R. C. Eddy, a contractor from Morgantown.[25] The site now houses a tire store and its parking lot.

2. Fairmont Theatre; 1922-23, Fred W. Elliot, architect; 1944. 410-416 Adams Street

Part of the site at 410-412 Adams Street was originally a vacant lot; a house at 414-416 Adams Street, which had been constructed around 1890 according to the Sandborn maps, had been used as a store room by the Kelley Music Company.[26]

Talk of constructing a new theatre for Fairmont on this site began in March of 1920. Samuel Spicer, a New York investor, secured an option on the lots on Adams Street just east of the Watson Hotel, and proposed to construct a theatre which would cost from $100,000 to $150,000, with a seating capacity of 1,500 people. It was to be a modern structure, equipped with a stage on which the largest productions could be given, and adapted for the use of motion pictures as well. They intended to use the slope of the lot to accommodate the raked seating in the theatre, and the stage would be at the level of the alley in the rear. "The house will be in keeping with the progressive spirit of Fairmont and the building will be worthy of a place in her greatest business street."[27] The first rendering of the building, used to attract investors to the project, resembled a Roman triumphal arch; it was a three-story structure with a two-story monumental Roman arch in the center for the entrance.[28] However, this was not the final design for the facade of the building.

The West Virginia Amusement Company was incorporated in June 1920 for the purpose of constructing the theatre. The intention was to begin the building by June 1920 and to have ready for opening the first of October 1920. The first architect hired to design the building was F. W. Dreher, of the firm of Dreher, Churchman, Paul and Ford of Philadelphia. By this time, the expected cost of the theatre had increased to $200,000. The building would have a white terra cotta facade, and would be equipped with a Wurlitzer-Hope-Jones pipe organ, to be used for music as well as for theatrical sound effects such as rain, thunder, and trains. It was thought that the theatre would be completed in a "short period of time."[29]

In September of 1920, the West Virginia Amusement Company had purchased the lot adjoining the Watson Hotel at 310-312 Adams Street, and was selling stock for the theatre's construction.[30] October came and went without even the beginning of the construction of the building. March 1921 headlines stated "New theatre is now assured is rumor prevailing," and that the plans were "to rush ahead the construction of the new playhouse" for the fall.[31]

In May of 1921, it was stated that a new theatre was assured for the city; the Amusement Company had purchased the property at 314-316 Adams Street, and the additional 43 feet of frontage was sufficient ground for the theatre. This gave the proposed building a total frontage of 90 feet and a depth of 165 feet. There was a change in the architect at this time; Mr. Fred W. Elliot of Columbus, Ohio was hired to design the theatre. He planned a structure with a seating capacity of 1,400. Mr. Kelley, who used space in the house on the site for storage for his adjacent music store, planned to extend his music store to the rear to make up for the space lost to the theatre. It was hoped to have the theatre open for the coming season.[32]

The name of the theatre, "The Fairmont," was decided upon in June 1921 at a meeting of the Amusement Company. This was done to advertise the city, just as the famous Fairmont Hotel did. It was also noted at this meeting that the cost of the new theatre would perhaps run as high as $350,000.[33] Still, no theatre materialized in this year, in spite of all the publicity and good intentions.

It was not until April of 1922 that the bids for the construction of the theatre were opened. The lowest bid of approximately $200,000 by Valley Engineering Corporation was accepted. The Amusement Company still had to sell stock for the company; although $100,000 had already been raised, they still needed to pay for and to secure title to the real estate before the other money would be available. It was thought that the construction would take seven months to complete, and they hoped to have the new theatre open for Christmas week.[34]

The campaign to finance the new theatre was on. The Chamber of Commerce, the Rotary, as well as other service organizations, gave the proposition their full support. It was noted that carloads of people had to go to Clarksburg, Wheeling, or Pittsburgh to see large theatrical production, which could not be shown here for lack of a proper facility. Fairmont, it was said, would benefit greatly by hosting these large productions, as well as being able to house state meetings they were missing out on. The operation of the theatre would have a positive impact on all trade in the city, the persuasive argument went, as the profits of the operation would be distributed back into the channels of trade. It would be owned and operated by people of the city, and there was a liberal plan for financing any potential investors.[35] The revised cost of the new theatre was $300,000: $100,000 for the land acquisition, and $200,000 for the construction.[36]

A contest was held by the Amusement Company for the five best short letters telling why Fairmont should have a modern theatre and why the citizens of Fairmont and the vicinity should own it; the cash prizes increased if the letter was accompanied by either money for theatre tickets or for stock. [37] With a big influx of cash to the tune of $150,000 from the Conservative Life Insurance Company of Wheeling, the project was finally well on its way to fruition.[38] The Fairmont Mining Machinery Company also subscribed to $10,000 worth of stock; this was seen as a mark of civic pride on the parts of the employees of the company.[39] Construction began on the theatre on May 29, 1922.[40]

One early problem with construction was an alleged encroachment of the building in the rear on Ogden Avenue. A survey of the property was made, and it was discovered that the theatre encroached 3/4 of an inch on one side of the lot, and 1/4 of an inch on the other side of the lot. In the interest of the public welfare and "to quiet vexatious questions", the city Board of Directors decided in favor of the Theatre, and it was allowed to remain as begun. [41]

In September of 1922, the West Virginia Amusement Company, apparently not pleased with the rate of progress on the new theatre, bought the contract for the construction from Valley Engineering Company; it placed Samuel D. Brady in charge of the construction and named William C. Hawkins superintendent of construction. Two shifts of workers were put on the job, in the hopes of having the building under roof by December 1, 1922. [42]

The next problem with construction involved the foundations. A strata of quicksand was discovered, and it caused considerable delay in constructing the pilings for the building. The first three feet of soil on the site was yellow dirt. Next, there was approximately fifteen feet of blue potters clay. It was below this clay that the vein of quicksand was discovered. To mitigate it, it was necessary to drive sheet pilings down about twenty-three feet; each of the thirty-five piers required thirty-six hours of time to perform this task. [43]

The other delay at this time was the lack of bricklayers. Even though there were eighty men working on the site, Mr. Hawkins needed as many as thirty-five bricklayers at once, going as far as New York to try to secure this type of worker. Because of the vast amount of construction in the country in the year 1922, this was difficult to do. "I haven't time to sleep," he stated. "My mind is never off this building a single moment. I must have bricklayers! That's my big trouble now!" [44]

By the beginning of November, the goal was to simply have the building under roof by December 1, 1922; the goal of opening the week of Christmas was out of the question, although the Virginia Theatre (316 Adams Street) was doing just that. The height of the walls in the rear of the Fairmont Theatre were about eighty feet tall at this point in time, and the walls in the front sixty feet tall. The trusses were expected to be placed within the week. [45]

"Fairmont's New Theater Being Rushed to Completion," the headlines read. The terra cotta work for the front facade was placed by the middle of November, as well as the steel frame for the marquee overhanging Adams Street. The walls of the theatre were twenty-two inches thick and extended down as deep as twenty-five to thirty feet to a solid bedrock foundation. [46] By the beginning of December, the heavy trusses supporting the roof were mostly in place, as well as much of the frame construction work. The side walls and the rear wall were completed, and the placement of the steel joists for the first floor had begun. [47]

The seats for the theatre arrived in January of 1923. They were manufactured by the American Seating Company; they were upholstered in tan velour, and the aisle seats had gold standards with an oval shaped plate on which the letter "F" was emblazoned. The 1,272 seats cost $17,000. A sample of the seats was displayed in the window of the Fairmont Furniture Company. [48]

The completed building designed by Fred W. Elliot was very different from the rendering by the first architect. It was now a three-story, five bay structure with Roman arched windows on the third floor, pairs of rectangular windows topped with a transom on the second floor, and three pairs of French doors and a store front on the first floor. There was an ornamental cornice between the first and second story windows, and a bracketed cornice at the roof. Pilasters in stone separated the windows on the second and third floors.

In May, it was announced that the official opening for the theatre was planned for June 4, 1923; the opening performance was to be the musical show "Helen of Troy, N. Y.," which would run for three days. It was to be followed by the senior high school play, "The College Widow." By this time, the auditorium was completed and the scaffolding removed; the major work remaining was the installation of the seats, the fitting of the marble for the lobby, the placing of the electrical fixtures and bronze railings, the hanging of the draperies, and the laying of carpet. The cost of the theatre had escalated to $400,000.[49]

As the workers were putting the finishing touches on the new theatre, it was noted that there were six rooms for rent in the building as well. Located on the upper floor, they were arranged in two suites of three rooms each. One had already been rented out before the theatre opened, and it was to be called the Mary Margaret Shop. It was to be established as a library, as well as an art shop.[50]

A pre-opening tour of the building gave an idea of the splendor of the new facility. The entrance to the building was through three pairs of French doors, onto the pure Venetian marble floors. The top floor housed a combination assembly hall and dance hall, which was 50 by 35 feet; this was to be rented. It had five arched windows as big as arched church doors. The floor below housed the six offices previously mentioned, and also a big restroom for communal use.[51]

The balcony level was divided into three sections, and had three exits. The balcony foyer had a "circle" rounded with white ivory balustrade. Above the circle was an "atriumdome," a great dome which held 135 inverted indirect lights. From this foyer, one could see down to the ground floor. The stage itself was 32 feet deep and 50 feet wide, and the hangings and the stage curtain were made of heavy gold velvet. There were nine dressing rooms, as well as a carpenter shop under the stage.[52]

" 'Helen of Troy, N. Y.' Beautiful Dancing Show Gives Premier Here Before First Audience in House," ran the headlines after the first performance in the new theatre on June 4, 1923. The ladies were in dazzling evening gowns and the gentlemen in smart black; they were rivaled only by the magnificence of the new facility. Flowers were sent by many of the businesses in Fairmont; one of the most magnificent baskets of flowers was from Fred Elliot, the architect of the building, who was also in attendance that evening. The opening was seen as a huge success.[53]

A week later, a large electric sign was hung at the new theatre, and the first motion picture, "The Rustle of Silk," was shown. The sign was said to rival those on Broadway, having nearly 200 lights.[54] On November 30, 1923, the Edla Shop opened at the theatre building. A total of 1,000 potted plants were given out at the opening. The shop was devoted to women's wear.[55]

In 1929, less than six years after its opening, the theatre was sold at public auction to Julius and Israel Golden, who owned Golden Brothers Department Store (331 Adams Street). For several months previous to that, it had been operating under a receivership. The proceeding which resulted in the sale of the property was instituted by two of the members of the West Virginia Amusement Company, who had built the structure. The Golden brothers bought the theatre for $256,000 cash. They intended to refurbish the place and operate it.[56]

The sale had been the biggest sale ever made in front of the Marion County Courthouse. The bidding had started at $100,000, and "continued snappy until the close." The only other bidder in the proceedings was the Conservative Life Insurance Company of Wheeling, which held the mortgage against the property. Originally, the lot and building had cost nearly $610,000.[57]

One week later, the Conservative Life Insurance Company of Wheeling acquired the Fairmont Theatre from the Golden brothers. A new local company, The Fairmont Theatres Company headed by Edwin Watson, was formed to take control of it, and would own and operate both the Fairmont and the Virginia Theatres. The new "talking" equipment ordered for the Virginia was to be installed in the Fairmont instead, and the opening show was scheduled to be the Al Jolson flick, "The Singing Fool." The street gossip said that the Goldens were enriched by $10,000 because of the transaction.[58]

For the opening of the premier "talkie" under the new management, the Fairmont Theatre was "high hatted and decorated like a college senior on Broadway" in April of 1929. The theatre was refurbished for the event, with the exterior washed and repainted. The box office, which originally had been in the lobby, was relocated to the right side of the entrance. A new lighting system was installed so that at the start of the motion picture the lights would dim gradually to blues. A new screen, porous for sound pictures, was also installed; two huge towers were erected behind the screen to support the "horns" which emitted the sounds and dialogue. Two new projection screens were also added. John Burchinal was the architect in charge of the remodeling.[59]

The magnificent theatre burned sometime around the year 1944, and the building currently on the site was built to replace it shortly thereafter. This structure is Art Deco in style, with simple geometric vertical and horizontal lines on the upper levels, and Carrara glass on the lower level. It is still used as a theatre, although the interior is divided into several individual auditoriums.

Proposed Fairmont Theatre (not constructed), 410-416 Adams Street, 1920.

Fairmont Theatre, 410-416 Adams Street in 1922.

3. Post Office, c. 1860; Fred C. Fleming residence, 1891; Singer Store, 1928.
418 Adams Street

A small wood frame house with a big outside chimney originally stood on the site, which was the home of Richard P. Lott. When he became Fairmont's postmaster in 1861, he constructed an addition to it; and the addition became Fairmont's first post office. Mr. Lott served as postmaster from 1861 to 1869, and the post office became a congregating place for young people, since it was located across the street from the Old Normal School (later known as Fairmont State College).[60]

When Fred C. Fleming built a brick structure on this site in 1891, this smaller house was moved into the back yard, and the addition which had served as the post office was removed at this time. When both of these houses were torn down in 1928, they were said to be one of the three remaining old homesteads on the city's main business street, and that the new construction was to be located on one of the most historic spots in the city.[61]

The structures were removed to make way for the two-story structure currently on the site, which was originally built to be used as business rooms and an apartment home.[62] There are two store fronts on the first floor, large rectangular windows on the second floor, and simple decorative brick coursing above the second floor windows. The building is still in use today.

Adams Street, 400 block looking east (right); Old Normal (middle background), 401-407 Quincy Street; Kenyon Hotel (left foreground), 312 Madison Street, in 1923.

4. Osgood's Store, 1921. 420-422 Adams Street

The buildings on this property prior to 1921 were small two story business houses. In 1921, Mr. D. M. Osgood purchased these properties with the intent of remodeling them. He purchased the property at 420 Adams Street from Mrs. Maggie E. Reger,[63] who had received the property as a gift from her half-uncle in 1909.[64] The other piece of property at 422 Adams Street was purchased two months later from the Barnes family,[65] who may have also obtained ownership in 1909 the same way, as a gift. The existing store room at 420 Adams Street was to be changed and another of the same size fitted up at 422 Adams Street, and both were carried the full 85 foot length of the lot. Four modern flat apartments were constructed over these store rooms.[66]

Work began on June 7, 1921, to transform the structure that had been used as a dwelling into a business house.[67] The structure had five bays and was three stories tall. The ground floor was to have a large double store room, with a large daylight basement room fronting 30 feet on Adams Street and running back to the depth of 85 feet. To do this, the old front was torn away and a new front constructed of calla stone. It was expected to be completed by September 1, 1921.[68]

Kelley's Music Store was to move into one half of the new Osgood Building, it was announced in December of 1921. It was to be one of the finest music stores in West Virginia. The first floor room was a spacious 35 feet wide and 85 feet deep, and housed the stock of pianos and grafonolas. It was even large enough to seat 300 people for a concert, it was stated. Grand pianos were to be the specialty of the new store, and the old store was going to be retained for storage purposes.[69] Within two years, Kelley's expanded to take the entire first floor of the building.[70]

Although still in use, the upper part of this building has been covered with gray stucco.

Osgood's Store (right), 420-422 Adams Street; and Barnes Property, Yost Building (left), 426-432 Adams Street. Crowd is watching scoreboard on Newspaper Building 401-407 Quincy Street in 1926.

5. Barnes Property, Yost Building; c. 1844 and c. 1890. 426-432 Adams Street

The property at 426 Adams Street dates from around 1890, according to the Sandborn maps; some of the properties at 428-432 Adams Street are said to date back to the 1840's. These are wood-frame structures, with various sizes of window openings on the second floor, and several store fronts on the first floor. They are currently covered with stucco and heavily remodeled. These were given by James F. Barnes to the family of his late half-brother as a Christmas present in 1909; at that time, the property (possible including the property at 422 Adams

Yost Building, 426-432 Adams Street. Photo taken just after streetcar wreck in 1927.

Street) was valued at $45,000.[71] The Sandborn maps show these structures interconnected in different configurations throughout the years. They also have had a variety of uses, including dwellings, groceries, stores, restaurants, and cleaners. Some sources claim that the buildings were used in the underground railroad during the Civil War.

The buildings, then called the Yost Building, were the scene of a tragic streetcar accident in May of 1927. A collision of a streetcar and an automobile at the top of the hill on Quincy Street at Madison Street cut the brake cable of the streetcar, which then rolled out of control down Quincy Street toward Adams Street. The tracks turned the corner at Adams Street, but the streetcar was traveling at such a great speed, probably near 40 m.p.h., that it jumped the tracks and crashed into the building. One woman was killed and approximately 18 others injured.[72]

These structures are still in use.

[1] Hoffman, p. 59.
[2] *Fairmont Free Press*, 1/20/1893.
[3] ibid., 7/28/1893.
[4] ibid., 9/8/1893.
[5] *Fairmont Index*, 1/3/1894.
[6] ibid., 1/3/1894.
[7] ibid., 1/10/1894.
[8] *Fairmont Free Press*, 1/12/1894.
[9] *Fairmont Index*, 3/21/1894.
[10] *Fairmont Free Press*, 4/27/1894.
[11] *Fairmont Index*, 5/16/1894.
[12] *Fairmont Free Press*, 1/25/1895.
[13] *Fairmont Index*, 7/11/1894.
[14] ibid., 8/13/1897.
[15] *Fairmont Times*, 2/25/1904, p. 1.
[16] ibid., 3/8/1916, p. 1.
[17] ibid., 4/18/1916, p. 1.
[18] ibid., 6/14/1916, p. 1.
[19] ibid., 8/15/1916, p. 2.
[20] ibid., 9/21/1916, p. 3.
[21] ibid., 12/30/1916, p. 1.
[22] ibid., 2/15/1918, p. 1.
[23] ibid., 4/15/1918, p. 2.
[24] ibid., 11/4/1919, p. 7.
[25] Spevock, p. 15.
[26] *Fairmont Times*, 3/12/1914, p. 2.
[27] ibid., 3/23/1920, p. 1.
[28] ibid., 7/6/1920, p. 8.
[29] ibid., 6/3/1920, p. 1.
[30] ibid., 9/25/1920, p. 7.
[31] ibid., 3/8/1921, p. 5.
[32] ibid., 5/15/1921, sect. 2, p. 1.
[33] ibid., 6/2/1921, p. 6.
[34] ibid., 4/12/1922, p. 1.
[35] ibid., 4/16/1922, p. 7.
[36] ibid., 4/17/1922, p. 8.
[37] ibid., 4/23/1922, p. 8.
[38] ibid., 5/8/1922, p. 1.
[39] ibid., 5/26/1922, p. 6.
[40] ibid., 5/29/1922, p. 1.
[41] ibid., 7/9/1922, p. 14.
[42] ibid., 9/14/1922, p. 12.
[43] ibid., 10/10/1922, p. 1.
[44] ibid.
[45] ibid., 11/3/1922, p. 12.
[46] ibid., 11/16/1922, p. 7.
[47] ibid., 12/2/1922, p. 6.
[48] ibid., 1/31/1923, p. 12.
[49] ibid., 4/29/1923, p. 7.
[50] ibid., 5/17/1923, p. 1.
[51] ibid., 5/27/1923, p. 1.
[52] ibid.
[53] ibid., 6/5/1923, p. 1.
[54] ibid., 6/12/1923, p. 12.
[55] ibid., 12/1/1923, p. 7.
[56] ibid., 3/3/1929, p. 1.
[57] ibid.

[58] ibid., 3/12/1929, p. 1.
[59] ibid., 4/13/1929, p. 1.
[60] ibid., 3/18/1928, p. 7.
[61] ibid.
[62] ibid.
[63] ibid., 4/10/1921, p. 1.
[64] ibid., 12/17/1909, p. 4.
[65] ibid., 6/8/1921, p. 1.
[66] ibid., 4/10/1921, p. 1.
[67] ibid., 6/8/1921, p. 1.
[68] ibid., 7/9/1921, p. 6.
[69] ibid., 12/11/1921, p. 11.
[70] ibid., 3/7/1923, p. 3.
[71] ibid., 12/17/1909, p. 4.
[72] ibid., 5/31/1927, p. 1.

Chapter 8

400 Block Adams Street, odd numbered buildings

1. Ogden Building, Billingslea Drug Store; c. 1889. 401-403 Adams Street

This site had a 1-1/2 story structure on it, according to the Sandborn map of 1884, which was used as a harness shop. By the time the 1892 map was drawn, it had been replaced by a two-story structure referred to as the Ogden Corner. From a drawing of it at the time, it had a bracketed cornice, segmented arched windows on the second floor, and a store front on the first floor. An ornamental metal balcony projected slightly above the store front at the second floor level.

Robinson and Co. had conducted their druggist business here from approximately 1889.[1] In 1892, the drug firm had been acquired by E. A. Billingslea, who then conducted the business at that location. The structure was used as a drug store until approximately 1915, when it was subsequently used as a dry goods store, shoe store, grocery, and other commercial enterprises throughout the years. The building was acquired by the City of Fairmont in 1976; it was demolished and the site is currently part of a city parking lot.

E. A. BILLINGSLEA & CO.'S PLACE OF BUSINESS.

Billingslea's Store, 401-403 Adams Street, c. 1894.

2. Piggly-Wiggly, c. 1889. 405-407 Adams Street

From the Sandborn maps, this building appears to have been built at the same time, if not in conjunction with, the adjacent building at 401-403 Adams Street; it had been traditionally used for a grocery store. Morgan's Grocery had operated there from around the turn of the century, until the business was acquired by the Piggly-Wiggly Corporation in March of 1922. This grocery chain was unique in that each of the stores were arranged identically, so that goods in one store were in the same location as the others. Also, each item was clearly marked with the price.[2]

The building has since been demolished, and the site is currently part of a city parking lot.

3. Eyster residence, c. 1885; Robb Meat Market, 1911. 409-411 Adams Street

A small two-story wood-frame structure was built on the site around the year 1885. It had been the home of the Eyster family for many years. In July of 1910, C. C. Robb purchased the Old Eyster lot for $13,000, to construct a three-story building to house his meat market on the first floor. The two upper floors were planned to be used as flats.[3] When the older building was being razed, it was thought to be possibly the oldest building on Adams Street, because of the huge timbers found in the construction that were thought to have been popular in the "early days."[4]

The new Robb Meat Market opened on January 26, 1911, and the public was invited to inspect the refrigeration plant and store; souvenirs were distributed to make the callers remember the occasion. The new building was a three story structure with a basement, and it was constructed with pressed bricks. It fronted 28 feet on Adams Street and extended 82 feet to the rear. The basement housed the refrigeration equipment and cold storage vaults. The upper floors each had two apartments. On the first floor were the rendering rooms, cooking rooms, and vaults. The store room itself was fitted with the very best sanitary cases and appliances.[5]

The business changed hands, and on December 17, 1926, the new Liberty Meat Market opened in the Robb Building. Hundreds of people attended the grand opening. Carl McElfresh's Orchestra provided the music for the opening, and souvenirs were distributed to everyone who visited: the men were given cigars, and the ladies were given a flower. The store had been completely renovated, redecorated and modern equipment was installed.[6]

The building has since been demolished, and the site is currently part of a city parking lot.

4. Dutton/Chisler Hardware, c. 1850; Hippodrome Theatre, Blue Ridge Theatre, 1911. 413-415 Adams Street

The original building on this site was a hardware store owned by Thomas Dutton, later owner by John Chisler. It was built around 1850. The site was leased from the Chisler heirs for the erection of an "airdome" theatre in May of 1911. The amusement company was headed by

Mr. H. C. Necessary of Grand Rapids, Michigan, and was composed of some Grand Rapids people and a local businessman. The old buildings, a two-story and a one-story structure, were removed to meet the demand for popular amusement, even though they were referred to as "landmarks of the city."[7]

It was planned to begin construction immediately, and to have the theatre opened on July 1, 1911. It was to be one story high, and the airdome was to be constructed on the rear. It was to be of brick and steel construction, to provide a fireproof building. The house was to be more of the nature of a hippodrome than a purely vaudeville and moving picture theatre.[8]

The initial performance in The Hippodrome Theatre was September 4, 1911, a little behind the original schedule. The very prominent feature of the theatre was the orchestra, composed entirely of professional musicians, thoroughly trained in the vaudeville business.[9] To prove how safe the building was, it was possible to empty the entire house in three minutes, since the exits were so well arranged.[10] Theatre safety had become an important issue because of highly publicized theatre fires that had taken many lives.

For several years, the theatre ran smoothly, opening in late August for the season, closing again in late June for the summer. It is presumed that the heat of the summer would have made it unbearable to sit through a performance in the days before mechanical ventilation and air conditioning.

Controversy erupted in 1916, when the lessee of the theatre, Mr. David Hellman, planned to present "The Lure" at the Hippodrome. Mr. Charles C. Robb, the principal stockholder of the Clarksburg Amusement Company (which at that time owned the theatre), threatened to revoke his lease if it were played at the theatre. It was thought that Mr. Robb was under the impression that the play was improper and would not add to the high character of the house which its owners were endeavoring to build. Mr. Hellman offered to submit the production to a rehearsal to any body of citizens that Mr. Robb would see fit to select.[11] Though the outcome of the controversy was not determined, a new company had leased the Hippodrome in February of 1917.[12] Censorship had come to Fairmont.

In April 1922, Sol Burka became manager of the facility and made significant changes. He renamed it the Blue Ridge Theatre, after the outfit in the 80th Division in which he had served overseas in the first World War. The interior renovations were to accommodate "first run photoplays" and included the installation of two projecting machines, and a projection screen, and enlarging the stage. On the exterior, he placed a ticket office in the center of the entrance, and installed a handsome marquee to the curb.[13]

The opening of the newly renovated theatre occurred on April 17, 1922. The feature attraction for the opening was Gloria Swanson in "The Great Moment." One hundred new seats were added, eighty in the balcony and twenty on the main floor, bringing the total capacity of the facility to 700. The insignia of the Blue Ridge Division was four mountain peaks with a pleasing skyline, representing the four states that comprised the division: West Virginia, Pennsylvania, Maryland and Virginia. This insignia was used extensively as decoration for the building.[14]

The stage was widened for large vaudeville acts and road shows, as well as to show pictures.

A four piece orchestra was to supply music for the afternoon and evening entertainments. Two, thirty-two inch suction fans were installed to change the air in the theatre every two minutes. Battleship linoleum was installed throughout the house, and all fire requirements had been met. There were seven exits available, and large fire extinguishers were installed.[15]

The lobby was finished in white enamel, and the front was remodeled. It was solid white, with nearly 600 electric lights, and advertisements of the films were included on the front. H. Parrack was the contractor in charge of the project.[16]

The success of this new endeavor was short-lived. On June 5, 1922, it was announced that the Blue Ridge Theatre was closing pending a trustee sale. Though the house became very popular with the movie fans of the district, the cost of remodeling was so great that Mr. Burka could not meet the demands of his creditors; "... his business difficulties reached such shape that .... he was sought by county officers, armed with warrants for his arrest on the charge of passing bad checks." He left for Pittsburgh on a train just as a group of officers began searching for him, though he vowed to make an attempt to satisfy his creditors and take over the theatre again. A public auction was scheduled for June 24, 1922, and it was probable that Charles C. Robb, who held the lease from the owners and who had sublet the theatre to Burka, was the chief bidder at the trustee's sale.[17]

Mr. Robb then ran the Blue Ridge Theatre as a successful amusement place, but in 1924 it was decided to close the playhouse permanently. The demand for "business rooms" in the city caused him to give up the amusement business, and he planned to transform the structure into a business block, as people had been besieging him to do for years. His plan was to put store rooms on the main floor, and either offices or apartments on the upper floor of the building, which was to be modernized in every particular. The real estate was owned by Miss Florence Arnett and Mrs. Laura Cole, sisters who live next door at 417 Adams Street, and was considered one of the most valuable pieces of property in the business section.[18]

One plan for the building was to transform it into a modern hotel. Mr. Charles E. McCray, who operated a chain of

Blue Ridge Theatre, 413-415 Adams Street, 1922.

hotels in the state, planned to link it with the apartments next door in the Robb Building, which would add 18 rooms to the proposed rooms, bringing the total to 58 sleeping rooms.[19]

That idea never fully materialized, because the Blue Ridge Grill was opened in December 1925 in the old Blue Ridge Theatre Building, which had been converted into store rooms and apartments. In addition to a soda fountain, candy counter, and lunch counter, the building also had a victrola for dancing, for which a floor was prepared. Upstairs, there was a private dining room for private gatherings.[20]

Later, in 1928, the building became the home of the A&P Store.[21] The building has since been demolished, and is currently part of a city parking lot.

5. Arnett, Cole Residence, c. 1855. 417 Adams Street

In a 1928 account, Mr. Thomas W. Fleming stated that this house was built in 1855 or 1856 by Thomas Dutton, who owned the hardware store next door at 413-415 Adams Street. He built the house for himself and his family; and it was a typical ante-bellum house: rectangular with a sloping roof, long front room, bedrooms and a kitchen. It was two stories in front, and dropped to one in the back. The house was later sold to J. C. Beeson, and then to John Chisler. Though it originally sat at the edge of the street, it was moved back from the street by Miss Arnett to allow for the widening of Adams Street and to accommodate the sidewalk. Additional rooms were also added, which greatly altered the original look of the building.[22]

The house has since been demolished and the site is currently part of a city parking lot.

6. G. W. L. Mayers residence, c. 1893; Elk's Club, c. 1925.
John C. Burchinal, architect. 421 Adams Street

On the 1884 Sandborn map, this lot was vacant, and in 1892, it was labeled "to be built." The house on this site was constructed by G. W. L. Mayers (who was a contractor in the city) as his two and one-half story, seven-room brick residence; it cost $6,500.[23] It was a Queen Anne style house, with multiple gable roofs, ornamental brackets for porch supports, and bay windows.

In 1904, the house was acquired by the Elks to provide a new lodge for them, and they moved from their previous quarters in the "Skinner Building" at 106-108 Adams Street. A building in the rear was made into the lodge room, while the residence was redecorated at this time by the Brady Construction company under the eye of Charles G. Yeager.[24] The construction was completed to the point that the Elks could move into part of it in May 1904.[25]

The Elks subsequently vacated the property in March 1918 when it moved to its newly constructed quarters on the top two floors of the Deveny Building (128-130 Adams Street). The property was then rented to the Salvation Army for its operations. The operations included a nursery for children, a home for delinquent girls, and accommodations for small boys who would otherwise be placed in jail waiting for trial or placed in an institution.[26]

G.W.L. Mayers residence, 421 Adams Street, c. 1894.

Although the Elks new rooms in the Deveny Building were luxuriously appointed, the quarters became were too small for their growing membership, which in 1923 exceeded 1,000 members. Though they considered four different sites, it was decided by ballot to construct a club house on their Adams Street property that they had vacated only five years earlier. It was anticipated that the structure would cost $300,000, but no difficulty was seen for the Elks to finance the building.[27]

In addition to the lodge room, the new facility was to include club rooms, dancing and recreation rooms, and a sizeable restaurant. The most noteworthy facilities to be added were one hundred sleeping rooms to provide quarters for bachelors. The site was preferable because of the increasing value of the real estate in that neighborhood due to the construction of many new buildings, including the Fairmont Theatre; it was a most desirous location in the city. The Exalted Ruler John C. Burchinal was instructed to appoint a building committee and to employ an architect for plans for the club house.[28]

In February of 1924, The Elks accepted the plans of architect John C. Burchinal for the construction of the $300,000 home. The original plan was for a building seven stories in the front and five stories high in the rear. It was proposed to be 80 feet wide on Adams Street, and extend back from the front 157 feet. A total of 74 bedrooms were planned, which would generate a good income for the Elks.[29]

Later in the year, the plans had changed. Now it was proposed to construct a three story high structure, only 48 feet wide by 165 feet long. This would allow for a 24 foot wide driveway and parking area on the east side of the building for the members' cars. The plans called for the retention and remodeling of the two and one-half story brick house, though it would not be recognizable after the improvements. The roof and attic of the house were to be razed, as well as the front wall of the second story. The front porch was to be rebuilt and the floors of the first floor lowered as well as remodeled on the inside to conform with the new building to be constructed in the rear. The structure of the building was to be steel frame veneered with rough textured brick veneer. There was to be an open porch on the front. Mr. Walter Eliason of Fairmont was chosen as the contractor.[30]

Plans were also made for the observance of the Eleven O'Clock Toast of the Elks by installing a series of clocks in the home, which would strike the hour and sound "Auld Land Syne" on their chimes, which signifies that the Elks are paying a silent tribute to their absent brothers. It was planned to mount a giant elk's head carved out of stone on the front of the building, and to mount a clock between the antlers, as a solemn testimonial of the love the Elks hold for their absent brothers.[31]

Grading for the structure began in April 1925, which was now estimated to cost $200,000. Some changes had been made in the plans for the building. The first floor would house the club rooms, and the kitchen was to be in the basement. Only fourteen sleeping rooms with baths were now planned for the third floor.[32]

Work on the foundation began on June 1, 1925, and the cornerstone for the structure was laid on June 18, 1925. "Work on the new building will be rushed ahead just as fast as is practicable..."[33]

Over two thousand people attended the cornerstone ceremony. The speakers told of the history of the organization, and two of the five living charter members of the organization, who had originally numbered twenty-five, were in attendance at the ceremony: W. T. Hartman and John H. Hough. A list of the articles and documents deposited in the cornerstone included lists of members and officers, historic photographs of Fairmont, historic coins, programs, and newspaper articles regarding the construction of the lodge. [34]

The completed structure is a three-story brick building. The front is divided into four bays, with pairs of rectangular windows on the upper floors, and segmented arched openings on the first floor. These open onto a porch which stretches across the entire front of the building; on this porch, one can see one of the bays of the original house. The simple brickwork creates three-story pilasters that separate the bays. There is a simple cornice just below the top of the roof. Part of the original stone foundation of

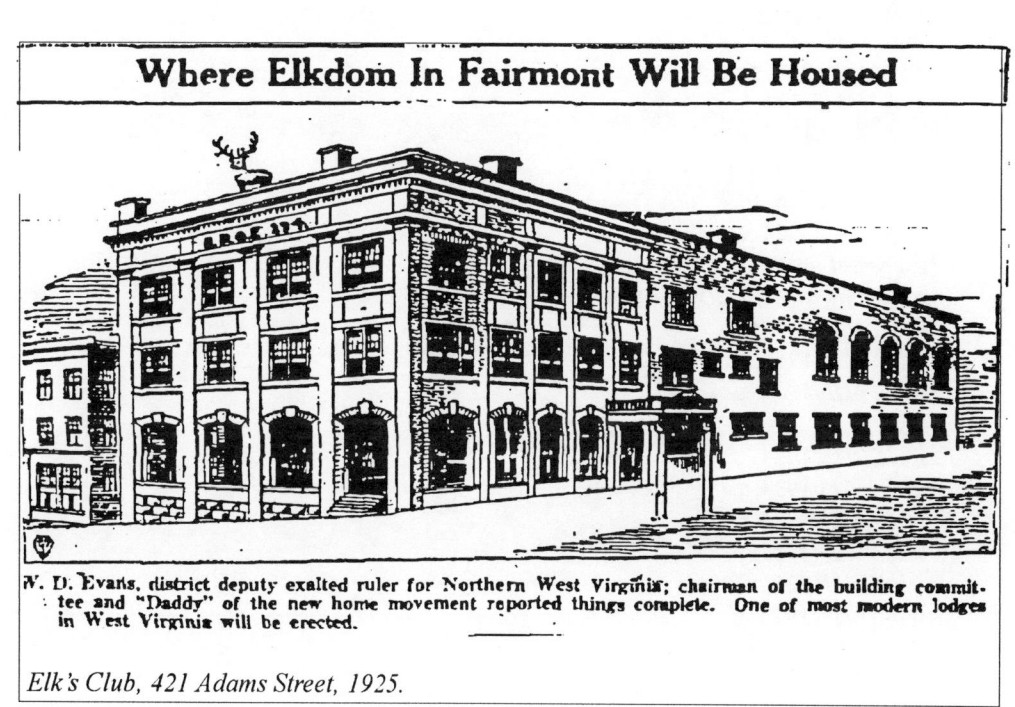

Elk's Club, 421 Adams Street, 1925.

the house may be seen on the west side of the structure.

The first meeting in the new Elks Home was on December 29, 1925. A new feature of the lodge was the serving of a business men's lunch every day except Sunday.[35] The luncheon service was so successful that they were serving over 200 meals per day. The new facility was also seen as filling a need in the community for a community center, and was also in demand as a meeting place for men. It was a social center for the community.[36]

Although changed by renovations, the building today is still used by the Elks.

---

[1] *Fairmont Index,* 4/15/1892.
[2] *Fairmont Times,* 3/28/1922, p. 12.
[3] ibid., 7/23/1910, p. 1.
[4] ibid., 7/29/1910, p. 1.
[5] ibid., 1/26/1911, p. 3.
[6] ibid., 12/18/1926, p. 9.
[7] ibid., 5/5/1911, p. 1.
[8] ibid.
[9] ibid., 8/31/1911, p. 8.
[10] ibid., 9/5/1911, p. 3.
[11] ibid., 12/13/1916, p. 2.
[12] ibid., 2/14/1917, p. 8.
[13] ibid., 4/9/1922, p. 7.
[14] ibid., 4/16/1922, p. 7.
[15] ibid.
[16] ibid.
[17] ibid., 6/5/1922, sect. 2, p. 12.
[18] ibid., 5/11/1924, sect. 2, p. 1.
[19] ibid., 4/17/1925, p. 1.
[20] ibid., 12/19/1925, p. 3.
[21] ibid., 2/5/1928, p. 7.
[22] ibid., 3/25/1928, sect. 2, p. 1.
[23] *Fairmont Index,* 1/3/1894.
[24] *Fairmont Times,* 3/2/1904, p. 5.
[25] ibid., 5/4/1904, p. 1.
[26] ibid., 2/11/1919, supplement.
[27] ibid., 4/25/1923, p. 1.
[28] ibid.
[29] ibid., 2/13/1924, p. 1.
[30] ibid., 12/3/1924, p. 1.
[31] ibid., 3/23/1925, p. 10.
[32] ibid., 4/15/1925, p. 1.
[33] ibid., 6/1/1925, p. 1.
[34] ibid., 6/19/1925, p. 1.
[35] ibid., 12/29/1925, p. 1.
[36] ibid., 1/4/1926, p. 1.

Part II—
Cleveland Avenue
(previously Barney Street and Parks Avenue)

Before it was called Cleveland Avenue, even before it was called Parks Avenue, the area of the street parallel to the river was referred to as New Dug Road. It wound down to the river bank, and a ferry took people across to the East Side, which was then the city of Palatine.[1] The 100 and 200 blocks of the street were later called Parks Avenue, and the street from the 300 blocks onward were called Barney Street. Sometime between 1912 and 1918, according to the Sandborn maps of those years, the entire street was renamed Cleveland Avenue.

The lower part of Cleveland Avenue (the 100 and 200 blocks) was Fairmont's "warehouse district" after the turn of the century. The property owners took advantage of the proximity of the railroad on the hillside below, and constructed buildings that accessed the railroad tracks at that level, approximately three stories below the street level. Produce could be transferred directly into the building, then brought up by elevator to street level to be distributed.

Chapter 9

100 Block Cleveland Avenue, even numbered buildings

1. Skinner's Tavern; c. 1847, 1903, 1904.
E. B. Fransheim, architect. 104 Cleveland Avenue

One of Fairmont's most famous hotels was Skinner's Tavern. The original or "historical" section was said to have been constructed in 1847 by Jas. Burns.[2] This was a two story wood frame building with a walk-down basement, located directly on the corner of Cleveland Avenue and Madison Street. During the 1850's, after the suspension bridge was constructed across the street (on Madison Street, also called Bridge Street) in 1852, this tavern became an important stopping place for people traveling between the National capital and points West. Many men of national repute found comfort in the tavern in those days.[3] It was chiefly noted for its good food and was mostly favored by transients, probably because the passenger station was just across the street from it.[4]

Mr. C. L. Skinner was the proprietor and landlord of the establishment around 1890. In 1891, it was noted that he had recently refitted and refurnished his hotel in "the most ample and elegant style," especially the dining room. The improvements had increased the number of guests in the hotel.[5] The hotel was so popular around this time that people were regularly turned away because it was full. Mr. Skinner also provided meals that were not generally found in restaurants, which included venison, wild turkey, and game of all kinds.[6] In May 1894, an addition was begun to the hotel. Twelve new lodging rooms were added to the north side of the property.[7]

In April of 1896, Benjamin G. Williams assumed charge of Skinner's Tavern. He planned to give the place a general overhaul to make it one of the best hotels in the State and the excellent reputation it had while Mr. Skinner was in charge.[8] These improvements included painting and repairing the bar to make it more inviting, the addition of bath rooms to the hotel, and a fresh coat of exterior paint. These were thought to greatly add to the comfort of the guests.[9]

In 1901, Ben Williams made plans for and began construction on a large addition to the "historical" Skinner's Tavern. The addition was to be a five-story brick structure containing 100 sleeping rooms, sample rooms, a fine bar, dining rooms (both general and private), and a well-equipped kitchen. It was to cost over $100,000 when completed, and T. L. Burchinal was the contractor for the project. From a drawing in the newspaper of the time, the completed building was to have a slightly protruding central section with feature windows and two symmetrical side wings of five bays.[10] The architect for the project was E. B. Fransheim of Wheeling. The addition was planned in four phases. The first was the west "wing" of the building and it contained the dining room and a number of bed rooms. It was constructed and was in use by

Skinner's Tavern (the original wooden section), 104 Cleveland Avenue, c. 1902.

spring of 1903.[11] The second phase was begun around 1903 and was the "central" section of the building. It contained an elevator which was to run to the fifth floor, the parlor, an ordinary, a European eating house, and a number of very handsome bedrooms.[12] This section was finished in the summer of 1904.[13] One of the new improvements to the hotel with the construction of the central section was the installation of a new telephone system in the hotel. All of the sleeping rooms were connected directly to a large central switchboard.[14]

The third phase of the addition to the hotel was to have been constructed between the new sections and the corner, and would have meant demolishing the "historical" Skinner's Tavern. This eastern "wing" would have balanced the building, which was planned to be symmetrical around the central section. It was never constructed. A fourth phase of the building was to be constructed up Bridge (Madison) Street from the corner.[15] It, too, was not constructed. The resulting building consisted of the west and central wing of the brick addition attached to the original wooden structure.

With the first two sections of the new building completed, the hotel became host to a number of banquets and conventions during the next several years. Also during this time, there were several minor fires, mostly in the older frame part of the building (the "historical" Skinner's Tavern).

In 1908, the Tavern was attempting to increase business, so it reduced its rates. Meals went from 75 cents to 50 cents; rooms with a bath went from $1.50 to $1.00, rooms without a bath from $1.00 to 75 cents.[16] This gave the desired results, as one month later it was noted that the hotels in the city were busy, especially the Tavern, which had cut its rates.[17]

In April 1909, Colonel B. G. Williams returned to manage Skinner's Tavern after an absence from it, probably during the time of the rate reduction. Mr. Williams set out to get the hotel back into first-rate condition. One of the things he did was to have the elevator repaired, which had been broken for some time, forcing the hotel patrons to walk up several flights of stairs to their rooms. The hotel was cleaned, and the dining room opened once more.[18]

It seemed like fires constantly plagued Skinner's Tavern. A small fire occurred in the restaurant and pool room in the old part of the building in November 1911, though little damage done.[19] Another, which occurred in February 1912, was due to a gas hose which burst in the wine cellar on the first floor; it spread into the second floor pool room, then to the attic and roof. Some of the roof timbers crashed onto the restaurant floor.[20]

The Tavern was sold to Col. B. G. Williams in September of 1912 for the sum of $85,650. In April of 1912, this sale was contested and a resale of Skinner's Tavern was ordered.[21] It appears that Col. Williams was indeed the eventual purchaser. Two years later, the property was purchased from him by Henry Schmulbach for the price of almost $100,000. Col. Williams was then seriously ill and was therefore forced to give up control of the property. Mr. Schmulbach intended to continue Mr. Williams' unique motto for the hotel: "I can't be beat unless you cheat." He also remodeled the facility at this time.[22]

Shortly after the purchase, R. Schmulbach announced that he intended to erect a building on the site of the old frame structure, the "historic" Skinner's Tavern. His intention was to construct a five story brick building, 54 feet by 76 feet, at a cost of $75,000; this may have been the planned east wing of the building. The ground floor was to be occupied by five store rooms, and the four stories above were to be divided into hotel rooms. It was intended for the construction to begin in the summer of 1915,[23] but this addition never occurred. A photograph in the newspaper from 1916 shows the first two sections of the 1903-1904 additions attached to the original frame structure of the "historic" Skinner's Tavern.[24]

Fires once more plagued the building. One occurred on August 7, 1916, in which an incendiary was thought to have been used. It originated on the second floor of the new part of the hotel in the dumb waiter shaft, and spread to the third and first floors; it was confined to the shaft and the dining room by the firemen. The fire was suspicious because it seemed that the alarm came in for the fire almost at the instance the fire began. Also, the dining room and kitchen were not being used at this time, and someone could have easily come in the unlocked stair door and gained access to the kitchen. There was no electric wiring in the shaft that could have started the fire there. In addition, sulphur matches were found on the first floor.[25]

Damage from the fire had not been heavy. The section of the building that had burned was in very bad repair. It was also noted that in the past fifteen years, the Tavern had escaped a half-dozen or more fires, and had probably been on fire more often than any hotel in the city. The building's survival in spite of this was due to the prompt arrival of the firemen throughout the years.[26]

Three months later, a more serious fire occurred. This time, the fire was discovered between the floors of the fourth and fifth stories of the new section of the building. Toilets on each floor, one above the other, made a flue for the flames, which swept up behind the marble from floor to floor; guests had discovered the flames. Damage to the building occurred from the firemen cutting into the walls to extinguish the flames, from the fire and smoke, as well as from the water used to extinguish it. At least five rooms on three different floor were damaged by the fire.²⁷

"Tavern Again on Fire Early This Morning," the headlines read in 1919. This time, the fire was discovered in the frame addition in the rear of the building that housed the hotel kitchen. The

Skinner's Tavern, 104 Cleveland Avenue, c. 1902.
This is the architect's drawing of the completed structure, but the east wing (on the right) that was to replace the wooden section was never constructed.

fire gutted this portion of the building, and then spread to the four-story frame portion of the building, used as quests rooms, in the rear of the modern brick portion facing Cleveland Avenue. The Tavern had been filled with guests that night, and those having rooms in the old wooden part of the building were "badly suffocated with smoke" before they could get sufficiently dressed to make their escape.²⁸

In 1924, the executors of the will of Henry Schmulbach were suing Benjamin G. Williams; the suit was to recover $40,000 and interest which the plaintiff alleged was due from the sale of Skinner's Tavern in 1912. It was said that the case was complicated and had been tried before. It had been in court for a number of years and had been tried several times, but nothing had been settled. The particulars of the case were not given.²⁹

Although the "historic" Skinners Tavern is gone, the 1903 and 1904 additions remain. It is currently owned by the Monongahela Lodge No. 148 Improved B.P.O.E. of the World, and is the oldest hotel building left in Fairmont.

2. Schmulbach Brewing Co., Thomas Transfer; c. 1900. 116-124 Cleveland Avenue

A small group of wood-frame buildings which existed on this site dated from around 1900. From around 1902 to 1912, some of the structures were used for Schmulbach's Brewing Company, according to the Sandborn maps of those years. Later, the site became the home of W. S. Thomas Transfer Company, which was located there at least through the 1930's.

The buildings no longer exist and the site is vacant.

[1] *Fairmont Times*, 7/14/1926, sect. 2, p. 1.
[2] Fleming, p. 13.
[3] *Twentieth Century Edition*, p. 24.
[4] Fleming, p. 13.
[5] *Fairmont Index*, 2/13/1891.
[6] ibid., 1/3/1894.
[7] ibid., 5/16/1894.
[8] *Fairmont Republican*, 4/2/1896.
[9] *Fairmont Free Press*, 12/17/1896.
[10] *Twentieth Century Edition*, p. 33.
[11] *Fairmont Times*, 6/17/1903, p. 2.
[12] ibid.
[13] ibid., 12/12/1903, p. 1.
[14] ibid., 1/19/1904, p. 6.
[15] ibid., 6/17/1903, p. 2.
[16] ibid., 10/22/1908, p. 1.
[17] ibid., 11/21/1908, p. 1.
[18] ibid., 4/3/1909, p. 1.
[19] *Fairmont West Virginian*, 11/2/1911, p. 1.
[20] *Fairmont Times*, 2/19/1912, p. 8.
[21] ibid., 5/29/1913, p. 2.
[22] ibid., 6/7/1915, p. 1.
[23] ibid., 6/18/1915, p. 1.
[24] ibid., 8/22/1916, p. 8.
[25] ibid., 8/8/1916, p. 1.
[26] ibid.
[27] ibid., 11/28/1916, p. 1.
[28] ibid., 8/9/1919, p. 1.
[29] ibid., 3/25/1924, p. 12.

Chapter 10

100 Block Cleveland Avenue, odd numbered buildings

1. Baltimore & Ohio Railroad Passenger Station, c. 1900. Cleveland Avenue

The Sandborn maps of 1892 and 1896 show a passenger station located between the railroad tracks and Cleveland (then Parks) Avenue at the corner of Madison Street. It was a one-story rectangular wood structure located near the street, just to the west of the cable suspension bridge. Adjacent to the passenger station (to the west) was a small freight depot.

The new passenger depot was constructed around 1900. According to the Sandborn map of 1902, the old depot was demolished, as well as a dwelling to the south of it. It was on the site of this dwelling that the new depot was constructed, located between the railroad tracks and the Monongahela River. Because it was set back from Cleveland Avenue, an access walkway over the tracks was constructed to connect the street to the second story of the building; the tracks were directly in front of the first floor of the building. This allowed room for additional tracks to be constructed between the depot and the street. A separate freight depot was also constructed (see below).

Baltimore and Ohio Railroad Passenger Station, 100 block, Cleveland Avenue, c. 1902.

The handsome new passenger station was first occupied on December 20, 1900. "It is safe to state that no body of people ever longed for the completion of a building more than have the 7,000 people in Fairmont who have had such poor accommodations in the past." The two-story building was constructed of hard red brick, had a low-pitched hip roof, and contained about fifteen rooms. When it opened, the top story was used as offices for the telegraphers, train dispatchers, the superintendent, and his chief clerk. The main entrance was near the bridge and the remainder of the room was used for the baggage wagons. All baggage was taken down below by elevator. At the bottom of the stairs was a window where one could see to checking one's baggage. The baggage rooms were very large and commodious. Downstairs was the ticket office with two windows, several waiting rooms, and a fruit stand. A large platform was later built in front of the depot for the passengers waiting for the various trains. The combined cost of both depots was nearly $50,000.[1]

This building no longer exists.

2. Baltimore & Ohio Railroad Freight Station, c. 1900. Cleveland Avenue.

The 1896 Sandborn map shows this as a empty site. When the new passenger station was constructed for Fairmont around 1900 (see above), a new freight station was also constructed. The new freight station was to the west of the passenger station, on Cleveland Avenue at the end of Jefferson Street (the Million Dollar Bridge was not constructed yet, and the street ended here), according to the 1902 Sandborn map. The upstairs rooms in the freight depot were occu-

Cleveland Avenue, 100 block looking east. Skinner's Tavern (left), 104 Cleveland Avenue; Baltimore and Ohio Railroad Freight Station (middle); and Passenger Station (right), c. 1908.

pied by the billing clerks and the company physician. Downstairs was the supervisor's office, the freight offices, and the waiting rooms. The combined costs of both depots was nearly $50,000.[2] When the Million Dollar Bridge on Jefferson Street was completed in 1922, it passed above the freight station.

    This building no longer exists on the site.

---

[1] *Fairmont Free Press,* 12/20/1900, p. 1.
[2] ibid.

Chapter 11
200 Block Cleveland Avenue, even numbered buildings

Note: The other buildings located on this block were generally minor structures or extensions of buildings located on Monroe Street or Adams Street, and are not included in this work.

1. Hart Produce, Fortney Drugs; 1900. 210 Cleveland Avenue

This three-story brick structure was constructed by Mr. John P. Hart for his wholesale produce company. It was completed in March 1900, and had a floor space of 64 by 36 feet.[1] The structure has seven bays. On the roof are three dormer windows, the middle one being the largest; these were originally topped with triangular pediments, which have since been removed.

In the 1920's and 1930's, the structure was occupied by Fortney drugs.

The Union Rescue Mission used the building in the 1940's as a dormitory.[2] The building is still in existence today.

[1] *Twentieth Century Edition*, p. 30.
[2] *Welcome Westinghouse*, sect. 7, p. 5.

Hart Produce, 210 Cleveland Avenue, c. 1902.

Chapter 12

200 Block Cleveland Avenue, odd numbered buildings

1. West Virginia Grocery and Candy Company, Smith-Race Groceries, Stevenson Groceries, Frank's Tire; 1901-02. 209 Cleveland Avenue

The 1902 Sanborn map notes that this structure was "being built." This brick building was 60 feet by 120 feet, and was six stories in the rear and three stories on Cleveland Avenue. The front of the building was divided into three sections with pilasters of brickwork. On the first floor, there were three store front windows; on the second floor, there was one window in each of the three building sections, which were surrounded by decorative brickwork; on the third floor were triple windows in each of the building sections. Above the third floor windows was a line of brick dentils.

The building was constructed by the West Virginia Grocery and Candy Company, and work began on it around May 1901. It was to take the place of their previous quarters on Fairmont Avenue and Second Street, which they had outgrown. The first floor accommodated the shipping department, and railroad cars could be brought up directly to its doors, since the lowest floor was on level with the railroad tracks. A cold storage plant was also constructed on this floor.[1]

The second floor of the new building was for storage of groceries. The third floor contained the offices of the company, as well as the stock of drugs, medicines, and candies. The fourth floor was used for the storage of general merchandise. Half of the fifth floor was partitioned off and utilized for the candy manufacturing department, the other half for the storage of containers for the products. The attic was used for general storage. Two large Otis elevators were installed for the ease of conveying merchandise. The company had expected to occupy their new quarters by February 1, 1902.[2]

The name of the company changed to the Smith-Race

Smith-Race Grocery, 209 Cleveland Avenue, c. 1908.

Grocery Company around 1907.³ By 1918, the building was occupied by the Stevenson Company, for the same purpose of supplying wholesale groceries.

Frank's Tire and Supply Company bought the structure from the Stevenson Company in 1965. On July 29, 1993, the structure, which was almost completely filled with used tires, burned and smoldered for four days. The remains of the building were later demolished.

2. Hose House, 1897. 215 Cleveland Avenue

This lot was purchased from C. J. Corbin in 1897, and a two-story wood frame hose house for the fire department was erected at a cost of $370.⁴ In 1903, the hose house was about to slip into Coal Run Hollow, and the city began looking for a new home for the fire department.⁵ It found a temporary home on Monroe Street, in a frame building in 1902, until the permanent

View of Fairmont from Monongahela River.

station was completed nearby (209- 213 Monroe Street).⁶

This building was replaced with a one-story wood-frame structure that was used for various storage purposes. The building no longer exists, and the site is vacant.

3. Corbin Groceries, Mountain State Candy Co.; c. 1890. 217 Cleveland Avenue

This structure was a three-story warehouse. It was the original location of Corbin Groceries[7] before it built a new building nearby (229-231 Cleveland Avenue). By 1912, it was occupied by Setron's Produce. A fire occurred in the structure on January 15, 1912. It was thought to have been caused by overheated stoves that were used to keep the produce warm in the cold weather.[8]

The Mountain State Candy Company occupied the building in the 1920's. A fire in January of 1923 started in the adjacent building at 227 Cleveland Avenue, and heavily damaged this structure. Although the Mountain State Candy Company was located in it, the building was still owned by the J. C. Corbin Company. The building was practically destroyed, but the firemen managed to save a part of it after a hard struggle.[9] The next day, the building was thought to be a total loss. Although it was valued at $5,000, it was not insured. The walls were still standing, but the floors were all burned out, and it was thought that it could not be repaired.[10]

This building no longer exists on the site.

4. Parks Avenue Hotel, Old Dewey Hotel; c. 1900. 227 Cleveland Avenue

This two story building was listed as the Parks Avenue Hotel on the 1902 Sandborn map. According to the 1906 map, it was used as a cigar factory. The 1912 and 1918 maps list it as a "tenement."

In the 1920's, it was referred to as the old Dewey Hotel. The Dattilo Fruit company acquired the building in 1922, and intended to construct a seven story concrete building on the site for its wholesale fruit business.[11] This did not occur. In 1923, the structure was destroyed by a fire which originated within the structure. At the time, it was occupied by five families, who were able to escape with their lives, but little else.[12]

The building no longer exists, and the site is currently vacant.

5. Corbin & Sons Groceries, c. 1910. 229-231 Cleveland Avenue

The site originally was occupied by a one-story dwelling, according to the 1902 and 1906 Sandborn maps. In 1910, the C. J. Corbin Company had a building constructed on the site to house its wholesale grocery business. It was two stories high on Cleveland Avenue, and went down four more stories to a level even with the B. & O. railroad tracks. This gave it great transportation facilities. The structure was constructed with white brick.[13] It has six bays on the second floor, and various openings on the first floor. All of the openings are segmented arch openings.

During the fire in 1923 at the adjacent Old Dewey Hotel (227 Cleveland Avenue), little damage was done to this building. The workmen of the company fought the fire in this building using their own hose and water from a standpipe to save the building. The thick brick wall of the building and the fire-fighting apparatus inside made the chance of its being damaged very slight.[14]

This building is currently use by the adjacent Jacobs-Hutchinson Hardware Company.

6. Jacobs-Hutchinson Hardware, 1923. 233-235 Cleveland Avenue

The Jacobs-Hutchinson Company acquired this vacant lot from W. M. Fleming in 1923 to construct a new building for its hardware company. It was to be a seven story building, with three stories on Cleveland Avenue.[15] It has six bays with segmented arched windows on the second and third floors, and various openings on the first floor. It is still occupied by this same company.

7. Arch Fleming Feed, Monon Valley Produce, c. 1918. 255-257 Cleveland Avenue

Arch Fleming had a building constructed on this site in 1917. It was a seven-story building, and cost around $40,000. The new building was a grain elevator to handle the supplies of Arch Fleming, who was a local grain dealer. A branch of the B. & O. Railroad was to be constructed up Coal Run Hollow to the new building.[16]

Contractors Wilbur H. Watson and Duke Brand of Barrackville completed the brick work on the building in November of 1917. The spur of the B. & O. Railroad had been completed to the building at this time, giving Mr. Fleming adequate facilities for loading and unloading cars. He also set the building back from Cleveland Avenue to load wagons without interference from the street traffic.[17] In the 1920's, it was used by the Monon Valley Produce Company.

The building no longer exists on the site.

8. Times and Index Building, c. 1900. Cleveland Avenue

This big frame building was about fifty feet square and stood three stories above the street and three stories below, and located approximately 170 feet from the intersection of Adams Street and Cleveland Avenue. It appears to have been constructed around 1900, according to the Sandborn maps. Smith and McKinney had moved their printing and publishing business here from a building on Adams Street, which had grown inadequate in size. This new office was well arranged for a printing office of its time. The street floor housed the publication office of *The Times* and *The Index*. There was plenty of room for job presses and equipment. Some of the composition for the newspaper was done by hand, but there had been some modern typesetting machines on hand as well. Private offices were partitioned off to take care of the editorial force and manager. On the second floor above the street, Col. Smith and Mr. McKinney had their offices, while on the third floor a number of lodges and various orders had their place of meeting.[18]

On March 19, 1903, fire destroyed the structure as well as the printing facilities of the

Fairmont Times Newspaper. [19] The newspaper then moved to 219 Monroe Street. The site has been vacant ever since.

9. Ravine Park, 1921. Cleveland Avenue (Coal Run Hollow)

The Ravine Park Amusement Center was established at this location in 1921. Work began in May of that year to clean up Coal Run Hollow in this area in preparation for establishing a park and playgrounds. The Ravine Amusement Company secured its charter and wanted to have the park running as soon as possible. It was the intention of the directors to construct a giant swimming pool and necessary bath houses, as well as to place hundreds of benches under the trees. A band stand and a pavilion were also planned, along with cinder paths that would wander through the level grounds where grass and flowers were to be planted. Because the park was located in the heart of the city, it was to be open six days per week. It was to be closed on Sundays, except for the swimming pool, for band concerts and for "other affairs which are not objectionable." There was to be no admission charge, thus making it the playground for the people of the city as well as those who came from a distance.[20] In June of that year, a merry-go-round was purchased for Ravine Park for $8,000; comments were that "it will be a beauty."[21]

Another new addition to Ravine Park, especially for those who did not dance, was The Cocoanut Grove. Tables and chairs were installed in place of the benches, and the entire space surrounded by a lattice wall. Scattered around were coconut trees, under which the tables were to be placed. Refreshments were served at the tables.[22] The manager of the park received notice on May 21, 1921 that the Ferris wheel that he had purchased in an Illinois town had been shipped and would be in operation in the park for the 4th of July.[23]

Because of the desire of "autoists" to drive into the park and to the pavilion, a permanent roadway from Locust Avenue was laid out. The "machines" were to be kept to this road and to the parking lot.[24]

For the 4th of July celebration in 1921, Ravine Park had planned some special entertainments. These included a band concert, dancing, a pony ride, and an old fiddlers contest.[25]

The park appears to have fallen into disuse around 1923. The site is used as a city parking lot.

Ravine Park, Times advertisement, June 27, 1922.

[1] *Twentieth Century Edition*, p. 37.
[2] ibid.
[3] *Fairmont Times*, 7/26/1907, supplement p. 3.
[4] *Welcome Westinghouse*, sect. 6, p. 8.
[5] *Fairmont Times*, 5/20/1903, p. 1.
[6] *Welcome Westinghouse*, sect. 6, p. 8.
[7] *Fairmont Index*, 2/13/1891.
[8] *Fairmont Times*, 1/16/1912, p. 1.
[9] ibid., 1/14/1923, p. 1.
[10] ibid., 1/15/1923, p. 1.
[11] ibid., 1/3/1922, p. 6.
[12] ibid., 1/14/1923, p. 1.
[13] ibid., 7/26/1910, p. 2.
[14] ibid., 1/15/1923, p. 1.
[15] ibid., 7/6/1923, p. 1.
[16] ibid., 6/12/1917, p. 2.
[17] ibid., 11/28/1917, sect. 2, p. 2.
[18] *Welcome Westinghouse*, sect. 1, p. 1.
[19] *Fairmont Times*, 3/19/1903, p. 1.
[20] ibid., 5/8/1921, p. 1.
[21] ibid., 6/4/1921, p. 7.
[22] ibid., 6/22/1921, p. 5.
[23] ibid.
[24] ibid.
[25] ibid., 9/4/1921, p. 10.

Chapter 13

300 Block Cleveland Avenue, odd numbered buildings

1. Arnett Residence, Electric Company Offices; c. 1900. 301 Cleveland Avenue

Mr. U. N. Arnett had purchased this property from the trustees of the M. E. Church, the Fairmont Development Company, and the Oliver Jackson heirs; he constructed his two and one half story residence on the site around the year 1900.[1]

When the Federal government was searching for a site for the new Federal Building in 1908, this and the adjoining Manley site (307-311 Cleveland Avenue) were originally chosen for the purpose. The government had decided to proceed with condemnation proceedings because of the high cost of the properties; Mr. Arnett wanted $34,000 for his.[2] This deal fell through, and the new Federal building was eventually located at 321 Monroe Street.

In 1914, the property was purchased from Mrs. U. N. Arnett by the Fairmont Building & Investment Company. They had had an option on the building for several weeks prior to the purchase, and the price was thought to be $40,000. Because it was on the corner of Main (Adams) Street and Barney Street (Cleveland Avenue), it was known as one of the best and most commanding locations in the city. The intent of the purchaser was not known at the time.[3]

The property was leased to the American Legion Post No. 17 in February 1922. It was remodeled for use as their home and club rooms on the second and third floors; the first floor was already leased to the Cass Electric Company. The American Legion was just in its fourth year of existence, to perpetuate the association and memories formed during the soldiers' service to the country during World War I.[4] In 1924, the Legion was relocated so the structure could be remodeled for use of the electric company.[5]

The building no longer exists on the site, and it is used for parking.

2. Manley Residence, 1894; Professional Building, 1916-7. L. C. Holmbe and Frederick Nickerson, architects. 307-311 Cleveland Avenue

Mr. Manley purchased this property in 1884 from Mrs. Jessie Hall, and in 1893 erected a handsome house upon it. This property, along with the adjoining property at 301 Cleveland Avenue, was considered by the Federal government in 1908 as the site for the new Federal Building. Mr. Manley wanted $20,000 for the property, which the government thought was too costly; it wanted to pay no more that $50,000 for the two lots, and the asking price of the two properties came to $54,000.[6] The Federal Building was eventually constructed at 321 Monroe Street.

In 1910, the First M. E. Church considered securing the property from Mr. Manley for construction of a new church; their location at 118-122 Adams Street was too noisy due to the

C. E. Manley residence, 307 Cleveland Avenue, c. 1894.

traffic. However, the "Manley lot" was thought to be too small for the church, and was rejected. Because it also owned a large lot on Fairmont Avenue, this ultimately became the location for their new church structure.[7]

In 1913, the Presbyterian Church purchased the "Manley lot" property from Mr. Manley. They, too, were considering the construction of a new church to replace the one at 301 Jackson Street,[8] but ended up building their new edifice on the site of the existing church. The Presbyterians then sold the lot to the Fairmont Building and Investment Company for the sum of $24,468.93.[9]

With this purchase, the Company owned two lots on Barney Street (Cleveland Avenue): this and the Arnett property. It was the intention of the company to erect a business building on the two lots. L. C. Holmbe and Frederick Nickerson, architects in Clarksburg, had drawn plans for the building, which was to be an eight story structure: four stories would be below the level of the street, and four stories would be above the level of the street. The building would be constructed for business rooms, and there were to be facilities for a moving picture show.[10]

In 1916, the announcement was made that the Fairmont Building and Investment Company was going to construct a modern, four-story fireproof office building, but on the Manley lot only. The exact location of the new South Side bridge had yet to be determined, which limited the construction to the one lot. It was the intent of the company that the building would be used by the professional men of the city; it was thought to be ideal for doctors, dentists, and lawyers, to name a few. The tentative plans were for the structure to be about 60 feet wide and 75 feet long. The upper floors were to be reached by ample elevator facilities and each floor would have approximately 25 rooms. The lower floor was to be arranged for shops and was to contain an arcade wherein all the shops would face.[11]

Two months later, in May of 1916, work on the property began. For several days workers moved the sod from the front of the property and transferred it to the rear of the site, where the Manley house was moved.[12] From the Sandborn map of 1918, one can see that they rotated the front of the house from the east to the south when it was moved to the rear of the site, though this residence now no longer exists.

The contract for the erection of the Professional Business Building was signed on September 28, 1916. Contractor J. L. Crouse, who was completing the new Fairmont State Normal school on Locust Avenue, was awarded the contract. The building was to cost considerably less than $90,000. At this time, it was determined that it would be a five-story structure. The first floor was to house business rooms, and the upper floors were to be offices. Some of the suites were to be constructed to the requirements of the tenants, and others according to the plans of the company erecting the building. It was to be fire-proof in its construction, with steel and reinforced concrete for its structure. The floors were to be concrete and the partitions hollow tile. The exterior was to be faced with brick. It was to be the second largest business block in the city. Construction was expected to be completed in ten months.[13]

The building is a five story, ten-bay, red brick building with simple rectangular windows and a cornice at the roof. Brick quoins extend from the second through fourth floors on the corners. The building did not open with the fanfare that other major structures in Fairmont had. This was probably due to the fact that World War I was raging at this time, and construction materials and workers may have been channeled to the war effort. It was probably fortunate to just have completed it during this time.

The structure is still in use as an office building.

3. Fairmont Dairy, Imperial Ice Cream, Jordan Autos; c. 1908. 337 Cleveland Avenue

The old Yeager building on this site was razed in 1908 to make way for some new structures; at the time, it was considered one of the oldest structures in the city. One of these new structures was the Fairmont Dairy Company's new building.[14] The contract for the construction of the new building on the corner of Jackson Street and Barney Street (Cleveland Avenue) was awarded to W. B. Ice & Brothers of Barrackville.[15] The structure was originally just two stories tall. It is a red brick, seven bay building and is still distinctive because the facade of the building curves around the corner of Cleveland Avenue to Locust Avenue.

By 1918, according to the Sandborn map of that year, the structure was occupied by the Imperial Ice Cream Company. The plant had fifty employees, and there was a need for more because of their thriving business. In 1922, they purchased land on the corner of Fifth Street and Virginia Avenue to erect a new, larger building, and moved out of the building.[16] Some time between 1922 and 1927, the third floor was added.

The building was next leased by the Jordan Fairmont Sales, which used the structure as offices and sales rooms for Jordan cars. It was remodeled to have hardwood floors, a vestibule entrance on Cleveland Avenue, large show windows facing both Cleveland and Locust Avenues, and a smaller show window for accessories facing on Cleveland Avenue. Jordan cars were also serviced here.[17]

The building is still in existence.

Imperial Ice Cream, 337 Cleveland Avenue in 1922.

[1] *Fairmont Times*, 11/16/1908, p. 1.
[2] ibid.
[3] ibid., 5/4/1914, p. 1.
[4] ibid., 2/5/1922, sect. 2, p. 1.
[5] ibid., 3/6/1924, p. 1.
[6] ibid., 11/16/1908, p. 1.
[7] ibid., 2/14/1910, p. 1.
[8] ibid., 2/20/1913, p. 3.
[9] ibid., 8/3/1915, p. 2.
[10] ibid.
[11] ibid., 3/8/1916, sect. 2, p. 7.
[12] ibid., 5/13/1916, p. 4.
[13] ibid., 9/29/1916, p. 1.
[14] ibid., 5/9/1908, p. 1.
[15] ibid., 7/21/1908, p. 1.
[16] ibid., 11/14/1922, p. 10.
[17] ibid., 2/27/1924, p. 7.

Chapter 14

400 Block Cleveland Avenue, odd numbered buildings

Marathon Oil Station, 401-403 Cleveland Avenue, c. 1923. To the left is the National Guard Armory, 8 Locust Avenue; to the right is the Trinity Church, 407 Cleveland Avenue.

1. West Virginia Grocery and Candy, American Steam Laundry, c. 1880; Standard Oil Station, 1922. 401-403 Cleveland Avenue

From 1983 to 1896, the West Virginia Grocery and Candy Company occupied the two and one-half story building at the corner of Barney Street (Cleveland Avenue) and Jackson Street. It was a wood structure with rectangular dormer windows, which protruded from the mansard roof. The building was truncated at the corner of Locust and Cleveland Avenue. Its business consisted of light groceries and confectionery, and was so successful that larger quarters were secured when a three story brick structure on the corner of Fairmont Avenue and Second Street was erected in 1896.[1]

The building was next occupied by the American Steam Laundry, according to the Sandborn map of 1896. Subsequent maps show it was used for storage.

The old candy factory was razed in April 1912. It had been an eye-sore and a fire menace to the community.

In 1922, an automobile service station was constructed on this corner by the Mountain State Oil and Gas Service, distributing Marathon products. This was their first station. Because it was set back from the acute angle of the intersection of Cleveland Avenue and Locust Avenue/Jackson Street, it was thought that Fairmont was fortunate to have such a building on this location, "as it would be dangerous to have another style of construction on that corner."[2]

The building was demolished and the site is vacant.

2. Colored Church, Trinity Church; 1911. 407 Cleveland Avenue

This church was constructed in 1911 to take the place of the original "Colored Church" located at 205 Monroe Street, which after forty years of use was too small and dilapidated. Part of the money for the new church came from the sale of the old building and property on Monroe Street; the price was between $10,000 and $15,000, because the area had become a popular business location in the city.[3] Another source of funds for the new church came from pledges by members of the church, whose sums were characterized as "sacrificial". The rest of the money came from an appeal to the public for "aid in this worthy cause." In the forty years of its existence in Fairmont, the church had never made appeals for money, and asking friends and well-wishers to rally to their support in the campaign did not seem like an unreasonable request.[4] The community responded. Instead of the modest $1,000 that was the original goal of the campaign, a sum of $5,600 was raised for the construction of the new church.[5]

The cornerstone of the church was laid on July 30, 1911. The names of the people who had contributed a dollar or more had their names inscribed on a tablet which was to be placed in the stone. The Meridian Lodge No. 34, A. F. and A. M. was in charge of the cornerstone ceremony, assisted by the lodges in Clarksburg and Morgantown. After the principal sermon, refreshments were served in the Dunbar School.[6] The building was dedicated on October 10, 1911.

The church is a buff-colored brick structure. It is Gothic in style, with its pointed-arch windows and doorways, castle-like towers, and battlements on the edge of the roof. The building has an auditorium that seats 250, and the basement has facilities for a church school, recreation, dining room, and kitchen. The church organ was installed in 1923.[7] It is still used as a church.

---

[1] *Twentieth Century Edition*, p. 37.
[2] *Fairmont Times*, 3/5/1922, p. 14.
[3] ibid., 4/8/1916, p. 1.
[4] ibid., 4/12 1912, p. 1.
[5] ibid., 9/26/1910, p. 6.
[6] ibid., 7/25/1911, p. 1.
[7] *Welcome Westinghouse*, front sect., p. 4.

Part III
Monroe Street

Although Monroe Street lacked the visibility of Adams Street, it provided attractive building sites conveniently located just off of the beaten path in Downtown Fairmont. Due to the severe drop-off to the south, the street was not extended to connect with Cleveland Avenue; it simply curves into Washington Street.

Chapter 15

200 Block Monroe Street, even numbered buildings

1. residence, c. 1905. 200 Monroe Street

This two and one-half story residence first appears on the Sandborn map of 1906; prior to that, it had been a vacant lot. It was used by the Musgraves, owners of the adjacent funeral home at 206 Monroe Street, as their residence during the 1920's. After the adjacent building was used for storage and eventually demolished, this building was the home of the Musgrave Springer Funeral Home. The Bell Telephone Company expanded its building to this lot.

Musgrave Springer Funeral Home, 200 Monroe Street, 1929

2. Musgrave Building, c. 1895. 206 Monroe Street

This was a vacant lot until the first structure appeared on the Sandborn map of 1896. The two-story building's function was listed as the Fairmont Republican Printing, with a lodge room on the second floor. By the 1902 Sandborn map, it was listed as an undertakers establishment, and was the home of the Musgrave Funeral Home for many years.[1] It was eventually demolished, and the Bell Telephone Company extended its facility to this lot.

3. YWCA Building, c. 1890.
210 Monroe Street

The building on this site was originally a residence, which first appeared on the 1892 Sandborn map. In 1921, the house was renovated and an addition was placed on the rear to convert it for use as the YWCA headquarters. The new facility provided a large cafeteria room and kitchen, club rooms, and an auditorium.[2]

The Bell Telephone Company expanded their facility onto this property.

4. Menear residence, c. 1890; Bell Telephone Company, 1916-17.
McKenzie, Voorhees and Gmelin, architects?   214 Monroe Street

The original building on this site was a residence constructed around 1890, known as the Menear home. In January of 1916, it was announced that the Bell Telephone and its "hello girls" would be moving from their offices on the second floor of the Skinner Building (110-114 Adams Street) into a new facility to be constructed on this site. The manager announced that their existing facilities were cramped because their subscribers list was rapidly expanding.[3]

The new building was to be 41 feet wide on Monroe Street and 48 feet deep. It was to be constructed so it could be extended to a maximum depth of 85 feet as the need for space increased. Although it was to be three stories in height, it was designed to be increased to four stories at a future date. Designed by a prominent (though unnamed) architect, it was to have a base of granite topped with gray tapestry brick, and a cornice and coping of gray terra cotta.[4]

The basement of the new building was to include the cable vault, where the underground cables would enter a fire- proof room, from which they would be fed to the upper floors. The emergency generator was to be located there as well, and there was to be emergency lighting throughout the hallways. The first floor was to house a small public space and the commercial offices of the company. The second floor was to house the terminal room where the cables would "fan out" on great steel racks and sorted numerically. The battery room would also be here. The third floor was to house the "brain of the telephone system", the switchboard, as well as the operators' sitting room.[5]

Few flammable materials were to be used in the building. The floorboards were to be eliminated and "battle-ship linoleum" was to be used instead. The windows were steel framed with wire glass for fire protection. The stairway was constructed of re-enforced concrete, and the doors all steel. [6]

The firm of Holbert and Spedden was chosen as the contractor for the construction, and the demolition of the Menear home occurred in March 1916.[7] The excavation for the basement was more complicated, since they had to blast solid rock to begin the foundation and to dig the conduit trench in Hull Alley. During the process, two windows in the adjacent Methodist Protestant Church (216-218 Monroe Street) were damaged. Luckily, the windows were the plain ones in the Sunday school addition, not the decorative stain glass ones. When powder was used

Bell Telephone Company, 214 Monroe Street, 1916.

in blasting, there was no damage to adjacent buildings. It was when they had to use dynamite that the damage occurred. The violent blasts had been jarring all the Monroe Street buildings. The city engineers said it was particularly dangerous for the City Building, "which is undermined and at one time threatened to crack." Rocks from the blasting were being thrown across the street.[8]

By December of 1916, the building was almost complete, at a cost of $40,000 for the building and an additional $51,000 for the equipment. The building was "absolutely fire proof throughout." In addition to the aforementioned construction, a fire escape was constructed on the rear of the building. The name "Bell Telephone" extended from the second story to the roof parapet in letters of white tile set in the brick.[9]

The telephone operators said good-bye to their old offices in the Skinner Building (110-114 Adams Street) on May 26, 1917, and the "cut over" of the new lines was made to the new equipment. There were no formal ceremonies, and the cutover was not even noticed by the subscribers. The new facility was occupied on May 27, 1917.[10]

The completed structure was made of beige brick and was three stories tall. On the two upper floors were five bays of rectangular windows. The first floor had a large expanse of glass in the center, a Roman-arched doorway to the right, and a smaller window to the left. There was a stone course between the first floor and the second floor, and a simple stone cornice near the roof line. The side along Hull Alley had eight bays of rectangular windows on all three floors. There is a granite base around the entire structure.

The first addition to the building was in 1925. W. H. Spedden was contracted for the three story addition to the rear of the building, which was planned from its inception. It was reported that the addition was to cost $80,000. The plans were made by the architecture firm of McKenzie, Voorhees and Gmelin of New York City,[11] who may also have been the original architects of the facility. By mid-March, the excavation for the work was almost complete.[12]

The Bell Telephone Company eventually expanded its operations with modern additions to take the frontage on Monroe Street from its original building to the corner of Washington

Street. The original building looks much as it did when it opened, with some moderate remodeling of the front of the first floor. It is still use by the telephone company.

5. Methodist Protestant Temple, 1896-7
J. Charles Fulton, architect. 216-218 Monroe Street

The original location of the Methodist Protestant Church was at 418 Quincy Street; in January of 1893, it was announced that a new church was to be constructed.[13] The chosen location had a one-story residence on it, which, according to the Sandborn map, had been built prior to 1884. Ground was broken in April of 1896 for the excavations of the foundation of the new church.[14] By May of the same year, work on the foundations of the building on Monroe Street was "rushing to completion."[15]

For a while, the fire bell for the nearby Fire Department had been located at the "new" Methodist Protestant Church. "The fire company requests us" (the newspaper) "to thank the church Committee for the use of their belfry for a time. Our readers should remember that the location of the bell has been changed that there may be no awkward waits, should a fire occur."[16]

The church was dedicated on August 8, 1897. Gathering at their old "church on the hill," the congregation had among them at least ten persons who were present at the dedication of the old church. "Fully three hundred and fifty men, women, and children walked in a body to 'The People's Temple', Monroe street..." It was the largest church in the city when constructed, and it was filled to capacity for the dedication.[17]

The church was designed by Mr. J. Charles Fulton of Uniontown, Pennsylvania, who blended Norman and Gothic architecture for the building. The superstructure stands one hundred and fifteen feet in depth and seventy-five feet in width. The main auditorium is octagonal in shape and seats four hundred and fifty. The lecture room and classrooms surrounding it can seat an additional four hundred persons. The auditorium also has a beautiful pipe organ. In the basement was the steam heating plant.[18]

The front of the building was constructed of Cleveland blue stone and Zanesville pressed brick, while the body of the building was made of the same stone and red stock brick. The sixteen foot square bell tower on the corner rises one hundred feet, with the pastor's study on the opposite side. The two are connected by a loggia with cut stone arches and columns, while the floor is blue Cleveland flagstone. The ceiling is yellow pine. The rear part of the building was arranged for "Sabbath school" and social purposes, and was as large as the main auditorium. The roof of the building was slate, requiring almost one hundred squares of the material.[19]

The doors from the loggia were heavy oak doors, while the pews in the auditorium were red oak. The hardware throughout the building, as well as the "electric chandelier", was antique copper. The pipe organ (built by the Salem Pipe Organ Company of Salem, Ohio) and the choir loft were paneled in red oak, as was the ceiling. The frescoing was done by Bryant Brothers of Pittsburgh and Columbus.[20]

One of the most noteworthy items is the building's stain glass windows. They were made of the best opalescent glass by S. S. Marshall and Brothers of Allegheny, Pennsylvania. Ten of them are portrait windows of heavy drapery glass. There are two large Roman windows measuring nine feet by fifteen feet. The one on Monroe Street, "The Ascension," was donated by Thomas W. Fleming and his brothers and sisters in memory of their father, Allison Fleming. The other, on Hull alley, is "The Nativity," and was placed by J. F. Barnes in honor of his parents and other members of his family.[21]

There were four smaller Roman windows opening onto the loggia: "Ascension" donated by the family of Matthew Fleming, "The Resurrection" donated by the family of Marshall Fleming, "Gethsemane" donated by the family of John Fleming, and "The Annunciation" donated by the King's Daughters. There were many other stain glass windows, all donated to the memory of departed members of the church.[22]

The total cost of the lot, building, and furnishings was $27,000, with Mr. M. L. Fleming being the largest single contributor of $1,000.[23] The mortgage was burned in July of 1903, and the ashes were placed in a bottle and kept in the pastor's study.[24]

The year 1903 was the diamond jubilee year for the church, marking the 75th anniversary of the church in the city. It was marked with a week long program of events.[25]

The building was constantly maintained. In 1907, the interior of the auditorium was redecorated, with olive and colonial colors used for the main background, and decorations of gold and crimson. The Sunday school rooms were also painted.[26] The auditorium was repaired and redecorated in 1909 as well.[27] The ceiling and the lighting were changed in 1911.[28]

By 1923, there were discussions of selling the church and building a new church in a different location. It was rumored that a fine price was offered for the property. Its

Methodist Protestant Temple, 216-218 Monroe Street.

location in the heart of the business sector was so noisy that the services were interrupted constantly by traffic. It was also seen as too small for the congregation, and a larger auditorium was needed.[29]

Instead of selling the building, it was renovated and an addition was constructed in 1925. The two-story high addition was added to the Sunday school section, and housed a large social hall on the first floor; sixteen new classrooms and a church parlor were located on the second floor. The auditorium as also completely redecorated and provided with a new lighting system. The W. H. Spedden company was in charge of the work. Until the work was completed, church services were held temporarily in the Masonic Temple (320 Jefferson Street).[30]

The centennial celebration of the church occurred in 1929. During the celebration, relics of the church were used or displayed. Several historic chairs were used to seat the dignitaries on the rostrum; they had been owned by Governor Francis H. Pierpont, John J. Moore, Allison Fleming, and Benoni Fleming. The evening's scripture lesson was read from a Bible that had belonged to Thomas Barnes, who was the founder of the church in this city; and another old Bible that had been owned by John Moor was also on display. The first organ of the church was used in this service as well.[31]

The building is still in use as a church.

---

[1] *Welcome Westinghouse,* sect. 4, p. 8.
[2] *Fairmont Times,* 10/2/1921, p. 2.
[3] ibid., 1/7/1916, p. 1.
[4] ibid.
[5] ibid.
[6] ibid.
[7] ibid., 3/17/1916, p. 1.
[8] ibid., 4/29/1916, p. 1.
[9] ibid., 12/30/1916, p. 1.
[10] ibid., 5/25/1917, p. 1.
[11] ibid., 2/19/1925, p. 7.
[12] ibid., 3/16/1925, p. 3.
[13] *Fairmont Free Press,* 1/6/1893.
[14] *Fairmont Republican,* 4/23/1896.
[15] ibid., 5/14/1896.
[16] *Fairmont Index,* 5/28/1897.
[17] ibid., 8/10/1897, p. 1.
[18] ibid.
[19] *Fairmont Free Press,* 2/24/1898.
[20] ibid.
[21] ibid.
[22] ibid.
[23] ibid.
[24] *Fairmont Times,* 7/13/1903, p. 1.
[25] *Fairmont Free Press,* 11/26/1903, p. 1.
[26] *Fairmont Times,* 3/2/1907, p. 2.
[27] ibid., 11/30/1909, p. 1.
[28] *Fairmont West Virginian,* 10/5/1911, p. 1.
[29] *Fairmont Times,* 10/5/1923, p. 1.
[30] ibid., 7/23/1925, p. 6.
[31] ibid., 9/7/1929, p. 1.

Chapter 16

200 Block Monroe Street, odd numbered buildings

1. Conoway's Feed Store, c. 1902. 201 Monroe Street

The 1902 Sandborn map noted this building as "foundation partly up," to be an agricultural implement warehouse. Because of the shape of the land, it is three stories on Monroe Street, and five stories on Parks (Cleveland) Avenue. It is a four bay, beige brick and stone building, with a first floor store front. There is a corbeled brick cornice near the roof. Although it had been a feed store through the 1910's, it was used as a furniture warehouse in the 1920's. It has reverted back to its original use, and is still functioning as a feed store today.

2. Methodist Episcopal Church, Colored; 1865. 205 Monroe Street

The building in which the M. E. Church, Colored was originally located was erected in 1865, and it was known as Jones Chapel. It was a little one story, one-room frame structure.[1] In 1883, the building and lot are valued at $1,000.[2] The church was founded here in Fairmont in 1869.[3] It was noted that the building was papered and painted, and much improved in appearance in 1895.[4] The structure jutted out into the street where Monroe and Washington Streets converge.

By 1909, the structure was beginning to show its age and was too small for the congregation. The location on Monroe Street had become valuable with the addition of several multistory buildings around it, and the building and lot were for sale. Plans for a new edifice were then incomplete.[5]

In the spring of 1910, the congregation was in negotiation for the sale of their church property on Monroe Street and to purchase a lot at the intersection of Barney Street (Cleveland Avenue) and Cherry Avenue to erect and furnish a modern church. The amount offered for their property was enough to cover the cost of the larger lot, and they had some additional funds at hand for the construction. However, they launched a campaign to raise $1,000 in thirty days to begin building operations. All of the church members had pledged sums, and then they appealed to the public in general to help them with this endeavor. "In the forty years of the existence of this church in Fairmont, it has never made appeals for money to any great extent, for the reason that it has never attempted anything of large proportions. The modest structure in which the congregation now worships was erected of very small cost and has stood for forty years with very little improvement. In coming forward then for the first time in the history of Modern Fairmont and asking friends and well-wishers to rally to its support in this campaign, the pastor and people feel that they are not making unreasonable requests and that when they call soliciting contributions they will find that they have not 'worn out their welcome'."[6]

Corner of Washington and Monroe Streets in 1923.

Within five months, the congregation had raised $5,600 for the construction of their new facility. It was a joyful day for the people, and they were given much credit for the sacrifices and spirit shown in the endeavor.[7] They moved into their new church at 407 Cleveland Avenue in 1911.

The old building was purchased by the James Specialty Company and used for their business until 1916. At that point in time, the property was purchased by Clarence D. Robinson and L. M. Davis for the sum of between $10,000 and $15,000. The new owners were planning to erect a large business building on the site, possibly in the spring.[8] This did not occur.

A new auto supply store, Brooks Specialty Company, opened at the location in March 1919.[9] It was used throughout the 1930's by automotive stores.

This building is no longer in existence.

3. Troy Steam Laundry, c. 1902. 207 Monroe Street

The Sandborn map of 1902 notes that the building on this site was under construction for the Troy Steam Laundry. The completed building consisted of a two-story section adjacent to the church, and a one-story section on the opposite side. The plant had a twenty horsepower steam engine, and a fifty- foot tall chimney. It operated at this location through the 1920's.

In January of 1929, Fairmont was hit by a windstorm. The Troy Laundry smokestack fell, with one section crashing into the walkway leading to the Police Station.[10]

The building no longer exists, and the site is used for parking for the adjacent police department.

4. Chisler residence, c. 1825;
City Building (Fire Station, City Hall, Jail), 1910-1916.
Walter Eliason, architect (original section);
Andrew C. Lyons, architect (addition)? 211-215 Monroe Street

The site of the City Building was said to have been the opening for the mine that in the olden days honeycombed under Monroe and Adams Streets.[11]

The first hue and cry for a new city building went up in 1903. At that time, the fire department and city jail, which were on Parks (Cleveland) Avenue, were "in great danger of tumbling into the Coal Run Hollow." The hose house was at least six inches off of its foundation in one day, had moved nearly six inches the night before, and three inches the night before that. The fire department was seeking a temporary home on Jackson Street, but it became evident that the city needed to build a hose house, a city lockup, and general city hall. Two locations on Monroe Street were considered, one where the colored M. E. Church stood (205 Monroe Street), and the other near the Times office (219 Monroe Street).[12]

Sam R. Nuzum offered to sell his lot on Monroe Street between the Troy Laundry (207 Monroe Street) and the Times Building (219 Monroe Street) to the City for $200 per foot; he owned approximately fifty feet. He also offered to allow the city to erect a temporary hose house on this lot free from rent.[13]

This second offer was snapped up, and work on constructing the temporary home of the fire department commenced the next day. The Chisler house on the lot, noted as being one of the oldest in the city, was razed. Said to be built in 1825, it was constructed of logs cut from the forests along Main (Adams) Street, and hewn with the old-fashioned broadax; there was no trace of saw or nails having been used the houses' construction.[14]

A number of citizens appealed to the fire committee at this time to build the temporary hose house large enough to accommodate a hook and ladder outfit in the future. A fire had recently occurred in the new six-story Cunningham Building (308-312 Jefferson Street) in 1902, which had almost destroyed it; the existing fire equipment was inadequate to fight the fire in this tall structure. Because of the construction of several tall buildings in the city, the acquisition of modern fire-fighting equipment was seen as necessary to provide fire protection and to help reduce fire insurance rates.[15]

The original plan for relocating the lock up cage for the city jail was to move it from the old building in its entirety. It was to be hauled up and placed on the lot, and the building constructed around it.[16] This caused much controversy. As the police were readying for the move, the residents claimed that too much cussing and raging from drunken prisoners would be heard on Monroe Street.[17]

The City was very sneaky about moving the old city jail to Monroe Street. Because of the outcry from the citizen when it was proposed, it was kept a "profound" secret until it occurred. The dirty old cages were to be placed in a little frame building which had been used for electric light supplies. It was only fifteen feet square, and the walls were thin. "All the curses and foul language of all the drunks can be plainly heard through the walls by the people of the colored church, the girls of the Troy laundry, the citizens' families living near, and the louder ravings and swearing will be audible as far away as the Protestant Temple."[18] All the protests were to no avail, however. Nothing stands in the path of progress.

The temporary fire department building (or "hose house") was completed in August 1903. It was large enough to accommodate a new, modern hook and ladder wagon, which was to arrive in early October of that year; and preparations were being made for additional stalls for the two extra horses needed to pull it. [19]

With the temporary home of the fire department and jail in place, the pressing need for a new city building wanned. It was not until three years later, in January of 1906, that it was proposed to buy the site from Mr. Nuzum. The building committee had looked at the site on January 27, 1906, as well as another location, a 45 foot by 120 foot lot on Madison Street near the Kenyon Hotel.[20]

In February 1906, it was decided to put to the people the question of whether the city would provide a sum of money sufficient to cover the expenditure of purchasing a site for a city building, and possibly a sum sufficient to erect a city building. This was seen as necessary, due to an act of the Legislature limiting the indebtedness of cities in the state. The city had already reached the limit of the lawful amount of indebtedness, and the amount to be expended for the site and building construction would be considerably over the limit.[21]

The lot that was chosen was the lot offered long ago by Mr. Nuzum. He owned a 40 foot by 80 foot lot, which he offered to the city for $12,000; two other smaller lots, which were seen as necessary for the construction of the building, brought the total for the property to $21,000.[22] The lots were purchased on March 30, 1906, after a vote of the peopled ratifying the proposed purchase by a three-fifths margin.[23]

The beginning of construction stalled. Although it was noted in April 1906 that the city prisoners would break up the stone on the Monroe Street lot for the new city building, [24] no other real progress occurred for several years. Prisoners were relocated to the rear of the fire station on Monroe Street in a house that had been rented to the proprietors of the Marietta Hotel (128-130 Adams Street).[25] In February 1907, the city made another payment on the site that they had purchased from Sam Nuzum, stating that the city jail may be erected "soon."[26]

The year 1909 saw the actual beginning of the saga of the construction of the City Building. City officials moved into their temporary quarters in the Jacobs Building (316 Monroe Street)[27] and the old jail was razed.[28] The contractor for the demolition, Mr. Huffman, was seriously hurt when the jail porch collapsed on him while he was working on it.[29]

The contract for the foundations of the new jail was awarded to Mr. Howell of Clarksburg.[30] By June of 1910, the new city building was "under advisement." The fire committee obtained estimates of the cost of the new building for the fire department and the city offices.[31] By August of that same year, Mr. Walter Eliason was working on plans for the 72 foot by 60 foot building which was to be two stories in height. The building was to be large enough to accommodate all the city offices and the city jail. After an inspection of the temporary quarters, it was stated that a new building would have to be erected or a small fortune spent in repairs of the existing facilities.[32]

The plans for the new city building were presented to the City Council at their meeting on August 3, 1910. The structure was to be two stories tall, but built so it could be made five stories tall if ever needed. It was to house the central fire station, the city jail with two rooms (one for men and one for women), all the city offices, the council chamber, and the police court room. A concrete vault for the city books and adequate room for all the offices needed by the city for the next twenty years was also to be provided. The estimate of the cost of the building was from $7,300 to $9,500. The "considering of the plans" for the new building was delayed until the next meeting.[33]

At the next meeting, the City Council approved $5,000 for the start of the construction of the new city building. Although the fire committee had asked for about $9,000 for the building, the council felt unable to appropriate that total amount; but thought it could afford to set aside $5,000, and the remainder the next year, with the understanding that the building was to be erected in two sections. One section was to contain the city offices and the jail, while the other was to house the firemen. Since both the jail and the fire station were in bad condition, it was a hard decision which to construct first.[34]

One wall of the new building was constructed immediately. In December of 1910, Mr. Hayes was constructing his bowling alley on the adjacent site (217 Monroe Street); he offered to split the cost of the party wall with the city. In essence, each party would pay the cost of nine inches of the eighteen inch wall. It was an offer that the city could not and did not pass up.[35]

In November of 1911, the fire department was moved into temporary quarters in the Deveny garage in the back of the Marietta Hotel (132 Adams Street) until the completion of the new Central Fire station, which was to be finished within three or four months. A sliding pole was installed from the sleeping quarters to the ground floor and stalls for the horses (to pull the fire wagons) were built at one side of the building.[36]

Work on the construction of the new building began in earnest in December of 1911. The first floor and side walls had been finished, and the three massive steel girders were in place for the erection of the second floor. The front of the building was to be "very pretty," with two large doors for the fire wagons to pass out, while on either side were the entrance doors. Above the two doors is a large stone bearing the inscription "Fire Station." A committee was appointed by the city council to look into the possibility of constructing the third story on the building, and this was added to the building at a cost of $2,000. The height was thought to contribute greatly to the appearance of the building, and was to be used as a public or town hall.[37]

Later that month, work was suspended on the city building due to the cold weather. Although the first floor was completed and the second floor laid, the brick work could not continue. However, the work was to be "hurried along."[38]

While unloading brick for the new building in January, a fireman suddenly died.[39] Work was resumed on the city building in late January of 1912. The brick masons were working on the third and last story of the building. It was anticipated that the city offices would soon be moved from the Jacobs Building (316 Monroe Street), as well as the fire department from the Deveny garage.[40] They were rushing the work on the city building in February. The brick work was done, and the roof was being installed.[41]

Even before the building was completed, plans were presented to the city council for the addition to the new building which would house the jail. It was proposed to be a two-story building with the intent of eventually being three stories. On the first floor of the building was to be the offices of the tax collector and the cages for the men prisoners. On the second floor, it was proposed to house the offices of the city clerk and the cages for the women prisoners. The proposed cost was $5,000 for the building, but no action was taken on the proposal at the meeting.[42]

By August of 1912, the city offices and the police department were located in the new city building. From a photograph in the newspaper at that time, one can see that the north section of the present-day building had been completed. This included the two "wagon" doors as well as two passenger doors, one on either side of the three-story building. It was decided shortly thereafter that the new jail was to be constructed beside of it.[43] This three-story addition added three bays on the south side of the building.

The preparatory work for the foundation of the new city jail was begun in October of 1912. The site was cleared for the new building that was to house the police headquarters, police court room and the cells for the women and men prisoners. It was to be a modern and up to date city jail.[44] The excavations began around October 16, 1912 for the three-story building which was to be similar to the adjacent city building.[45] After these preliminary decisions, there was no action on the addition for two years.

Progress came to Fairmont's fire department when, in July 1914, the city bought a much-needed motor driven fire truck.[46] At this time, too, work was renewed on the city jail. The first thing that was done was to tear away the foundation that had been laid for several years (since 1912). When it had been laid, it was the original plan to erect the addition to the city hall on a level with Monroe street, making room on the first floor for the accommodation of the city prisoners. Since that time, it had been deemed advisable by the commissioners to excavate down to a level with Parks (Cleveland) Avenue, changing the quarters for the jail to this location, making the entrance from Parks (Cleveland) Avenue instead of Monroe Street. To do this, it was necessary to put in a new foundation. The plans for the entire addition to the city building were being drawn by Architect Andrew C. Lyons.[47]

The actual work on the addition to the city building began on April 7, 1915. The new section, which was being "rushed to completion," was to contain five stories on Parks (Cleveland) Avenue and three on Monroe Street. The first floor on Parks (Cleveland) Avenue was to contain the city's plumbing shop and was to house the employees of the water department, their tools, and equipment. The second floor was to contain the city jail.[48]

The first floor of the addition on Monroe Street was to contain the offices of the city collector in front and the second and third floors were to contain offices for the use of the various departments of the city. The new building was of brick and stone, with the city constructing most of the building itself.⁴⁹ It matched the original section of the building so it is almost impossible to distinguish it as two parts.

Within two weeks, the masons were busy on the site. The first floor of the building on Parks (Cleveland) Avenue was to be stone, and the city commissioners selected a buff-colored pressed rough brick for the rest of that elevation. The front elevation on Monroe Street was to be the same red brick as the original section of the building. The addition was to be almost as large as the original section, and was to provided badly needed space for the city.⁵⁰

By September of that year, it was announced that the addition was to be completed by December 1, 1915. The annex was to be called the "City Building" and was to be distinct from the original section, which was to be called the "Fire Department." With the exception of the offices behind the hallway on the second floor and the public auditorium on the third floor, the whole building was to be for the Central Fire Company.⁵¹

The entrance to the City Building was on the first floor. The office at the front was the business department, and the police department was located to the rear. The county commissioners offices were on the second floor of the annex. A public hall was located on the third floor, with an outside stairway to reach it; the auditorium was to be used for lectures, entertainments, or social affairs.⁵²

After the City Building was completed in December 1915, the fire department remodeled the rooms that had been previously occupied by the police department. The partitions of the small offices were removed to create a large room, and the building was painted as well.⁵³ Work on the jail portion of the building must have been halted for the winter, and was resumed in April 1916.⁵⁴ The jail portion was expected to be completed in June 1916. Described as "pala-

Fairmont Fire Department (temporary), 211-215 Monroe Street, c. 1908.

tial," the commissioners planned to have a formal opening of the jail; once prisoners were admitted, it would be locked up tight, so this would be the public's only chance to see it.[55]

On August 16, 1916, it was announced that, with the completion of the jail, the city building was at last completed. At that time, it was said to have been designed by W. S. Mayers, consulting engineer, who also supervised the construction.[56] It took six years to complete.

Above: City Building (Fire Station, City Hall, Jail), 211-215 Monroe Street, c. 1919.
Right: City Building, rear of 211-215 Monroe Street on Cleveland Avenue, c. 1919.

During World War I, the third floor of the city building was rented to the Red Cross. There had been a great many people in attendance at the work meetings since the relations between Germany and the United States had been broken off. The women were making garments, rolling bandages, and preparing other necessary equipment to give aid and comfort to the wounded on the battlefields.[57] After the war, the third floor was used as the gymnasium for the YWCA, which was located across the street.[58]

The building is still used by the Fire Department, although most of the other city functions have relocated to the Harper-Meredith Building (200 Jackson Street).

5. Hays Building, Majestic Building; c. 1910, 1912. 217 Monroe Street

A small one-story warehouse appeared on this site on the 1906 Sandborn map, where there had been just a vacant lot on previous maps. Mr. J. Hays (also spelled "Hayes") constructed a large-scale building on this site beginning in 1910. The brick building was originally two stories tall; the first story was ninety feet long and housed bowling alleys. The second story was eighty feet long and was rented by the Moose Lodge. The City of Fairmont took advantage of the offer of Mr. Hayes to split the cost of a party wall between the proposed structures on the sites, by each paying for nine inches of the eighteen inch wall; the City was constructing the City Building on the adjoining lot to the south.[59]

By January of 1911, the bowling alleys were being "pushed to completion," and plans were in the works for the grand opening of "four of the finest alleys in the State." It was to be the biggest opening night that had ever been offered in Fairmont. The entry fee was one dollar, but the first prize was a silver loving cup (which had been on display in the window of Mr. Wise's store on the corner of Adams and Monroe Streets). Second, third, and fourth prizes were cash prizes, and for the single high roll the prize was a cut glass water set. Mr. Hayes also planned for bowling for the ladies, and intended to set aside Tuesday and Friday afternoons for their use.[60] The opening occurred on February 11, 1911.[61]

Mr. Hayes was already planning to greatly enlarge and remodel the building by July 1912. He had purchased the land extending in the rear of the building to Parks (Cleveland) Avenue, and proposed to extend the building to it. The addition was five stories high on Parks (Cleveland) Avenue, and three stories on Monroe Street; the original two-story front was taken out of the building and a new front similar to the fire department was installed. The new addition was to house apartments. An old stable on Parks (Cleveland) Avenue was razed to make room for it.[62]

The new, improved Hayes Building was opened in February 1913. The four bay brick structure had a store front on the first floor, rectangular windows on the second floor, and Roman arched windows with keystones on the third floor. A bracketed cornice supported a small shed roof, which was topped with a brick arcade, to make the building as tall as the adjacent fire department. An inlaid stone, inscribed with "A. J. Hays," is located between the second and third floor.

The original four alleys had been closed for several months while the work was being done to the structure. The length of the Monroe Street floor increase, allowing the alleys to be moved back. This gave plenty of room in the front of the building for seats for spectators. The new alleys were of the latest design, with complete regulation fixtures and a modern, up-to-date bowling parlor in operation.[63]

By 1919, the bowling alley was gone, and the building was converted to business use. In August of 1919, the Union Store opened at this location. The store only carried suits, for both men and women. Mr. M. Levine of New York was the manager of the store. Souvenirs were given to all who attended the opening.[64]

Hays Building, 217 Monroe Street, c. 1920.

In 1924, the Standard Building and Loan Association opened its doors in the Hayes building, in the room formerly occupied by the New Palace Market. This "commodious room centrally located" was thought to be an ideal location for the financial institution.[65]

By the 1920's, the building was referred to as the Majestic Building in city directories, and housed offices, as well as the American Red Cross at one time.

The building is undergoing renovations.

6. Jacobs-Hutchinson Hardware, Times-Index Printing Company; 1901. Andrew C. Lyons, architect. 219 Monroe Street

This site had been an empty lot until The Jacobs-Hutchinson Hardware Company constructed the building on the site in 1901. Andrew C. Lyons was the architect, as noted in a drawing of the building. The company had been doing business in the Hall Block (132 Adams Street) until its successful operation outgrew the location. They completed their three-story brick building just ninety days after they had acquired title to the ground.[66] The structure was a three-bay brick building. Openings on the first and second floor were rectangular, but the third floor windows were Roman arched openings with brick crossettes creating "voussoirs." Above the third floor windows was a sign for the Jacobs-Hutchinson Hardware Company, and above that was a bracketed cornice with a rectangular pediment, inscribed with the date 1901. Finials were also placed on the roof.

The Jacobs-Hutchinson Hardware company remained here for only two years, until they

Jacobs-Hutchinson Hardware Company, 219 Monroe Street, c. 1902.

moved into the new Jacobs-Hutchinson Block (201-207 Adams Street) in 1903. After their building on Cleveland Avenue burned on March 19, 1903, the *Fairmont Times* and *Index* Printing Company found its new home in this building.[67] Originally renting the premises, the company purchased the building from C. E. Smith, Earl Smith, and their mother Mrs. M. V. Smith, in 1921. The firm had been contemplating the construction of a new newspaper building, but the cost was prohibitive. Therefore, they abandoned the idea and instead purchased the building they had rented for eighteen years. The location was ideal, "located but a step from Main Street." Soon after the time of purchase, they renovated and rearranged the interior of the structure, and added new, modern equipment.[68] The newspaper remained here until 1926, when *The Times* and *The West Virginian* merged and moved into the Old Normal School Building (401-407 Quincy Street).

This building was later converted to commercial use, though it is currently vacant.

7. Sample Building, 1900. 221 Monroe Street

The *Fairmont Free Press* and Fairmont Printing Company moved into the Sample Building when it was completed in 1900.[69] Originally, it was a three story, three bay beige brick structure; a pediment above the bracketed cornice at the roof line included the words "Sample 1900". Although the windows on the second floor were rectangular, those on the third and first floors were Roman arched windows. In 1914, the *West Virginian* newspaper moved into the Sample Building, where it remained until 1918, when it moved to the Old Normal School Building on Quincy Street.[70]

The structure was used after that time for commercial endeavors. The See Denham First Company, a purveyor of paints, papers, furniture, and furnishings for the home, moved into the structure and had its opening in March 1919.[71] In 1923, Ice and Hardesty's shoe store was in the location.[72]

Sometime between 1918 (as seen on the Sandborn map of that year) and 1924, a fourth story was added to the building. This addition eliminated the "Sample 1900" pediment above the roof line. Although the brick of the additional floor is slightly different in color, another row of Roman arched windows was added. A bracketed cornice remains at the roof line, and may be the "recycled" original.

The Knights of Columbus, leaving their previous headquarters above the Crane Drug Store (322 Adams Street), leased the three upper floors of the building, with the shoe store still occupying the first floor. The K. of C. converted the third floor to a large rest and reading room, with provisions for cards, pool and other amusements. The fourth floor was remodeled to house a large lodge room, also be used for social events. The Lodge intended to rent the second floor for office purposes.[73]

In February 1925, it was announced that the Elks would be moving into the second floor of the Sample Building. The lease on their quarters in the Deveny Building (128-130 Adams Street) expired on February 28. This was temporary quarters until their new facility at 421 Adams Street was completed. The Elks used the second floor for their club rooms, and made arrangements with the Knights of Columbus to use the fourth floor lodge room.[74]

"The local herd of Elks huddled in new pastures yesterday," as they met for the first time in their temporary quarters. The rooms were a bit small, but those in charge of financing the new building were pleased over the fact. They believed that the membership would be more apt to demand more room and to advance their money to secure a larger facility if the temporary facility was a bit crowded, thus facilitating the construction of the new home.[75] The building is currently used for offices.

Sample Building, 221 Monroe Street, 1914.

[1] *Fairmont Times*, 9/26/1910, p. 6.
[2] *Hardesty's Historical and Geographical Encyclopedia*, p. 310.
[3] *Fairmont Times*, 7/31/1911, p. 4.
[4] *Fairmont Republican*, 7/11/1895.
[5] *Fairmont Times*, 12/31/1909, p. 4.
[6] ibid., 4/12/1910, p. 1.
[7] ibid., 9/26/1910, p. 6.
[8] ibid., 4/8/1916, p. 1.
[9] ibid., 3/9/1919, p. 4.
[10] ibid., 1/7/1929, p. 1.
[11] ibid., 7/13/1924, sect. 2, p. 1.
[12] ibid., 5/20/1903, p. 1.
[13] ibid., 5/21/1903, p. 5.
[14] ibid., 5/22/1903, p. 1.
[15] ibid.
[16] ibid.
[17] ibid., 8/4/1903, p. 1.
[18] ibid., 11/3/1903, p. 1.
[19] ibid., 8/28/1903, p. 7.
[20] ibid., 1/27/1906, p. 2.
[21] ibid., 2/28/1906, p. 1.
[22] ibid.
[23] ibid., 3/31/1906, p. 1.
[24] ibid., 4/18/1906, p. 1.
[25] ibid., 11/8/1906, p. 5.
[26] ibid., 2/13/1907, p. 2.
[27] ibid., 2/2/1909, p. 1.
[28] ibid., 8/31/1909, p. 1.
[29] ibid., 9/6/1909, p. 1.
[30] ibid., 9/20/1909, p. 1.
[31] ibid., 6/8/1910, p. 1.
[32] ibid., 8/2/1910, p. 5.
[33] ibid., 8/4/1910, p. 1.
[34] ibid., 8/10/1910, p. 3.
[35] ibid., 12/14/1910, p. 6.
[36] ibid., 11/17/1911, p. 1.
[37] ibid., 12/22/1911, p. 1.
[38] *Fairmont West Virginian*, 12/29/1911, p. 8.
[39] *Fairmont Times*, 1/6/1912, p. 1.
[40] ibid., 1/24/1912, p. 8.
[41] ibid., 2/21/1912, p. 8.
[42] ibid., 6/19/1912, p. 8.
[43] ibid., 8/22/1912, p. 2.
[44] ibid., 10/12/1912, p. 2.
[45] ibid., 10/16/1912, p. 2.
[46] ibid., 7/21/1914, p. 2.
[47] ibid., 7/28/1914, p. 8.
[48] ibid., 4/8/1915, p. 7.
[49] ibid.
[50] ibid., 4/26/1915, p. 3.
[51] ibid., 9/30/1915, p. 2.
[52] ibid.
[53] ibid., 12/18/1915, sect. 2, p. 1.
[54] ibid., 4/12/1916, p. 5.
[55] ibid., 5/13/1916, p. 4.

[56] ibid., 8/16/1916, p. 8.
[57] ibid., 2/10/1917, p. 3.
[58] ibid., 9/22/1922, p. 8.
[59] ibid., 12/14/1910, p. 6.
[60] ibid., 1/26/1911, p. 6.
[61] ibid., 2/11/1911, p. 5.
[62] ibid., 7/2/1912, p. 2.
[63] ibid., 1/30/1913, p. 5.
[64] ibid., 8/22/1919, p. 4.
[65] ibid., 8/27/1924, p. 4.
[66] *Twentieth Century Edition*, p. 20.
[67] *Farmers Free Press*, 6/27/1912.
[68] *Fairmont Times*, 10/29/1921, p. 1.
[69] *Fairmont Free Press*, 11/1/1900.
[70] *Welcome Westinghouse*, p. 1.
[71] *Fairmont Times*, 3/13/1919, p. 4.
[72] ibid., 11/4/1923, sect. 2, p. 8.
[73] ibid., 3/2/1924, p. 4.
[74] ibid., 2/2/1925, p. 8.
[75] ibid., 3/2/1925, p. 3.

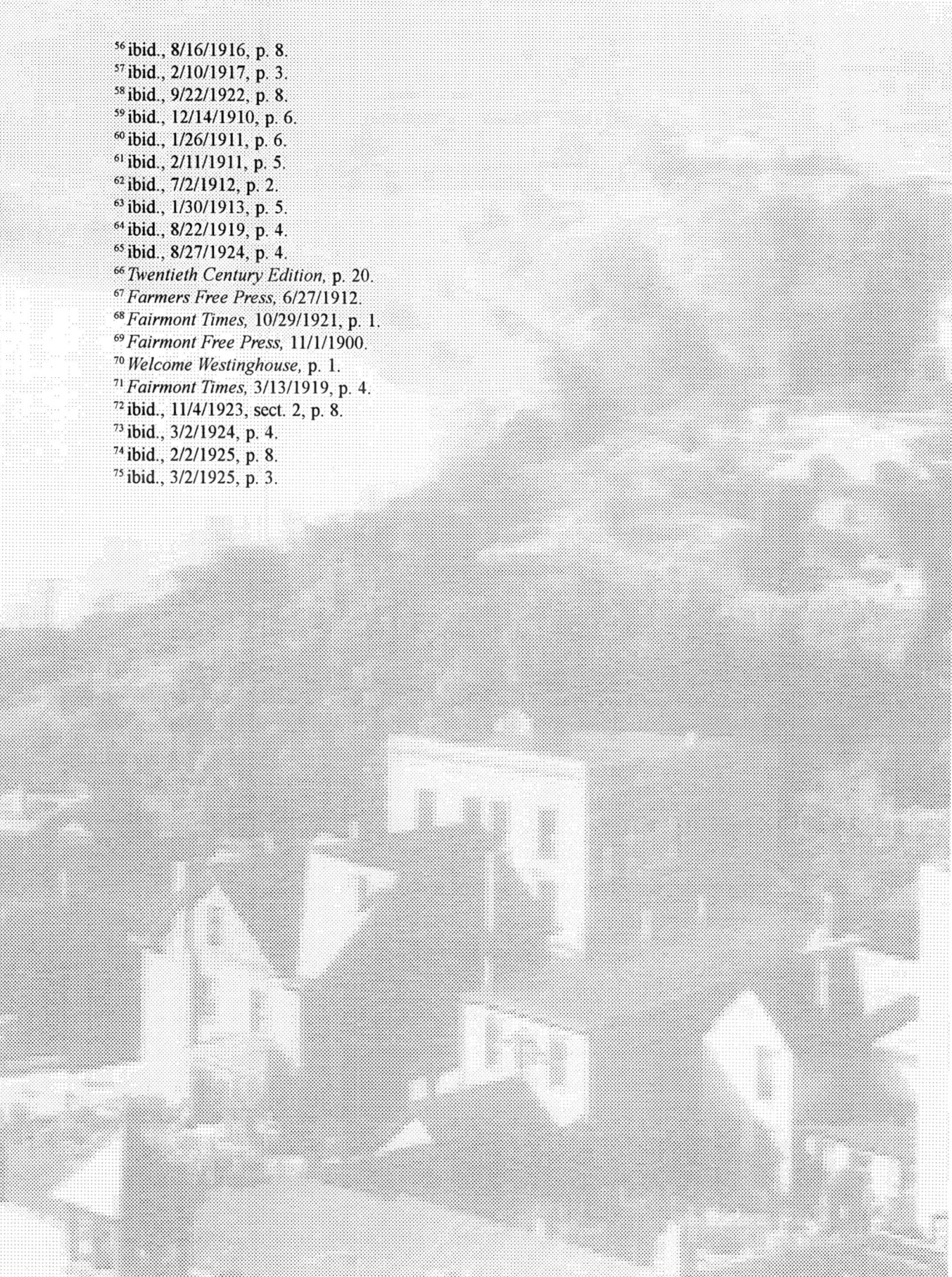

Chapter 17

300 Block Monroe Street, even numbered buildings

1. George M. Jacobs Building, 1903.
Andrew C. Lyons, architect. 312-316 Monroe Street

This five story, nine bay structure was designed by Andrew C. Lyons and constructed in 1903. It is a Neo- classical commercial block, with terra cotta decoration on the roof consisting of two flanking triangular pediments and a balustrade between them. The fifth floor windows consist of flanking trios of rectangular windows, with ornament over the center one, creating a Palladian window effect. The center trio of windows on the fifth floor are Roman arched windows. The first floor of the facade has been completely covered over with modern materials, and none of the original two store fronts, nor the original central Roman arched doorway to the lobby, are visible.

George M. Jacobs purchased the lots just west of the new Jacobs-Hutchinson Block at 201-209 Adams Street, which he had had erected in 1902; the lots cost $18,000. When the purchase was announced in May of 1903, it was also reported that Mr. Jacobs was going to build a skyscraper on the site at once. When asked if he were going to put up a building on the lots this year, he replied "No, I think not."[1]

Four days later, it was announced that Mr. Jacobs had let the contracts that day for the construction of a fine office building on his Monroe Street lots. The five story building would join up with the Jacobs-Hutchinson Block, and in fact would be a continuation of it. Holbert and Spedden, who were the contractors for the Jacobs-Hutchinson Block were awarded the contract for $40,000, and the building was to be completed by January 1, 1904. Andrew C. Lyons, it was announced, was the architect; he was also the architect of the Jacobs-Hutchinson Block.[2] Two days later, work began to prepare the lot for the foundations.[3]

The structure was planned as a mixed-use building; the first floors were to be commercial enterprises, and the upper floors were to be rented for professional offices of all types. In the succeeding months, many of the offices were leased in anticipation of the completion of the building. In October of 1902, the carving work on the building was almost completed; it was designed at the office of A. C. Lyons, and was executed by Mr. John Stokes of Washington, D. C.. Mr. Stokes had been a stone carver for forty years when he was executing the work; he had been one of the carvers on the art studio building in Chicago, the Buffalo art studio institute, the Congressional Library in Washington, and many other handsome structures. The carving on the Jacobs Building was said "to be the finest of its kind in this section of the country."[4] The building appears to have been completed late in 1903.

A man was badly smashed in an elevator accident in the Jacobs Building in February 1904. A Mr. B. F. Simpson was taking the elevator down from fifth floor when he lost control of the machine and it started to the bottom at a high rate of speed. Knowing he would be severely injured at the bottom if he stayed on, he saw the third floor door open and jumped. He fell in such a position that the top of the cage caught him and gave him "a very severe squeeze." The elevator went on to the bottom, where it struck, smashing the floor.[5]

Also in that month, a blaze threatened the entire downtown area. Embers from a fire used to keep workers warm on Monroe Street, near the new Jacobs Building, were carried by the wind and caught fire. It was extinguished by the fire department without incident.[6]

After the building's completion, businesses moved in. The opening for Mr. R. H. Blacka's Racket Department Store occurred on Saturday, April 23, 1904; it was located in the 312 Monroe Street store front, in the rear of the People's Bank (201 Adams Street).[7]

On Tuesday, April 19, 1904, the first edition of the reorganized West Virginian newspaper was published on the first floor of the new Jacobs Building, located in the 316 Monroe Street store front at Porter Alley.[8] It had moved from its location over Cochran's Jewelry Store at 226 Adams Street. It remained here until 1914, when it relocated to the Sample Building at 221 Monroe Street.[9]

Offices of the City were temporarily moved into the Jacobs Building in February of 1902, during the construction of the City Building on at 209-213 Monroe Street. Previously located in the Smith-McKinney Building (313-317 Adams Street), those offices were located on the second floor, above the *West Virginian* newspaper offices at the 316 Monroe Street store front. The new quarters consisted of five rooms, one large and four small. The large one overlooked the county jail and court house, and they had considered constructing a "bridge of sighs" of sorts, to connect the room and the courthouse. The big room was to be used as the council chamber and the municipal court room, and was thought to be large enough to accommodate many spectators. The front room was assigned to the city engineer, street commissioner, and water commissioner. The second room was fixed up for police headquarters. The next room was to be used by the clerk. The newspaper writer seemed to be appalled at the annual rent of $600, which included lights, heat, and janitor service, referring to the new space as "the Hotel De Ville of the people of Fairmont."[10]

The very next month, a serious fire occurred in the building, which endangered the entire business section of Fairmont, as well as the lives of two men. It was discovered by the night watchman around five in the morning in an office on the third floor. Had it not been for the him, the fire might have been more serious. The night watchman had been in the police headquarters room on the second floor when he detected the smoke.[11]

Two men who had rooms on the fifth floor were awakened by smoke in their rooms. They quickly dressed, but were unable to reach the street because of the thick smoke which poured up the stairway and the elevator shaft. They called down to the firemen in the street to raise a ladder to rescue them, but by then the fire was already under control. The men were later brought down the stair by the firemen. There was no fire escape on the part of the building in which they were located, and they had been cut off from the stair by the fire.[12] The major losses in the building were limited to the office of a representative of a book company, who was

George M. Jacobs Building, 312-316 Monroe Street, c. 1908.

underinsured. The building itself suffered only minor damage, thanks to the quick work of the fire department.[13]

The Union Business College opened its facility on the entire fifth floor of the Jacobs Building in the latter part of 1910.[14] This school boasted hundreds of graduates who held positions of trust and responsibility in many of vocations and businesses in the area. It was thought of as an important adjunct to the commercial and business interests of the city.[15]

Because of the growth of its business, Hartley's Department Store, located in the adjacent Jacobs-Hutchinson Block, leased the first floor room and basement in the adjoining section of the Jacob's Building (312 Monroe Street).[16] The newly-acquired space in the adjoining Jacobs Building gave the department store a Monroe Street entrance, and it was connected to the main building by an enclosed passage way. The entrance to the rooms upstairs in the Jacobs Building were accessed from the second floor by an elevated passageway referred to as the "Bridge of Size" (a play on the "Bridge of Sighs" in Venice, Italy), and they planned to lower this passage at a later date for convenience.[17] There were no sales rooms added above the second floor in the Jacobs Building at that time because it would have been impossible to transport customers until additional elevator service could be secured; it was seen as being out of the question at that time, as "it would be unpatriotic in the Hartley view to attempt to get huge elevators shipped into Fairmont with the present demands upon transportation facilities,"[18] referring to the realities of World War I.

The enlarged store was thrown open to the public on March 22, 1918, and it had increased its area by twenty-five percent, from 30,000 square feet to 40,000 square feet. This event was referred to as an "at home," since it was seen as entertaining the many friends of the store.[19]

On January 18, 1976, a blaze erupted in the basement of the Sport Store, which occupied one of the sections of the building. The alarm was sounded by a seven-year-old poodle named Dolly, who lived with her owners on the fifth floor of the building. Heavy smoke spread from the Sport Store to the adjacent Chamber of Commerce, and into the Jones' Store (which had taken the quarters previously occupied by Hartley's Department Store).[20] The fire engaged all floors of the building, and the second through fifth floors are currently condemned. The first floor is used for county offices, and the upper floor are used for storage only.

---

[1] *Fairmont Times,* 5/23/1903, p. 2.
[2] ibid., 5/27/1903, p. 1.
[3] ibid., 5/29/1903, p. 1.
[4] ibid., 10/21/1903, p. 1.
[5] ibid., 2/8/1904, p. 7.
[6] ibid., 2/15/1904, p. 1.
[7] *Fairmont West Virginian,* 4/22/1904, p. 2.
[8] ibid., 4/19/1904, p. 6.
[9] *Welcome Westinghouse,* p. 1.
[10] *Fairmont Times,* 2/2/1909, p. 1.
[11] ibid.
[12] ibid.
[13] ibid.
[14] ibid., 10/11/1910, p. 7.
[15] ibid., 12/12/1916, p. 1.
[16] ibid., 10/19/1917, p. 2.
[17] ibid., 3/19/1918, sect. 2, p. 1.
[18] ibid.
[19] ibid.
[20] *Fairmont Times-West Virginian,* 1/19/1976, p. 1.

Chapter 18

300 Block Monroe Street, odd numbered buildings

1. Post Office, Marion County Library; 1913-4.
Joseph Knox Taylor, architect, 321 Monroe Street

The site was originally occupied by four small one-story dwellings, according to the Sandborn map of 1884. These were torn down for the erection of the Post Office.

Talk about building a new post office for Fairmont began around 1906. The city had been growing at an astronomical rate, and there was a need for a larger facility than the first floor of the "Skinner Building" (106 Adams Street) could provide. Many sites, a few considered good, were offered to the government for the new facility. Several free sites were offered in the First Ward (East Side), which itself was growing, and wanted the prestige of having the new facility located across the river from the central business district.[1] In December 1906, the Post Office moved to the first floor of the new Masonic Temple Building (316-320 Jefferson Street), which they had leased. But talk of constructing a new Post Office and Federal Building continued.

A government architect for the project had been chosen, and he was in the city in May of 1909 to look over the proposed sites for the post office.[2] Joseph Knox Taylor, whose name appears on the cornerstone of the building, was the architect for the project. It is noteworthy that Taylor had been in partnership in the 1890's with Cass Gilbert, architect of the West Virginia State Capitol, as well as the Woolworth Building in New York, and the state capitols in Minnesota and Arkansas. The two architects had an office in St Paul, Minnesota at that point in time.[3]

It was finally in June of 1909 that the Hall property on the corner of Monroe Street and Porter Alley, just above the Opera House (325 Monroe Street), was selected to be the site of the new post office building. It was purchased from the S. W. Hall heirs for $31,000.[4] It was noted that a few old dwellings existed on the property, but their removal and the construction of the new building would add much to the looks of the city.[5]

Although the owners of the property had received the check for their property in 1909,[6] there was a delay in the construction of the building. It was not until 1912 that the drawings were ready for bid. The story-and-a-half building was to be constructed with the $93,000 available for it.[7] By May of that year, the drawings were said to be practically completed and that bids were to be solicited around the first of June. The contract contained a provision that work must be started on the building within thirty days, so it was thought that the work would commence in July 1912 and finished in early 1913.[8]

By March of 1913, the placment of the concrete pillars and joining rods of steel was finished and everything was ready for the masonry to be laid.[9] The building was constructed by Westchester Engineering Company of White Plains, New York at an entire cost of $89,173.20.

With the purchase price of the site at $31,000, the total cost of construction (lot and construction) was brought to $120,173.20.[10]

The new Post Office building was thrown open to public inspection on June 27, 1914 before its official opening. From the hours of 7 pm to 10 pm, Fairmonters saw the interior of the building, as well as "behind the scenes" of the Post Office. It was opened from cellar to garret. A fine view of the new building was printed on post cards, then on sale at the local stores for a penny; and it was said that it was about the best view of the building seen lately.[11]

Approximately 3,000 people visited the new facility on that day. Over two thousand souvenir post cards showing the building were given away. It was the policy of those who designed and built the local Post Office to spend the money appropriated on the interior of the building, where it would result in the greatest benefit to the employees and patrons of the office. "While the outside appearance of the building is not so impressive, the interior is of unusual fine finish and the building is equipped with all modern conveniences." The post master, Col. A. Howard Fleming, was on hand to receive the visitors, as was the staff, who showed them all over the building.[12]

The structure is Neo-classical in style, with Roman arched windows flanking a Roman arched entrance. The red brick is contrasted with stone quoins and stone pilasters, as well as stone dentils below the stone cornice. A stepped pediment at the roof emphasizes the center.

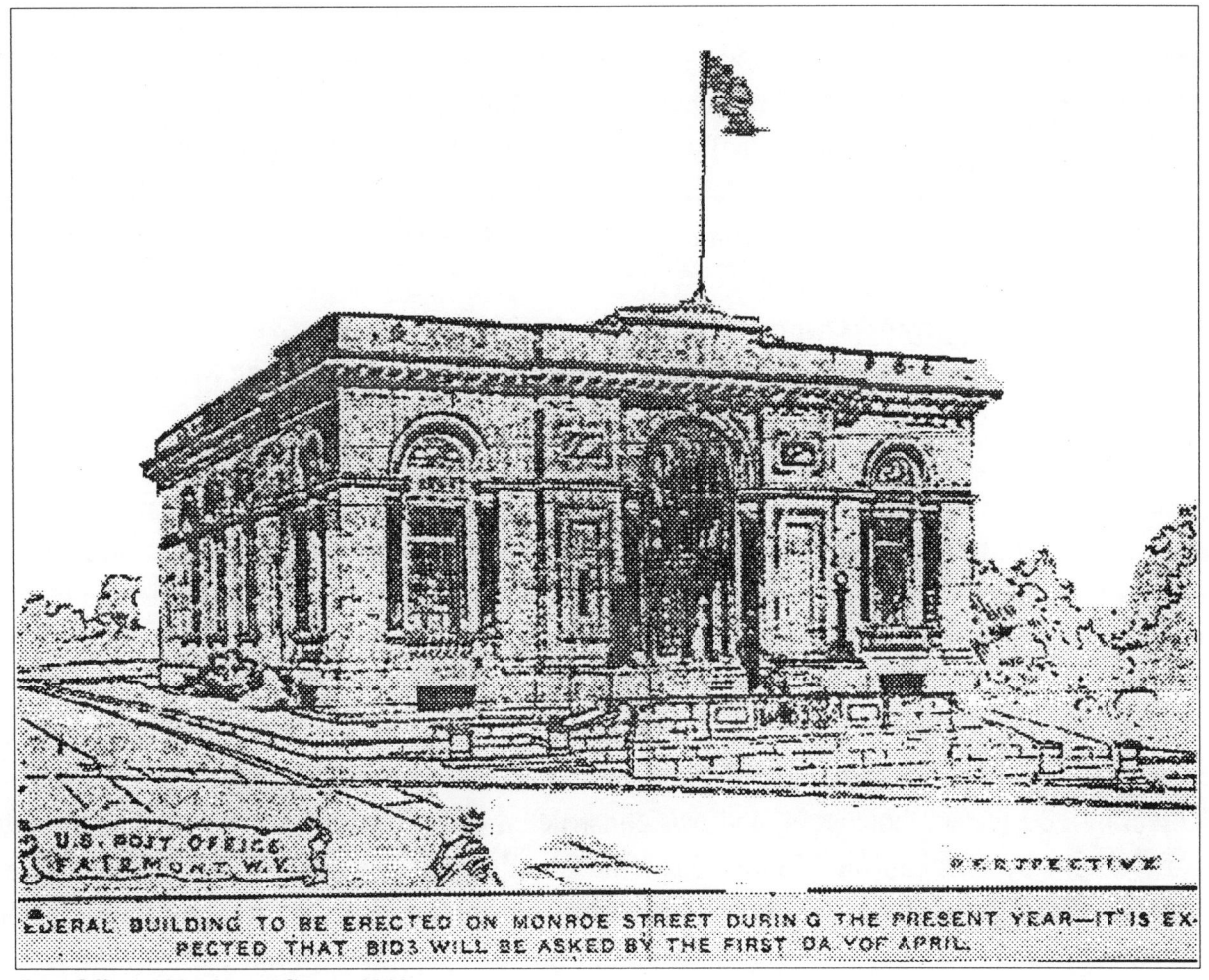

Post Office, 321 Monroe Street, 1912.

The Post Office officially opened for business on July 1, 1914. The new location added to the general confusion in the city, as the city's sixteen saloons were closed the night before.[13]

There had been much criticism regarding the architecture of the new Post Office Building in Fairmont, and it had been compared to a pottery building or a garage. This was due in part to the building only being one story tall, because there was no Federal court included in it, as had been originally discussed. However, the citizens agreed that the interior of the office was well arranged and one of the most handsome in the country. In comparison to the new Post Office in Morgantown, which was two stories tall, Fairmont's new Post Office was also much larger.[14]

The building was furnished throughout with the most up- to-date modern fixtures that could be purchased. The equipment included four Seth Thomas clocks, one Cincinnati Time Recorder, and a Columbia cancelling machine. The post master's office was furnished with a large double vault.[15]

It took only a month and a half for the intersection of Monroe and Meredith Streets by the Post Office to become a dangerous traffic location, especially for automobile owners. The drivers of the automobiles were said to be entirely too careless in many instances and the public made complaint. A serious accident was narrowly averted, when a young woman and her little child were nearly run down by a rapidly moving car coming out of Meredith Street. The drivers did not pay enough heed when driving through that street, and horns were seldom blown. Drivers had been cutting from Barney (Cleveland) Street through Meredith Street to get their mail, exiting on to Monroe Street, and vice versa. "The attention of the city authorities has been called to the general carelessness of the chauffeurs at this point."[16]

The building was vacated by the Post Office in the 1940's when the new Federal Building facility was constructed at the corner of Fairmont Avenue and Second Street. The building later became the Marion County Public library,[17] which is its current use.

2. Grand Opera House, 1902; I.O.O.F. Building, 1921-22.
J. E. Allison, architect. C. H. Snider, architect of remodeling. 325 Monroe Street

The earliest documentation of a structure on this site comes from the 1884 Sandborn map, which notes that the small structure there was used for the J. Nuzum and Company as a furniture factory. On the 1892 Sandborn map, it was said to be used as a storage house, and in 1896 as a store. This building was razed to make way for the new Fairmont Opera House, to take the place of the one that had burned in December 1901 at 312 Madison Street, referred to as "The Rink."

The Fairmont Opera House was designed by Architect J. E. Allison of Pittsburgh, and constructed by T. L. Burchinal of Fairmont at a cost of $60,000 to $70,000. The building was 60 feet by 100 feet in dimension, and was constructed of buff brick and stone.[18] The structure had a stepped gable end on Monroe Street and battlements on the eave on Jackson Street. Because of the slope of the site, there were store fronts along Jackson Street on the first floor, with the theatre proper beginning on the second floor. The windows of the theatre were Roman arched on the second floor, and circular on the upper levels.

Opera House, 325 Monroe Street, c. 1902.

The seating capacity of the house was between 1,400 and 1500. The seating room consisted of a bowl floor, orchestra circle, fourteen boxes, balcony, and gallery. There were also ladies' parlors, toilet rooms, manager's office, check rooms, and other necessary ante-rooms. The dressing rooms and orchestra room were arranged under the stage, with ten dressing rooms, two toilet rooms, and one orchestra room. The stage was thirty-three feet by sixty-two feet in dimension and was equipped with necessary fly galleries, rigging loft, storage rooms, and, at that time, the most modern scenic switch board for stage purposes. The switch board was mounted with the "latest" electric appliances and a complete set of dimmers.[19]

Special attention was given to the heating and ventilation of the house. A low pressure gravity steam heating system was installed to insure the comfort of the patrons. The building was liberally lighted by electricity and gas, with a total of between 400 and 500 lights. The building was equipped with fire escapes, which allowed the house to be emptied in less than two minutes.[20]

The interior was handsomely decorated in stucco relief and color. The main entrance was on Jackson Street, and a separate entrance and stairway was provided for the gallery. Over the main entrance was a handsome porte cochere that extended across the pavement, and the loggia had a tile floor. Handsome art glass added greatly to the decorative effect of the house.[21]

The gentlemen who were responsible for the construction were those who made up the Fairmont Opera House Company: J. Thomas Miller, Sam R. Nuzum, M. A. Jolliff, E. F. Hartley, John A. Clark, A. A. Hamilton, L. C. Powell (all of Fairmont); and L. S. Horner of Clarksburg.[22] The theatre opened in January 1902.[23]

Only two years after it opened, in January of 1904, the owners had additional fire exits constructed on the building. The "Iroquois Theatre horror in Chicago" was the main reason for this addition; a fire in this theatre had cost many lives when the exit doors refused to open. The people of Fairmont did not want a disaster such as this occurring in their city. It was proposed to add six new fire escapes to the theatre immediately. They were to be placed at different intervals in the first balcony and on the main floor, to greatly eliminate the danger of a stampede which then existed in the playhouse. The main improvement was another general exit for the main floor, which was to be constructed at the spot where the ladies' retiring room was located. It led to a platform that was extended out from the previous main entrance.[24]

Within three days of the proposing the change, the City Council met at the Grand Opera house, along with a majority of the directors of the Grand Opera House Company, its manager, and Architect Lyons. The party looked around the theatre house for over an hour, and met that evening to determine whether or not to grant the opera house people permission for the revisions. After much discussion, permission was granted for the new exits.[25] Within two weeks, two of the new exits were completed.[26]

The rest of the fire escapes were completed in July of 1904. Joseph Kohlmier of Cleveland was in charge of the construction of iron balconies around the Grand Opera House, which made all of the new fire escapes practical. There were now eight in number. In addition to the new balconies, an iron ladder had been run from the ground to the top of the building to be used by firemen in the event a fire should ignite near the roof. The ladder was located near the stage entrance. A one hundred foot hose attached to a reel was also kept on the top of the building, which could be easily attached to the city hose. Some of the directors of the Opera House Company inspected the work, and were much pleased with it.[27]

Besides the theatre proper, other commercial enterprises occupied the lower part of the building and were accessed from Jackson Street. One of these was the Opera House Restaurant. An advertisement for it stated that it had opened up again, and would serve its customers as usual in first-class style. "It is for both ladies and gentlemen." [28] Another business, The Grand Opera House Saloon, W. G. Bosserman, proprietor, was closed by the constable pending the result of certain civil actions. It seems that two of its creditors had not been paid; The Grand Opera House Company was owed $270 in back rent, and the Citizens' Dollar Bank was owed $86.70 for an overextended account. It was thought that there would be additional suits brought in a short time.[29] A new undertaking firm was formed in Fairmont in 1909. Williamson Undertaking had their office and morgue located in the Grand Opera House building.[30]

Fire remained a grave danger for the building. In February of 1906, a fifth attempt in three months to burn the theatre was reported. Passerbys noticed smoke coming from the building and reported the fire. The firemen discovered a lively fire burning in a small check room in the rear of the house under the balcony stairs. It was extinguished without incident, and thought to have been begun by incendiary means. [31]

In the days before radio and television, the theatre was a source of communications with the outside world. The election returns in November 1906 were read between acts at the theatre.[32]

"Near Panic at Grand Opera House," read the headlines in 1909. During a school entertainment at which twelve hundred people were in attendance (one third of whom were school children), the cry "fire" was raised. A child who had been playing in the orchestra had a fit and fell over; a woman in the balcony cried fire, and people began to rush for the exits. The exits were in good working order, but the children were in most danger of being trampled by the hysterical adults. However, cooler heads prevailed and assured the crowd that it was a false alarm. The rush was checked, order resumed, and the play allowed to proceed.[33]

In June of 1910, the Grand Opera House was leased to a pair of gentlemen named Moore and Robinson. These men, from Wheeling and Clarksburg, respectively, had organized a string of theatres in West Virginia and Ohio to bring the best attractions to them.[34]

Under the new management, the theatre was to be overhauled from the dressing rooms to the front entrance during the summer months. New scenery, new dressing rooms and many new and modern things for the stage were to be installed. The wonders were to be worked in the auditorium, where the interior was to be repainted, new carpets laid, and the house made brighter and more cheerful in appearance. It was estimated that three or four thousands dollars would be spend on these improvements.[35]

The Grand Theatre, as it was later called, underwent further renovations in 1916. It was closed for a month for the work, which included a redecorated lobby, a great cathedral pipe organ, new decorations in the interior of the house, and new equipment in practically every department of the theatre. The pipe organ was to be the first installed in a theatre in the city; it was to be the biggest single feature that had ever before been offered in the city in the way of a picture accompaniment to the Paramount pictures shown here. It was to be used for concerts as well. The lobby was rebuilt and finished in cream white and gold, with a contrast of great potted palms and statuary. Several changes were to be made to the exterior of the building as well. These changes were to make the theatre more attractive, since the theatre business has not been a remarkably well-paying in Fairmont for a number of years. [36]

The new, improved theatre opened at the end of July 1916. A new rotary converter was installed to produce a beautiful clear white picture and to eliminate the "flicker and dark spots." In addition, new electric lighting fixtures were installed throughout the house, with exquisite tinted inverted bowl light fixtures. A new electric sign was installed on the front of the building, which made a striking appearance from Main (Adams) Street. A great sky-rocket mechanical sign was to be placed on the roof as well. New velvet carpet was laid on all open spaces in the theatre, and a strip of it was to be placed across the street in front of the building, as was done in the most exclusive theatres in larger cities.[37]

In spite of all the improvements over the years, the theatre was closed and the building was sold to the Odd Fellows Lodge in 1920. Initially, there were two options for the building. The first was to construct two additional stories to the building for the club and lodge rooms to be located above the theatre, keeping the playhouse open for business. The other, which at the time seemed more likely, was to remodel the existing building, doing away with the stage and auditorium, and establishing two stories for lodge purposes under the existing roof.[38] The later scheme prevailed.

At a meeting of the Odd Fellows Lodge in January of 1921, it was decided to convert the amusement house into a lodge home. The Grand Opera House, it was said, was to be lost to Fairmont for all time as a theatre. The plan was to remodel it into a Odd Fellows temple, with a business floor taking the place of the main auditorium of the theatre, adding an additional floor for offices above that, and with the two top floors devoted to the use of Odd Fellows organizations.[39]

The property was purchased for $40,500, and there had been a rumor that the lodge was subsequently offered $81,000 for the property. In addition to the Grand Opera House, the Odd Fellows also owns the Jackson Hotel property (119-121 Jackson Street), the top part of the Thomas W. Fleming Building (200 Adams Street), and Maple Grove Cemetery. The society was said to be one of the richest secret orders in Fairmont and to have a membership of 570 members.[40]

At a meeting of the Odd Fellows on July 14, 1921, approximately a quarter of the $55,000 worth of bonds that were issued for the remodeling of the Grand Opera house were sold. The plan for the building was to locate the lodge room on the fourth story of the building; the banquet hall, committee rooms, club rooms and library on the third floor; offices on the second floor; and business rooms on the first floor and in the basement. The architect for the work was C. H. Snider. Bids for the work were to be opened two weeks after the meeting.[41]

A report on the status of the work appeared in the newspaper in December of 1922. People were wondering what the inside of the new Odd Fellows hall would look like, thinking that they just may as well have "fashioned an entirely new building on the old opera house location ... because so very much of the old building was discarded." Merely the outer shell of the building was being used, and even the foundation had reinforced footings added in sixteen places.[42]

The entire inside of the building was new, with every inch of the old lumber torn out. In place of this, steel beams were erected so that the building was considered entirely fireproof, all a cost of possibly $90,000 (and $42,000 for the purchase of the building). Where did all of this money come from, a reporter asked. "Shucks," answered the superintendent in charge, "there's oodles of money."[43]

Seventy new windows were cut into the side walls of the old opera house, and the top of the building was raised nine feet to accommodate high ceilings on the top floor for the lodge room. The building was finished on the outside in stucco or kellastone so that it presented "a beautiful appearance," and raised the standard of all future builders near this location.[44]

The completion of the building was expected to occur June 1, 1923. Although the work had begun in June 1922, there had been some difficulties in getting the materials. Most of the old material in the building had been disposed of. Even the old opera chairs, on which many a Fairmonter had sat, had been sold. Fifteen to eighteen men were employed to work on the building.[45]

The front entrance of the building was on Monroe Street, where the entrance of the theatre had been located. There was a vestibule, then a revolving door leading to the lobby, which then led to the elevator. Another entrance would lead to the big store room which was to occupy the entire first floor. S. R. Holbert, the contractor, had a small office with an entrance of Jackson Street, where he was constantly found during the construction.[46]

At this time, the spaces of the building were planned. There were to be five floors from the Jackson Street elevation. The first floor was to be a large store room, suitable for a department store. The second floor would accommodate sixteen up-to-date offices with two windows each and modern conveniences. A roomy corridor would lead to these rooms. The third floor would accommodate the magnificent banquet hall of the Odd Fellows, as well as the pool and billiard rooms, lounging room, reading room, and kitchen. The fourth floor would have the lodge room on it, and it was to have four stages. The fifth floor would accommodate the paraphernalia rooms, one committee room, one candidate room, one ante room, and one regalia room.[47] The cost of the entire project was said to have been $175,000.[48]

I.O.O.F. Building, 325 Monroe Street, 1923.

The Odd Fellows met in their new building for the first time in July 1923. The new lodge room was furnished with plastered walls and mahogany wainscoting. The ceiling was of galvanized iron and painted ivory. Chandeliers and wall lights were used to illuminate the room, and the floor was covered with cork carpet. Two Otis elevators were installed. and the furniture from the old lodge had been moved to the new one.[49]

The installation of new officers, held on September 24, 1923, was the first public event in the new building, and was attended by hundreds of people. The building had been transformed into an imposing and magnificent new structure. Although the new elevator had been installed, it had not yet been inspected, so it was necessary for everyone to walk to the top floor where the entertainment took place. The installation ceremony included speeches, the installation service, solos, and refreshments. Donations were sought to pay off the $27,000 still owed on the building. Even at this date, the building was not yet completed. The outside was still to be stuccoed and the inside still lacked the finishing touches.[50]

On June 2, 1924, the West Virginia Business College, the forerunner to Webster College, opened for business on the third floor of the I.O.O.F. Building.[51] By 1927, the College had grown so large that it had to secure an additional room in the building and secure extra equipment. That September, their enrollment was 164 students. A new athletic director had been employed to coach both basketball teams, as well as other forms of physical education.[52]

The building was also noteworthy for being the first meeting place of the Church of Christ in Fairmont on July 14, 1927.[53]

The building was razed in 1980 for a parking lot.[54]

[1] *Fairmont Times*, 8/22/1906, p. 8.
[2] ibid., 5/18/1909, p. 1.
[3] Cohen, p. 62.
[4] *Fairmont Times*, 7/1/1914, p. 2.
[5] ibid., 6/18/1909, p. 1.
[6] ibid., 12/14/1909, p. 3.
[7] ibid., 2/19/1912, p. 1.
[8] ibid., 5/12/1912, p. 1.
[9] ibid., 3/5/1913, p. 8.
[10] ibid., 7/1/1914, p. 2.
[11] ibid., 6/26/1914, p. 1.
[12] ibid., 6/29/1914, p. 2.
[13] ibid., 7/1/1914, p. 2.
[14] ibid.
[15] ibid.
[16] ibid., 8/14/1914, p. 2.
[17] *Welcome Westinghouse,* sect. 5, p. 2.
[18] *Twentieth Century Edition,* p. 22.
[19] ibid.
[20] ibid.
[21] ibid.
[22] ibid.
[23] *Fairmont Times,* 7/26/1907, sect. 2, p. 7.
[24] ibid., 1/4/1904, p. 7.
[25] ibid., 1/7/1904, p. 1.
[26] ibid., 4/21/1904, p. 2.
[27] *Fairmont West Virginian,* 7/23/1904, p. 8.
[28] ibid., 9/6/1904, p. 2.
[29] *Fairmont Times,* 1/14/1906, p. 1.
[30] ibid., 6/29/1909, p. 1.
[31] ibid., 2/13/1906, p. 1.
[32] ibid., 11/6/1906, p. 1.
[33] ibid., 6/8/1909, p. 1.
[34] ibid., 6/20/1910, p. 1.
[35] ibid.
[36] ibid., 6/20/1916, p. 2.
[37] ibid., 7/21/1916, p. 6.
[38] ibid., 3/21/1920, sect. 2, p. 1.
[39] ibid., 1/12/1921, p. 5.
[40] ibid.
[41] ibid., 7/15/1921, p. 1.
[42] ibid., 12/31/1922, p. 3.
[43] ibid.
[44] ibid.
[45] ibid.
[46] ibid.
[47] ibid.
[48] ibid., 2/20/1923, p. 2.
[49] ibid., 7/18/1923, p. 8.
[50] ibid., 7/25/1923, p. 1.
[51] ibid., 5/20/1924, p. 11.
[52] ibid., 9/8/1927, p. 12.
[53] *Welcome Westinghouse,* sect. 1, p. 6.
[54] *A History of Marion County, West Virginia,* p. 2.

Part IV
Jefferson Street

Jefferson Street is the main cross street of Adams Street, made even more significant by the location of the Courthouse on the corner of Adams and Jefferson Streets. It was a very popular business location. The street originally ended with a steep hill at Cleveland Avenue to the south, just across from the B. & O. Freight Station. The construction of the Million Dollar Bridge at the south end of Jefferson Street in 1921 elevated the end of Jefferson Street, making Washington Street the last intersection; the street now passes over Cleveland Avenue and where the B. & O. Freight Station had existed (now gone). The extension of the street across the river to the East Side via the bridge makes Jefferson Street one of the gateways to the city.

Chapter 19

200 Block Jefferson Street, even numbered buildings

1. Fairmont Hotel; 1916-17, 1920.
Milburn, Heister & Company, architects. 200-214 Jefferson Street

The structures originally on this site were one-and two- story dwellings from the 1800's, according to the Sandborn maps. They remained on the site until the construction of the Fairmont Hotel began.

The first talk of a new hotel for Fairmont started in 1912. There was a great need for a modern hotel for the city, since it was growing so quickly and so many visitors needed accommodations. A rendering of the proposed eight- story facility was displayed in M. D. Christie's store window (300 Adams Street), and the site for it was stated to be at the corner of Jefferson and Washington Streets.[1] The rendering, which appeared in the Fairmont Times newspaper, showed the structure and stated that the plans for the hotel "have practically been decided upon ... and will resemble exactly the photograph above, which was taken from the plans."[2]

After this first "bravo," it was three years before a serious plan for a new hotel emerged again. In November of 1915, it was rumored in local building circles that a new hotel was to be built. A reference was made to the fact that there had been talk of it at one time, but it was indefinitely postponed. This was due to some conditions arising which made those behind the project believe that such an investment might not have been profitable. One reason for the talk of the new hotel was that there had recently been over 5,000 visitors in the city, crowding the existing hotels.[3]

Two days later, it was announced that more activity had occurred on the idea of a new hotel. A "very influential concern" had taken up the matter, and was willing to furnish a site at the actual cost which was paid for the property, and was also willing to take $50,000 worth of stock in the hotel company. The site was characterized at advantageous to business men because of its accessibility, though it had not been definitely decided upon.[4]

At the Chamber of Commerce meeting on December 9, 1915, discussion of the new hotel occurred, with nearly one hundred of the city's leading businessmen in attendance. Though he was not in attendance, George T. Watson sent Robert C. Cunningham as his representative to state that if the members of the organization could raise $150,000 for the new hotel, the interest he represented would raise a like sum. Mr. Cunningham announced it was his own opinion that Mr. Watson would raise $200,000 if the other business interests would raise $100,000. The general consensus was favorable to the idea, and thought such a sum could be raised without delay. Mr. Watson limited his offer to construction on the site at Jefferson and Washington Street on the lot recently purchased for that purpose, and that the offer was only valid for quick action on the part of the businessmen.[5] The financial campaign began on December 13, 1915.[6]

It was a whirlwind campaign to raise the funds for the construction of the new hotel, without equal in the history of cities the size of Fairmont. The Watson interests had announced that they would subscribe $200,000 if the public would raise an additional $100,000. This was accomplished in two days. Subsequently, Senator C. W. Watson, who had himself assisted in the campaign and had subscribed for $50,000 worth of stock, announced that if the people of the town would add an additional ten thousand to the cause, that he would raise an additional $40,000, making the total sum for the hotel $350,000. The offer was snapped up, and $5,000 was immediately raised. In addition to local people who were contacted by telephone and telegraph wire, several firms in Baltimore, who made a feature of Fairmont stocks, purchased some of the hotel company stock.[7]

The stock investors began to organize the project on December 16, 1915. Preliminary committees were formed to begin the work even before the charter was to be secured, and engineers were called to prepare blueprints of the lot. An executive committee was named, as well as sub-committees on grounds, architects, and organization. "Arrange your plans so that your hotel may be added to without trouble. Within five years, Fairmont will be so large that the hotel you are now building will not be half large enough to take care of the business," stated Senator C. W. Watson.[8] This foresight paid off only three years after the building's completion, when an addition was made to its height.

By December 30 of that year, the tenants occupying the existing buildings on the site of the new structure were given the customary thirty days notice to vacate. This meant that the grading on the lot could begin within a little over a month. Blueprints of the site showing the elevations had been made and general ideas for the hotel compiled by the members of the committee in charge of the preliminary plans; these were mailed to over 25 of the leading architects of the country, requesting plans. In addition, the corporation papers were sent to Charleston, asking for a charter.[9]

A meeting of the stockholders took place on February 7, 1916 to elect officers and directors. Mr. Brooks Fleming, Jr. was chosen president of the company, and he made it understood that it would be his policy to rush the work as fast as possible. The board also inspected the twenty sets of plans that had been submitted by the architects, hoping to make a final decision within a week.[10]

The officials of the new hotel company decided to seek the aid of the citizens of Fairmont in selecting a plan for the new hotel. The plans were on display in the Watson Building (301-311 Adams Street), and the public, whether stock owners or not, were invited to see the plans and give their opinions as to the best one for the city. After viewing the plans, the public would have an opportunity to tell the officers and directors of the hotel company their views.[11]

At least three hundred citizens inspected the twenty sets of architectural drawings on display in the Watson Building at the open house held on February 16, 1916, and the public was in awe over them. The drawings were noted as "marvels for beauty and modernness and that they are far more lavish than was expected." Representatives of the architects were also in attendance at the open house to explain the merits of their drawings, and they and the hotel company representatives were besieged with questions regarding the plans. The most noticeable feature of the open house was the surprise of the visitors over the excellence and extent of the proposed hotel, having no idea that such a magnificent hotel was in store. The drawings were excellent, and many showed the building on the site in such a clever manner that it appeared to be a photograph of the real magnificent structure erected at Jefferson and Washington Streets.[12]

The executive committee then met with representatives of the architects, who were from New York, Washington, and various cities from the East, Ohio, and Pennsylvania. The committee was to report to the board of directors within a few days after the meetings with the choice of the architect and what plans would be utilized in the construction of the hotel. It was the intention to have the structure completed in 1916.[13]

A prominent hotel man on his visit to Fairmont underscored the importance of having a good hotel in the city. The hotel is the first home of the visitor, he said, and gives him his first and most lasting impression of the city; it is the front door to the city. Many a hotel has put a city on the map. It behooves the people of a city, he continued, to give their financial and moral support to a fine hotel and display the proper civic pride in order to induce outsiders to visit their city, either on business or pleasure. Cities grow chiefly by drawing population from the outside, the visitor said, not by natural increase. An outsider never invests until he or his agents personally visit and inspect the property and its surroundings.[14]

On March 8, 1916, the directors of the hotel company announced that it had awarded the contract for the architects and plans to the firm of Milburn, Heister & Company of Washington, D. C. for the new hotel. The firm was well-known and especially notable in hotel drafting and construction. The plans that the firm had submitted were to the directors' liking, though the architects were sent back to their Washington offices to make revisions. Work on the new hotel was scheduled to begin by May 15, 1916. To expedite matters, the steel for the structural framework was purchased at this time. This had a two-fold benefit: the hotel company could get a good price for the steel, since the price for the material was rising in price almost daily (probably due to the World War); and there would be no delays in securing the material at the time it would be needed.[15]

The plans for the hotel were for a building five or six stories in height and containing approximately 150 sleeping rooms. It was to be fireproof, and equipped with the latest sanitary devices. The first floor was to contain a spacious lobby, large dining room, manager's office, and kitchen. There was to be a mezzanine floor with a balcony, which would include parlors; on the front of the building at this level would to be a large veranda which could be opened in the summer and enclosed with glass in the winter for a sun parlor. The building would also contain a banquet hall, the location of which had not been decided upon.[16]

The final plans for the hotel were announced on March 21, 1916, and the architect was returning to Washington with "the last revisions." The bids were to be asked for and received by the middle of April. Much attention was given to the plans, as any mistake was seen to be very costly in the future. One major detail was the location of the banquet hall and ballroom, which had originally been located on the sixth floor; this was changed to the first floor for convenience and efficiency.[17]

The final, final plans for the hotel were announced on March 23, 1916. Besides the finest ball room and banquet hall in the South, the building also was to contain a men's cafe on the first floor for the busy patron's noonday lunch. The ballroom and banquet hall were to be located on the second floor, and connected to the mezzanine so that patrons who were not dancing could be seated on the balcony off the mezzanine and overlook the floor below. Guests coming to a banquet would go to the mezzanine to discard their wraps, then step down a flight of private stairs or take an elevator to the hall below.[18]

The last house was moved off of the site in April, and digging the foundation of the building began.[19] Changes to the plan were once again requested by the Fairmont Hotel Company, and then they authorized the architect to proceed with details of the drawings and the preparation of specifications. It seems that the delay was due to information regarding pricing that had to be obtained before the final decision could be made.[20]

The excavations were proceeding even as the plans were being revised, and much water was found under the new hotel site. It seems there was an old mine chamber at the location.[21]

The final transfer of the property for the new Fairmont Hotel occurred on June 14, 1916, when the secretary of the hotel company placed the deed, which transferred the property from the original owners to the hotel company, on file in the county clerk's office for official recordation. The plans and specifications were to be immediately sent forward to the numerous contracting and building firms which had indicated their desire for consideration in the awarding of the contract.[22] The contractors were requested to have their bids in the hands of the hotel company in early July 1916. Some of the most successful and well known builders in the United States had requested permission to bid on the hotel's construction.[23]

The contract was awarded the George A. Fuller Company of New York and Washington on July 24, 1916. They had made a specialty of hotel construction, and had built the famous Greenbrier at White Sulphur Springs, West Virginia, and the new Homestead at Hot Springs, Virginia. They were one of eleven firms who had submitted bids, and were to begin the work within the week. It was the hope of the contractor to have the building under roof before winter and to complete the entire structure within eight months. The contract was well within the budget, leaving extra funds available for furnishings and other equipment. Since the steel had been ordered in advance and was already on the site, there would be no delay in awaiting that material.[24] The contract was closed on July 25, 1916. While there was no time limit to the construction period, it was understood that the hotel would be completed in nine months time, and would be thrown open for business by July 4, 1917.[25]

The building superintendent for the new hotel construction, Mr. S. M. Beaumont, arrived in town on July 26, 1916; he spent the day getting information regarding local contractors and local supply firms.[26] The building permit for the structure was obtained the very next day. It provided for the construction of a building with five stories and a mezzanine, with a Washington Street frontage of 135 feet and a Jefferson Street frontage of 150 feet. It was to be constructed of steel, brick, stone, and concrete, and was to contain approximately 125 bedrooms.[27]

The contracting firm had a splendid reputation for its construction work. It had erected more than three hundred structures of the most notable buildings throughout the United States, and had offices in at least seventeen major cities. Among the many hotel buildings it had constructed were the Biltmore, the Plaza, and the Breslin in New York City; the Blackstone and the La Salle in Chicago; and the New Willard, the Raleigh, and the Powhatan in Washington, D. C.. One of its famous non-hotel buildings was the Flatiron Building in New York City.[28]

The first block of the new hotel building was laid on September 27, 1916. "The placing of the initial block was not without formalities for it rests on bronze coins." A representative of the Fairmont Chamber of Commerce, a representative of the City Board of Affairs, and a representative of the Fuller Construction Company all placed Lincoln pennies under the brick. Representatives of the Bricklayers' Union placed an Indian head coin to keep company with the Lincoln coins. With this formality over, the brick work proceeded.[29]

Fine progress was made on the building in spite of some difficulties. Although the ground was known to be somewhat rocky, the amount of solid sandstone that was discovered in the excavation was a surprise. In addition, an old abandoned coal mine under a portion of the lot required much planning to safely overcome. It was finally decided to make a concrete fill in the mine. No less that 450 cubic yards of material had been placed within the confines of the mine under the hotel lot. The old mine first had to be pumped and cleaned out before the concrete could be placed. It extended about ninety feet from the entrance back into the interior of the mine, and the width widened out from eight feet the opening to about thirty-five feet at the end, where solid stone walls six feet in depth had been erected. Concrete was poured to fill the area up to the roof of the old mine. At this time, the concrete column foundations had been placed and a big derrick which had been erected a few days previous was putting the structural steel in place. The framework for the entire building was expected to be standing within a month.[30]

By February 1917, the work on the hotel was progressing well, and the furniture and furnishings were ordered, to be delivered in June. A Mr. R. L. O'Neal was being considered for the position of the hotel manager.[31]

Plans for the big opening of the Fairmont Hotel began in May 1917. Officials of the Chamber of Commerce were considering a huge banquet for the event.[32] At first, it appeared that a July 4th opening would be possible, but the opening date was pushed back because some of the finishing materials were delayed.[33] Opening day was July 16, 1917. Stores in the city closed early so their employees would have an opportunity to see the hotel on its opening day.[34]

"Opening of 'The Fairmont' A Red Letter Day In The City's Civic Improvement," read the headlines of newspaper. The opening of the $400,000 structure was from 3 to 6 pm, and 8:30 pm to 12 am, and thousands of people attended. Music was provided by the Greater Fairmont Band in the afternoon, and Vincent's Orchestra in the evening. Guides were enlisted from the citizenry to show visitors the building. The tour began on the fourth floor and proceeded downward to the basement. A dance commemorating the occasion began at 9 pm. [35]

The structure rests on concrete footings, and the exterior walls from the first floor line to the ground are faced with Peerless Bedford Indiana limestone. All of the rest of the exterior is faced with red brick. Most of the floors in the building were marble, with the stairs made of gray Tennessee marble. The building was heated by the direct low pressure steam heating system. There were two passenger elevators. The building was designed and constructed to be fireproof in every detail, and was amply provided with fire- proof stairs and fire escapes. A telephone was provided in every room.[36]

The ground floor is on level with Washington Street, and accommodated four store rooms, as well as a barber shop, a billiard room, the boiler house, service rooms, and an entrance to the hotel connecting with the elevator. The first floor housed the main entrance from Washington Street, as well as two store rooms on Jefferson Street and the "Coffee Shop", a department of The Fairmont. Also on this floor was the ballroom, the dining room, and the kitchen. A flight of stairs from the main lobby led to the mezzanine floor, which housed the ladies' parlors.[37]

The second, third, and fourth floor plans were identical, and housed the guest rooms. Each floor was provided with seven rooms with bath tubs, six rooms with showers, and fourteen rooms with hot and cold water, but no showers or tubs. To take care of the rooms without baths, gentlemen's and ladies's toilets were provided. The roof of the building was constructed so that it could be made into a roof garden, or the building could carry several additional stories.[38]

The Fairmont Hotel had fulfilled all expectations with its splendor, and it was estimated that 10,000 people had visited it at the opening.[39] Seventy-five guests stayed in the hotel on that first night,[40] and on August 23, 1917, all of the rooms in the new hotel were taken.[41] Later in the month, the hotel was overflowing; sixty-two guests had been turned away.[42]

By August 1919, the prediction that the hotel would need to be enlarged came true. A two-story addition to the top of The Fairmont would give the building an additional 68 rooms.[43] The addition of these two floors would be too much for the heating plant, so a new, immense boiler was ordered for the hotel as well.[44]

The Fairmont Hotel and the Watson Hotel (400 Adams Street) were acquired by the Fairmont Hotel Corporation in 1919. Both of these structures were to have additions. The Frederick T. Ley Company was the contractor for The Fairmont Hotel, and it was estimated that it would require only twenty-seven weeks to complete the work.[45] The roof was ripped off of the building in January 1920, though arrangements had been made that the work would progress without the slightest inconvenience to the occupants of the hotel.[46]

The addition to The Fairmont Hotel was opened in November 1920. The hotel's capacity was increased to 179 rooms with the $244,000 addition. Each room in the addition was provided with a bath or shower. Some rooms were also configured to provided suites of two or three rooms, for those "who prefer the hotel life to housekeeping in the winter months." There had been difficulties in obtaining furnishings as well as building materials; this is probably due to the recent end of World War I, when civilian construction was limited to conserve materials and workers for the war effort. [47]

On December 22, 1928, WMMN first broadcast from a studio on the mezzanine floor of The Fairmont Hotel. The station was obtained through the co-operation of Senator M. M. Neely (thus the call letters of the station) and Judge Ira E. Robinson of Grafton, chairman of the

Fairmont Hotel, 200-214 Jefferson Street, 1919.

Federal Radio Commission. Mr. Clyde S. Holt was the owner and operator of station.[48]

In 1935, the American Hotel Company took over the hotel. A corporate reorganization also occurred in 1941.[49] On June 1, 1984, the former Fairmont Hotel was dedicated as the East View Apartments,[50] its current use.

2. G. C. Murphy Building Addition, 1950.
216-218 Jefferson Street

The 216 Jefferson Street site is said to have been the site of the log cabin home of Boaz Fleming, on whose farm the city of Middletown, later to be named Fairmont, was established and laid out in regular form in 1817. From the 1880's, it had a dwelling on it that was later used as a boarding house and then as a Chinese laundry, according to the Sandborn maps.

The 218 Jefferson Street site had been a vacant lot, according to the Sandborn maps, until approximately 1918, when the one-story building was constructed and used as an electrical supply store. Both structures were demolished to make way for the one-story brick Murphy Building addition in 1950, which connected to the back of the 314-320 Adams Street building at the rear, creating an "L"-shaped building. The building is vacant.

3. Crane residence, c. 1880; The Princess Theatre, 1915.
220 Jefferson Street

A dwelling was located on this site from the 1880's. It was used around 1906 as a Chinese laundry. The Majestic Theatre Company purchased the site, then referred to as the Crane homestead, in 1911. Their intent was to construct a modern playhouse, with an entrances on both Jefferson and Main (Adams) Streets. The theatre was planned to be a family theatre for "refined vaudeville," and an architect (unnamed) at the time was working out the details of the building. The proposed building would be 60 by 135 feet, and it would have two store rooms in it as well as the theatre lobby. Since the property was located on Jefferson Street as well as on an alley, it was thought to be made safe from any danger of fire. The purchase price was $30,000.[51]

Three weeks later, the Majestic Theatre Company met and elected its officers. The plans for the new building were being drawn, and the construction was said to commence at an early date. The existing building on the site was soon to be removed.[52]

A delay on the construction ensued. In January 1913, the city council denied the building permit for the building, citing that the plans were contrary to the provisions of the fire ordinance.[53]

Work was not begun on the building until June 1915. The structure was to be of modern design and equal to those in the metropolitan cities. It was projected that it would cost $10,000 to construct. The house used as a Chinese laundry was to be demolished, and the construction was thought to take three months. The capacity of the house was to be over 700, with 450 seats on the main floor and an additional 250 in the balcony.[54]

Although the architect's plans were not yet complete, the demolition of the existing brick building on the site had begun, and the construction of the new theater followed closely. The design was to be based on the Orpheum Theatre in Clarksburg, which greatly impressed the owner on his extensive trip of surrounding cities to see their theatres. The building was to be fire proof, with plenty of exits and aisle room, so it would be possible for all the people to get out of the house in two or three minutes.[55]

At this time, the building was planned to be 32 by 95 feet, with a 25 foot tall ceiling. The stage was to be 16 by 30 feet. While the theatre was planned to be used for "moving pictures," it could also be changed into a vaudeville house with very little cost, it was stated.[56]

Work on the new theatre was delayed because the material for the gravel roof had been delayed in shipment. It was hoped to have the structure open by the first of October. The seats were said to be of special interest, as they were very large and roomy, and finished in Circassian walnut, with iron work a beautiful grey trimmed with old gold. The aisles would be thirty inches wide, "and will be received as a blessing by those people who are tired of squeezing into narrow aisles in an effort to get to a seat in a darkened house."[57]

The Princess Theatre opened for business on October 14, 1915. The new brick building was opening with the film, "The Heart of Maryland," and had a seating capacity of 600, with 175 of those seats in the balcony. Besides the wide aisles, the public was pleased to hear that one would not have to pass more that three chairs to reach any seat in the house. Also, there were no posts in the auditorium, so there was a clear and uninterrupted vision of the screen.[58]

In addition to the auditorium, there was also a ladies' retiring room, the walls of which were surrounded with huge mirrors. For safety, there were three exits, making it possible to empty the house in a minute and a half. The operating booth was modern and fire-proof, and modern fire escapes were also to be provided.[59]

The lighting for the interior was by elaborate chandeliers on the ceiling, with nicely shaped side lights along the walls. On the outside were three great arc lights, which were to make this area of the city appears as bright as day. A new sidewalk was also added to the outside of the building.[60]

The Princess Theatre operated successfully through the 1910's and 1920's, until it was renovated into the Princess Recreation Room in 1925. Noted as Fairmont's newest recreation room, it had seven pool tables, and reported the latest sporting news returns by ticker service. A business men's lunch was served from 11 am to 2 pm, with lunch counter service at all hours. "A good place to spend an idle hour," the advertisement read.[61]

A fire occurred in the basement of the building, which was the Cabaret Bar, in October 1978. The building was destroyed by fire in October 1990 when it was the Varsity Club. It is currently a parking lot.

---

[1] *Fairmont Times*, 6/20/1912, p. 2.
[2] ibid., 7/1/1912, p. 1.
[3] ibid., 11/30/1915, p. 2.
[4] ibid., 12/2/1915, p. 2.
[5] ibid., 12/10/1915, p. 1.
[6] ibid., 12/13/1915, p. 1.
[7] ibid., 12/15/1915, p. 1.
[8] ibid., 12/16/1915, p. 1.
[9] ibid., 12/31/1915, p. 1.

[10] ibid., 2/8/1916, p. 1.
[11] ibid., 2/10/1916, p. 1.
[12] ibid., 2/17/1916, p. 1.
[13] ibid., 3/2/1916, p. 1.
[14] ibid.
[15] ibid., 3/9/1916, p. 1.
[16] ibid.
[17] ibid., 3/21/1916, sect. 2, p. 1.
[18] ibid., 3/23/1916, p. 3.
[19] ibid., 4/6/1916, p. 1.
[20] ibid., 4/18/1916, p. 1.
[21] ibid., 4/21/1916, p. 1.
[22] ibid., 6/15/1916, p. 1.
[23] ibid., 6/24/1916, p. 1.
[24] ibid., 7/24/1916, p. 1.
[25] ibid., 7/26/1916, p. 1.
[26] ibid., 7/27/1916, p. 1.
[27] ibid., 7/28/1916, p. 1.
[28] ibid.
[29] ibid., 9/27/1916, p. 1.
[30] ibid., 12/22/1916, p. 1.
[31] ibid., 2/14/1917, p. 2.
[32] ibid., 5/14/1917, p. 1.
[33] ibid., 6/29/1917, p. 6.
[34] ibid., 7/14/1917, p. 2.
[35] ibid., 7/16/1917, p. 1.
[36] ibid., p. 5.
[37] ibid.
[38] ibid.
[39] ibid., 7/17/1917, p. 1.
[40] ibid., p. 8.
[41] ibid., 8/23/1917, p. 2.
[42] ibid., 8/30/1917, p. 2.
[43] ibid., 8/6/1919, p. 8.
[44] ibid., 9/22/1919, p. 3.
[45] ibid., 11/4/1919, p. 7.
[46] ibid., 1/14/1920, p. 6.
[47] ibid., 11/17/1920, p. 4.
[48] ibid., 12/22/1929, sect. 2, p. 1.
[49] *Welcome Westinghouse*, sect. 1, p. 2.
[50] Spevock, p. 79.
[51] *Fairmont Times*, 5/1/1911, p. 1.
[52] ibid., 5/23/1911, p. 1.
[53] ibid., 1/22/1913, p. 8.
[54] ibid., 6/7/1915, p. 1.
[55] ibid., 6/29/1915, p. 2.
[56] ibid.
[57] ibid., 8/31/1915, p. 8.
[58] ibid., 10/11/1915, p. 1.
[59] ibid.
[60] ibid.
[61] ibid., 8/22/1925, p. 4.

Chapter 20

200 Block Jefferson Street, odd numbered buildings

1. Governor Fleming residence, American Legion: c. 1860. 207 Jefferson Street

Governor A. B. Fleming residence, 207 Jefferson Street, c. 1908.

Governor A. B. Fleming had purchased this two-story building from Col. William Hood in the 1860's for use as his home.[1] It was made of brick, and had twelve rooms, not including the laundry room and bath room. Governor Fleming added a spacious Colonial porch to "the old house," and most of the interior trimwork was made of oak and sycamore. It was wired for electric lights, plumbed for natural gas and water, and heated by steam.[2] The brick front and basement extension were added later to the building when it was remodeled by the American Legion Post 17, which currently occupies the building.

2. T. Worth Fleming Residence, c. 1848.
217 Jefferson Street

This is said to be the site of Boaz Fleming's wolf trap, which was the first structure erected in what is now downtown Fairmont in the year 1789. The trap was a large pen made of logs, with a tilt-plank and a bait-pole. The wolf went up the plank to get the bait, the plank tilted and threw him down into the pen. The walls of the pen were ten feet high and slanted inward at the top. Once in the pen, the wolf was doomed and could not get out.[3] Boaz Fleming sold the lot in 1824 to Andrew E. McCray, and it was identified in a paper of negotiation as the "wolf trap lot opposite my cabin." McCray constructed his house on this property in 1825. Mrs. T. Worth Fleming is said to have told Glenn Lough that the McCray house had been partly constructed from the oak logs which Boaz Fleming used to build his wolf trap, specifically, the sills in the front hall and the front wall of the dining room. The McCray family occupied the house until April 2, 1831, when it was sold to Benjamin "Hatter Ben" Fleming for $150.[4] Another source stated that this residence was constructed by "Hatter Ben" Fleming in 1848,[5] so it is unclear whether there had been one or two residences at this location. Yet another source states that it was not established whether the house was constructed by "Hatter Ben" Fleming, or his son, T. Worth Fleming.[6]

This property, a two-story wood frame structure, was demolished in November 1964 because it was deemed a fire hazard.[7] The lot is currently vacant.

3. "Hatter Ben's" Store House, c. 1828; store, 1927.
219-223 Jefferson Street

This two-story wood frame structure was said to have been constructed by 1828 by "Hatter Ben" Fleming. In a letter to his wife in 1828, he stated that he had sold all his hats and was going on a hunting expedition. Since he had built this house for the storage of his hats, it was believed that it was standing at the time the letter was written. It at least was said to be several years older than the house next door, which may have been built by "Hatter Ben" in 1848.[8]

After it ceased being used for hat storage, the little frame house had been used for various purposes. It was occupied for a time by Torrey's Boot and Shoe Shop; then used as a dwelling; and, from approximately 1923 until 1927, it was used as a restaurant. When the building was being torn down in 1927, the workers found the frame timbers hewn and fastened together with wooden pegs. They were said to be as sound as the day that they had been erected, except for the sills, which had come into contact with the ground. The house had been built of yellow poplar, recognized as one of the finest West Virginia building materials because of its lasting qualities. A new brick structure, two stories in height and 26 by 40 feet, was constructed on the site in 1927.[9] It has been used for a variety of commercial enterprises, and is still in use today.

4. Haymond Building; c. 1890, c. 1904.
225-229 Jefferson Street

This lot was vacant on the Sandborn map of 1884, but appeared on the map of 1892 as a three story structure. The earliest mention of the structure was in 1890, which noted that George Morrow has moved his household goods from the Haymond Building on Jefferson Street to a different location. [10] At this time, the four-bay, brick building had a decorative cornice at the roof, a metal balcony at the two center windows on the third floor, and a metal balcony running the width of the building on the second floor; the first floor was very much as it appears today, with its arched windows and steps. [11]

Bennett and Leonard had their "tonsorial parlor" (barber shop) located there in 1893. The furniture was all new and was of the newest and latest design. There was also a first-class bathroom, always in readiness for the use of the public. "This is a deserving firm and merits the excellent trade it is getting." [12] The Democratic headquarters was located on the third story of the building to the left of the hall in the fall of 1896. [13]

The F. & M. Telephone exchange was located in the building from around 1896, according to the Sandborn map. Dr. D. D. L. Yost had his offices located in the Haymond Building in 1901, specializing in chronic and constitutional diseases. [14]

Sometime between 1902 and 1906, according to the Sandborn maps, a fourth story was added to the building. The windows on this new floor are Roman arched windows, as opposed to the segmental arch windows seen on the other three floors.

An explosion occurred in the building on May 30, 1907. Some of the Consolidated Telephone Company operators, who worked in the building, complained that they had become cold during the night. The superintendent took a candle and went to the basement

Dr. Yost's Office,
225-229 Jefferson Street, c. 1902.

to light a fire in the furnace. Immediately after he entered the door, there was an explosion, which shook the entire building and knocked him to the floor. He was taken to Dr. Yost's offices, and an ambulance took him to the Cook Hospital, where he appeared to be able to recover. Even though the entire building was shaken, there was very little damage done to it, and the building was not set on fire. It was assumed that the gas had not been completely turned off from the furnace, and the accumulated gas exploded when it came into contact with the candle.[15]

Although the upper floor had consistently been the offices of various lawyers during the years, the lower floor had several different uses. It had been used as a tailor, barber shop, and a restaurant, according to city directories from the 1920's. The building is currently vacant.

---

[1] *A History of Marion County, West Virginia*, p. 2.
[2] *Fairmont Index*, 1/3/1894.
[3] *Fairmont West Virginian*, 11/12/1964, p. 1.
[4] ibid.
[5] *Fairmont Times*, 11/9/1927, p. 1.
[6] ibid., 11/16/1964, p. 1.
[7] *Fairmont West Virginian*, 11/12/1964, p. 1.
[8] *Fairmont Times*, 10/9/1927, p. 1.
[9] ibid.
[10] *Fairmont Index*, 11/14/1890.
[11] ibid., 4/15/1892.
[12] ibid., 1/3/1894.
[13] ibid., 8/25/1896.
[14] *Twentieth Century Edition*, p. 24.
[15] *Fairmont Times*, 5/31/1907, p. 1.

Chapter 21
300 Block Jefferson Street, even numbered buildings

1. Nuzum Building, c. 1900.
306 Jefferson Street

Originally, a small two-story wood frame building existed on this site, which housed a cigar factory and a job printer at one time, according to the Sandborn maps of 1884 and 1896, respectively. By the 1902 map, however, the structure had been replaced by a four-story brick building, with a distinctive truncated corner on the southwest corner of the building.

The building had been used by the Consolidated Coal Company and the Fairmont & Clarksburg Traction Company during the construction of the adjacent Watson Building (301-311 Adams Street), which lasted from August 1909 to April 1911. The building was purchased by Sam R. Nuzum in 1911.[1] Lloyd Samples then moved his printing shop to the building in 1912, and placed a new electric sign on Jefferson Street to advertise his business.[2]

In 1919, the structure was purchased by Brooks Hutchinson, who planned to spend $50,000

Jefferson Street, 200 block looking north, December 3, 1921.
The occasion was a public wedding to promote Trade Expansion Week.

renovating it. The first floor was to be turned into a modern drug store to be managed by Earl Fortney, and the three upper floors were to be made into two- and three-room "flats."[3]

The building was purchased in the 1970's by the First National Bank of Fairmont and, along with the adjoining buildings, was demolished for the bank drive-thru facilities.

2. Cunningham Block, Hotel McAlpin, Home Furniture Company; 1901-2. 308-312 Jefferson Street

This site was originally occupied by two two-story, wood frame structure which were constructed around 1890, according to the Sandborn maps. They were removed for the construction of the Cunningham Building.

The six-story brick structure was at the time of its construction the highest business building in Fairmont. It was planned as two separate "business houses;" the section to the south (308 Jefferson Street) was five bays, and the section to the north (312 Jefferson Street) was four bays. Each "house" had a distinctive broken pediment on the top of the roof, as well as expansive windows on the five upper floors. Mr. Robert L. Cunningham, who had the structure erected, intended to put his own business in one section of the building, and to rent the remainder for store and offices purposes.[4]

On November 15, 1902, Mr. Cunningham did just that. He moved his undertaking business from the corner of Jackson and Monroe Streets to the sixth floor and part of the fifth floor of the 312 Jefferson Street section of his new building.[5] T. J. Ruddy opened his furnishing company in the building during that month as well, in the 308 Jefferson Street section.[6]

Less than a year after the new building opened, a major fire occurred in the Cunningham Block, which gutted the north section of the building. Each of the five floors was badly damaged, the new elevator equipment of the building was ruined, and the building had to be completely overhauled before it could be occupied again. The fire was discovered shortly after noon on the third floor. It was impossible for the occupants of the building to exit by the stairs, so they had to go down the exterior fire escape.[7]

The firemen were hindered in the job of extinguishing the fire due to the lack of proper equipment. At that time, it was thought that the losses would have been greatly reduced had the fire department had a hook and ladder outfit. An insurance man also stated that the citizens of the city had to pay extra costs on their insurance amounts, and that this extra cost would easily buy and maintain a modern fire fighting outfit.[8] Shortly thereafter, a horse-drawn hook and ladder wagon was obtained in 1903 at a cost of $1,200.[9]

On December 1, 1903, W. H. Billingslea moved his furniture store from the Jacobs-Hutchinson Block (201 Adams Street) to the Cunningham Block because his section of the building had been sold to the People's Bank. He acquired the stock of the T. J. Ruddy Furnishing Company, and opened up the business in the Cunningham Block as the Coal City House Furnishing Company.[10]

In 1906, the adjoining Manley Hotel was prospering so much that it needed more space.

Cunningham Block (right), 308-312 Jefferson Street and Manley Hotel (left), 314 Jefferson Street in 1910.

Mr. Manley leased all six floors of the 312 Jefferson Street portion of the building to expand his hotel by thirty-five rooms. The first floor store room was to be used as a saloon. Mr. Cunningham's undertaking business was to be moved to the new Manley Building that was in the course of erection across the street (313-317 Jefferson Street).[11]

The Ideal Theatre was located in the 308 Jefferson Street store front around the year 1915.[12] For the 1916 election, the second floor above the Ideal Theatre was used as the Democratic headquarters for the county.[13]

By 1917, the McAlpin Hotel opened independently in the 312 Jefferson Street portion of the building that had previously been used by the Manley Hotel.[14] The Home Furniture Company opened its business in the 308 Jefferson Street portion of the building in 1919.[15]

In 1929, fire once again struck the building, and gutted the section owned and occupied by the Home Furniture Company. The fire was discovered by the president of the company, who had visited the store after attending a show at the Virginia Theatre, at approximately 9:00 pm. It appeared to have started between the ceiling of the third floor and the floor of the fourth floor, in the rear of the building and near the elevator shaft. Although the fire department responded quickly and utilized their aerial truck on the flames, the building could not be saved. The fire appeared to have gone up the elevator shaft and through the roof. The adjoining building to the north, the McAlpin Hotel, suffered some damage by water dripping through the adjoining wall. The other nearby structures, the Bethlehem Building (314 Jefferson Street) and the Fortney Drug Store (306 Jefferson Street), did not suffer any damage.[16]

The building was purchased in the 1970's by the First National Bank of Fairmont and, along with the adjoining buildings, was demolished for the bank drive-thru facilities.

3. Manley Hotel, Bethlehem Building; 1901-3.
314 Jefferson Street

The original two-story, wood frame building on the site was constructed around 1890, and was used for coffin storage, and flour and feed, according to the Sandborn maps of 1892 and 1896, respectively. This structure was demolished to make way for the Manley Hotel.

Mr. Charles E. Manley, who had been the county sheriff for many years, had the six-story, two-bay brick building constructed as a hotel. It was 25 by 126 feet, and was to have a total of 58 rooms, 47 of which were to be sleeping rooms. No expense was being spared to make the hotel sumptuous in all particulars, including construction, equipment, and appointments; the hotel was to be conducted on the European plan (a fixed rate for lodging and service). The contractor for the building was T. L. Burchinal.[17]

The hotel opened on February 16, 1903. It was furnished throughout with the finest of carpets, oak and birds' eye maple furniture, and brass and iron bedsteads.[18] At the opening, there were 75 people registered at the hotel.[19] Shortly after it opened, it was granted a license for a bar in the facility.[20]

The first lady who was registered at the hotel was a Miss Olive Eddy of Amos. The hotel register claimed the honor of being the last place the name, Miss Olive Eddy, was written, for Miss Eddy was shortly thereafter married to Mr. Burt Porterfield of Butler County, Pennsylvania.[21]

The parlors and reception rooms were on the second floor. The dining room was on the first floor leading from the office. Another dining room was on the second floor, which was also to be used as a ball room. It was handsomely finished in mahogany, and had fine frescos by Charles Yeager of Fairmont. In the basement, there was a finely equipped bar, to which there was an entrance from the office and also from the street. Throughout the building, there were conveniences of all kinds. There were telephones on every floor, toilet rooms, and good heating facilities. The hotel was also equipped with a water filter, which was said to give the water a sparkle similar to mineral water.[22]

The Hotel Manley advertised the availability of rooms single or "en suite," with or without a bath. The rates were $2.50 or $3.00 by the day. It boasted of electric elevators, steam heat, electric light, call bells, inter-communication telephones, and all outside rooms. It was "modern in every appointment," a most central location, and was conducted on the American Plan (a fixed sum for room and meals combined).[23] The building was the site of many banquets, including the Undertakers Banquet,[24] the YMCA banquet,[25] and an Easter dance.[26]

The hotel was so successful that it needed to expand. In October of 1906, Mr. Manley leased the north portion of the adjoining Cunningham Block (310 Jefferson Street), which had been erected at the same time as the hotel. By cutting through the separating wall in several places, it was relatively easy to connect the halls of the two buildings, which gave the hotel 35 badly-needed additional rooms.[27]

On March 2, 1907, the Manley Hotel changed hands. It was sold by Mr. Manley to Mr. A. E. Shaw for approximately $75,000. Mr. Shaw planned some important improvements and innovations for the hotel, including rearranging the lobby so that a separate entrance for ladies would be provided and more room for lounging established. The hotel had long been popular with travelers because it had been free from gambling and had never had undesirable characters loafing about its public rooms. Mr. Shaw also intended to add the European plan (a fixed rate for lodging and service) to the place and would establish a first-class restaurant on the second floor of the building in the room used as a banquet hall.[28]

"American plan meals are a thing of the past for the present at the hostelry," stated the newspaper in November of 1916. In the rear of the lobby, a fine restaurant was installed. The restaurant was to be first class in every particular, and a lunch counter in front of the pool room was maintained for those desiring meals while the main room was closed. There was not much demand for meals on the American plan (a fixed sum for room and meals combined), and there was a new demand for the business men's lunch. The dining room which has been used for the American plan meals was to be divided into additional sleeping rooms. The total number of rooms at the hotel would then be twelve rooms with baths, forty-five outside rooms, and twenty court rooms.[29]

The Manley Hotel closed its dining room in June of 1917. The increase in cost for food made it unprofitable, even though it was on the Continental plan (a la carte). The hotel was crowded, but there was "light eating."[30]

In November of 1920, the Manley Hotel was sold and converted into a modern office building. The Bethlehem Coal Company acquired the property from the Shaw Hotel Company, and remodeled the interior of the structure to convert it into a first-class office building. It contained the central offices of the Bethlehem Coal Company. This was an indication for the need of more office buildings in the city.[31] After seventeen years of successful operation, the Manley Hotel closed its doors on November 16, 1920.[32] By August of 1921, the renovations were nearly complete to convert the building into the Bethlehem Coal Company offices. The first floor of the building was occupied by the Marion Hardware Company.[33]

The building was purchased in the 1970's by the First National Bank of Fairmont and, along with the adjoining buildings, was demolished for the bank drive-thru facilities.

Manley Hotel, 314 Jefferson Street, c. 1902.

4. Masonic Temple Building, 1906-7.
Baldwin and Pennington, architects.
316-320 Jefferson Street

The original buildings on this site constituted three dwellings and a few outbuildings from the 1890's, according to the Sandborn maps.

The first indication of plans for the construction of a large-scale building on this site occurred in 1905. The owners of the property, the Watson-Malone-Miller Company, proposed to construct a building on the site and sell two floors of the building to the Y.M.C.A., which was seeking a permanent home. It was also suggested at this time that the Federal Government would use the ground floor for a post office, and the remaining five floors were to be devoted to apartments.[34] This plan was rejected by the Y.M.C.A., and they located their new home over the bridge (100 Fairmont Avenue, which is the current Moose Lodge).[35]

"Two New Local Skyscrapers," read the headlines of the paper on April 16, 1905. The Watson-Malone-Miller Company announced plans to construct two buildings: one on Jefferson Street and one on the corner of Jefferson and Main (Adams) Streets. The corner building was to be the new home of the Bank of Fairmont. The Jefferson Street building was to constructed first (this was the location that had been offered to and rejected by the Y.W.C.A.). The new plan was to construct an eight-story steel frame structure, built as nearly fire-proof as possible. It was to cost $100,000 and to be completed by March 1, 1906. The Bank of Fairmont was to move into the building while the construction of its permanent home on the corner of Jefferson and Main (Adams) street was in progress, which would begin after the first skyscraper was completed.[36]

The Masonic Lodge was offered the two upper floors (the seventh and eighth) of the building on Jefferson Street, and the remainder would be constructed as apartments. If the Masonic Lodge did not accept the offer, the entire building was to be constructed as apartments. The architect for the project was Lon C. Smith, who was in the process of completing the plans.[37] Workers began clearing the site of the Jefferson Street skyscraper on April 21, 1905; they cleared the lot, knocking down the fencing and removing the buildings that were there.[38]

Plans changed once more. In July 1905, Fairmont Lodge No. 9 A. F. & A. Masons purchased the excavated lot on Jefferson Street from the Watson-Miller-Malone Company, to construct a Masonic Temple "which will be an ornament to the city." The building was to be "rushed to completion" (as it seems every building in Fairmont was) to have the first floor ready for occupation by March 1, 1906. The building was to be five or six stories tall, though because of the banquet hall to be included in the plans, would appear to be one story taller. A price of $20,000 was paid for the lot.[39]

Masonic Temple Building, 316-320 Jefferson Street, 1906.

The Masons had been in search of new quarters. Their rooms in the J. L. Lott Building (330-332 Adams Street) at the corner of Adams and Madison Streets were well-furnished, but too small for the fast-growing lodge. They had considered renting one or two of the upper stories of the building to have been constructed on the Jefferson Street lot, but the lodge wanted a new home that it could call its own.[40]

The new building was to be 55 feet by 110 feet and constructed of brick and steel. The first floor was to be for business purposes, to be occupied by "one of the most important industries in the city." One or two floors would be used for offices, and perhaps a floor or two of apartments. The upper floors were reserved for the lodge and a large banquet room. The banquet room could be rented for any function. Every man in the lodge was ready to subscribe to stock for the construction of the new building.[41]

The architects for the building were the Baltimore, Maryland firm of Baldwin and Pennington, who also designed the Y.M.C.A. Building (100 Fairmont Avenue), which is currently used for the Moose Lodge. Ephraim Francis Baldwin was also noteworthy for designing many railroad stations, especially in Maryland, for the Baltimore and Ohio Railroad.[42] The contract for the erection of the new Masonic Temple Building was awarded to the Brady Construction Company of Fairmont.

Masonic Temple Building, Times *newspaper illustration, 1907.*

The work was scheduled to begin in September 1905 and to be completed in June 1906. It was to be one of the prettiest buildings in the city. The outside was to be constructed of brick, stone, and terra cotta. Although only five stories high, it was to be higher that any other building in the city, because of the high ceilings in the lodge room and in the banquet hall.[43]

The basement of the building was to be rented for various enterprises. The first floor was to be finished for "some business." The second and third floors were to be fitted up for offices, many of which already had been rented. The fourth floor was to be made into a magnificent banquet hall, 52 feet by 77 feet, which could hold 600 guests. A large banquet hall was needed in the city at this time. The kitchen would be adjacent to it. The fifth floor of the building was to be the lodge room, for Masonic use only. It was to be 52 by 71 feet, and was to be the grandest in the State. Besides the large lodge room, the fifth floor was to contain the necessary paraphernalia rooms.[44]

The construction of the building was delayed because of bad weather, which precluded the foundation builders from doing anything in the wet weather. When it was learned that the steel for the structure was likely to arrive about six months late, the building committee began looking for new options. Because the Masonic Temple Building was to be built in a rush, the Brady Company sub-let the contract to a company who it was thought could have the building under roof in two months. The National Fireproofing Company would use reinforced concrete instead of steel girders and beams.[45]

Reinforced concrete was a relatively new construction method, but it had been pronounced as safe as steel as well as adding to the fire-proof characteristics of the building. The architects for the building, the firm of Baldwin and Pennington of Baltimore, were consulted on the matter, and they were very much in favor of the substitution. Although the Security Bank

Building (209 Adams Street), constructed in 1904-5, had concrete floors, it appears that this was the first complete structure of reinforced concrete in building construction in Fairmont.[46]

As soon as the foundations were completed, the National Fireproofing Company began the reinforced concrete work. The workmen did not wait for the brick walls to be built, and the concrete work was pushed along. The roof was on the building by the time the brick work was completed. Thus, the delay on the building was lessened, and this was agreeable to the Brady Construction Company.[47]

Plans for laying the cornerstone of the new Masonic Temple began in early November 1905. Since the foundations were being hurried along, it was thought that the ceremony could be held on Thanksgiving day. Worshipful Master T. Wilbur Hennen was to invite the Grand Master and other Grand Lodge officers to participate. An invitation was extended to all the surrounding lodges to be present on the occasion, and "the Masonic emblem is expected to flash in Fairmont as never before."[48]

Near the end of November, it was thought that the cornerstone could be laid in the middle of December, since the foundation work could not be completed in time for the original Thanksgiving day date.[49] This date also passed without the ceremony taking place. In January 1906, the concrete workers had begun to work on the Masonic Temple. They were making the frames for holding the concrete in place, and the floor and entire frame work was to be a single piece of "the new kind of masonry,"[50] reinforced concrete.

Snow prevented the Brady Construction Company crews from getting back to work on the building in the spring of 1906. Although the intention was to have the first floor ready by March 1, 1906, there were delays because of changes in the plans and because of the weather. Most of the material was on hand at this point in time: terra cotta, reinforcing iron, and dozens of other kinds of materials were occupying several vacant lots near the building site. They just needed the weather to cooperate.[51]

On March 16, 1906, it was announced that the contractors would be ready for the laying of the cornerstone in a short time, and the Masons began preparations for the ceremony within two weeks.[52] It was later announced that the cornerstone ceremony would take place on Monday, April 9, 1906. Although the Grand Master, George W. McClintic of Charleston could not be present, he issued his proxy to Hon. O. S. McKinney of Fairmont, who was to be in charge of the event.[53]

"Despite The Drenching Showers Masons Laid Cornerstone for New Temple," read the headlines. More than 200 Masons were at the site for the ceremonies, after marching there from their old lodge quarters at the corner of Adams and Jefferson Streets. They were joined by hundreds of bystanders. Grand Master McKinney addressed the crowd, mentioning that earlier lodge quarters were located close to the new building, in the eastern room of the upper chamber of the old Presbyterian church (thought to be near the corner of Jefferson and Adams Streets). Mr. E. C. Kerr of Fairmont, the oldest living member of the local lodge to attend the ceremonies, said that when he joined the lodge in 1850, they met in the second story of a little building in the rear of what in 1906 was Nuzum Grocery, which was located in the Skinner Building

(110-114 Adams Street). The lodge later moved to the Presbyterian church.[54]

The ceremony continued with the lowering of the cornerstone, along with a sealed box containing records of the various Masonic lodges, current issues of daily and weekly newspapers and various other articles, "certain memorials of the period at which it was erected, so that in the lapse of ages, if the fury of the elements of the slow but certain rages of time should lay bare its foundation, an enduring record may be found by succeeding generations to hear testimony to the energy, industry, and culture of our time."[55]

The Grand Master spread the cement, the deputy Grand Master applied the square, the senior grand warden the level, and the junior grand warden the plumb. Then the corn was scattered as an emblem of plenty, the wine was poured as an emblem of joy and gladness, and the oil as an emblem of peace. Because of the bad weather, the rest of the ceremonies, which would have been public, were conducted in the old lodge quarters, thus depriving the public from hearing the orator of the occasion, Hon. E. M. Showalter.[56]

Part of Mr. Showalter's remarks ring true even today. "The day for dingy, misshapen, contracted buildings with us is in the past. We must have modern, spacious, fireproof structures, with light and ventilation, and equipment in our business blocks, in our churches, in our educational institutions, and in our temples. Commerce, society, civilization make those calls upon us and make them urgent, and we cannot and we will not turn a deaf ear."[57]

Masonic Temple Building, 316-320 Jefferson Street, 1916.

Work on the building continued. In September, it was thought that the first floor would be complete, and on that date the Post Office would move from the "Skinner Building" (106 Adams Street).[58] In December, it was noted that the move was delayed awaiting the arrival of a postal inspector from Washington.[59] On December 11, 1906, it was announced that the Post Office would not move until the first of the year, since the postal inspector had not arrived.[60] On December 17, 1906, it was announced that the Post Office was now in its new quarters in the Masonic Temple Building.[61]

The basement of the building was ready for occupancy in January of 1907. A pool and billiard room, and bowling alley were planned for the floor, to be opened for business in February.[62]

In May of 1907, the dedication of the new Masonic Temple Building was announced for May 23. It had just recently been completed, and two days were planned for the festivities. The first day was to include throwing the building open for public inspection, the second for the dedication proper in the Masonic lodge room for the lodge members.[63]

An invitation to the public to visit the new Masonic Temple on June 5, 1907 was published in the newspaper. Visitors were to be shown through the building from the basement to (and including) the roof. This included the lodge rooms, banquet hall, office rooms, Post Office, and bowling alleys. An orchestra was to provide music during the event. The postmaster, A. Howard Fleming, was to allow the public to see the inner workings of the Post Office. The dedication ceremonies the next day were limited to the Masons and their ladies, owing to the large number of them expected to attend.[64]

The public inspection of the new building was a huge success. There was a steady stream of visitors to the building, and members of the Masonic building committee and other members of the Lodge were there to show the visitors around. Dowden's Orchestra provided the music throughout the afternoon and evening.[65]

The visitors to the Temple were taken by the Otis hydraulic elevator to the upper story and first looked over the city from the roof. Between this and the fifth floor were the two rooms occupied by Architect Giffin, who was the supervising architect for the construction. On the fifth floor was the lodge room, which was the part of the building for the Masons only after the lodge moved into it. This is where the orchestra was stationed, and seats were arranged for 400 people.[66]

On the fourth story was the banquet hall with reception and retiring rooms, as well as the kitchen. The hall was to be open to public meetings, receptions, and balls. The third floor consisted of apartments, and included 17 large rooms. On the second floor, there were 17 well-arranged offices, nearly all of which had been taken by the opening of the building.[67]

Watson Banquet in Masonic Temple ballroom in 1911.

The first floor was used entirely by the Post Office, which was the best equipped in the state. A souvenir booklet was printed and distributed to the visitors; it contained photographs of the rooms and the work force, as well as interesting data regarding the building. The basement held the Temple bowling alleys and pool room, as well as the mechanical equipment.[68]

The most auspicious occasion for the Masons of Fairmont was the dedication of the Masonic Temple building the next day. The extensive lodge room was filled to capacity; it was estimated that nearly 1,000 masons and their ladies were in attendance. Speeches that evening included a brief history of Masonry in Fairmont, the city's growth, and the grandeur of the new building. "The grandeur of the outer walls were shown to be symbolic of the great teachings and workings of the inner order which has done much for the upbuilding of humanity for many generations past." The grand lodge ceremonies were then performed and the hall was dedicated in due and ancient form. After the speeches, the entire party exited to the banquet hall below for the reception.[69] The total cost of the structure was $122,000.

The rooms located on the lower floors were filled with Fairmont's commercial offices. The banquet hall in the building became the favorite place for social life in Fairmont. Many organizations had their dances, balls, and performances there. In the 1910's, balls were held in the Masonic Temple ballroom, but alcohol was banned. "At every formal ball 'breath-smellers' were posted by the elevator in the Masonic Temple to detect and report any violator of the rule. When a young blade was found guilty he was immediately ejected if he were a stag, but permitted to stay, on pain and penalty, if he were the escort of an acceptable girl, but his name was dropped from invitation list of future dances."[70]

With the completion of the new Post Office at 321 Monroe Street, the quarters that once provided the most up-to-date postal facility in the state were vacated on June 30, 1914.[71] This left the first floor empty for a short while. On May 1, 1915, the Ross Furniture Company moved into the building and was ready for business. The company had been established in 1887 by Sam R. Nuzum, and later organized as the Fairmont Furniture Company. In 1904, H. J. Ross became identified with the business, and eventually the Fairmont Furniture Company was taken over by the Ross Furniture Company. The business had been conducted at "the old stand" (117-119 Adams Street), but Mr. Nuzum was contemplating the erection of a big business block on that site, so the move was made. The firm of Holden and Spedden was hired to construct a mezzanine floor to double the space of the floor.[72]

A description of the renovated building at the time of the opening of the Ross Furniture Store seems to confirm that this was when the facade was revised. The original layout of three segmented arched windows was changed to one segmented arched window on the left and one large window (encompassing two original windows) on the right. "A feature of the main floor is the light. A large plate glass almost as high and extending the width of the front lets the daylight into the room, making it as light as day."[73] This enlargement of the window area necessitated changing the brickwork; the crossettes surrounding the two original windows were reworked into horizontal ribbons around this area; the original crossettes around the segmented window on the left remain. This change was documented in a newspaper photograph from 1921.[74]

In September 1917, the Women's Club of Fairmont leased the auditorium of the Masonic Temple for its general club meetings and department meetings. The kitchen and dining equipment were seen as being very convenient for the demonstrations conducted by the home economics department. The move from their quarters in the Watson Hotel (402 Adams Street) was expected to be completed in October.[75]

The furniture business on the first floor of the Masonic Temple Building was good, and more floor space was needed. In 1920, the Ross Furniture Company augmented its floor space by leasing the second and third floors of the Manley Building which was located directly in the rear of the Masonic Temple Building on Porter Alley (now Meredith Street). The walls were cut through to establish this communication between the two buildings.[76]

The Masons sold the building in 1975, and vacated the premises.

The building was placed on the National Register of Historic Places in April 1993. It currently houses a used merchandise store.

5. Residence; c. 1880, c. 1894.
322-324 Jefferson Street

The original part of this two-story wood frame house, set back from the street approximately 25 feet, was constructed prior to the 1884 Sandborn map. With the requirement that structures in the business district be constructed of brick after the Great Fire of 1876, this building may pre-date the fire. The front section, with its distinctive double bay windows, was constructed between 1892 and 1896, according to the Sandborn maps of those years. It had been a residence until the 1920's, when it was then used for a variety of commercial endeavors. It still exists on the site.

---

[1] *Fairmont Times*, 4/27/1911, p. 3.
[2] ibid., 10/23/1912, p. 2.
[3] ibid., 5/19/1919, p. 4.
[4] *Twentieth Century Edition*, p. 38.
[5] *Fairmont Times*, 11/15/1902, p. 4.
[6] ibid.
[7] ibid., 7/11/1903, p. 1.
[8] ibid.
[9] *Welcome Westinghouse*, sect. 6, p. 8.
[10] *Fairmont West Virginian*, 7/23/1904, p. 7.
[11] *Fairmont Times*, 10/9/1906, p. 1.
[12] ibid., 5/25/1915, p. 1.
[13] ibid., 7/20/1916, p. 1.
[14] ibid., 7/29/1917, p. 2.
[15] ibid., 3/9/1919, p. 4.
[16] ibid., 4/20/1929, p. 1.
[17] *Twentieth Century Edition*, p. 37.
[18] *Fairmont Times*, 2/13/1903, p. 1.
[19] ibid., 2/17/1903, p. 1.

[20] ibid., 2/18/1903, p. 1.
[21] ibid., 2/19/1903, p. 1.
[22] ibid., 2/20/1903, p. 5.
[23] R. L. Polk & Company, 1904, p. 8.
[24] *Fairmont Times*, 7/11/1903, p. 1.
[25] ibid., 2/24/1904, p. 1.
[26] ibid., 4/2/1904, p. 8.
[27] ibid., 10/9/1906, p. 1.
[28] ibid., 3/2/1907, p. 5.
[29] ibid., 11/1/1916, p. 2.
[30] ibid., 6/1/1917, p. 4.
[31] ibid., 11/13/1920, p. 1.
[32] ibid., 11/17/1920, p. 6.
[33] ibid., 8/24/1921, p. 8.
[34] ibid., 3/8/1905, p. 1.
[35] ibid., 4/10/1905, p. 2.
[36] ibid., 4/16/1905, p. 1.
[37] ibid.
[38] ibid., 4/21/1905, p. 2.
[39] ibid., 7/5/1905, p. 1.
[40] ibid.
[41] ibid.
[42] Potter, p. 131.
[43] ibid., 9/16/1905, p. 1.
[44] ibid.
[45] ibid., 10/26/1905, p. 1.
[46] ibid.
[47] ibid.
[48] ibid., 11/10/1905, p. 1.
[49] ibid., 11/23/1905, p. 1.
[50] ibid., 1/2/1906, p. 1.
[51] ibid., 3/14/1906, p. 7.
[52] ibid., 3/16/1906, p. 5.
[53] ibid., 3/28/1906, p. 1.
[54] ibid., 4/10/1906, p. 1.
[55] ibid.
[56] ibid.
[57] ibid.
[58] ibid., 9/8/1906, p. 6.
[59] ibid., 12/8/1906, p. 12.
[60] ibid., 12/11/1906, p. 6.
[61] ibid., 12/17/1906, p. 1.
[62] ibid., 1/26/1907, p. 8.
[63] ibid., 5/2/1907, p. 1.
[64] ibid., 6/5/1907, p. 1.
[65] ibid., 6/6/1907, p. 1.
[66] ibid.
[67] ibid.
[68] ibid.
[69] ibid.
[70] Hoffman, p. 106.
[71] *Fairmont Times*, 6/30/14, p. 1.
[72] ibid., 4/6/1915, p. 2.
[73] ibid., 5/5/1915, p. 3.
[74] ibid., 6/19/1921, p. 6.
[75] ibid., 9/14/1917, p. 6.
[76] ibid., 2/11/1920, p. 8.

Chapter 22

300 Block Jefferson Street, odd numbered buildings

1. Manley Building; c. 1880, c. 1906.
315-317 Jefferson Street

From the 1880's, the southern portion of this lot was vacant, and the northern portion had a two-story structure on it that was used for a variety of commercial enterprises, according to the Sandborn maps. Around the year 1906, the northern lot was rebuilt and southern lot was developed in conjunction with it to create a three-story structure that was known as the Manley Building. The structure had commercial businesses on the first floor, and apartments on the upper floors, according to the Sandborn maps. This building no longer exists, and the site is part of the Harper-Meredith City County Building, which was constructed in 1982.

2. C. L. Smith residence, c. 1892.
319 Jefferson Street

This two-story pressed brick structure with native stone foundation first appeared on the Sandborn map of 1892. It was the residence of C. L. Smith, publisher of the *Fairmont Index* newspaper. It had a distinctive projecting two-story bay. The interior of the house was trimmed in oak, and there were five bed chambers and a bathroom on the second floor. The house was plumbed for natural gas and water, lighted with electricity and heated by steam.[1] It had been used as a dwelling through the 1900's. This building no longer exists, and the site is part of the Harper-Meredith City County Building, which was constructed in 1982.

C. L. Smith residence, 319 Jefferson Street, c. 1894.

3. Kunst Residence, c. 1890. 321 Jefferson Street

The original structure on this site was a one-story dwelling set back from the street. Some time around 1892, according to the Sandborn map, a new two-story structure was built up to the street. It had been constructed and continually used as a dwelling. Fairmont city directories from 1915 to 1933 list the inhabitant as Dr. Kunst. This building no longer exists, and the site is part of the Harper-Meredith City County Building, which was constructed in 1982.

4. U. A. Clayton Residence, Moose Club; c. 1890. 323 Jefferson Street

The original structure on this site was a small one- story structure. A two-story Victorian brick structure was constructed on the site around the year 1890 for Mr. U. A. Clayton, who owned a planing mill.[2] It was used as a residence until October 3, 1918, when it was sold to the Moose Lodge for $25,000. They extensively remodeled the building to be used for their lodge quarters, which opened on January 18, 1919.[3] This building no longer exists, and the site is part of the Harper-Meredith City County Building, which was constructed in 1982.

U. A. Clayton residence, 323 Jefferson Street, c. 1894.

5. commercial building; c. 1880, c. 1890. 327-329 Jefferson Street

A two-story structure existed on the northern portion (329 Jefferson Street) of this site on the Sandborn map of 1884. A one-story addition was constructed beside (327 Jefferson Street) around the year 1890. These two buildings remained through the 1950's. Throughout the years, they were generally used as a tin shop and a hardware store, among other commercial uses, according to the Sandborn maps. This building no longer exists, and the site is part of the Harper-Meredith City County Building, which was constructed in 1982.

---

[1] *Fairmont Index*, 1/3/1894.
[2] ibid.
[3] *Fairmont Times*, 1/12/1919, p. 8.

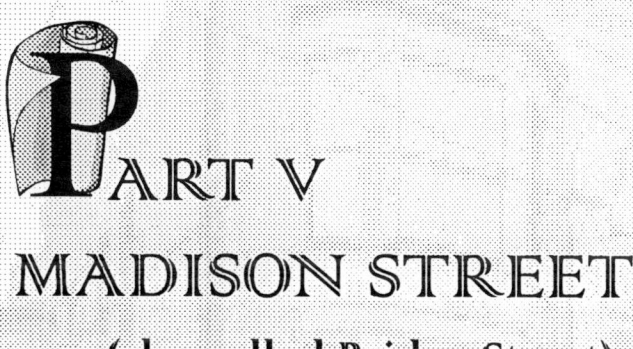

Part V
Madison Street
(also called Bridge Street)

Long ago, Madison Street was important because the first bridge across the Monongahela River, an iron suspension bridge, was constructed at its southern terminus in 1852. In fact, it was often referred to as "Bridge Street." The B. & O. Railroad Passenger Station was also located next to the old suspension bridge on Cleveland Avenue. The street became a convenient and popular location for hotels, as well as the saloons associated with them. The hotels competed for patrons by operating "busses" to meet the trains. Because of the steepness of the terrain near the station, it was a wild, rough ride up "Rocky Hill," which characterized lower Madison Street.[1]

Chapter 23

200 Block Madison Street, even numbered buildings

NOTE: The buildings comprising the rest of this block were modest one- and two-story structures that had a variety of uses, such as barbers, tailors, laundries, shoe repairs and others. Very little information is known about these structures, and they are not included in this work. The buildings have been demolished, and the sites are parking lots.

1. Roush House, c. 1890.
200-202 Madison Street

From the Sandborn map of 1892, it appears that this building was a three-story dwelling before it was used as a restaurant. On February 16, 1902, W. H. Roush opened his restaurant and rooming house at this location at the southeast corner of Madison and Washington Streets. It was seen as a most desirable location, since it was within one block of the B. & O. Railroad Passenger Station (Cleveland Avenue) and overlooked the Monongahela River. Although it was a modest hostelry, Mr. Roush followed the old axiom, "Cleanliness is next to Godliness."[2]

In 1916, Mr. Roush made improvements to his hotel to handle the large and increasing trade that was coming to this popular eating emporium. Greater facilities were added to the hotel;[3] and, from the Sandborn map of 1918, this appears to have been a two-story wrap-around addition on the south, west, and north sides of the building.

In July 1917, Mr. Roush moved his restaurant to the first floor of the McAlpin Hotel (310 Jefferson Street).[4] In 1922, 47 members of the striking Culinary Workers Union took over the operations of the Ideal Restaurant, at the old Roush location, which had been owned by Mr. Edward F. Ford. The Culinary Workers wanted to operate the restaurant in order to keep the members of the union in employment. They had an auspicious start, feeding 400 people the first day of their operations.[5]

According to the city directories, this establishment was known as the Baldwin Hotel, the Boyer-Irvine Hotel, and the St. Charles Hotel. In the 1939 directory, the address is no longer listed, and the building no longer appears on the 1950 Sandborn map; it is assumed that the building was demolished around this time. The site is currently a parking lot.

---

[1] Fleming, p. 14.
[2] *Industrial Fairmont in 1908*, p. 64.
[3] *Fairmont Times*, 5/24/1916, p. 2.
[4] ibid., 7/29/1917, p. 2.
[5] ibid., 7/2/1922, p. 2.

Chapter 24

200 Block Madison Street, odd numbered buildings

1. Gans Hotel, Hotel Marion, Mountain City Hotel; 1900.
201-209 Madison Street

A two-story dwelling existed on this site, on the southwest corner of Madison and Washington Streets, on the 1892 and 1896 Sandborn maps. It was replaced by the three- story Gans Hotel, which was constructed in 1900. The hotel opened in November of that year.[1]

In April of 1905, the hotel, which was then known as the Marion Hotel, was heavily damaged by a fire that was thought to have begun by a fuse burning out in the engine room in back of the hotel. A nearby livery and a house also suffered damage, as flames from the fire shot up above the roof of the hotel. In addition to the roof, the window shades and part of the interior was also on fire. The main damage to the building was due to the water used to extinguish it.[2] In 1910, the hotel changed hands again. The former Marion Hotel was going to open up as a "stag hostelry," for men only, as the Hotel Antler. Renovations to the building were planned.[3]

The building underwent renovations again when it was operated by W. L. Lunch as the Madison Hotel. At this time, in 1916, a dining room was installed.[4] In 1918, the name of the establishment was changed to the Carrico Hotel.[5]

In March of 1920, the new Carrico Hotel dining room was opened with much fanfare. Roses and carnations were given as favors to the people who visited the dining room during the formal opening, and music was furnished as well. The new dining room had a seating capacity of 55 people at marble-topped tables, and had fourteen stools at its marble-topped counter. Mr. Carrico was also arranging for the installation of hot and cold water in all rooms of the New Carrico Hotel, since he had recently purchased the property.[6]

Beginning in the mid-1920's and through the 1940's, the establishment was known as the Mountain City Hotel, according to the city directories. This building no longer exists, and the site is a parking lot.

2. Murphy-Deveny Building, 1912-13.
215-221 Madison Street

Mr. F. M. Murphy and Mr. T. A. Deveny bought this property from the Christie family in 1912. The old two-story homestead on the site, (known as a landmark in the city), as well as an old grocery store on the site, were removed to make way for the new building. The new building was a three story high brick structure, designed for four business rooms on the ground floor, and modern apartments on the second and third floors. Work on the foundation had begun in

July of 1912.⁷ By 1913, several business had already located to the structure, including the United Shoe Store and the Leader Shoe and Men's Clothing store.⁸

In February of 1915, fire struck the Murphy-Deveny Building. It appears to have started in the basement by a hot water heater that had exploded. The fire was contained to the basement and first floor of the big structure, though thousands of dollars of damage was done to the building. The stock of both the United Shoe Store and the Leader Clothing Store was destroyed or very badly damaged, but it was thought that both firms had insurance. The heavy timbers in the basement were burned, and the wall between the two stores on the first floor was burned through in places and the plaster soaked with water. The tenants on the upper floors were frightened and evacuated, but no one was injured. Because of the dense smoke in the building, the firemen's lantern would not burn, so they used flashlights, some of which they had borrowed from spectators.⁹

In 1915, it was announced that George A. Walter was to open a new ten cent store in the Murphy-Deveny Building. The room in the building had previously been occupied by the Fairmont Produce Company, but was being renovated for its new purpose.¹⁰

Another fire occurred in 1926, in which the stocks of two of the four stores on the first floor, Wolf's Leader Shop (which had opened up in place of Deitz's Leader Shop) and Sidlers Clothing Store, were destroyed. The destruction was actually caused by two fires occurring within two hours of each other on January 18, 1926. People in the upper floor apartments, as well as in the Virginia Theatre which abutted the rear of the Murphy-Deveny Building, left the buildings because smoke from the fire had infiltrated the spaces.¹¹

Fire eventually destroyed this building. On April 17, 1982, two businesses, The Wiz nightclub and Chick's Bargain Center, were destroyed in the blaze. The Wiz nightclub location had once been the location of the State liquor store.¹² The site is currently part of a parking lot.

3. Booher's Saloon, c. 1890. 223-225 Madison Street

On the 1884 Sandborn map, there was a small, one-story frame building on the site in which meats were sold. On the 1892 map, it had been replaced with a two-story brick building, though used for the same purpose. In 1900, Mr. Morgan had bought it for $8,000. Two years later, in 1902, F. M. Murphy bought this property from Mr. Morgan, which had been used for J. L. Booher's saloon, for $21,000.¹³

At first, Mr. Murphy announced that he was going to construct a four-story "stag hotel" (for men only) on the site.¹⁴ This apparently did not occur. Mr. Murphy continued to operate the saloon here, as well as bath rooms on the second floor of the building, which were proving popular in 1911.¹⁵

During the 1910's and 1920's, a variety of different stores occupied the two store fronts on the first floor, such as restaurants, clothing stores, and jewelers, according to the city directories.

The building no longer exists, and the site is part of a parking lot.

[1] *Fairmont Free Press*, 11/15/1900.
[2] *Fairmont Times*, 5/3/1905, p. 1.
[3] ibid., 7/16/1910, p. 1.
[4] ibid., 12/2/1916, p. 2.
[5] ibid., 4/25/1918, p. 2.
[6] ibid., 3/9/1920, p. 2.
[7] ibid., 7/27/1912, p. 2.
[8] ibid., 1/10/1913, p. 5; 10/31/1913, p. 8.
[9] ibid., 2/2/1915, p. 1.
[10] ibid., 11/22/1915, p. 1.
[11] ibid., 1/19/1926, p. 1.
[12] *Fairmont Times-West Virginian*, 4/17/1982, p. 1.
[13] *Fairmont Times*, 10/20/1902, p. 1.
[14] ibid., 5/28/1910, p. 1.
[15] ibid., 2/11/1911, p. 1.

Chapter 25

300 Block Madison Street, even numbered buildings

1. Standard Garage, Fairmont Recreation Corporation; 1911.
310 Madison Street

A two-story dwelling existed on the site from the 1880's. In 1911, George T. Watson and Walton Miller leased the property from the Fairmont & Clarksburg Traction to construct a new home for the Standard Garage Company. The building was 45 feet by 110 feet, and was a garage that featured the output of the Packard and Oldsmobile factories.[1] The fire-proof building opened in June of 1911. Five years later, there was no longer room for people to store their cars, only room for the cars which were for sale. [2] This location, though convenient, became too small for the growing company; in the spring of 1919, the Standard Garage moved its facilities to the old National Guard Armory at 8 Locust Avenue.[3]

The Fairmont Recreation Company was the next business to occupy the building. In October of 1920, they had a contest for the best suggestion of a name for the new amusement center, with a prize of $50. The hall, which was the largest in the state, was equipped with pool and billiard tables, a soda fountain, and a lunch counter. It opened on October 14, 1920,[4] and operated at that location through the 1950's, according to city directories.

This building no longer exists, and the site is part of a city parking lot.

2. "The Rink," Opera House: c. 1885;
Kenyon Hotel, Madison Hotel: 1903. 312 Madison Street

During the 1880's, the roller skating craze hit the town, and the members of Patriarchs Militant, the uniformed body of the Odd Fellows, decided that the town needed a combination armory for the order and a skating floor. The old "rink," on the site of the Kenyon Hotel, was planned and built. The building was a monstrous affair for those days. It was narrow, long, and possessed a rounded roof that was "good to look at."[5] The Davis Light Guards used the building for practicing its drills.[6] At first, roller skating occupied the rink for a number of seasons, but finally the craze died out, and theatrical shows began to travel the territory; it was then decided to transform the skating rink into a theatre.[7] This was the second location for a theatre in Fairmont; the first was the "Town Hall Theatre" on the second floor at 200 Adams Street. This transformation was accomplished by placing a stage in the rear, raising the floor beginning at the stage and ending at the Madison Street end, and erecting a tiny balcony in the rear, with the ticket offices and store rooms underneath. No opera chairs were purchased, but a few hundred of the "kitchen variety" were purchased and nailed together in long strips, each strip constituting the seating arrangement on one side of the middle aisle.[8]

Fairmont had no electric lights in the 1880's and early 1890's, so the stage and auditorium were lighted with oil lamps. For the footlights, a long row of lamps was placed. For dark scenes on the stage, pieces of tin were placed on a rod between the stage and the lamps, and when the stage was darkened, the rod was turned so that the tins flapped up again and the lamps shut off their rays. Scenery rolled over poles at the top of the stage, and the noise was so loud that it could be heard all over the auditorium.[9]

There were only two dressing rooms, one for men, the other for women. During one big burlesque, there were so many chorus girls that many of them went into a stable in the rear of the theatre to change their costumes. At times, the horses in these stables would break up a performance by restlessly tromping on the wooden boards of the floors in their stalls.[10]

The Opera House, as it was known in the 1890's, was updated to better accommodate performances. In April of 1893, it was announced that the building was to be repaired and renovated to permit a gallery. This was thought to fill the requirements of the town for years to come.[11] By October, the stage had been raised to permit using the largest scenery. The inside of the house had been neatly painted and the whole structure cleansed. New opera house chairs were also installed.[12]

In December 1901, the Opera House was destroyed by fire. The fire was first spotted above the stable in back of the Opera House. The alarm was quickly sent in, the fire wagon arrived in a short time, and a hose was run from the plug at the corner of Madison and Adams Streets, but it was impossible to save the Opera House; attention was turned to saving the buildings nearby. Because there was no wind that early morning, many buildings were saved. It was immediately decided to build a new and up-to-date theatre on the site of the old one.[13] Although a new Opera House was constructed shortly thereafter, it was located on the site at 325 Monroe Street.

The old Opera House site was vacant until the Kenyon Hotel was constructed on the site in 1903. It was a four- story brick structure. The facade was divided into three parts; the central section had a Roman arch entrance opening on the first floor, pairs of rectangular windows on the second and third floors, and two arched windows that together formed a Roman arch on the fourth floor. The two side sections had store fronts on the first floor, and had projecting bays on the second, third, and fourth floors. The building was topped with a decorative cornice at the roof. Bay windows were also incorporated on the sides of the structure.

The new Kenyon Hotel in the Nelson-Galligher Building was opened to the public in November 1903, and a number of visitors were shown throughout it by the proprietors, Mr. Chas. Coffman and Mr. C. C. Cunningham. The hotel contained thirty-six sleeping rooms, nine bath rooms, two parlors, two kitchens, a dining room, an office, and a lobby. It was nicely furnished throughout and was equipped with all modern improvements and conveniences.[14]

The building underwent renovations in 1906 when a new proprietor took over the operation.[15] During the next three years, however, the hotel gained a rather notorious reputation. In August of 1907, the Kenyon Drug Company, located in the Kenyon Hotel Building, was given a stiff fine for selling liquor on Sunday: $200 for each count.[16] A gambling room was found in

Kenyon Hotel (left), 312 Madison Street and residence, 310 Madison Street (right), c. 1905.

the Kenyon Hotel in April of 1908. [17] The Kenyon Drug Company was again fined $200 for selling liquor in 1908;[18] and in 1909, the license of the Kenyon was revoked.[19]

The Kenyon Hotel was sold by the Reed family to Mrs. Illa Burke of Morgantown. The hotel was remodeled and the lobby and all the rooms were repapered and painted. An elevator was to be installed (which did not occur) and they were also considering adding another story on the building (which also did not occur).[20] In addition, the entire plumbing system had been gone over, and hot and cold running water had been put into every room, "a feature that was never thought of in the good old days when the Kenyon was in the height of its glory."[21] According to the city directories, this was probably the time when the name was changed to the Madison Hotel.

The building was demolished, and the site is currently a city parking lot.

3. Jolliff Residence, Frey Funerals; c. 1910.
320 Madison Street

This was a vacant site until the dwelling of Marcellus A. Jolliff was constructed around the year 1910, according to the Sandborn maps. It was a two-and-one-half story brick structure with three roof dormers. The center dormer contains a Palladian window. The front porch has a pediment entrance, and it is supported by Ionic columns. The building was later owned by Joe Jolliff Frey, and it was converted into a funeral home in the 1960's, which is the building's function today.

[1] *Fairmont Times,* 4/20/1911, p. 5.
[2] ibid., 5/1/1916, p. 8.
[3] ibid., 4/13/1919, p. 4.
[4] ibid., 10/10/1920, p. 2.
[5] ibid., 5/27/1923, p. 1.
[6] ibid., 10/28/1927, sect. 2, p. 1.
[7] ibid., 5/27/1923, p. 1.
[8] ibid.
[9] ibid.
[10] ibid.
[11] *Fairmont Index,* 4/7/1893.
[12] ibid., 10/25/1893.
[13] ibid., 12/4/1901, p. 1.
[14] *Fairmont Times,* 11/9/1903, p. 5.
[15] ibid., 7/10/1906, p. 6.
[16] ibid., 8/20/1907, p. 1.
[17] ibid., 4/4/1908, p. 1.
[18] ibid., 11/24/1908, p. 1.
[19] ibid., 2/4/1909, p. 1.
[20] ibid., 2/12/1929, p. 1.
[21] ibid., 11/11/1929, p. 4.

Chapter 26

300 Block Madison Street, odd numbered buildings

1. Tin shop, Mountain City Mill, c. 1890; restaurant, 1904.
305 Madison Street

In the late 1880's and early 1890's, a one-story tin shop was located on this site; in the late 1890's, it was incorporated in to the Mountain City Mill Company, according to the Sandborn maps. In December of 1904, Mr. George Yeager, who owned this part of the old Mountain City mill building (which was adjacent to the rear of his store, the Yeager Department Store at 331 Adams Street) decided to remove the old structure because of the danger of fire. The other section of the old mill property (309-315 Madison Street) was owned by Brownfield and McCray.[1]

The old tin shop was replaced by another one-story building that was used as a restaurant for years, according to the Sandborn maps. During the 1920's through the 1950's, it was the Union Lunch, according to the city directories.

The building no longer exists, and the site is part of a parking lot.

2. Mountain City Mill, c. 1880; Virginia Hotel, 1929.
309-315 Madison Street

This was part of the mill operations that was a two- story structure known as the Madison Mill Company on the 1884 Sandborn map, and was a three-story structure known as the Mountain City Mill Company on maps thereafter. This was the section that was owned by Brownfield and McCray.[2] The 1902 Sandborn map notes that the mill was to be converted into stores; and the 1906 Sandborn map shows three storefronts located in the three-story building. According to the city directories, the store front at 309 Madison Street was used for a saloon, the store front at 311 Madison Street was used as a loan/jewelry store, the store front at 311 Madison Street was used as a hardware store.

Lipson Jewelry opened in the old Mountain City mill building on March 8, 1906.[3] In 1916, the store was robbed and the burglars got "a big lot of jewelry." The store was entered from the front door, using a crow bar from the Presbyterian Church construction site (301 Jackson Street) and the robbers opened the door by "jimmy action."[4]

On January 4, 1928, the old Mountain City Mill Building was destroyed by fire; the unofficial estimate of the damage was $50,000. For years the structure had been considered one of the serious fire menaces in the city; the old building was constructed with a framework of heavy wooden beams, with pine partitions, and was made entirely of wood with no fire walls or other fire protection.[5]

All the businesses on the first floor were damaged, as well as the adjacent restaurant building

(305 Madison). The upper floors of the three-story building were used as a rooming house and apartments. Everyone appeared to make it out of the building safely. Embers from the fire carried across Madison Street and dropped on the roof of the Kenyon Hotel (312 Madison Street), but that building did not catch on fire. The cold temperatures hampered the fire-fighting effort, but there was also no wind to carry embers.[6]

C. E. McCray decided to rebuild on the site. In January 1929, he received a building permit for a $40,000 business building on Madison Street.[7] The building that was constructed on the site was named the Virginia Hotel, after Virginia McCray, the late wife of C. E. McCray. It was a four-story steel and brick structure. The first floor was used for the hotel lobby, as well as for three store fronts, with the forty rooms of the hotel on the upper stories. Nine of these rooms had a private bath, and all were equipped with telephones. For every eight rooms not possessing a private bath, there was a public tub, shower bath, and two public toilets.[8]

Walter Eliason drew up the plans for the structure and acted as the superintendent in its erection. A large foundation supported the building, which could carry an additional six stories. The basement walls were four feet thick, the first through third walls three feet thick, while the upper walls were a foot thick. Heat was supplied by a large steam heating system. An elevator was to be installed in the building.[9] The first floor store fronts were occupied by the Farley Clothing Company, the Lipson Jewelry Store, and the McCray Hardware Company.[10]

This building no longer exists on the site; it is a parking lot.

3. store, c. 1900.
317-319 Madison Street

This site originally housed a small one-story harness store from around 1892. Around 1900, a two-story brick building was constructed. It had two store fronts on the first floor, five bays on the second floor. It was used for various commercial enterprises, including dry goods, clothing and groceries, according to city directories.

This building no longer exists, and the site is part of the Post Office, which was designed by Alpha Associates of Morgantown and dedicated in 1987.

4. McCray Building, c. 1900. 323-325 Madison Street

A dwelling from the 1880's stood on this site until a three-story building was constructed around 1900. The first floor of the structure was divided into two store fronts. The upper stories had five bays of windows, and there was a decorative cornice at the roof line. In the city directories, it was referred to as the McCray Building. The two store fronts held various commercial enterprises, such as a bakery, a dry goods store, a clothing store, and a hardware store.

This building no longer exists, and it is the site is part of the Post Office, which was designed by Alpha Associates of Morgantown and dedicated in 1987.

5. American-Italian Building, 1921.
329-335 Madison Street

This corner block originally housed a residence from the 1880's. The house was moved to the west end of the site (along Jackson Street) for the construction of the American-Italian Building in 1921. The Italian American Investment Company leased the property from Mrs. Patrick H. Bennett, and were required to construct a building at least two stories high.[11] The structure was of tile and brick veneer construction, fronting 85 feet on Madison Street and 100 feet on Jackson Street. There were four store rooms fronting on Madison Street, and two more on Jackson Street on the first story. The second story had a lodge room and eight offices. The completion date was set for October 1, 1921.[12]

The first floor of the building was expected to open on November 1, 1921; it was to be occupied by the Paige Motor Sales, the Fairmont Tailor Shop, the Goldberg Clothing store on Madison Street; and by a Lincoln car dealership and a Piggly Wiggly store on Jackson Street. The second floor was expected to be opened a short time after that.[13]

Fire damaged the building on December 9, 1928. It was thought to have originated in a small room on the second floor of the building, started by boys who were attempting to cook food. It was assumed that the boys broke the gas line to the range at a point where a bushing was used to make the connection with the appliance. Only this room on the second floor was affected by the fire itself, though heavier damage occurred on the first floor due to both the fire and the water used to extinguish it.[14]

This building no longer exists, and it is the site is part of the Post Office, which was designed by Alpha Associates of Morgantown and dedicated in 1987.

6. Dunbar School, 1903.
near 400 block of Madison Street (on Jackson Avenue)

A meeting was called in 1868 by the older colored citizens in the city to take steps to have a school. A small building had been used, but it did not seem to meet their desires. A lot was purchased from Thomas Stone for $125, and each colored man of the community was to give so many days' work free. The excavation was done on Saturdays, since it was the only day the men could get off. After this was done, contributions began to come in. Several citizens donated material for the construction, and several people donated money. This was in addition to the small contributions that the colored men took out of their scant earnings, and by festivals given from time to time.[15]

The donations soon became exhausted, and the group wrote to the Freedman's Bureau for help. They sent General Harris, who looked the situation over and became so impressed with the earnestness of their efforts that he agreed to give $200. This, with the money advanced by Jake Gould, cashier of the bank, enabled them to complete the building. The entire cost was about $725, which was paid off in about three years by contributions and by holding festivals.

The school opened in 1869, with approximately 27 pupils. "Perhaps no school in the country has come up through greater struggles to its present status than this school, and no school owes more to the race than the pupils of Dunbar School. It is up to the boys and girls of Fairmont to make good to the memory of those old pioneers who builded greater than they knew."[16] The structure was 25 feet by 32 feet in dimension, according to the 1902 Sandborn map.

This frame building became too small for the school's needs, so it was removed, and a new one constructed on the site for approximately $6,500 in 1903. The corner stone of the structure was laid on August 23, 1903 with imposing ceremonies by the Mountain City Lodge No. 3,538, G. U. O. of O. F. The president of the Board of Education gave a short address, and the stone was placed. Inside the stone was placed various documents and coins of the year.[17] The building was a two-story brick structure in a T-shape, later referred to as Dunbar School.

The new Dunbar School was subsequently constructed on Cleveland Avenue, and this building was used by the Nazarene Church. The building no longer exists, and the site is a parking lot.

---

[1] *Fairmont Times,* 12/1/1904, p. 1.
[2] ibid.
[3] ibid., 8/4/1929, p. 4.
[4] ibid., 8/30/1916, p. 8.
[5] ibid., 1/5/1928, p. 1.
[6] ibid.
[7] ibid., 1/30/1929, p. 1.
[8] ibid., 6/30/1929, p. 1.
[9] ibid.
[10] ibid., 12/2/1929, p. 7.
[11] ibid., 4/29/1921, p. 1.
[12] ibid., 6/17/1921, p. 12.
[13] ibid., 10/23/1921, p. 11.
[14] ibid., 12/10/1928, p. 1.
[15] ibid., 9/18/1917, p. 8.
[16] ibid., 9/18/1917, p. 8.
[17] ibid., 8/24/1903, p. 7.

Part VI—
Quincy Street

Although located at the "head" of Adams Street, Quincy Street was primarily a residential street. Those non- residential uses that were located on it, the Normal School and Methodist Protestant Church, were more suitable neighbors for the adjacent residences than the commercial endeavors that lined Adams Street would be.

Chapter 27

400 Block Quincy Street, even numbered buildings

Note: the rest of this block was filled with residential structures, and are not included in this work. They have all been demolished.

1. Governor Pierpont's residence, c. 1844.
402 Quincy Street

This two-story wood frame structure is said to have been built approximately twenty years before the Civil War. It was a simple gable structure, with the gable end facing Quincy Street, located on the corner of Quincy and Pierpont Streets. Francis H. Pierpont was one of Fairmont's most famous citizens, as he served as the Governor of the Restored Government of Virginia; his statue is in Statuary Hall, Washington, D.C.[1]

Governor Pierpont and his family occupied this residence, and his four children were born here. During Jones' Raid in 1863 during the Civil War, it was said that Pierpont's private library was burned in the street in front of his office.[2] Other accounts say that a Bible was taken from the parlor of the house by the Confederates, tied to a horse's tail, and was dragged through the streets.[3] Yet another account stated that the house had been pillaged during the raid.[4]

In 1886, Governor Pierpont's wife died, and ten years later he left the house to his heirs and spent the last three years of his life in Pittsburgh with his daughter Anna.[5]

The house was acquired by Mrs. M. B. Barr, and used as her residence. In 1910, she decided that the house was too large for her use, and she put it on the market for sale. At this time, there was a renewed interest to purchase the house and maintain it as a historical place in the city, which had been discussed a few years prior to this time as well. "There is no building in Fairmont with as many historical incidents attached and the purchase of it as a relic of the Civil War would be a patriotic move."[6] Nothing came of the idea.

In 1924, the house came into the spotlight again. At that time, it had been recently sold, and a business block was to be erected on the corner. A suggestion was made to move the former residence of the Governor to the location selected for the county Four-H camp. Members of the county court doubted if the old timbers could be removed from the site and be erected elsewhere.[7] Again, nothing was done.

The house was neglected, became deteriorated, and eventually became an eye-sore to the community. In June 1933, the house was declared a fire hazard by officials of the state fire marshal's office and was razed. Only a few gavels were made from the old lumber and distributed to historical societies.[8] The site is currently houses the city bus facility.

2. Methodist Protestant Church, c. 1833, 1852.
418 Quincy Street

The Methodist Protestant Church, 418 Quincy Street.

The Methodist Protestant Church was organized in Fairmont in 1829. The first services were held in Thomas Barnes' old horse-mill in Barnsville. A few years later, this lot was donated to the congregation by Governor Pierpont, and a frame building was erected.[9] This was thought to be sometime after 1833.[10]

On June 2, 1852, a brick structure was completed on this site to replace the old frame one, at a cost of $2,110. It was dedicated on July 25, 1852.[11] This building became known as "The Church on the Hill."[12] Its gable end faced Quincy street, and it had Gothic arch windows. Early photographs of it, around the 1870's, show the building topped with an octagonal lantern; in later photographs, this is missing.

The "Church on the Hill" was noteworthy because its basement was the first location for the Fairmont Normal School (later known as Fairmont State College) when it opened in 1865, and before its own building was constructed across the street.[13]

In 1869, this church was the site of the first negotiations to reunite the two separated branches of the Methodist church, the Ohio conference and the Pittsburgh conference. The cause of the separation, slavery, had been removed, and it was a matter of proper legal and ecclesiastical procedure to reunite the two bodies. The reunion was later consummated in Baltimore in 1877.[14]

A new church was constructed for the congregation at 216-218 Monroe Street in 1896-7. The congregation met in the old church for the last time on August 8, 1897. After the program, old and young alike, fully three hundred and fifty men, women, and children walked in a body from the old church to "The Peoples' Temple."[15]

The site was later sold to Mr. C. L. Smith, who constructed a residence on it.[16] The Sandborn maps of 1902 through 1927 show the structure being used as a dwelling. The building no longer exists on the site, and it is part of the parking lot of an adjacent commercial building.

---

[1] *A History of Marion County, West Virginia*, p. 346.
[2] ibid.
[3] *Fairmont Times*, 7/14/1910, p. 3.
[4] ibid., 3/18/1924, p. 11.
[5] *A History of Marion County, West Virginia*, p. 386.
[6] *Fairmont Times*, 7/14/1910, p. 3.
[7] ibid., 3/18/1924, p. 11.
[8] *A History of Marion County, West Virginia*, p. 386.
[9] *Fairmont Times*, 12/12/1925, p. 5.
[10] *A History of Marion County, West Virginia*, p. 90.
[11] *Hardesty's Historical and Geographical Encyclopedia*, p. 309.
[12] *A History of Marion County, West Virginia*, p. 90.
[13] Dunnington, p. 14.
[14] *Fairmont Times*, 12/12/1925, p. 5.
[15] *Fairmont Index*, 8/10/1897, p. 1.
[16] Fleming, p. 11.

Chapter 28

400 Block Quincy Street, odd numbered buildings

Note: the rest of this block was filled with residential structures, and are not included in this work.

1. Old Normal School, High School, Newspaper Building: 1867-69, 1873.
401-407 Quincy Street

Fairmont State College was first organized as the Fairmont Normal School in 1865. It was first located in the basement of the Methodist Protestant Church (418 Quincy Street).[1] In 1867, a lot was purchased from Judge E. B. Hall for $1,500[2] on the northwest corner of Adams and Quincy Streets, and the construction of the building began. The cornerstone was laid on August 15, 1867, and the ceremonies included a speech by Senator Charles Sumner of Massachusetts.[3]

The building was a brick structure containing a basement and two stories, and was located on Quincy Street approximately sixty feet from the corner of Adams Street. It measured 68 by 40 feet, and was planned to accommodate 150 students. The basement was to hold two rooms for the primary department, the first floor two larger rooms, and on the second floor one very large room and two recitation rooms. During the construction, the school was held in rented quarters on the southeast corner of Adams and Madison Streets. Work was completed on the building and classes were first held in the new building April 1869.[4]

An act of the Legislature of February 23, 1869 provided that some or all of the public school children would be taught under the direction of the Normal School in order to serve as a model school, and that the district could share the Normal Building under an agreement to be made between the Board of Education and the Regents. When it first opened in 1869, approximately 100 children attended. The demand for more space brought about by the addition of the public school instigated the planning for a new wing, larger than the original building.[5]

The new wing of the Normal School was begun during the summer of 1872 and completed in June of 1873. It was a three-story brick structure, measuring forty by eighty feet, and was larger than the original building.[6] This portion of the structure was located adjoining the original building and directly on the corner of Adams and Quincy Streets. The entire cost of the Normal School building was approximately $20,000, with the State providing half the amount and the school district of Fairmont the remainder.[7]

The growing enrollment of the Normal School during the 1880's began to strain the physical facilities. It was jointly owned and occupied by the Normal School and the public schools of Fairmont district. By 1890, it was apparent that one or the other of the two would have to vacate and erect new quarters. The two entities decided to sell the State's interest in the building to the Fairmont school district and to erect a new building for the Normal School. The voters of the

Fairmont Independent District overwhelming approved that bond issue to make the purchase possible. The New Normal building was constructed on the southeast corner of Fairmont Avenue and Third Street, and the Normal School occupied the new structure on March 23, 1893.[8]

The building on Quincy Street was then entirely devoted to the public school system, and students from the Second and Third Wards attended here. It was referred to as the Central School Building. Although it was an old and worn structure by 1902, it had been renovated and improved to make it a comfortable and attractive building. The high school and grammar school were both housed in it.[9] In 1906, it was used only as the Second Ward grammar school, since a new high school had been constructed on the corner of Fifth and Benoni Streets.[10]

By 1908, there was general concern about the building. It had been repaired for the school year, but there had been a lot of work done on it, and it was noted that the structure needed constant repairs because of its age.[11] All schools were inspected by the mayor and the fire chief, who stated that the building, now called the Second Ward School, was unsafe. Doors were found opening inward, there were narrow hallways, and the stairways leading to the upper floors were steep and winding. The fire chief ordered fire drills to be conducted as part of the pupils' training.[12] Approximately a month later, a fire drill was conducted at the Second Ward school building, and it showed efficiency.[13]

By 1911, there was a call for a new school for the Second Ward. This was recommended by the Chamber of Commerce, which stated that it was the only ward that did not have a modern building, and that its attendance was the largest.[14] Two days later, an inspection was made of the schools. The Second Ward building (Old Normal) was found to be a deathtrap, and the sanitary conditions were poor. It was a unanimous decision by the group of people inspecting the building that a new one was needed.[15]

The new Thomas C. Miller School was completed in the spring of 1914, which replaced the Old Normal building as the Second Ward School. The Board of Education announced that the old site was to be offered in the spring at public sale, as the law required. Because the building was at the head of Main (Adams) Street, and Main Street frontage was growing more and more difficult to secure every year, it was thought that several buyers would be interested in the property.[16]

The West Virginian Newspaper moved into the former Normal School building in 1918 from its quarters in the Sample Building (221 Monroe Street). On August 1, 1926, the companies which published *The West Virginian* and *The Times* merged, and *The Times* joined *The West Virginian* in the building (The Times moved from its previous quarters at 219 Monroe Street). The papers continued to be published separately, with *The Fairmont Times* published as the morning newspaper and a representative of the Democratic party, and *The West Virginian* as the evening paper and the representative of the Republican party.[17] The business offices, circulation department, and advertising department were located on the first floor of the building, and the editorial rooms on the second floor.[18]

In 1929, the third floor of the building was leased by the Fairmont Community Players to convert Fraternity Hall into a little theater as its permanent home.[19]

The Times-West Virginian assumed its present name on September 13, 1931, and the edito-

Old Normal School, 401-407 Quincy Street, c. 1902.

rial staff of *The West Virginian* took over its publication. The Fairmont Newspaper Publishing Company moved to new offices constructed at the corner of Ogden Avenue and Quincy Street in 1954.[20]

R. C. Eddy Contractors of Morgantown dismantled the building in 1956.[21] An apartment building now occupies the site.

---

[1] *A History of Marion County, West Virginia*, p. 14.
[2] Dunnington, p. 100.
[3] Turner, p. 6.
[4] ibid., pp. 6-8.
[5] ibid., p. 9.
[6] ibid., p. 14.
[7] Dunnington, p. 100.
[8] Turner, pp. 38-39.
[9] *Fairmont Times*, 11/19/1902, p. 2.
[10] ibid., 5/8/1906, p. 6.
[11] ibid., 7/22/1908, p. 2.
[12] ibid., 8/6/1908, p. 1.
[13] ibid., 9/23/1908, p. 1.
[14] *Fairmont West Virginian*, 12/6/1911, p. 1.
[15] ibid., 12/8/1911, p. 1.
[16] *Fairmont Times*, 3/13/1914, p. 1.
[17] *Welcome Westinghouse*, p. 1.
[18] *Fairmont Times*, 8/16/1926, p. 1.
[19] ibid., 7/11/1929, p. 1.
[20] Hoffman, p. 91.
[21] Spevock, p. 15.

Part VII—Locust Avenue and Jackson Street

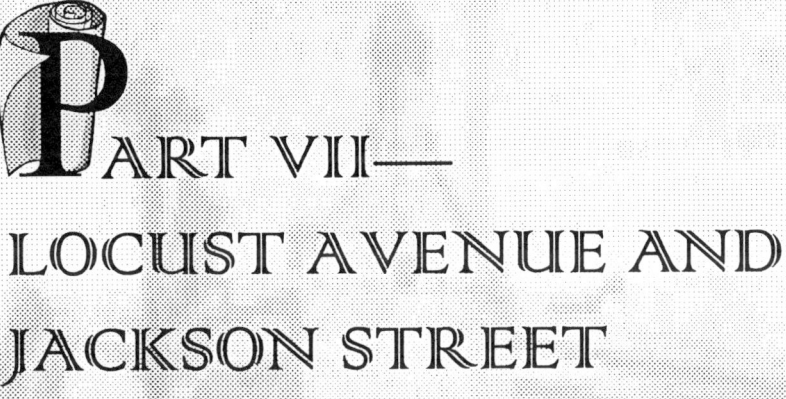

Locust Avenue

Although Locust Avenue is technically out of the selected study area, this block of Locust Avenue was sometimes referred to as "Jackson Street, at Locust Avenue." There are a number of structures located adjacent to the intersection of Cleveland Avenue and Jackson Street that deserve to be mentioned, as they are related to the commercial nature of the downtown Fairmont area. This chapter, therefore, will cover those structures.

Jackson Street

Jackson Street was regarded as the poor stepsister to Adams Street. Historically, it was home to more utilitarian or industrial businesses, and had fewer monumental buildings located on it. It was never the high-visibility location that Adams Street was, and this jealousy become evident after the illuminating arches were constructed at the intersection on Adams Street in 1907. The businesses on Jackson Street petitioned the city to erect two illuminating arches on Jackson Street at the Jefferson and Monroe Street crossings. "The business people of that thoroughfare believe that their street has about as many natural advantages as Main Street and for that reason they have started a boom." The boom was to be further amplified by weekly band concerts during the summer.[1] But Jackson Street never usurped or even matched the prestige of Adams Street.

Chapter 29

Locust Avenue

1. Mumford Electric, Mumford Apartments; c. 1910, c. 1915. 2-6 Locust Avenue

On this lot, and on the adjacent Fairmont Dairy Company lot at 335 Cleveland Avenue, the old Yeager building stood; in 1908, it was one of the oldest structures in the city. It was demolished. Mr. C. E. Mumford owned this part of the lot, and it was his intention to construct a three-story brick building, which would be located in between the Dairy and the National Guard Armory (8 Locust Avenue). The first floor was to be for business quarters, and the upper floors for apartments.[2]

The building was erected in two stages. The 1912 Sandborn map shows a two-story structure on the northwest side of the lot; the 1918 Sandborn map shows this section as a three-story structure (a story added), and a matching structure constructed to the southeast of it. This matching section was constructed in the spring of 1913. Mr. Mumford intended to rent the new first floor business room (next to his), and the use the upper floors as apartments.[3] The completed structure was a three-story building, with six bays on the two upper floors, and two store fronts on the first floor. There was a decorative cornice at the roof line.

According to the city directories, the structure was used for the Mumford Plumbing & Electrical Company, and the upper floors were known as the Mumford Flats. The building was located "on the square", according to a newspaper advertisement.[4]

This building was demolished in 1995 and the site is vacant.

2. National Guard Armory, Standard Garage; 1912-13.
Wyatt and Nolting, architects.
8 Locust Avenue

In 1906, the need for an armory in Fairmont for the National Guard of West Virginia first came to light. Three men, Captain John Henshaw, Captain M. M. Neely, and Lieutenant H. S. Lively, were instructed by the Adjutant General's office to secure such a building. On October 23, 1906, a deal was closed with E. M. Showalter and Willard J. Rowland for the purchase of their lot on Jackson Street (Locust Avenue) near the stone bridge (over Coal Run). The 74 foot by 86 foot lot was $5,500, and the cost of the new building was to be approximately $10,000.[5]

The original plan was to construct a two-story building with a basement; with the first floor was to be constructed of either stone or brick, while the second floor was to be frame construction. The first floor was to be used for the guard organization, and was to have a drill hall 70 feet by 85 feet in size, with no posts dividing the space. In the rear and in the basement would be property rooms of the organization and practice room for the First Regiment band. The second floor was to be utilized for a dance hall, skating rink, meeting place, and theater. It was also to be free of posts and complete with a movable stage and auditorium chairs. A bowling alley was to be maintained, either on the first floor or in the basement, as well as shower and needle baths for both the soldiers and the bowlers. The proposed armory would be one of the largest in the country, and would compare favorably with the armory in Morgantown.[6]

Later that year, the men in charge of the proposed armory visited several existing armory buildings to get ideas for the new armory in Fairmont.[7] They recruited a famous architect, Mr. Nolting of the firm of Wyatt and Nolting of Baltimore, to design the structure; they were the designers of the Fifth Regiment Armory of the Maryland National Guard in the city of Baltimore. The cost of the structure had skyrocketed from the original amount of $10,000 to $25,000. The arrangement of the building had changed as well. Now it was proposed to construct a one-story building, but that story was to be about thirty feet high. A skating rink and dancing hall would be included on the first floor, and a bowling alley in the basement. The building would be about 85 feet by 110 feet, and occupy nearly the entire lot. The location was said to be on Jackson Street, at Locust Avenue, near the Coal Run Bridge.[8]

Preparatory arrangements for the new armory did not occur until August of 1908. It was noted that the plans for the building would entail the outlay of $35,000 to $40,000 for the completion of the building, which may have been the cause of the delay. The stones from the old bridge pier here (assumed to be the old stone bridge nearby) had been purchased for the foundation stones of the proposed building, and were hauled onto the lot on Locust Avenue where they were stored until ready for use. These stones were very large and heavy, and were thought to make the best sort of foundation.[9]

By the end of 1912, the Armory Building, now stated to be on Locust Avenue near Barney (Cleveland Avenue) and Jackson Streets, was nearly complete. The two-story brick building was under roof.[10]

The front of the Armory is distinctive, with two projecting corner "towers" that look medieval in nature due to the battlements at the top of the wall. The central Roman arch entrance was flanked by two storefronts. On the second floor were six bays of rectangular windows.

The National Guard Armory was used by the public for the first time on January 14, 1913, when the Fairmont Poultry and Pet Stock Association opened it sixth annual exhibition in the building. It was seen as an ideal structure for such exhibitions, and it promised to fulfill the need for such buildings that had existed in the city for some time. It afforded a very large floor space, and it was thought that it would be in demand as a gathering place for public meetings, an excellent basketball floor for independent teams, and a fine dance hall, as well as an excellent home for the local military companies. It also made a great improvement of that part of Coal Run over its former condition.[11]

The formal opening of the National Guard Armory was to take place in the latter part of March 1913. A public opening during the day and a military ball at night was planned. Companies H and I had already placed their property in the basement of the armory, where there were four property rooms (two for each Company). A splendid indoor shooting range was in the basement, as well as the toilet rooms, the shower baths, and other baths. The kitchen in the rear was designed to prepare big banquets that were to be given in the drill room of the Armory; the drill hall was said to be one of the best in the State. The floor of it was made of Michigan rock maple to stand up to the harsh treatment, and there were no columns to interrupt the space. There was a balcony with raised floors to accommodate spectators in the drill room. There was a band room in the rear of the balcony, which was to be the headquarters of the First Regiment band.[12]

During the following three years, the Armory was the site of many community activities, including basketball games, agriculture shows, poultry exhibitions, band concerts, and dances. It was a gathering place for the young men of the city. Then, the local militia was incorporated in the United States military forces during World War I, and the armory was not used.[13]

In the spring of 1919, it was announced that the Standard Garage would locate into the Armory Building from its previous location at 310 Madison Street. Work was done to convert the building for the new use. A 3,000 gallon tank was buried in concrete at the lower corner of the building facing Locust Avenue. They put a Bowser system pump on the curb. The cellar of the building was changed into a work shop, and a rear entrance made with a 20 foot driveway created around the lower side.[14]

The stairway heading up to the balcony was left intact, with wall showcases full of accessories and sliding doors; they reached from the main floor to the balcony. The office on the right of the main entrance was to be used as the garage office; and the one on the left to be used as a show room for continuous display of an automobile, its floor covered with druggets (a coarse floor cloth) to protect it. The main room and storage room were to hold up to 150 automobiles. The second floor was fixed up as a stock room for automobile parts. The balcony was arrange for the display of tires, as well as more bulky articles such as fenders, running boards, and engine hoods.[15]

The Standard Garage had moved into its new quarters in May of 1919. In addition to the existing building, it constructed an oil house of Japanese design. The walls were of stucco and the roof was a very artistic affair coming out over the sidewalk. It was conveniently located for car owners to get the oils that were needed in the operation of their cars. The company was the local home of the Packard, the Hudson, the Dodge, and the Buick.[16]

The building is still in use today.

3. Jackson Feed Mill, c. 1894. 5-9 Locust Avenue

According to the Sandborn maps, a two-story wood frame structure, which was 40 feet by 70 feet, existed on the site. It was the home of Oliver Jackson's Feed mill. Mr. Jackson had moved his operation from its location on Parks (Cleveland) Avenue just east of the old suspension bridge, as noted on the Sandborn map of 1892. Mr. Jackson operated his mill at the Locust Avenue site from around 1894 through approximately 1915.

On November 1, 1922, it was announced that the Novelty Roller Rink would open on Locust Avenue opposite the Standard Garage (8 Locust Avenue), which would make this the likely location. This was to replace the rink that had been located in Ravine Park (near Cleveland Avenue). The interior was to be much wider and longer than the previous rink, had a railing all around the space, and room for spectators in back of the railing. Heating arrangements had been made, as well as provisions for caring for the wraps of those skating. The skating surface had been prepared, eliminating rough and uneven places, and a brass band had been secured for the opening. The manager was intent on entertaining his guests throughout the winter session.[17]

This building is no longer in existence.

4. American Laundry, Terrace Apartments; 1911.
Holmboe and Lafferty, architects
11-15 Locust Avenue

In February of 1911, the American Laundry announced that it would construct a new building on Locust Avenue near Coal Run. It was a four-story steel, brick, and stone structure. The basement and first floor were to be used by the laundry, and the two upper stories were to be used for ten apartments, ranging from eight to three rooms. The entrance to the apartments was to be from Rhea Terrace. The building was designed by Holmboe and Lafferty of Clarksburg, and the contract for its construction was awarded to C. W. Dowling of Marietta, Ohio. The structure was to be 40 feet by 106 feet, and was expected to cost approximately $40,000.[18]

The building was to be absolutely fire proof. All floors were to be heat and sound proof as well. Each apartment has its own entrance, so that they are independent of each other. Around the upper side of the building there was a driveway leading from Locust Avenue to the rear where the stables were originally erected. Here, all of the horses used by the laundry company and all of the wagons were kept.[19]

This structure is unique in that the south facade facing Locust Avenue, which was the entrance to the laundry, has Roman arch windows and a classical pediment over the central doorway. The entrances to the apartments on the west from Rhea Terrace have projecting classical porticos to protect the entrances. The apartments and the lower level commercial space are still occupied.

American Laundry and Terrace Apartments, 11-15 Locust Avenue in 1921.

[1] *Fairmont Times*, 5/13/1907, p.1
[2] ibid 5/9/1908, p. 1.
[3] ibid., 3/12/1913, p. 5.
[4] ibid., 5/29/1921, sect. 4, p. 8.
[5] ibid., 10/24/1906, p. 1.
[6] ibid.
[7] ibid., 12/12/1906, p. 9.
[8] ibid., 12/15/1906, p. 1.
[9] ibid., 8/10/1908, p. 1.
[10] ibid., 12/5/1912, p. 2.
[11] ibid., 1/15/1913, p. 2.
[12] ibid., 2/5/1913, p. 2.
[13] ibid., 10/28/1927, sect. 2, p. 1.
[14] ibid., 4/13/1919, p. 4.
[15] ibid.
[16] ibid., 5/2/1919, p. 4.
[17] ibid., 10/29/1922, sect. 2, p. 1.
[18] ibid., 2/8/1911, p. 5.
[19] ibid.

Chapter 30

100 Block Jackson Street, even numbered buildings

1. Crane Building, Jackson-Dotts Building; 1925.
116-118 Jackson Street

Through the early 1900's, according to the Sandborn maps, this site had two one-story sheds on it; they were used for Reeds Sales and Feed, and for a livery. Mr. B. F. Reed had previously owned the stables, and had many horses there in the old days when horses were used extensively for travel. The lot was acquired by W. R. Crane, and he had the old stable razed in June of 1924 to erect a new business building in the summer. The building was to be erected by Earl Jackson and Joseph T. Dotts, who had leased the ground for a number of years.[1] This four-story brick structure has five bays on the upper floors, and two large store front areas on the first floors.

Jackson-Dotts Building (right), 116-118 Jackson Street and Kisner Building (left), 120 Jackson Street, c. 1988.

In September 1925, Fairmont's new dance hall opened in the Jackson-Dotts Building, and scores of dancers enjoyed the music of the Ambassador Orchestra from Clarksburg. Jackson Auditorium, as the dance hall was known, was located on the second floor of the building, and access to it was through a court between the Post Office grounds (321 Monroe Street) and the Odd Fellows building (325 Monroe Street). The hall was a large, roomy place and the largest of any hall in the city, with the exception of the open-air pavilion in Ravine Park (Cleveland Avenue). There were no posts in the hall to obstruct dancing, only a lighted fountain set in the exact center of the room. There was also a place provided for non- dancing spectators at one end of the hall, and a large stage on which the orchestra sat, at the other end.[2]

The building was subsequently used for the Craig Motor Company in the 1930's, according to city directories. It still exists today.

2. Fleming Mill, c. 1890; Kisner Building, c. 1924.
120 Jackson Street

In the 1890's, part of this property had been used by O. J. Fleming for his planing mill, according to the Sandborn maps. It was a vacant lot though the 1900's to 1920. Around the year 1924, this three-story, six bay brick building was constructed.

The first floor was inhabited by the used car department of the Central Automobile Corporation in 1926. It was in this year that the Full Cut Underwear Company located its new factory in the Kisner Building, as it was known then. "A new star has been fixed in Fairmont's industrial firmament," stated the newspaper article. This factory manufactured men's athletic underwear and later it was expanded to include the manufacture of women's "Rayon silk underthings." The company occupied the second and third stories and the mezzanine of the structure. The sewing machines were installed on the third floor, and the second floor held the pressing room, the packing room, and the shipping offices. The offices and stock rooms were located on the mezzanine floor of the first story.[3]

To put the building in readiness for the factory, an additional entrance was made to the building, placing a door in a window opening on the walkway below the Post Office (321 Monroe Street), beginning in Monroe Street and extending back to what was the parish hall of the Episcopal church. The location of the factory was seen as ideal, and the building was seen as ample in size for the business. Since the building was new, it would make a pleasant atmosphere for the workers.[4]

The Fulkut Plant began working on April 12, 1926 The work of preparing the building, including the installation of the machinery, carpentry, plastering the walls, installation of the electrical work for lights and the machinery was completed. The building was large enough for the installation of 125 sewing machines, which was less that the number of machines that the company had brought to Fairmont from New York.[5]

By July of the same year, plans were being made to enlarge the factory. The underwear plant was doing well and rapidly growing. The owner wanted to convert the second floor of the Kisner building into a garment making room and to move the cutting department and some other departments downstairs.[6]

The building still exists and is currently occupied.

---

[1] ibid., 6/5/1924, p. 10.
[2] ibid., 9/10/1925, p. 7.
[3] ibid., 3/7/1926, p. 1.
[4] ibid.
[5] ibid., 4/12/1926, p. 1.
[6] ibid., 7/29/1926, p. 1.

Chapter 31

100 Block Jackson Street, odd numbered buildings

1. Amos Carriage Works, c. 1890.
111-115 Jackson Street

The 1892 Sandborn map shows the left-hand side of this building in existence as the George Amos Carriage Manufacturing Company. Business must have been good, because the 1896 map shows an addition to the right hand side. The completed building was a two-story high, five bay structure with decorative brackets hold the roof line cornice. It was converted in to commercial use as a hardware store and grocery store in the 1900's, and used as a grocery warehouse in the 1920's, according to the Sandborn maps.

The building no longer exists.

2. Majestic Hotel, Jackson Hotel; 1903.
George Giffin, architect.
119-121 Jackson Street

A one story dwelling existed on this site in the 1880's. In 1903, A. M. Berns and B. F. Simpson were having a new hotel building erected on the site, to be called The Majestic. Located across the street from the Grand Opera House (corner of Monroe and Jackson), it was to be a four story stone front building. The foundations were completed in March of 1903, and was expected to cost between $35,000 and $40,000 when completed. The architect for the structure was Mr. George Giffin.[1] Later, plans were changed to make it

Jackson Hotel, 119-121 Jackson Street, 1907.

a six-story structure, to contain about fifty bedrooms and was to be "first-class in every particular."2

Although it originally opened as the Majestic Hotel, it was later reopened as the Jackson Hotel. This occurred in 1905. Each of the thirty-six rooms had new furniture, and each was provided with a stationary washstand with hot and cold water attachments. On each floor were two bath rooms, all light and airy, and furnished with porcelain tubs. The carpets for the rooms were purchased with an eye to the color of the walls, as well as the brass beds and beddings.3

An electric elevator furnished all the floors with "hoisting power." The doors to the elevator were solid wood, which could not be opened from the outside, to eliminate any accidents from the elevator shaft. The cage itself was a handsome piece of work in steel and wrought iron.4

The hotel office was located on the second floor. It was a homey place with a natural gas log provided in the fireplace. Each room in the house was furnished with a radiator, and steam heat was used to keep the building warm. The dining room was also located on the second floor. An ordinary and a private dining room were off to one side of the main dining room.5

An advertisement in January 1906 noted that the hotel's rates were $2 per day, and provided free automobile service to guests. There were also commodious sample rooms for "Commercial men" to display their goods, and short and long distance telephones.6

Even though the elevator was thought to be fool-proof, an accident occurred in November 1909, in which Charley Carr fell through the elevator shaft from the first floor to the bottom of the shaft. He had opened the door to the elevator shaft by mistake and stepped in. Luckily, he only received a broken leg.7

In 1914, the Jackson Hotel changed hands. The hotel, which was one of Fairmont's newest and most popular, was overhauled and refitted from cellar to garret.8 The hotel reopened as the Neininger Hotel in April of 1916. Mrs. Neininger had been a hotel manager in Beaver, Pennsylvania before taking charge of the hotel in Fairmont. The hotel had fallen into bad repute, and she was hired to run it on a strict and clean basis to win back the trade that it once had.9

At this time, the hotel was renovated. The walls were painted and papered, the dining room in the establishment was opened with a great Japanese style chandelier in the center of the dining room. "Since Mrs. Neininger has taken charge, she has secured a number of patrons among the better element of the city who are glad of the opportunity offered them in securing quarters in the excellent situation near the business district that the Neininger enjoys, and at the moderate rates that are prevailing at the house."10

Jackson Street at Monroe Street (bottom left) in 1923.

In the 1930's and 1940's, the building was known as the Temple Apartments, according to city directories.

In January 1978, a fire occurred in the H & S Building, as it was known then. The interior top three floors of the building collapsed. The building was undergoing remodeling of the apartments in the building. The building was a total loss,[11] and was demolished in June 1978.

3. Monongahela Candy Company, c. 1900. 123-125 Jackson Street

This site had a one-story dwelling from the 1880's on it originally. The building which replaced it was constructed around 1900; it was used for various commercial enterprises through the next fifteen years or so, such as a saloon, a furniture store, and a produce warehouse, according to the Sandborn maps. It was a two-story, five bay brick building.

By 1918, the Monongahela Candy Company inhabited the building. Besides wholesale confectioneries, it also carried a complete line of cigars and cigarettes.[12] The company owned the building until the 1970's. It has since been demolished.

4. apartments, c. 1920. 129-131 Jackson Street

The original structure on this site was a two-story wood frame building that was used for a variety of functions, according to the Sandborn maps. R. L. Cunningham Undertaker and Embalmer was located here from the late 1890's until 1902, when he moved his business into the new building he had constructed at 310 Jefferson Street.[13] In 1911, Omen's First Regimental Band moved to the second floor of this building;[14] and later that year, Mr. Omen opened a music store in the building.[15]

The four story structure that currently exists on the site was constructed some time between 1918 and 1927. The front of the building actually faces Monroe Street, and it's three bays wide. The structure is noteworthy because of its ornamental metal balcony railings that are found on the second, third, and fourth floors in the center bay. Motor companies and tire companies occupied the lower floor throughout the years, and the upper floors were apartments.

The first floor of the building is used for commercial enterprises.

---

[1] *Fairmont Times*, 3/9/1903, p. 8.
[2] ibid., 12/12/1903, p. 1.
[3] ibid., 4/15/1905, p. 1.
[4] ibid.
[5] ibid.
[6] ibid., 1/30/1906, p. 2.
[7] ibid., 11/16/1909, p. 3.
[8] ibid., 7/8/1914, p. 1.
[9] ibid., 4/5/1916, p. 6.
[10] ibid.
[11] *Fairmont Times-West Virginian*, 1/17/1978, p. 1.
[12] *Fairmont Times*, 5/22/1921, sect. 3, p. 8.
[13] ibid., 11/15/1902, p. 4.
[14] ibid., 9/16/1911, p. 2.
[15] *Fairmont West Virginian*, 11/25/1911, p. 1.

Chapter 32

300 Block Jackson Street, odd numbered buildings

Note: The structures located on both sides of the 200 block and on the even numbered side of the 300 block of Jackson Street were generally one-and two-story wood frame structures. Very little information was available regarding them, and they are not discussed in this work. The structures on the even-numbered side of the 200 block have been demolished for the Harper-Meredith Building (200 Jackson Street) and parking lot; those on the even-numbered side of the 300 block have been demolished for the Post Office and its parking lot. A few buildings yet remain on the odd numbered side of the 200 block.

1. Presbyterian Church;, 1878, 1916-17.
W. H. Nichlas, architect. 301 Jackson Street

The first two church buildings of the Presbyterian Church were both located near the corner of Adams and Jefferson Streets (301 Adams Street). The Jackson Street site was originally purchased for use as the parsonage.[1] The second of these church buildings on Jefferson Street was pulled down to provide materials for the third one at the corner of Jefferson and Jackson Streets, which was constructed in 1879 for $3,000.[2] This structure had a gable roof with the gable end facing Jackson Street, and a tall tower with a spire on the southwest corner, and a smaller one on the southeast corner. The window and door openings, and blind arches were Gothic in character.

When the church building was constructed, the Masons were in charge of the cornerstone ceremonies. The stone was set at the Jackson-Jefferson corner of the building. The customary iron box, with documents of the day, was placed. It was a large event in the history of the small town. The Normal School, which has then at the corner of Quincy and Adams Streets, dismissed for the occasion. The laying of the brick walls by the contractor, G. W. L. Mayers soon followed; his son, W. S. Mayers, carried one-third of the brick from the previous building (Jefferson and

First Presbyterian Church.

Presbyterian Church, 301 Jackson Street, c. 1892.

Adams Streets) to be used in this building.[3]

An addition to the building was made in 1892 to include a Sunday school room, at a cost of $1,200. To raise this money, bricks for the building were sold at five cents a piece. A large part of the sum was obtained this way, and Miss Ella Greiner won a prize by selling the most bricks. Part of the lot on the other side of the parsonage was also sold to help pay for the Sunday school. This land was later bought back to make room for the Sunday school of the 1916 church.[4]

Presbyterian Church (left), 301 Jackson Street and Snyder Motor Company (right), 313-319 Jackson street, c. 1988.

When the Sunday school room was completed, there was a partition built at the back wall. The partition was removed in 1894 when it was discovered that the Sunday school room as well as the main auditorium would be needed to seat the growing congregation. A rolling door was placed in the area after the partition was removed, but in never worked because it was too unwieldy to lift.[5]

Circular pews were placed in the church in 1889, and they were the first of that shape in Fairmont. Prior to that, they had been straight back. The old bell in the tower was made of cast iron and lasted until one New Year's Eve, when it died with the old year. The tower had been struck by lightning no less than six times.[6]

When the church was first constructed, a parlor organ had been used, until the beginning of the century when a small pipe organ was purchased by J. M. Hartley on one of his mercantile trips to New York. "The instrument made melodious music as long as the colored boy stayed at the bellows. But not all the Presbyterian hymns were of the rousing revival order and once in a while the African pumper would drop into dreams of Old Uncle Remus."[7]

In the 1890's, the church was carpeted throughout, and was lighted by electric lights. There was also a commodious lecture room, with chairs, carpet, and it was lighted by gas.[8]

The first word of constructing a new edifice was incidentally exposed by the pastor in his sermon in November of 1905. Their structure was too small for the congregation, and there was a plan on foot to construct a new one.[9] The call was repeated during the sermon in which Reverend Stoetzer celebrated his seventh anniversary as pastor in 1907.[10]

In 1912, it was announced that a new Presbyterian church would be constructed on Fairmont Avenue between Third and Fourth Streets;[11] but the property in question was given up after some deliberations, and the matter of a new church was dropped for a time.[12]

The Presbyterians had purchased the Manley lot on Cleveland Avenue (307 Cleveland Avenue) around 1914 with the thought of constructing their new church at that location, but in 1915, they sold it to the Fairmont Building and Investment Company.[13]

In 1915, it was decided to erect the new church on the site of the existing church. W. H. Nichlas of Cleveland, Ohio, was chosen as the architect.[14] The plans of the architect were accepted by the church in February 1916.[15]

John M. Kisner & Brothers Company were awarded the contract for razing the old edifice and constructing the new one at the same location. Demolition was to begin April 10, 1916. The church met in the YMCA auditorium in the interim.[16]

April 6, 1916 was the date of the last assembly in the old Presbyterian church building.[17] Within a week, the razing had begun; the roof was off, the windows were out, and the organ had been dismantled.[18] The battered brick heap that had once been the church was noted as "ruins worse than Rheims Cathedral." Under the debris could be seen pick marks in the clay made back in 1878. The cellar of the old church was never entirely dug out, since there was a large bank of clay beneath the building. "The marks of the mattix of a bygone age are still seen." Excavation for the new church on the old parsonage lot was also under way, and an old cistern of the parsonage was discovered.[19]

The Presbyterians then launched their financial campaign to finance the new church. They were attempting to raise $50,000 in one week.[20] The first day of the campaign netted $22,000 in subscriptions.[21] By the end of the five-day event, $50,610 had been raised, and the members of the First Presbyterian church raised their voices in the soul-stirring strains of the Doxology.[22] The church was expected to cost around $100,000.[23]

After the financial concerns were over, the matter of the construction of the church was at hand. Sandstone for the new church came from the Kingwood quarries, and it was the first like it to be used in a West Virginia building. [24]

The cornerstone laying occurred on August 25, 1916. The Grand

Livery (left), 313-315 Jackson Street; blacksmith (middle) 317-319 Jackson Street; Jones Funeral Home (right), 321-329 Jackson Street, c. 1905.

Lodge of the A. F. & A. M. of West Virginia was in charge of the ceremony. The Knights Templar were in uniform to act as escort for the Grand Lodge, and all the emblematic ceremony of the order was given at the laying of the stone. Inside the stone was placed many of the articles taken from the old stone of the 1878 church. In addition to these old articles, many articles of the 1916 era were added to it. [25] These included a list of the membership and associates of the church, and a list of the contributors to the new church fund, and copies of the newspapers of the day.[26]

The church was to be one of the finest in West Virginia. It was constructed of famous Kingwood stone, a quartzite of genuine antique yellow color, and was quarried in Preston County. The stone is as strong and durable as granite and belongs in the class. It is one of the few stones with a texture like the famous Ham Hill stone of England. The roof of the church was made of Spanish red tile, and the trimmings of the entire structure were of the Bedford lime stone.[27] The structure is still Gothic in character, and still has its towers, though they do not have spires.

The structure in 82 feet by 116 feet; the Sunday school room 90 feet by 30 feet, and the main auditorium 76 feet by 76 feet. The auditorium seats 512 persons, and the balconies seat 242. The lighting for the building was provided by many large skylights and windows, as well as an illumination system for night. Ventilation was accomplished through an electric fan system. It was heated by steam from several large boilers in the basement.[28]

The basement had room for the Stoetzer Mission Band, the largest dining room in town, kitchen, boiler room, ladies parlor, and a large room for the beginners department. The feature in the latter room was a fountain which was surrounded by flowers. The Sunday school room had a system of folding and rolling doors to provide twenty-five separate rooms.[29]

The main entrance to the church is from the corner of Jefferson and Jackson Streets. Three handsome stained glass windows are in the main auditorium; the one facing on Jackson Street had a beautiful figure of the Master. Off of the main auditorium was the pastor's study, choir room, and session room, as well as others.[30]

The church was dedicated in October 1917, and the total cost was $110,002.[31]

The church is still in use by the congregation today.

2. Snyder Motor Company; 1921, 1927.
Dodge Brothers Company, architects.
313-319 Jackson Street

In the 1880's, this site was occupied by a livery at 313-315 Jackson Street. In the 1890's, this was the livery of Simeon Bright, then J. M. Conaway; later in the early 1900's, it was the livery of A. J. Reynolds, according to the Sandborn maps.

A blacksmith existed at 317-319 Jackson Street. In the 1880's, it was a one-story wooden structure, which was replaced by a two-story brick building around 1894.

In 1921, L. Snyder, the local representative of the Dodge Brothers Motor Cars, built one of the most up-to-date garages in the city. It was three stories in height, and occupied a space 46 feet by 116 feet. On the first floor was the display room and storage space. The second floor was the repair ship, and on the third floor a job painting department. The plans for the garage were drawn by the Dodge Brothers Company architects, and the construction was under their supervision.[32] This was the 317-319 Jackson Street location.

In 1927, L. Snyder completed a new building adjoining the previous Snyder Motor Company garage and show room on Jackson Street. It cost approximately $40,000.[33]

The adjacent Presbyterian church purchased this property in 1995 and demolished the two buildings for a parking lot.

3. Jones Funeral Home, Standard Furniture Company; c. 1904.
321-329 Jackson Street

The early buildings on this site consisted of a two-story undertaking establishment and a two-story dwelling. These were last seen on the 1902 Sandborn map; by 1906, they had been replaced with a three-story brick structure of eleven bays. The building was distinctive because it was set up as three separate "store houses." The store front on the east had a protruding bay

Standard Furniture Company (bottom left), 321-329 Jackson Street; residence (middle), 331 Jackson Street; Heinze Cleaners (on corner), 333-337 Jackson Street; St Peter's Catholic Church (on opposite corner), 401-407 Jackson Street, c. 1923.

with three windows on the second and third floors.

Early after the building opened, the store front with the bay was occupied by R. C. Jones Undertaking.[34] The 1918 and 1912 Sandborn maps show the two storefronts to the west occupied by the National Biscuit Company. Beginning in the 1920's, these two storefronts were used by the Standard Furniture Company, which eventually expanded into the store front to the east.

This building was demolished, and the site is used as a parking lot.

4. residence, c. 1880.   331 Jackson Street

A dwelling had existed on the site from the 1880's. In 1921 when the adjacent Heinze Cleaners was constructed, they moved this original building off of the site, and moved the house that had been on the Heinze Cleaners site to this site. This is evident when comparing the Sandborn maps of 1918 and 1927.

The site is now used as a parking lot.

5. Heinze Cleaners, 1921-22.
333-337 Jackson Street

A dwelling was constructed on this site around 1895. It was moved to the adjoining site on 331 Jackson Street when the Heinze Cleaners building was constructed in 1921-22 This was the location of their cleaning and dyeing establishment in Fairmont. The building was constructed of concrete, brick and fire glass, with a distinctive concrete frame and infill panels of brick and glass in a modern horizontal manner. It fronted 50 feet on Jackson street and rose to three stories running back to the depth of 60 feet. A one story high section was located at the rear, which was used exclusively for dyeing and cleaning. The company was to clean everything in the way of wearing apparel except hats.[35] The first floor of the building had first class offices, one suite occupied by the company and the other one to be rented. The third floor was to be used for cleaning carpets. The Concrete Steel Bridge Company of Clarksburg constructed the building.[36]

In March 1922, the Heinze Cleaners moved from its previous location on Monroe Street to its new home on the corner of Jackson and Madison Streets.[37] In the 1930's, the Standard Furniture Store expanded its operations to this building.

This building was demolished and is now used for a parking lot.

---

[1] *Fairmont Times*, 4/7/1916, p. 2.
[2] *Hardesty's Historical and Geographical Encyclopedia*, p. 310.
[3] *Fairmont Times*, 4/7/1916, p. 2.
[4] ibid.
[5] ibid.
[6] ibid.
[7] ibid.

Jackson Street, 400 block, c. 1922.

[8] *Fairmont Index,* 1/13/1894.
[9] *Fairmont Times,* 11/20/1905, p. 7.
[10] ibid., 1/14/1907, p. 1.
[11] ibid., 5/2/1912, p. 1.
[12] ibid., 1/28/1913, p. 2.
[13] ibid., 8/3/1915, p. 2.
[14] ibid., 7/22/1915, p. 1.
[15] ibid., 2/9/1916, p. 1.
[16] ibid., 3/29/1916, p. 1.
[17] ibid., 4/6/1916, p. 3.
[18] ibid., 4/12/1916, p. 1.
[19] ibid., 4/25/1916, p. 8.
[20] ibid., 6/24/1916, p. 1.
[21] ibid., 6/27/1916, p. 1.
[22] ibid., 7/1/1916, p. 1.
[23] ibid., 8/25/1916, p. 6.
[24] ibid., 7/8/1916, p. 8.
[25] ibid., 8/22/1916, p. 1.
[26] ibid., 8/25/1916, p. 6.
[27] ibid., 4/28/1917, p. 7.
[28] ibid.
[29] ibid.
[30] ibid.
[31] ibid., 10/15/1917, p. 1.
[32] ibid., 3/21/1921, p. 5.
[33] ibid., 7/17/1927, p. 10.
[34] *Industrial Fairmont in 1908,* p. 33.
[35] *Fairmont Times,* 8/24/1921, p. 8.
[36] ibid.
[37] ibid., 3/13/1922, p. 6.

Chapter 33

400 Block Jackson Street, even numbered buildings

1. National Guard Armory, 1927 412-414 Jackson Street

This site had a residential structure on it from the 1890's until 1927. It was demolished to make way for the new National Guard Armory (the old one had been located at 8 Locust Avenue). The contractor for the work was Walter Eliason. By July of 1927, the excavating and foundation work had been completed, even ahead of schedule. There was no scarcity of labor in the city, and they were awaiting the steel to continue the work. It was hoped to have the building ready for occupancy by September 1, 1927.[1] It was thought that the building would cost in the neighborhood of $35,000.[2]

The first floor of the building was to be used for the drill room, and was 72 by 112 feet in size. Below that was the rifle range. The first event to be held in the building was a big auto show, because the size of the building made it possible to make it the greatest automobile exposition ever held in the state.[3]

The new Armory was to be open for the big auto show week beginning October 16, 1927. By the end of September, the great auditorium was under roof, and the material for the floor of the drill hall, white maple lumber of the finest grade, had arrived and was being installed. The store rooms and offices in the front portion of the building were almost complete. The lower floor of the building was not to be partitioned off until after the automobile show, to give the event the use of both the first and lower floors.[4]

Other activities were planned for the new, large space. Among these were an indoor circus and dances. The National Guard itself signaled its formal occupancy of its new home by giving a grand military ball. This included a Boy Scout review before the dance, a guard mount by the local Guardsmen, a concert by the 201 Infantry Band of Morgantown, and a Grand March, led by the prominent visitors with music furnished by the band. After the formal functions concluded, the new building was to be devoted to its intended purpose: the home of the National Guard. Drill was held each Monday night, with the building being available other evenings for public functions.[5]

The building has been demolished, and now the site is used for a parking lot.

2. Skating Rink, garage; c. 1905. 418 Jackson Street

This had been a vacant lot for years. Around the year 1905, a one story structure with a basement was constructed. According to the 1906 Sandborn map, the top floor was used for a skating rink and the lower floor was used for a dance hall. In 1917, there was some discussion of turning the old Casino property into a city market for producers to dispose of their product and for the needs of the public.[6] This does not appear to have materialized. By 1918, it was used for a garage.

In 1922, the property, referred to as the Casino Rink property and also the home of the Fairmont Motor Car Company, was sold for $52,000. Although the purchaser, Mr. Fred W. McIntire, intended to erect a three-story building on he site,[7] it does not seem to have materialized. The property was used as a motor company and a garage in later years, according to city directories. The building is gone and the site is currently used as a parking lot.

3. Salvation Army, 1905.
420 Jackson Street

A two-story shed on the site was replaced by a two-story brick structure in 1905. It was constructed for the Cordray Carriage Company for the manufacturing and sale of their products: buggies, which ranged in price from $125 and up; and light wagons, adapted to the requirements of merchants and others. The company also repaired all kinds of vehicles. The structure was originally only two stories high, but their trade had increased to such an extent that it was necessary to enlarge the premises by adding another story to the building. The entire building had 960 square feet of floor area.[8] The structure had three bays on the two upper floors, and two store fronts on the first floor.

In 1925, the property was purchased from Lawrence McCray for the home of the Salvation Army.[9] The building no longer exists on the site, and it is used for parking.

---

[1] *Fairmont Times*, 7/11/1927, p. 1.
[2] ibid., 7/17/1927, p. 10.
[3] ibid., 9/22/1927, p. 4.
[4] ibid., 9/25/1927, p. 1.
[5] ibid.
[6] ibid., 8/8/1917, p. 2.
[7] ibid., 9/13/1922, p. 14.
[8] *Industrial Fairmont in 1908*, p. 59.
[9] *Fairmont Times*, 3/12/1925, p. 11.

Jackson Street in 1918. St. Peter's Catholic Church in center.

Chapter 34

400 Block Jackson Street, odd numbered buildings

1. St. Peter's Catholic Church Complex.
Church: 1856, 1902-04; Badgeley and Smith, architects.
Parochial School: 1912.
Rectory: 1922-23; John C. Burchinal, architect.
Parochial School Annex: 1927-28; Carl Reger, architect.
401-407 Jackson Street

The corner of this block went from a sleepy little church in 1856 to a church complex in twenty-six years of active construction. The original church building on this site was located on the corner of Jackson and Madison Streets. It was a 30 foot by 50 foot gable-roofed brick structure, and the lot was purchased for $125. The cornerstone was laid in May 1856, and the structure was dedicated in the spring of 1857.[1] By 1894, it was too small to accommodate the increasing congregation. "The lecture room a few years ago would seat comfortably all the worshipers, but of late this room as well as the gallery is crowded."[2]

In August 1897, Father Boutlou secured the Fleming property adjoining the church for

$5,100 and made plans for the new church. The cornerstone was laid in 1902.[3] Although the foundation was completed in the late fall of 1902, the work was stopped during the winter. The architects for the church, Badgeley and Smith of Baltimore, prepared the plans and specifications, and were ready to accept bids in March 1903. It was hoped to have it completed by the autumn of 1903.[4]

In April of 1903, it was announced that the contract for the new Catholic church was let to T. L. Burchinal.[5] By the end of April, work resumed on the construction. The brickwork was done by contractor J. F. Phillips, who used brick from the Hutchinson-Barnes Brick Company.[6] The brickwork was begun on June 11, 1903.[7]

The contract for memorial windows for the new church was closed in July 1903. The Tyrolese Art Glass Company of Innsbruck, Province of Tyrol, Austria, was chosen for the work. The windows were a very handsome design.[8]

By the middle of August 1903, the brickwork on the church was almost complete, and the placing of the roof began soon after that. The basement was finished for immediate occupancy that fall, and the main part was thought to be finished for occupancy the summer of 1904.[9] By the end of the year, the Catholic church moved from its temporary quarters on Monroe Street to its new basement, as it awaited the completion of the rest of the structure.[10]

January 1904 found the fresco work on the church finished. It was done by Mr. Alfred Ronchetty of Chicago.[11] The beautiful memorial windows were completed in March of that year,[12] and the Catholic Church was dedicated on November 20, 1904.[13] The cost of the church was $44,000; by the end of 1907, the debt on the new church was fully paid.[14]

The structure is in the Beaux Arts style. The white stone base is surmounted by red and buff colored brick with Neo-classical details including Roman arch windows, triangular pediments, and a distinctive curved pediment for the major gable of the church, which faces Jackson Street. On the southwest corner is a tower, the top part of which is striped, with alternating layers of red and buff brick. The tower is surmounted by a copper dome with a Latin cross. Pilasters on the exterior walls are also formed by the alternating layers of red and buff brick.

In April of 1910, the church acquired the property of Laura Jackson on Madison Street, adjacent to the church, for the sum of $10,000. It was the intent of the church to establish a new Catholic school on the property.[15]

The cornerstone for the new school building was laid on May 26, 1912, and there was a large attendance. A procession of local and visiting clergy and altar boys was formed at the church, and went to the scene of the cornerstone laying. Bishop Donahue delivered a brilliant and inspiring address. The cornerstone box was laid with the usual ceremony, and contained a historical sketch of the church, sketches of the different church societies, names of contributors to the school fund, copies of local papers, and other documents. The new building was to be a three-story brick structure with finished basement. There were to be six rooms, and an auditorium on the third floor.[16]

The church acquired more property in 1919. The property was that of the late Mrs. Maria Haymond on Jackson and Madison Streets, adjoining the church and school; it was acquired for

$12,000. There were no immediate plans for the property, but it gave the congregation possession of a valuable site.[17]

In July of 1922, it was announced that St. Peter's Church was to build a new rectory.[18] It was constructed on Jackson Street between Quincy and Madison Streets. It was a twelve-room residence, built of face brick and finished with a green Spanish tile roof. John C. Burchinal of Fairmont was the architect and A. E. Hanley of Clarksburg was the general contractor for the structure. On the main floor of the building was a large vestibule at the entrance, and to the right were the reception room and office, while to the left was the dining room. There was also a large pantry, kitchen, and housekeeper's apartment on the main floor. The second floor had four bedrooms and two study rooms. The house was replete with bath room facilities and other modern conveniences. A large enclosed porch was built on the side of the house in view of the church, directly off from the pastor's office.[19]

The old rectory was removed from the site and relocated further east on the property; the grounds between the old and new rectories were terraced and improved. An old brick residence which had stood on the adjoining lot had been razed some time previous to this date; the bricks and other material from it were used in the construction of a cottage near the entrance to Holy Cross Cemetery. The Cottage was occupied by the caretaker of the cemetery.[20]

The new rectory was completed and an open house for the congregation was held on September 6, 1923.[21] The building was completed at a cost of approximately $27,000.[22]

The next construction project for the church was the annex to the school which housed the high school and gymnasium, which was begun in the spring of 1927. Carl Reger of Morgantown was the architect who designed the building, Louis D. Schmidt of Fairmont was the superintendent for the construction, and L. A. and Leonard Riley of Shinnston were the contractors for it.[23]

The auditorium, which would double as the gymnasium, was located on the first floor, and six or more classrooms were located directly over it. Although the plans were not yet complete, the structure was to be annexed to the existing school building and have a frontage facing on Quincy Street, but would not extend to the street front. A garage on the church property was removed to make way for the new building. The structure was constructed of the same kind of brick used in the church and school buildings.[24]

By July of 1927, steam shovels were excavating the site for the foundations of the school annex, which was the largest single structure for which a building permit has been issued in that year. It was to cost approximately $50,000.[25] L. D. Schmidt of Fairmont was the superintendent of construction on the project, and it was also decided to name the school the Father Boutlou Memorial High School, in honor of the pastor whose dream it had been to have a parochial high school.[26]

The new school opened with a dinner and entertainment on January 17, 1928.[27] The formal dedication took place on May 13, 1928, with the Bishop of Wheeling in attendance. The structure is 100 feet long and 60 feet wide, constructed of brick and steel with maple floors and sand finish and plaster composition roof. The lower level houses the auditorium/gymnasium, equipped with a stage. The upper floor, which connects with the second floor of the main building, contains four classrooms, all with good outside light. The entire building was heated by steam, and the class rooms have the Shipp window ventilators which force fresh air through the radiators for constant fresh air.[28]

The church complex is still in use by the congregation.

2. R. C. Jones Funeral Home, c. 1905.
421 Jackson Street

This structure first appears on the Sandborn map of 1906. It had been the residence of Thomas S. Haymond. In 1922, R. C. Jones had purchased the property to convert it to use as a funeral home.[29] The building still exists today.

---

[1] *Welcome Westinghouse,* front sect., p. 10.
[2] *Fairmont Index,* 1/3/1894.
[3] Lough, p. 681.
[4] *Fairmont Times,* 3/11/1903, p. 1.
[5] ibid., 4/2/1903, p. 1.
[6] ibid., 4/30/1903, p. 1.
[7] ibid., 6/12/1903, p. 2.
[8] ibid., 7/15/1903, p. 8.
[9] ibid., 8/17/1903, p. 8.
[10] ibid., 12/9/1903, p. 8.
[11] ibid., 1/19/1904, p. 2.
[12] ibid., 3/28/1904, p. 2.
[13] ibid., 11/21/1904, p. 1.
[14] Lough, p. 681.
[15] *Fairmont Times,* 4/12/1910, p. 1.
[16] ibid., 5/27/1912, p. 3.
[17] ibid., 8/11/19, p. 7.
[18] ibid., 7/19/1922, p. 2.
[19] ibid., 11/9/1922, p. 2.
[20] ibid.
[21] ibid., 9/7/1923, p. 3.
[22] ibid., 6/27/1923, p. 2.
[23] ibid., 1/14/1928, p. 2.
[24] ibid., 4/10/1927, sect. 2, p. 1.
[25] ibid., 7/17/1927, p. 10.
[26] ibid., 7/27/1927, p. 1.
[27] ibid., 1/14/1928, p. 2.
[28] ibid., 5/13/1928, p. 1.
[29] ibid., 9/10/1922, p. 2.

Part VIII
Washington Street

Washington Street was primarily residential in nature. Most large buildings on the street actually fronted on the more important cross streets. The commercial structures on the street were utilitarian in nature and construction. Therefore, most buildings on the street are not covered in this work due to a lack of information on them.

Chapter 35

200 Block Washington Street, even numbered buildings

1. "Indian Building," prehistoric; Methodist Episcopal Church, Episcopal Church; c. 1842, 1879 220 Washington Street

This site was originally that of the "Indian Building", which was a prehistoric structure estimated by archaeologists to have been over 400 years old at the time it was discovered. It was approximately 40 feet by 12 feet 5 feet, and was made of stone mortared with a mixture of clay and mussel shells.[1]

The Methodist Episcopal (M. E.) Church, referred to in the old days as the "Old Side" Church, is said to have been first built on this site in 1842. The old frame church was significant because it was here that the first court was ever convened in the County, and it was used for the court until the brick courthouse on Adams Street could be completed,[2] which occurred in 1844.[3]

Around the year 1854, this church was purchased by the Protestant Episcopal Church, as the M. E. Church moved to 118-122 Adams Street. The old church was pulled down and a new one, the present building, was constructed in 1880 at a cost of $5,000.[4] This was the first brick church built within the town in Fairmont.[5] It is a neo-Gothic style structure, with Gothic arched windows; the northwest tower was originally capped with a 40 foot tall spire. In 1892, the ladies of the church were endeavoring to raise funds to purchase a bell for the tower.[6] By December of that year, the bell had been ordered, and the church was also

Christ Episcopal Church, 220 Washington Street, c. 1908.

being plumbed for natural gas heating.[7] In 1895, a handsome new carpet was installed in the church as well.[8]

In 1910, the Christ Episcopal church, as it was then called, had purchased property at the corner of Gaston Avenue and Second Street for the erection of a new church to take the place of the old one on Washington Street.[9] An additional piece of property on the corner of Second Street and Virginia Avenue was also purchased. Plans for a new church building were prepared and a subscription campaign was carried out. However, the project was abandoned because of World War I.[10]

The idea for a new church lay dormant for a time, until a new site was donated to the church at Fairmont Avenue, Ninth Street, and Gaston Avenue. The new building was completed, and the church on Washington Street was filled for the last service on July 24, 1927.[11]

The old Episcopal Church was leased by the Christian Science Society for their services in January of 1928. The terms of the lease were for one year.[12] Work of repairing the old building for the new inhabitants had begun in February. The high belfry, which was one of the outstanding architectural features of the old building, was razed to the height of the roof of the church at this time. The belfry was thought to have been in a dangerous condition, so it was torn down rather that repaired. The belfry had been home to a score of birds for several years; its removal left the birds without a home, and there was considerable excitement among them as it was torn down. In addition, many loose bricks at the eves of the church roof were repaired, as they were in danger of falling to the street.[13]

The building is currently used as the Union Mission chapel.

---

[1] *A History of Marion County, West Virginia*, p. 73.
[2] Fleming, p. 11.
[3] *A History of Marion County, West Virginia*, p. 2.
[4] *Hardesty's Historical and Geographical Encyclopedia*, p. 310.
[5] Dunnington, p. 96.
[6] *Fairmont Index*, 11/25/1892.
[7] *Fairmont Free Press*, 12/16/1892.
[8] *Fairmont Republican*, 8/15/1895.
[9] *Fairmont Times*, 4/5/1910, p. 1.
[10] ibid., 7/25/1927, p. 1.
[11] ibid.
[12] ibid., 1/31/1928, p. 1.
[13] ibid., 2/26/1928, sect. 2, p. 4.

APPENDIX A - BUILDING INDEX

* denotes building no longer in existence

PART I - ADAMS STREET

Ch. 1 100 block - even numbers
- *1. 100-102 Adams Street Carr Building Andrew C. Lyons, architect 1900
- *2. 104 Adams Street Geo. M. Jacobs Building, Citizens Dollar Bank, Fairmont State Bank Andrew C. Lyons, architect 1900
- *3. 106-108 Adams Street "Skinner Buildings" Andrew C. Lyons, architect? c. 1895
- 4. 110-114 Adams Street Skinner Building Andrew C. Lyons, architect? 1892-3
- 5. 118-122 Adams Street Methodist Episcopal Church, Hennen Building 1854, 1896, 1911, 1916
- 6. 124 Adams Street alley infill building c. 1917
- 7. 126 Adams Street Marietta Hotel Annex c. 1898
- 8. 128-130 Adams Street Continental Hotel, Marietta Hotel, Deveny Building John Burchinal, architect 1916-17

Ch. 2 100 block - odd numbers
- *1. 101 Adams Street Mansbach's Store c. 1897
- *2. 103 Adams Street Home Savings Bank Andrew C. Lyons, architect 1897-8
- *3. 105 Adams Street Fitch Block c. 1898
- *4. 107 Adams Street Old Fred Fleming Building c. 1900
- 5. 109-113 Adams Street Fleming Building, American Building, Hartley's Store Emil R. Johnson, architect (remodeling) 1911-2, 1929
- 6. 115 Adams Street Nuzum Building Annex c. 1880, 1901
- 7. 117-119 Adams Street Nuzum Block, Morrison's Store, Hartley's Store, 1928
- *8. 121 Adams Street store c. 1894
- *9. 123 Adams Street Peoples Bank, Palace Restaurant c. 1854
- *10. 125 Adams Street store c. 1905
- *11. 127-135 Adams Street Hall Block 1893-5

Ch. 3 200 block - even numbers
- 1. 200-202 Adams Street Town Hall Theatre, T. W. Fleming Building, Odd Fellows Hall c. 1870
- 2. 204 Adams Street T. W. Fleming Building, Iseman's Store c. 1870
- 3. 206 Adams Street alley infill c. 1940
- 4. 208 Adams Street First National Bank Cashier's Residence, Jones' Store 1875, 1917
- 5. 210-212 Adams Street First National Bank, Fairmont Trust Company, Adams Office Supply 1898
- 6. 214-216 Adams Street T. F. Hall Building c. 1875
- 7. 218-220 Adams Street Fountain Saloon, McCrorey's Store 1909
- 8. 222-224 Adams Street Hatter Ben's Big Brick, Underselling Store, Goodman's Store c. 1845
- 9. 226-230 Adams Street Fleming/Cochran Building 1875-6
- 10. 232-236 Adams Street Commerford Building c. 1878

Ch. 4 200 block - odd numbers
- 1. 201-207 Adams Street Jacobs-Hutchinson Block: People's Bank, Hartley's Store, Jones' Store Andrew C. Lyons, architect 1901-2 National Register of Historic Places
- 2. 209 Adams Street Fairmont Trust Company, Home Savings Bank 1904-5
- 3. 215 Adams Street Marion County Jailer's Residence and Jail, Marion County Historical Museum E. J. Woods, architect 1909-12 National Register of Historic Places (Jailer's Residence only)
- 4. 217-221 Adams Street Mountain City House, Marion County Courthouse Joseph Warren Yost and Frank L. Wood, architects 1897-1900 National Register of Historic Places

Ch. 5 300 block - even numbers
1. 300-302 Adams Street Christie's Drug, Hartley's Store c. 1877
2. 304-306 Adams Street millinery store, barber c. 1880
3. 308 Adams Street Chisler Building c. 1880
4. 310 Adams Street store c. 1880, 1902
5. 312 Adams Street Osgood's Store c. 1880
6. 314-320 Adams Street G. C. Murphy Building 1932, 1939
7. 322 Adams Street Dowden Building c. 1880
8. 324 Adams Street Marion Hardware, Virginia Theatre c. 1880, 1922
*9. 326 Adams Street market, Lipson's Jewelry c. 1880
*10. 328 Adams Street saloon, restaurant c. 1880
*11. 330-332 Adams Street J. W. Lott Building, Masonic Temple c. 1879

Ch. 6 300 block - odd numbers
1. 301-311 Adams Street Presbyterian Church, Bank of Fairmont, Watson Building
  Horace Trumbauer, architect 1909-11
*2. 313-317 Adams Street Smith & McKinney Building 1892
*3. 319 Adams Street Fleming Home and Building c. 1890, 1929
*4. 321 Adams Street residence, Kaufman's Store c. 1880
5. 323 Adams Street Brownfield Building c. 1880, 1923
6. 325 Adams Street Holt-Rowe Building c. 1880, c. 1910, 1921
7. 327 Adams Street Brownfield Building c. 1895, 1919, 1926
*8. 329 Adams Street Prendergast's Saloon, Golden Brothers Annex c. 1890, 1924
*9. 331 Adams Street Swisher & Carpenter's Store, Yeager's Store, Jones' Store, Golden
  Brothers Store Andrew C. Lyons, architect 1896

Ch. 7 400 block - even numbers
*1. 402-408 Adams Street Shot Tower, Watson Hotel Leiner and Faris, architects 1894
2. 410-416 Adams Street Fairmont Theatre Fred W. Elliot, architect 1922-23, 1944
3. 418 Adams Street Post Office, Fred C. Fleming residence, Singer Store c. 1891, 1928
4. 420-422 Adams Street Osgood's Store 1921
5. 426-432 Adams Street Barnes Property, Yost Building c. 1844, c. 1890

Ch. 8 400 block - odd numbers
*1. 401-403 Adams Street Odgen Building, Billingslea Drug Store c. 1889
*2. 405-407 Adams Street Piggly-Wiggly c. 1889
*3. 409-411 Adams Street Eyster residence, Robb Meat Market 1911
*4. 413-415 Adams Street Dutton/Chisler Hardware, Hippodrome Theatre, Blue Ridge Theatre 1911
*5. 417 Adams Street Arnett, Cole residence c. 1855
6. 421 Adams Street Mayer residence, Elks Club John Burchinal, architect c. 1893, 1925

PART II - CLEVELAND AVENUE

Ch. 9 100 block - even numbers
1. 104 Cleveland Avenue Skinner's Tavern E. B. Fransheim, architect 1903, 1904
*2. 116-124 Cleveland Avenue Schmulbach Brewing Company, Thomas Transfer c. 1900

Ch. 10 100 block - odd numbers
*1. Cleveland Avenue Baltimore & Ohio Railroad Passenger Station c. 1900
*2. Cleveland Avenue Baltimore & Ohio Railroad Freight Station c. 1900

Ch. 11 200 block - even numbers
- 1. 210 Cleveland Avenue Hart Produce, Fortney Drugs 1900

Ch. 12 200 block - odd numbers
- *1. 209 Cleveland Avenue West Virginia Grocery & Candy Company, Smith-Race Groceries, Stevenson Groceries, Frank's Tire 1901-02
- *2. 215 Cleveland Avenue Hose House 1897
- *3. 217 Cleveland Avenue Corbin Groceries, Mountain State Candy Company c. 1890
- *4. 227 Cleveland Avenue Parks Avenue Hotel, Old Dewey Hotel c. 1900
- 5. 229-231 Cleveland Avenue Corbin & Sons Groceries c. 1910
- 6. 233-235 Cleveland Avenue Jacobs-Hutchinson Hardware 1923
- *7. 255-257 Cleveland Avenue Arch Fleming Feed, Monon Valley Produce c. 1918
- *8. Cleveland Avenue Times and Index Building c. 1900
- *9. Cleveland Avenue Ravine Park 1921

Ch. 13 300 block - odd numbers
- *1. 301 Cleveland Avenue Arnett residence, Electric Company Offices c. 1900
- 2. 307-311 Cleveland Avenue Manley residence, Professional Building L. C. Holmbe and Fredrick Nickerson, architects 1916-17
- 3. 337 Cleveland Avenue Fairmont Dairy Company, Imperial Ice Cream, Jordan Autos c. 1908

Ch. 14 400 block - odd numbers
- *1. 401-403 Cleveland Avenue West Virginia Grocery and Candy, American Steam Laundry, Standard Oil Station c. 1880, 1922
- 2. 407 Cleveland Avenue Colored Church, Trinity Church 1911

PART III - MONROE STREET

Ch. 15 200 block - even numbers
- *1. 200 Monroe Street residence c. 1905
- *2. 206 Monroe Street Musgrave Building c. 1895
- *3. 210 Monroe Street YWCA Building c. 1890
- 4. 214 Monroe Street Menear residence, Bell Telephone Company McKenzie, Voorhees & Gmelin, architects? 1916-17
- 5. 216-218 Monroe Street Methodist Protestant Temple, J. Charles Fulton, architect 1896-7

Ch. 16 200 block - odd numbers
- 1. 201 Monroe Street Conoway's Feed Store c. 1902
- *2. 205 Monroe Street Methodist Episcopal Church, Colored 1865
- *3. 207 Monroe Street Troy Steam Laundry c. 1902
- 4. 211-215 Monroe Street Chisler residence, City Building Andrew C. Lyons, architect? 1910-16
- 5. 217 Monroe Street Hays Building, Majestic Building c. 1910, 1912
- 6. 219 Monroe Street Jacobs-Hutchinson Hardware, Times-Index Printing Company Andrew C. Lyons, architect 1901
- 7. 221 Monroe Street Sample Building 1900

Ch. 17 300 block - even numbers
- 1. 312-316 Monroe Street George M. Jacobs Building Andrew C. Lyons, architect 1903

Ch. 18 300 block - odd numbers
- 1. 321 Monroe Street Post Office, Marion County Library Joseph Knox Taylor, architect 1913-14
- *2. 325 Monroe Street Grand Opera House, I.O.O.F. Building J. E. Allison, Coy H. Snider, architects 1902, 1921-22

PART IV - JEFFERSON STREET

Ch. 19 200 block - even numbers
    1. 200-214 Jefferson Street Fairmont Hotel Milburn, Heisler, & Company, architects 1916-17, 1920
    2. 216-218 Jefferson Street G. C. Murphy Building Addition 1950
    *3. 220 Jefferson Street Crane residence, Princess Theatre c. 1880, 1915

Ch. 20 200 block - odd numbers
    1. 207 Jefferson Street Governor Fleming residence, American Legion c. 1860
    *2. 217 Jefferson Street T. Worth Fleming residence c. 1848
    3. 219-223 Jefferson Street "Hatter Ben's" Storehouse, store c. 1828, 1927
    4. 225-229 Jefferson Street Haymond Building c. 1890, c. 1904

Ch. 21 300 block - even numbers
    *1. 306 Jefferson Street Nuzum Building c. 1900
    *2. 308-312 Jefferson Street Cunningham Block, Hotel McAlpin, Home Furniture Company 1901-2
    *3. 314 Jefferson Street Manley Hotel, Bethlehem Building 1901-3
    4. 316-320 Jefferson Street Masonic Temple Building Baldwin and Pennington, architects 1906-7 National Register of Historic Places
    5. 322-324 Jefferson Street residence c. 1880, c. 1894

Ch. 22 300 block - odd numbers
    *1. 315-317 Jefferson Street Manley Building c. 1880, c. 1906
    *2. 319 Jefferson Street C. L. Smith residence c. 1892
    *3. 321 Jefferson Street Kunst residence c. 1890
    *4. 323 Jefferson Street U. A. Clayton residence, Moose Club c. 1890
    *5. 327-329 Jefferson Street commercial building c. 1880, c. 1890

PART V - MADISON STREET

Ch. 23 200 block - even numbers
    *1. 200-202 Madison Street Roush House c. 1890

Ch. 24 200 block - odd numbers
    *1. 201-209 Madison Street Gans Hotel, Hotel Marion, Mountain City Hotel 1900
    *2. 215-221 Madison Street Murphy-Deveny Building 1912-13
    *3. 223-225 Madison Street Booher's Saloon c. 1890

Ch. 25 300 block - even numbers
    *1. 310 Madison Street Standard Garage, Fairmont Recreation Company 1911
    *2. 312 Madison Street "The Rink", Opera House, Kenyon Hotel, Madison Hotel 1903
    3. 320 Madison Street Jolliff residence, Frey Funerals c. 1910

Ch. 26 300 block - odd numbers
    *1. 305 Madison Street Tin shop, Mountain City Mill, restaurant c. 1890/1904
    *2. 309-315 Madison Street Mountain City Mill, Virginia Hotel c. 1880/1929
    *3. 317-319 Madison Street store c. 1900
    *4. 323-325 Madison Street McCray Building c. 1900
    *5. 329-335 Madison Street American-Italian Building 1921
    *6. near 401 Madison Street Dunbar School 1903

PART VI - QUINCY STREET

Ch. 27 400 block - even numbers
> *1. 402 Quincy Street Governor Pierpont's residence c. 1844
> *2. 418 Quincy Street Methodist Protestant Church c. 1833, 1852

Ch. 28 400 block - odd numbers
> *1. 401-407 Quincy Street Old Normal School, High School, Newspaper Building 1867-9, 1873

PART VII - LOCUST AVENUE/JACKSON STREET

Ch. 29 Locust Avenue
> *1. 2-6 Locust Avenue Mumford Electric, Mumford Apartments c. 1910, c. 1915
> 2. 8 Locust Avenue National Guard Armory, Standard Garage Wyatt and Nolting, architects 1912-3
> *3. 5-9 Locust Avenue Jackson Feed Mill c. 1894
> 4. 11-15 Locust Avenue American Laundry, Terrace Apartments Holmboe and Lafferty, architects 1911

Jackson Street

Ch. 30 100 block - even numbers
> 1. 116-118 Jackson Street Crane Building, Jackson-Dotts Building 1925
> 2. 120 Jackson Street Fleming Mill, Kisner Building c. 1924

Ch. 31 100 block - odd numbers
> *1. 111-115 Jackson Street Amos Carriage Works c. 1890
> *2. 119-121 Jackson Street Majestic Hotel, Jackson Hotel George Giffin, architect 1903
> *3. 123-125 Jackson Street Monongahela Candy Company c. 1900
> 4. 129-131 Jackson Street apartments c. 1920

Ch. 32 300 block - odd numbers
> 1. 301 Jackson Street Presbyterian Church W. H. Nichlas, architect 1916-17
> *2. 313-319 Jackson Street Snyder Motor Company Dodge Brothers Corporation architects 1921, 1927
> *3. 321-329 Jackson Street Jones Funeral Home, Standard Furniture Company c. 1904
> *4. 331 Jackson Street residence c. 1880
> *5. 333-337 Jackson Street Heinze Cleaners 1921-2

Ch. 33 400 block - even numbers
> *1. 412-414 Jackson Street National Guard Armory 1927
> *2. 418 Jackson Street Skating Rink, garage c. 1905
> *3. 420 Jackson Street Salvation Army 1905

Ch. 34 400 block - odd numbers
> 1. 401-407 Jackson Street St. Peter's Catholic Church Complex
>> Charles G. Badgeley and Smith, John Burchinal, Carl Reger; architects 1902-4, 1912, 1922-3, 1927-8
> 2. 421 Jackson Street R. C. Jones Funeral Home c. 1905

PART VIII - WASHINGTON STREET

Ch. 35 200 block - even numbers
> 1. 220 Washington Street "Indian Building," Methodist Episcopal Church, Episcopal Church 1880

APPENDIX B - BIBLIOGRAPHY

A History of Marion County, West Virginia. Fairmont, West Virginia: Marion County Historical Society, 1986.

Balderson, Walter L. *Fort Prickett Frontier and Marion County.* Fairmont, West Virginia: 1975.

Board of Affairs, Fairmont, West Virginia. *Report of the Several Departments Under Commission Form of Government, Fairmont, West Virginia.* Fairmont, West Virginia: Fairmont Printing Company, 1919.

Cohen, Stan and Andre, Richard. *Capitols of West Virginia: A Pictorial History.* Charleston, West Virginia: Pictorial Histories Publishing Co., 1989.

Dunnington, George A. *History and Progress of the County of Marion.* Fairmont: 1879. Reprinted 1992, Morgantown Printing and Binding Co., Morgantown, West Virginia.

Fairmont Commercial Newspaper. Fairmont, West Virginia.

Fairmont Free Press. Fairmont, West Virginia.

Fairmont Index Newspaper. Fairmont, West Virginia.

Fairmont Republican Newspaper. Fairmont, West Virginia.

Fairmont Lodge No. 9 A. F. and A. Masons, Fairmont, West Virginia: One Hundredth Anniversary 1849 - 1949 Fairmont, West Virginia: Printing and Office Supply Company, 1949.

Fairmont Times Newspaper. Fairmont, West Virginia.

Fairmont Times-West Virginian Newspaper. Fairmont, West Virginia.

Fairmont West Virginian Newspaper. Fairmont, West Virginia.

Farmers Free Press. Fairmont, West Virginia.

Fleming, Allison Sweeney. *Memories of Fairmont.* Fairmont, West Virginia: 1950.

Hardesty's Historical and Geographical Encyclopedia of Harrison and Marion County. Chicago, Illinois and Toledo, Ohio: H. H. Hardesty & Company, 1883.

Hoffman, Joseph E., editor. *Marion County Centennial Yearbook 1863-1963* Fairmont, West Virginia: Fairmont Printing and Binding Company, 1963.

Industrial Fairmont in 1908. Fairmont West Virginian Newspaper, April 1908.

Lough, Glenn D. *Now and Long Ago: A History of the Marion County Area.* Morgantown, West Virginia: Morgantown Printing and Binding Company, 1969.

Potter, Janet Greenstein. *Great American Railroad Stations.* New York, New York: John Wiley & Sons, Inc., 1996.

R. L. Polk & Company, Publishers. *Fairmont, West Virginia Directories.* Pittsburgh, Pennsylvania: 1901, 1904, 1915, 1925, 1929, 1933, 1939, 1949.

Sandborn Map and Publishing Company, Limited. *Maps of Fairmont, West Virginia.* New York, New York; 1884, 1892, 1896, 1902, 1906, 1912, 1918, 1927, 1950 (correction).

Spevock, Frank. *45 Years of Diary Notes 1947 - 1992.* Charleston, West Virginia: Color Craft Printing, 1992.

Turner, William P. *A Centennial History of Fairmont State College.* Fairmont, West Virginia: Fairmont State College, 1970.

Twentieth Century Edition. Fairmont West Virginian Newspaper, January 10, 1902.

Welcome Westinghouse - Monongahela Valley Progress Edition. Fairmont Times-West Virginian Newspaper, August 2, 1941.

APPENDIX C - PHOTOGRAPH CREDITS

Ron Chrislip: p. 42, 64, 72, 117, 129, 178, 189, 246.

Fairmont Index Newspaper: p. 26, 38, 52, 58, 61, 75, 98, 108, 116, 120, 121, 141, 146, 166, 237, 238, 272.

Fairmont Times Newspaper: p. 4, 7, 11, 62, 105, 119, 123, 134, 135, 137, 138, 144, 147, 163, 168, 174, 176, 191, 199, 205, 224, 228, 229, 232, 255, 265, 269, 295, 296.

Jeanne-Marie Higinbotham: p. 49.

Industrial Fairmont in 1908: p. 31, 82, 122, 156, 159, 187, 196, 218, 287.

Debra B. McMillan: p. 160, 267, 273.

Report of the Several Departments Under Commission Form of Government, Fairmont, West Virginia: p. 9, 21, 84, 187, 214.

Twentieth Century Edition: p. 20, 32, 50, 54, 62, 114, 151, 153, 156, 158, 190, 201, 220, 227, 259.

Welcome Westinghouse: p. 102.

J. Earl Windsor: p. 1, 19, 39, 47, 68, 70, 93, 100, 106, 115, 136, 170, 182, 222, 231, 270, 274, 278, 281.

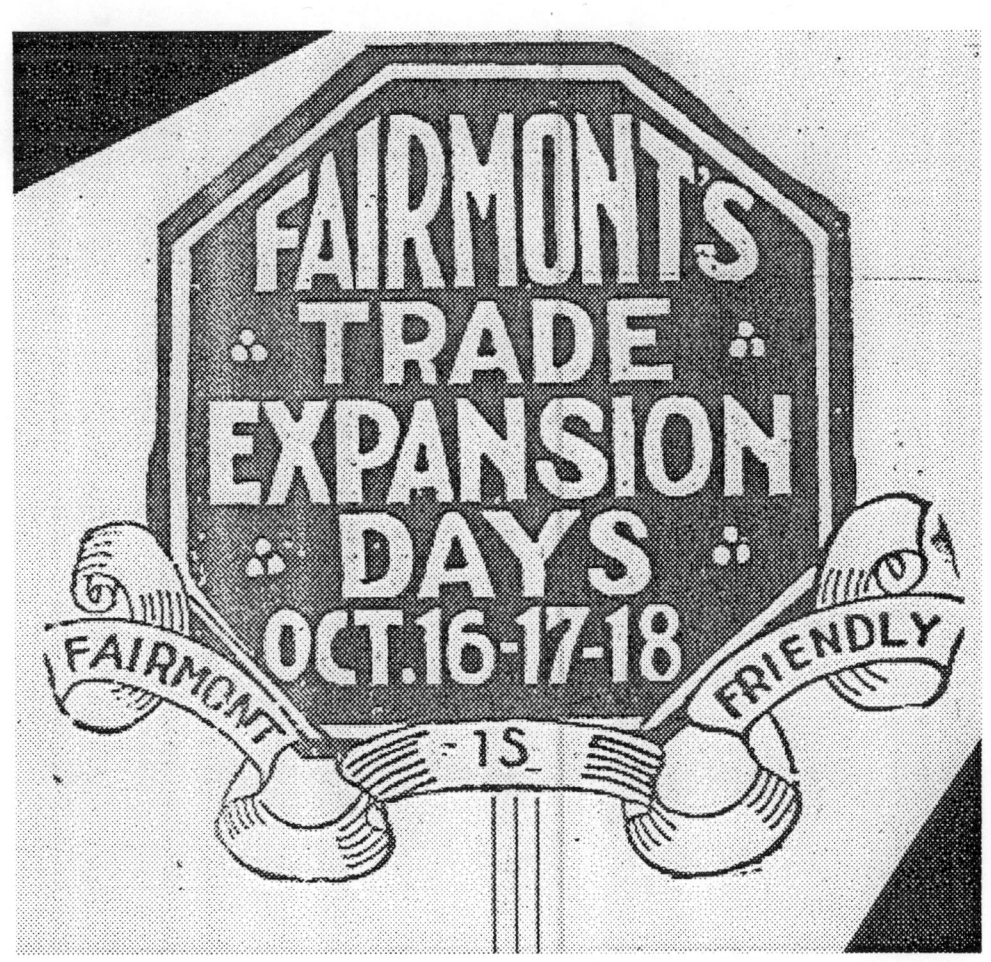

Times newspaper advertisement, October 24, 1916.

An Ornament to the City

Times newspaper advertisement, January 27, 1923.

Index

A

A. and P. Store 58
A. B. Scott & Co 71
A. Howard Fleming's jewelry store 99
A. L. Parrish drug store 22
Adams, George 112
Adams Office Supply 42, 43
Adams Street 18
Al Hartman's Orchestra 50
Albert, D. D. 73
Alford-Graham Shoes 43
Allison, J. E. 200
Alpha Associates 249, 250
American Building 82
American Department Stores Corporation 45, 82
American Hotel Company 214
American Laundry 265
American Legion 218
American Seating Company; 132
American Steam Laundry 170
American- Italian Building 250
Amos, George Carriage Manufacturing Company 269
Ancient Order of United Workman 43
Anderson, Boyd 34
Anderson, J. E. 115
Anderson Restaurant 49, 52
Arch Fleming Feed 162
Armory Building 263
Arnett, Florence 144
Arnett Residence 165
Arnett, T. W. 120
Arnett, U. N. 165
Arnett, W. E. 33

B

B. & O. Freight Station 113
B. & O. Railroad Passenger Station 239
Badgeley and Smith 281
Badgley, Charles G. 45
Baldwin and Pennington 229
Baldwin, Ephraim Francis 229
Baldwin Hotel 240
Baltimore & Ohio Railroad Freight Station 156
Baltimore & Ohio Railroad Passenger Station 155
Baltimore and Ohio Railroad 10
Baltimore and Ohio Railroad Company 99
Bank of Fairmont 60, 63, 110, 228
Barnes family 136
Barnes, James F. 137
Barney Street 149
Barr, M. B. 254
Beaumont, S. M. 211
Beaux Arts style 282
Beckman's Store 102

Beeson, J. C. 145
Bell Telephone Company 25, 174
Berman and Polan 75
Berns, Charles 33
Bethlehem Coal Company 226
Biller, John 128
Billingslea Drug Store 141
Billingslea, E. A. 141
Billingslea, W. H. 79
Blair, H. T. 67
Block, Dan 101
Blue Ridge 143
Blue Ridge Grill 145
Blue Ridge Theatre 142
Blumberg, Michael 69
B'nai B'rith 44
Boaz Fleming 10
Bobet News 107
Bon Ton store 115
Booher's drug store 75
Booher's saloon 242
Bossie's Orchestra 34
Bowen, Mayor 36
Boyer-Irvine Hotel, 240
Brady Construction Company 229
Brady Construction company 145
Brady, Samuel D. 132
Brand, Duke 162
Bridge of Sighs 81, 91
Bridge of Size 81, 196
Bright, Simeon 275
Brooks Specialty Company 181
Brown, Arch 99
Brownfield and McCray 248
Brownfield Building 118
Brownfield, G. H. 118
Burchinal, John 35
Burchinal, T. L. 60, 121, 150
Burka, Sol 143
Burke, Illa 246
Burns, James 68
Burns, Jas. 33
business houses 18
Busy Bee Restaurant 51, 75

C

C. A. House music store 24, 49
C. and M. Land Company 57
C. B. Carney 97
C. L. Smith residence 237
Cabaret Bar 216
Cafe Watson 128
Campbell's Shoes 102

Carney drug store 73
Carr Building 19
Carrico Hotel 241
Cashier's Residence 60
Casino property 279
Casino Rink property 280
Cass Electric Company 165
Casterline and Hoge 79
Casterline and Hoge's Racket Store 79
Casterline, S. M. 72
Central Automobile Corporation 268
Central Fire Company 186
Central School Building 258
Chamber of Commerce 114
Chick's Bargain Center 242
Chinese Laundry 215
Chisler Building 99
Chisler Hardware 142
Chisler, John 142, 145
Chisler residence 182
Christ Episcopal Church 288
Christian Science Society 288
Christie's Drug 97
Church, M. E. 165
Church on the Hill 255
Church Theatre 28
cigar factory 68
Citizens' Dollar Bank 202
Citizens Dollar Savings Bank 21
City Building 182
Civil War 254
Clark Coal & Coke Company 25
Clark, Harry B. 103
Clark, John A. 201
Clark Safe & Vault Company of Pittsburgh 80
Clarksburg Amusement Company 143
Clayton, U. A. 238
Clothes Shop 48
Coal City House Furnishing Company 223
Coal Company Building 110
Coal Run Hollow 19, 163
Cochran's Jewelry Store 195
Cocoanut Grove 163
Cole, Laura 144
Cole Residence 145
Colonial Theatre 29, 30
Colonial Trust Company 80
Colored Church 171
Commerford Building 73
Commerford, Michael M. 73
Community Bank & Trust Company Building 42, 43
Communtzi's Confectionery 58, 107
Comuntzis, Nicholas J. 58
Conaway, J. M. 275
Concrete Steel Bridge Company 277
Conoway, J. F. 127
Conoway, W. W. 46
Conoway's Feed Store 180

Conservative Life Insurance Company 131
Consolidated Coal Company 222
Continental Hotel 33
Corbin & Sons Groceries 161
Corbin Groceries 161
Cordray Carriage Company 280
Costianes, Nicholas 58
Courtney's 23
Craig Motor Company 267
Crane Drug Store 191
Crane homestead 215
Crane, W. R. 107
Crawford, L. L. 118
Criss, M. B. 28
Crouse, J. L. 167
Culinary Workers Union 240
Cunningham Block 80, 223
Cunningham Building 111, 223
Cunningham Undertaker and Embalmer 271

D

D. F. Everett drug store 22
D. L. Morrow's boot and shoe store 118
Daffin's Confectionery 102
Dan Block, tailor 24
Dattilo Fruit company 161
Davis, L. M. 181
Davis Light Guards 57, 244
Davy Levi's pool room 75
Deitz, E. 24
Deitz, J. H. 24
Deitz's Leader Shop 242
Democratic State Headquarters 63
Deveny Building 29, 33, 145
Deveny skyscraper 35
Deveny, Thomas A. 28, 33
Dixie Shoe Store 50
Dixie Theatre 23, 30, 72, 104
Dodge Brothers Motor Cars 275
Dohney, John 127
Dollar store 24
Donahue, Bishop 282
Dotts, Joseph T. 267
Dowden Building 102, 103
Dowden's Orchestra 57
Dowling, C. W. 265
Downing, Robert 57
Dr. Fitch building 43
Dreher, F. W. 130
Dunbar School 171, 251
Dutton, Thomas 142

E

East View Apartments 214
Economy Shoe Store 100
Eddy, Olive 225
Eddy, R. C. 130

Edla Shop 133
Egan's Shoe Store 30
Electric Company Offices 165
Electric Theatre 23
Eliason, Walter 99, 117, 147, 182, 183, 279
Elks Club 23, 35, 113
Elliot, Fred W. 130, 131
Exclusive Garment Shop 102
Eyster residence 142

F

F. & A. Masons 24
F. & M. Telephone 220
F. Klaws Toggery Shoppe 120
Fairmont & Clarksburg Traction Company 222, 244
Fairmont Bank 51
Fairmont Building & Investment Company 165, 167
Fairmont Coal Company 111
Fairmont Community Players 258
Fairmont Dairy Company 168, 262
Fairmont Development Company 115, 165
Fairmont Elks 35
Fairmont Fire Department 113
Fairmont Free Press 190
Fairmont Furniture Company 48, 132, 233
Fairmont Hotel 118, 130, 208, 212
Fairmont Hotel Corporation 213
Fairmont Light and Gas Company 113
Fairmont Lodge No. 9 A 24
Fairmont Lodge No. 9 A. F. & A. Masons 228
Fairmont Mining Machine Company 45, 111, 131
Fairmont Motor Car Company 280
Fairmont Newspaper Publishing Company 259
Fairmont Opera House 200
Fairmont Post of the American Legion 107
Fairmont Recreation Company 244
Fairmont State Bank 21
Fairmont State College 135, 257
Fairmont State Normal School 45, 167, 257
Fairmont Tailor Shop 250
Fairmont, The 131
Fairmont Theatre 104, 130
Fairmont Theatres Company 134
Fairmont *Times* 28
Fairmont *Times and Index* Printing Company 190
Fairmont Trust Company 60, 64, 82, 83, 107
Fairmont *West Virginian* 73
Fanus Jewelry Company 71
Farley Clothing Company 49, 249
Farmer's Bank 51
Farmers Room 86, 91
Federal Building 165
Federal Radio Commission 214
Finger's Garment Store 102
First M. E. Church 165
First National Bank of Fairmont 51, 60, 63, 223
First National Building 43
First Presbyterian church 274
First Warders 22
Fisher, W. A. 75
Fishers Jewelry store 75
Fleming, A. B. 110
Fleming, Allison 43
Fleming, Ben 68
Fleming, Bert 66
Fleming, Boaz 110, 214
Fleming, Brooks 209
Fleming Building 122
Fleming Flower Store 30
Fleming, Fred C. 99, 135
Fleming Grocery store 116
Fleming, Hatter Ben 219
Fleming Jewelry 43
Fleming, Joseph P. 118
Fleming, Matthew 85, 87
Fleming Mill 268
Fleming, T. W. 58, 79, 106
Fleming, Thurston W. 69
Fleming, Worth 66
Fleming/Cochran Building 71
Ford, Edward F. 240
Forman, Israel 115
Fortney Drugs 158
Fortney, Earl 74, 223
Fountain Hotel 66
Fountain Restaurant and Bakery 66
Fountain Saloon 66
Frangos, George 58
Frangos, William A. 58
Frank's Tire and Supply Company 159, 160
Fransheim, E. B. 150
Frederick T. Ley Company 213
Frey, Joe Jolliff 247
Friendly Furniture Store 83
Fulkut Plant 268
Fuller Construction Company 111, 212
Fulton, J. Charles 177

G

G. C. Murphy Building 101
G. C. Murphy Building Addition 214
Gans Hotel, 241
Gas and Light Company 111
George A. Fuller Company 211
George M. Jacobs Building 194
Giffin, George 269
Gift and Art Shop 98
Gilbert, Cass 198
Gilmore, Henry P. 67
Globe Rubber Stamps Works of Fairmont 80
Glumicich, Milan 34
Goldberg Clothing store 250
Golden Brothers Department Store 120, 122, 133
Golden Corner 122

Golden, Israel 133
Goodman, Simon D. 69
Gotses, Spiro 52, 117
Gould, Harry L. 122
Governor Fleming residence 218
Governor Pierpont's residence 254
Grand Lodge of the A. F. & A. M. of West Virginia 274
Grand Opera 30
Grand Opera House Company 202
Grand Opera House Saloon 202
Grand Theatre 30, 203
Great Atlantic and Pacific Tea Company 58
Great Fire of 1876 71, 73, 96, 99, 106
Great White Way 52
Greenbrier 211
Greer, Mrs. H. Glen 47
Grocery, Nuzum 25

H

H. & H. Drug Company 98
Hall Block 111, 189
Hall Hardware store 44
Hall Harness store 67
Hall, Homer 74
Hall, J. Lee 44
Hamilton, A. A. 201
Hamilton, Glen B. 98
Hammond Fire Brick Company 45
Hando's Restaurant 107
Harper-Meredith Building 92, 188, 272
Harper-Meredith City County Building 238
Harrison's Department store 122
Harrrison, A. 122
Hart Produce 158
Hartley & Morrow 79
Hartley, E. F. 201
Hartley, H. J. 46
Hartley, Harry J. 81
Hartley, J. M. 127
Hartley, Joseph Milton 81
Hartley's Department Store 196
Hartley's Store 97
Hatter Ben's Big Brick 68
Hawkins, W. E. 43
Hawkins, William C. 132
Hayden and McCoy, Attorneys 69
Haymond Building 220
Haymond, Maria 282
Hays Building 188
Hays, J. 188
Heinze Cleaners 277
Hellman, David 143
Henderson, Harriet 27
Hennen Building 27
Hennen, T. Wilbur 28
Henshaw, John 262
Highgate 111

Hippodrome 30
Hippodrome, The Theatre 143
Hippodrome Theatre 142
Holbert & Spedden, Builders 79
Holbert and Spedden 175
Holbert, S. Ray 79, 86
Holmbe, L. C. 167
Holmboe and Lafferty of Clarksburg 265
Holt, Clyde S 118
Holt, Clyde S. 98, 214
Holt Drug Company 98
Holt Rowe Novelty Company 118
Holt-Rowe Novelty Company 98
Home Furniture Company 225
Home Savings Bank 42, 82, 85
Homestead 211
Hood and Clelland Hardware 102
Horace Trumbauer 110
Horner, L. S. 201
Hose Company 33
Hose House 160
Hotel Antler 241
Hotel De Ville of the people of Fairmont 195
Hotel Manley 226
Hough, James F. 48
Howell, C. P. 86
Hub Clothing Store 51
Hull Alley 175
Human Fly 84
Huntington Banks 42
Hutchinson, Brooks 222
Hutchinson, Brooks S. 74
Hutchinson, Clyde E. 79
Hutchinson, Elizabeth 10
Hutchinson, M. L. 79

I

I.O.O.F. Building 205
Ice and Hardesty's shoe store 191
Ideal Theatre 30, 224
Idlers Clothing Store 242
Imperial Ice Cream Company 168
Indian Building 287
Ingram, Nola 34
International Company 37
Irwin, John W. 89
Iseman, Sam B. 32, 59, 127
Italian American Investment Company 250

J

J. C. Corbin Company 161
J. C. McCrorey & Company 35
J. E. Watson 104
J. L. Hall Hardware Company 44
J. L. Lott Building 228
J. L. Mott Iron Works of New York 90
J. M. Hartley & Son 45, 79

J. Nuzum and Company 200
J. W. Lott building 106
Jackson, Earl 267
Jackson Hotel 269
Jackson, John 75
Jackson, Laura 282
Jackson's Feed mill 264
Jacobs Building 73, 183
Jacobs, George M. 20, 79
Jacobs, J. M. 79
Jacobs-Hutchinson Block 45, 79
Jacobs-Hutchinson Company 162
Jacobs-Hutchinson Hardware Company 80, 189
Jailer's Residence 85, 87
James Westwater & Company 89
Jim Martin's 74
John M. Kisner & Brothers Company 274
John M. Kisner Lumber Company 45
Johnson, Emil R. 45
Johnson system 83
Johnston's Studio 30
Jolliff, M. A. 201
Jolliff, Marcellus A. 247
Jolliffe, G. L. 25
Jolliffe, J. Vaughn 128
Jones and Nuzum of Fairmont 103
Jones' Department Store 60, 61
Jones' Dress Shop 64
Jones, E. C. 44, 60, 121
Jones Economy Store 66
Jones Funeral Home 276
Jones, General 10
Jones' Raid 254
Jones' Store 121
Jordan Fairmont Sales 168

K

Kaufman, Harry 118
Kaufman's Store 118
Keiser, C. D. 35
Kelley Music Company 130
Kenyon Drug Company 245
Kenyon Hotel 244
Kerns, James 85, 87
Kerr, E. C. 24, 230
Kidwell, Dr. Zedekian 69
Kingwood 274
Kingwood stone 275
Kinney Shoe Store 24
Kisner Building 268
Klaw's Department store 102
Kline Shoes 102
Knights of Columbus 107, 191
Knights of Pythias 44, 115
Knights Templar 275
Kohlmier, Joseph 202
Kunst Residence 238

L

L. T. Feaster, Jeweler 23
Lamb, Leonard 85
Lanham, H. H. 28
Leader Shoe and Men's Clothing store 242
Lee Reinheimer & Brothers Clothing 107
Leiner & Faris 126
Leopold & Company 42
Levell, John 126
Lewis A. Herman's store 100
Liberty Meat Market 142
Linn, Harry G. 73
Linn Realty Company 103
Linn, Russel 103, 105
Linn, Turk 23
Lipson Jewelry 105, 248
Little Nemo 23
Lively, H. S. 262
Lloyd, Frank 90
Lloyd, T. H. 75
Loch Lynn Construction Company 128
Loch Lynn Hotel 128
Lodge Number 9, A. F. & A. M 89
Lott Building 106
Lott, Richard P. 135
Loue, T. C. 51
Lough, Glenn 219
Lunch, W. L. 241
Luther, J. H. 66
Lyons, Andrew C. 19, 28, 79, 121, 182, 185, 194
Lyric Theatre 23

M

M. D. Christie's store 208
M. E. Church, Colored 180
MacArthur, C. E. 79
Mack's Orchestra 48, 52
Madison Hotel 241
Madison Mill Company 248
Main Street Fairmont program 11
Main Street News Stand 30
Majestic Building 188
Majestic Hotel 269
Majestic Theatre Company 215
Mammoth, The 48
Manley Building 224
Manley, George W. 33
Manley Hotel 128, 225
Manley Hotel Building 103
Manley lot 166
Mansbach Store 42
Marianna, John W. 22
Marietta Hotel 26, 32, 128
Marietta Hotel Annex 32, 59
Marietta, Marcus 33
Marietta Restaurant 34

Marion County Chamber of Commerce 26
Marion County Courthouse 73
Marion County Historic Society 81
Marion County Historical Museum 87
Marion County Jail and Sheriff's Residence 87
Marion, General Francis 10
Marion Hardware Company 102, 103, 227
Marion Hotel 241
Markowitz, Mr. 24
Martin and Leaf Grocers 24
Martin Brothers 22
Martin Brothers Cash Grocers 25
Martin Brothers Drug store 23
Martin, Fred T. 25
Martin, James A. 74
Marvin Fink Store 118
Mary Margaret Shop 133
Masonic Hall 106
Masonic Lodge 110, 228
Masonic Temple 106
Masonic Temple Building
    22, 25, 48, 83, 111, 198, 229, 231
Masons of Fairmont 106
Maundy Feast of the Masons 31
Maunz and Crawford 75
Mayers, George W. 89
McAlpin Hotel 225, 240
McClintic, George W. 230
McCray Building 249
McCray, Charles E., Jr 28
McCray Hardware Company 249
McCray, L. F. 120
McCray, Lawrence 280
McCray's Colonial Theatre 30
McCrorey Building 35, 64
McCrorey's Store 68
McCrory Five and Ten 65
McCrory, J. G. 67
McIntire, Fred W. 280
McKenzie, Voorhees and Gmelin 176
McKinney, O. S. 106, 230
McKinney, Owen S. 116
Menear home 175
Merchants' Carnival 57
Meredith, Judge W. S. 73
Meridian Lodge No. 34, A. F. 171
Methodist Episcopal (M. E.) Church 27, 287
Methodist Protestant Church 175, 177, 253, 255, 257
Milburn, Heister & Company 210
Miller, J. Thomas 201
Million Dollar Bridge 207
Moebs, Joseph 128
Monon Valley Produce 162
Monongahela Candy Company 271
Monongahela Lodge No. 148 153
Moose Club 238
Moose Lodge 34, 229

Morgan, M. Earle 23
Morgan's Grocery 142
Morrison Department Store 49
Morrison, O. J. 49
Mountain City Drug Store 73, 74
Mountain City Hotel 65, 71, 73, 128, 130, 241
Mountain City House 87, 88
Mountain City Lodge No. 35, 38, G. U. O. of O. F. 251
Mountain City Mill Company 248
Mountain Lake Park 128
Mountain State Candy Company 161
Mountain State Oil and Gas Service 171
Mumford Flats 262
Mumford Plumbing & Electrical Company 262
Murphy-Deveny Building 241, 242
Musgrave Springer Funeral Home 174
Mutual Home & Savings Association 42

N

Nathan, Ben 43
National Guard Armory 262, 263, 279
National Register of Historic Places 83
Natural Gas Company 25
Nazarene Church 251
Necessary, H. C. 143
Neely, M. M. 46, 214, 262
Nelson Theatre 30, 101, 104
Nelson-Galligher building 245
New Carrico Hotel 241
New Dug Road 149
New Hennen Building 30
New Palace Market 189
Newark Shoe Store and Schoolnics 116
Nickerson, Frederick 167
Normal School 253
Noss Family 57
Novelty Roller Rink 265
Nuzum & Ross 48
Nuzum Building 222
Nuzum furniture store 47
Nuzum Grocery 231
Nuzum, Sam R. 48, 201

O

O. J. Morrison's 24
Odd Fellows Lodge 203
Ogden Corner 141
Ohmer Sons & Company 80
Old Dewey Hotel 161
Old Grand Opera House 104
Old Normal School Building 135, 190
"Old Side" Church 287
Omen's First Regimental Band 271
Omni Associates 47
O'Neal, R. L. 128
Opera House 198
Orpheum Theatre 215

Osgood, D. M. 136
Osgood, Rose 51
Osgood's Store 100, 136

P

Packard, Frank L. 89
Page, Abram 89
Paige Motor Sales 250
Palace Coffee Shop 117
Palace Jewelry Store 75
Palace Pool Parlor 100
Palace Restaurant 52, 117
Panama Pacific Exposition 101
Parks Avenue Hotel 161
Parrack, H. 144
Patriarchs Militant 244
Pedersen, Ralph 92
People's Bank Building 79, 111
People's Bank of Fairmont 51
People's National Bank 82
People's Temple 177, 256
Phillips, John F. 25, 57, 86
Pierpont, Francis H. 254
Pierpont, Governor 10
Piggly-Wiggly Corporation 142
Pitcher, Frankie 57
Porter Alley 47, 195
Porterfield, Burt 225
Post Office 198
Powell, L. C. 201
Prendergast's saloon 120
Presbyterian Church 106, 110, 166, 272
Presidents' Grid 8
Preston County 275
Princess Theatre 30, 216
Professional Business Building 167
Protestant Episcopal Church 27, 287

R

R. C. Eddy Contractors 259
R. C. Jones Funeral Home 284
R. E., Dr. McCray 28
R. H. Blacka's Racket Department Store 195
Racket Store 79
Ravine Amusement Company 163
Ravine Park Amusement Center 163
Ray's Jewelry 100
Reeds Sales and Feed 267
Reger, Carl 283
Reger, Maggie E. 136
Reinheimer, Lee 73
Reitman's Market 42
Restored Government of Virginia 254
Revolutionary War 10
Rexall Remedies 74
Reynolds, A. J. 275
Riheldaffer, Alex 99

Rink, The 57, 200
Robb Building 142
Robb, C. C. 142
Robb Meat Market 142
Robinson and Co. 141
Robinson, Clarence D. 63, 181
Robinson, Clarence L. 57
Robinson, Ira E. 214
Ronay Jewelry 100
Rosier, Joseph 46
Ross Furniture Store 48, 233
Roush House 240
Rowand's Store 102, 116
Rowland, Willard J. 262
Rownd, John H. 81

S

S. M. Kisner and Sons Company 45
Salvation Army 280
Samas, George 58
Sample Building 37, 107, 190, 258
Sample, Henry C. 7
Samples, Lloyd 222
Sandborn Insurance 20
Satterfield, Lee N. 91
Scarlats, Sam 117
Schmidt, L. D. 92
Schmidt, Louis D. 283
Schmulbach, Henry 152
Schmulbach's Brewing Company 153
Second Ward School 258
See Denham First Company 191
Setron's Produce 161
Sharp-Hamilton-Arnett company 59
Shaw Hotel Company 226
Shertleff and Welton Shoe store 43
Sherwood Barber shop 99
Shot Tower 126
Showalter, E. M. 231, 262
Showalter, Emmet 46
Shroyer, Ed 75
Shurtleff & Welton, a shoe store 43
Silling & Associates 92
skating rink 279
Skinner Building 21, 231
Skinner, C. L. 150
Skinner, Charles L. 25
Skinner's Tavern 150
Smart Shoppe 51
Smith and McKinney Building 44, 111, 115, 195
Smith, F. J. 118
Smith-Race Groceries, 159
Snider, C. H. 204
Snyder, L. 275
Snyder Motor Company 276
Spedden, W. H. 21, 79, 118
Spicer, Samuel 130

St. Charles Hotel 240
St. Peters Catholic Church Complex 24, 281, 283
Standard Building and Loan Association 189
Standard Furniture Company 276, 277
Standard Garage Company 244, 264
Stevenson Groceries 159
Stokes, John 194
Stout's Shoes 43
Stoy the Tailor 25
Sturm and Watkins 89
Swisher & Carpenter's Store 96, 120

T

T. F. Hall Building 65
T. L. Burchinal 23
T. Worth Fleming Residence 219
talking pictures 101
Taylor, Joseph Knox, 198
Tetrick and Randall, 53
The Fair 25
The Goodman Store on the Level 70
The Great White Way 18
The Index 75
The West Virginian 190, 258
Thomas C. Miller School 258
Thomas F. Watson Hotel 127
Thomas Prendergast's Saloon 96
Thomas W. Fleming Building 204
Thompson, Daniel M. 87
Times and Index Building 162
Times-Index Printing Company 189
tin shop 248
Torrey, J. L. 75
Torrey's Boot and Shoe Shop 219
Town Hall 57
Town Hall Theatre 244
Traction Company 111
Troy Steam Laundry 181
Truesdale, Agnes 23
Trumbauer, Horace 111
Twin Rouss Store 21
Tygarts Valley Brewing Company 33

U

U. A. Clayton Residence 238
"Uncle Moose" Fleming's grocery store 71
Uncle Tom's Cabin 57
Underselling Store 67
Union Business College 196
Union Clothing Store 32
Union Mission Chapel 27, 288
Union National Bank 82
Union One Price Clothing Store 19
Union Rescue Mission 158
United Shoe Store 242
United Woolen Mills of Parkersburg 23

V

Valley Engineering Company 132
Valley Engineering Corporation 131
Varsity Club 216
Virginia Tea Room 104
Virginia, The 103
Virginia Theatre 102, 104, 225, 242
Vonderhaas, George 128

W

W. B. Ice & Brothers 168
W. C. Shafer's Photograph and Art Studio 25
W. H. Nichlas of Cleveland, Ohio 274
W. R. White School 33
W. S. Thomas Transfer Company 153
Watson Building 68, 110, 209
Watson, C. W. 209
Watson, Edwin 134
Watson Hotel 32, 126, 128
Watson, J. E. 111
Watson Skyscraper 114
Watson, Thomas F. 126, 127
Watson, Wilbur H. 162
Watson-Malone-Miller Company 227
Weber's Flowers 30
Webster College 205
West Virginia Amusement Company 104, 130, 132
West Virginia Business College 205
West Virginia Grocery and Candy Company 159, 170
West Virginia Office Complex 47
West Virginia Publishing Company 36
Westchester Engineering Company 198
Western Union 30, 111
William Miller & Sons of Pittsburgh 111
Williams, B. G. 67, 150, 151
Williamson Undertaking 202
Wiz, The nightclub 242
WMMN 46, 118, 213
Wolf's Leader Shop 242
Women's Club of Fairmont 234
Wood, W. D. 33
Woods, E. J. 85
Woolworth store 36
Wyatt and Nolting of Baltimore 263

Y

Y.M.C.A 227
Yeager & Company 121
Yeager, Charles 84, 145, 226
Yeager Department store 122, 248
Yeager, George 121, 122, 248
Yeager, Samuel S. 121
YMCA 46, 98, 107
Yost Building 138
Yost, Joseph Warren 89